Muddling Through

Peter Hennessy is Professor of Contemporary History at Queen Mary and Westfield College, University of London, and Chairman of the Kennedy Memorial Trust. His books include *Cabinet*, *Whitehall* and *Never Again: Britain 1945–51*, for which he was awarded both the Duff Cooper Prize and the NCR Prize in 1993, and his examination of the British constitution, *The Hidden Wiring*, was published by Gollancz in 1995 (revised edition Indigo, 1996).

For many years he was a journalist, with spells on *The Times*, the *Financial Times* and *The Economist*. He has written columns for the *Independent*, the *New Statesman*, and *Director* magazine, was a regular presenter of the BBC Radio 4 *Analysis* programme 1986–92, and in 1994 wrote and presented the Wide Vision Productions/Channel Four Television series *What Has Become of Us?*

Peter Hennessy was educated at Marling School, Stroud; St John's College, Cambridge; the London School of Economics and Harvard (where he was a Kennedy Memorial Scholar 1971–2). He lives in north-east London with his wife and two daughters and has taught History at QMW since 1992.

States of Emergency
(with Keith Jeffery)

Sources Close to the Prime Minister
(with Michael Cockerell and David Walker)

What the Papers Never Said

Cabinet

Ruling Performance
(co-editor with Anthony Seldon)

Whitehall

Never Again

The Hidden Wiring

PETER HENNESSY

Muddling Through

*Power, Politics and the Quality of
Government in Postwar Britain*

INDIGO

First published in Great Britain 1996
by Victor Gollancz

This Indigo edition published 1997
Indigo is an imprint of the Cassell Group
Wellington House, 125 Strand, London WC2R 0BB

A catalogue record for this book is available from the British Library.

ISBN 0 575 40102 8

Designed and typeset by Production Line, Minster Lovell, Oxford
Printed and bound in Great Britain
by Guernsey Press Co. Ltd, Guernsey, Channel Isles

97 98 99   10 9 8 7 6 5 4 3 2 1

For my BBC Radio Three and BBC Radio Four Analysis
producers who made much of this volume happen:

Caroline Anstey, Simon Coates, Julian Hale, Mark Laity,
Zareer Masani, David Morton, Frank Smith,
Fraser Steel and Anne Winder
and
for Sue Thompson who kept us all going.

As we were leaving the House [of Commons] that night, he [Winston Churchill] called me into the Chamber to take a last look round. All was darkness except a ring of faint light all around under the Gallery. We could dimly see the Table but walls and roof were invisible. 'Look at it,' he said. 'This little place is what makes the difference between us and Germany. It is in virtue of this that we shall muddle through to success and for lack of this Germany's brilliant efficiency leads her to final destruction. This little room is the shrine of the world's liberties.'

From the Diary of McCallum Scott, March 1917

Contents

Preface: Thinking Aloud   9

Introduction: Humbugging our Way   13

Part One: Crown Power

1   Jewel in the Constitution? The Queen, Parliament
    and the Royal Prerogative   16
2   The Back of the Envelope: Hung Parliaments, the Queen
    and the Constitution   34

Part Two: The Uneasy Fusion

3   Permanent Ballast in the Constitution   55
4   Teething the Watchdogs: Parliament, Government
    and Accountability   63
5   No End of a Lesson?   80

Part Three: Where in the World?

6   'A Bloody Union Jack on Top of It'   99
7   A Canal Too Far   130
8   Out of the Midday Sun? Britain and the Great Power Impulse   150

Part Four: Portraits

9   Living with Clem   171
10 Living with Winston   187
11 Living with Anthony   204
12 The Last Edwardian   220

13   A Countryman in Downing Street   235
14   The Scarlet Thread   246
15   Be Prepared   268
16   Knowing Their Little Tricks   279
17   The Last Retreat of Fame: Mrs Thatcher as History   290

Epilogue   298
Notes   301
Index   309

Preface

Thinking Aloud

[Haley] was, indeed, ideally suited to serve the conception of broadcasting which the British people have chosen for their own. Here was to be found satisfaction for all his most cherished beliefs in the efficacy of self-education, in the dissemination of culture, in the pervasive influence of honest reporting – in short, of liberalism.

Anonymous *New Statesman* profile of Sir William Haley, 1954[1]

[Ellen Wilkinson] wanted Britain to become a 'Third Programme' nation.

Lord Redcliffe-Maud recalling the Minister of Education, 1945–7, in 1981[2]

The 1944 Education Act taught me to read and think. The National Health Service has given me nice teeth and the BBC gave me Shakespeare and Beethoven.

Gillian Reynolds, 1989[3]

There's always a drill. I've been coming here since 1948 and there's always a drill.

Enoch Powell, as rebuilding in Broadcasting House interrupted the recording of a BBC Radio Four *Analysis* programme, 1990[4]

The BBC has a special place in my affections. As with Gillian Reynolds it shaped me and, in some ways, made me. The Home Service (later Radio Four) is the best place in the world to eavesdrop on others thinking aloud in a sustained fashion, and, as I discovered a generation after first absorbing its vibrations, it is unquestionably the place in which to indulge in a spasm of public thinking of one's own.

The Home Service/Radio Four has since the Second World War provided a rich running commentary on national and international life – so much so that it has become part of our national identity, the disseminating source to which the thoughtful and the discriminating turn at moments of shock or when rites of passage are in motion. For example, I still cannot quite see how the electorate could engineer a change of government without the extraordinary Brian Redhead arbitrating the transfer of power from Studio 4A in Broadcasting House.[5]

I was tickled (in a grim way) rather than surprised to learn that the final check the commander of a Royal Navy Polaris or Trident submarine would make deep under the waters of the North Atlantic to determine whether a United Kingdom still existed before opening his sealed orders on retaliation after a pre-emptive nuclear strike would be to tune in to the Radio Four *Today* programme. If after a highly secret number of days there is no Jim Naughtie, John Humphrys, Anna Ford or Peter Hobday, those last instructions from a by now deceased Prime Minister will be opened – a final if macabre tribute to a broadcasting service *sans pareil*. I used sometimes to wonder if Mrs Margaret Thatcher as Prime Minister knew about this particular subsidiary function of *Today*, a programme of which she was a regular but rarely satisfied listener. (Her Press Secretary, Bernard Ingham, refers to 'its ill-considered output' in his choleric memoirs.[6]) Indeed, Mrs Thatcher had grave doubts about the modern BBC as a whole,[7] and was prone to decry its prime source of funding, the licence fee, as 'taxation without representation'.[8]

Throughout the late 1980s the BBC was for me a barbican of reason and balance amid a depressingly polarized cycle in the rhythm of British political life. The Radio Four *Analysis* programme, which became my professional home in 1987 and remained so until 1992, was the kind of redoubt that I like to think Ellen Wilkinson and William Haley would have recognized as a part of that high cultural fabric they wished the country to share. Life on *Analysis* was a fairly intensive existence with, roughly speaking, a three-week turnaround for each forty-five-minute documentary which, usually, would embrace hour-long interviews with a dozen or so authorities or witnesses. Lifting up my eyes from scriptwriting, I would sometimes gaze at the boxes and tapes containing the transcripts and tapes of past *Analyses* accumulated since the programme's inception in 1970 and ponder both on the richness of it as a still growing archive and on the near impossibility of retrieving it for a later and a wider audience. I would ponder, too, on the sheer quality of the *Analysis* producers – though there was no *Analysis* stereotype, no trace of central casting in their varied (and often volatile) make-up. They taught me a great deal, stretched me quite ruthlessly when the occasion required and were the best and funniest of companions on the long journeys.

This volume, or the bulk of it, is a belated attempt to do something about such musings by offering a bill of fare which bears so visibly the distinctive stamp of that gem of a programme. That is why it is dedicated to my *Analysis* friends and to Julian Hale who, though not an *Analysis* man, set out with me in 1989 in search of the practitioners of premiership.

Producing this book has depended on rare talents of a different kind. I owe a huge debt of gratitude to my editor, the incomparable Sean Magee, who persuaded me that there was a book in this particular cluster of artefacts; to Gillian Bromley, whose editorial skills are such that she could turn a set of old telephone directories into something palatable; to Katrina Whone, who makes sure everything happens on time with a special charm; to Liz Lynch, who made legible much the material in this volume; to Tony Raven, my favourite indexer and to my typesetter, Charlie Webster, with whom it is a pleasure to be working once more. They know the kind of 'dependency culture' I inhabit and how lost I would be without them.

Peter Hennessy
Walthamstow and Mile End
May 1996

All but two of the chapters in this book have their genesis in programmes first broadcast on BBC Radio Three or Radio Four. The exceptions are 'Permanent Ballast in the Constitution', a lecture delivered on 26 June 1995 at the Civil Service College at Sunningdale to mark the College's twenty-fifth anniversary, and 'The Last Retreat of Fame', first published in July 1991 in *Modern Law Review*, volume 54, number 4. Both are republished with kind permission.

Introduction

Humbugging Our Way

Compare the story of Britain in the twentieth century with that of her supposedly successful competitors, France or Germany or Japan. They made a ghastly hash of their countries, alongside which Britain, whether due to the qualities of her people and institutions or to her insular character or more likely to the combination of both, came relatively unscathed through immense transitions and vicissitudes: we defeated our aggressors, we preserved our constitution and we humbugged our way with self-satisfaction through everything.

Enoch Powell, 1987[1]

An Englishman's mind works best when it is almost too late.

Lord D'Abernon, undated[2]

Historians have a horror of the stereotype and the parody. They seem to be more at ease with the notion of national identity, especially when able to demythologize the 'invented' bits of a country's 'tradition',[3] than with ruminations on national character. But there is a distinct trait exhibited by many set in authority over us in the twentieth century, whether minister of the Crown or member of one of the Crown services, an approach which eschews the rational, the written, the planned or the strategic. It is the exceptions to this stereotype of understated, pragmatic, occasionally inspired *ad hoccery* and last-minute improvisation that stand out – the Lloyd Georges, the Churchills and the Thatchers.

We are, in Churchill's phrase, a 'muddling through'[4] nation in terms of so much of our policy-making. 'We just *are* a back-of-envelope type race,'[5] as Philip Ziegler put it, when operating the conventions and procedures of our elusive constitution. The humbug comes in the pretence that this is not only deliberate, but desirable and successful too – though, as a Whitehall-watcher, I have been struck by the contrast between the public complacency and the private anxiety (and candour) about such matters, especially on the part of those who worked in areas where the lack of financial and industrial muscle at the disposal of Premiers and Cabinets who wished Britain to cut a dash in the world way out of line with its GDP per head (which, so far, is every occupant of the postwar Number Ten and most occupants of the twenty or so ministerial seats around the Cabinet table) was, and still is, cruelly exposed.

I have long suspected that one of the cardinal rules of the British way of government is that panic must always be portrayed as poise and desperate improvisation as the pragmatic product of centuries of wisdom and experience. 'Muddling through' is a polite expression of such realities. A delightful example of *sub rosa* candour came over the lunch table in the mid-1990s. One former Treasury knight, talking of a recently deceased predecessor in that terrible overseas finance job in Great George Street, recalled telling Sir X that he, Sir Y, at moments of sterling meltdown used to think back with admiration of Sir X's ability to remain calm as Britain's financial sinews stretched to breaking point. Sir X thanked Sir Y for the compliment but confided 'It was always one great continuous fuck-up, but we pretended it wasn't.'[6]

That burst of most un-Treasury-like language (a kind that would *only* be used between consenting mandarins in private) could almost be the motto, perhaps the *recitative*, behind what follows in this volume. Because, though the *Analysis* programme never succumbed to a please-pass-the-Valium kind of indulgence by wallowing in Britain's relative decline or its creaking political and administrative systems, it none the less had a justifiable tendency to hover over the great intractables of late twentieth-century Britain. It did so for two reasons: first, because of the tendency of much of the media to follow the trivial and the transient; and secondly, because so many current vicissitudes simply cannot be understood without an understanding of the undertow of the past. History was very much a motor of the *Analysis* approach.

The following adaptations of *Analysis* programmes, which are interleaved with BBC Radio Four historical specials and some BBC Radio Three discussions as well as articles, speeches and lectures on associated topics, are arranged in a fluid fashion: they start with the ancient, but still live, question of Crown power and personal monarchical prerogative; flow over the human players of the central government game (both elected and appointed) and the institutional playgrounds in which they exercise their skills and impulses; pause for a while to look at that pronounced desire to punch heavier than our weight in the world (and at some of its consequences); and finish up with portrayals of nine Prime Ministers who presided over the fluctuating fortunes of post-1945 Britain.

Part One

Crown Power

The British Constitution has always been puzzling, and always will be.
                                               HM Queen, early 1990s[1]

The Monarchy Question has taken the 1990s by storm – though, despite the misfortunes that have assaulted the Royal Family in battalions, I remain convinced the institution will survive.[2] When, with my boss and producer, Caroline Anstey, I sat down in the studio with Enoch Powell and Tony Benn in the spring of 1989 to discuss matters pertaining to the royal prerogative, we probably struck our listeners as the eccentric in pursuit of the arcane. By the time Simon Coates and I set out with tape-recorder to pursue the Queen's two remaining personal prerogatives (the power to dissolve Parliament and the power to appoint a Prime Minister) just over two years later, flickers of interest were apparent, but because of potential political volatility at the forthcoming election rather than any resurgent republicanism or cataract of personal revelation about the House of Windsor. We were, quite accidentally, ahead of the game (in my case, a rare but pleasant sensation), with the additional bonus of the Cabinet Secretary, Sir Robin Butler, acknowledging later in public that the transcript of our programme reflected the latest insider thinking in Palace, Cabinet Office and Downing Street circles about these ancient Crown powers.[3] The material which follows, therefore, should be treated as a pause for thought before the storm.

1

Jewel in the Constitution?

The Queen, Parliament and the Royal Prerogative

If we leave literary theory, and look to our actual old law, it is wonderful how much the sovereign can do . . . If any one will run over the pages of Comyn's Digest *or any other such book, title 'Prerogative', he will find the Queen has a hundred such powers which waver between reality and desuetude, and which would cause a protracted and very interesting legal argument if she tried to exercise them. Some good lawyer ought to write a careful book to say which of these powers are really usable, and which are obsolete. There is no authentic explicit information as to what the Queen can do, any more than of what she does.*

Walter Bagehot, 1867[1]

The British monarchy is one of the most and the least discussed institutions in the land. The idea of 'a *family* on the throne' is 'interesting', Bagehot wrote: 'It brings down the pride of sovereignty to the level of petty life.'[2] 'Interesting' is certainly an understatement from the perspective of the late twentieth century: a glance at any single week's worth of tabloid newspapers suggests the word 'obsessional' would be more appropriate. Yet the sovereign's political powers – the so-called royal prerogatives – are scarcely discussed at all in the popular sense. They are deemed a fit topic for the PhD thesis rather than the glossy magazine. Here, to adapt Bagehot again, 'daylight' has never really been let in 'upon magic'.[3] Once the English fought wars about the power of the monarchy; today, for the most part, it arouses little more than a hum of conversation among constitutional experts. For most people – when they think about it at all – the matter has long been resolved on the basis that, in the end, on any matter of substance, Parliament has the final say: the monarch can 'advise, encourage and warn' the Prime Minister,[4] and that's all.

Sixteen eighty-eight, the year of the Glorious Revolution, is the key date people remember as marking the moment when the Crown relinquished nearly all of its prerogative powers and became a constitutional monarchy. By way of a personal celebration of the 300th anniversary of that year, in 1988

Tony Benn sponsored a Bill to bring the remaining Crown Prerogatives firmly under the control of Parliament. The scope of these prerogatives, when listed by Mr Benn, surprised many observers, including as they do the power to declare war, to make peace, to ratify treaties and to recognize foreign governments. Mr Benn's Bill, as he realized himself, had no chance of being passed, but it did stimulate discussion on the political role of the Crown. His critics argued that his Bill was irrelevant because in practice the Queen's prerogative powers are exercised by the Prime Minister and members of the Cabinet – elected politicians, who are answerable to Parliament for their actions. Apart from the so-called 'personal prerogatives' – the admittedly important powers to dissolve Parliament and appoint a Prime Minister, which the monarch, in theory at least, still retains – all the other prerogatives have long since passed from Buckingham Palace to Whitehall. But should they now move a bit further, across Parliament Square and into the House of Commons itself? Should the Speaker of the House of Commons have the sole responsibility for dissolving Parliament and appointing a new Premier? Or is it the case that the personal prerogatives are in fact fully circumscribed by convention? To what extent is it true that, as Enoch Powell has argued, the nature of parliamentary democracy as it has developed in the House of Commons is inseparable from monarchy? Why does Mr Benn believe that the question of royal prerogatives actually matters?

It matters because we still live under a feudal constitution. Actually it is a written constitution because the Common Market law takes precedence over our law now. But, if you look at it from the point of view of the people – and I've always been a believer in the sovereignty of the people – the people can't elect the head of state: the American people can; the people can't elect the Senate or House of Lords: the American people can; and the House of Commons has become a part of the 'dignified' part of the Constitution because the powers of the Crown have been transferred to the Prime Minister without accountability, except of a most tenuous kind. And so it is very important. Common Market membership has resuscitated the prerogatives; when Heath signed the treaty of accession it hadn't ever been published, and all the powers of law-making are now exercised in secret under prerogative powers. So it's a very, very big issue indeed.

Does this square with Enoch Powell's understanding of how things actually work?

Tony Benn and I are both hard-necked maintainers of the overriding sovereign power of the House of Commons and that's why we're both opposed to membership of a European Economic Community, which is incompatible with it, and also, I suppose, to rulings of the European Court, which could strike down Acts of Parliament and force Acts of Parliament upon an unwilling House of Commons. So I doubt whether there's any real issue of principle between myself and Tony Benn. I think there is a big issue of practicability, however, and my only argument, had I been able to, or wished to, join in the debate on his Bill, would be to say that the consequence of it was going to be to weaken the House of Commons by so clogging it up that it could scarcely live or breathe. We work, you see, by the principle of confidence, and by challenging confidence, by the ability to challenge confidence, to withdraw confidence, the House of Commons at all times, and thus the electorate eventually, retains the ultimate control over these powers which in real life have simply got to be exercised without reference to resolutions taken by an assembly.

From the way the Bill was written, it is clear that Tony Benn was worried that the power to make peace or declare war was a Crown prerogative and not actually dependent on prior consultation and a vote in the House of Commons. He points out that Britain went to war in the Falklands without Parliament explicitly voting to authorize it, whereas the Americans do have to go through that authorization process; and that there was no authorization at the time of Suez, either. But, he says, the peace and war argument is to an extent theoretical; what really worries him is the question of treaty-making powers.

It is worth going back, not only to Heath's signature of the treaty of accession, which was published after he signed it, but to the fact that every single Common Market directive and regulation under which we now work has been brought into effect without being debated. Enoch says Parliament can't interfere in everything; I agree, but then, we've handled expenditure for a long time by picking the items we want. The point is that, if we did want to pick an issue like heavy lorries, where the law of Europe was contrary to our interests, we wouldn't have the right to pick it. And therefore we don't discuss it. To be in the House of Commons now is to watch the impotent body observing decisions taken over their heads by people, some of whom sit there, but who are not accountable to them; and of course, the ultimate instrument of overthrowing a government is one that no party will take because the price they would pay would be so great. So, you're frozen by votes of confidence into assenting to things you don't want, decided by people you don't control; and that is nothing whatever to do with parliamentary democracy.

What of Enoch Powell's point that the place would get clogged up? For example, the Bill also covered honours and appointments, which would be transferred from the monarchy to the House of Commons. If the Commons had to ratify the appointments of ministers, judges and senior civil servants and to control the grant of honours, wouldn't it find this a full-time occupation? Tony Benn thinks not.

Take John Tower, the Secretary of Defense that wasn't in America: the Senate examined his record – I'm not commenting on it – but that had the right to confirm or not, and I think the right to confirm major appointments of judges and so on was right. As far as the honours are concerned, it's very simple: you table a motion of thanks, which would be the honours list, if you like, once a year, and Parliament passes it after a few speeches and then you all repair to Westminster Hall and have a nosh-up with all the people.

Enoch Powell finds this prospect contrary to the very idea of parliamentary debate:

I'm really quite shocked at the idea of Tony Benn approving of an unamendable motion before the House of Commons. Surely the essence of debate in the House of Commons is that you debate amendable motions. You debate motions to which you can propose amendments. If the House of Commons is really going to control honours, then it has to have the right to pick and choose on a list which is submitted to it and say, 'We're not going to have so and so, we're going to have somebody else instead,' and you must be in the position, if the thing is genuine at all, to debate that. I think this is the underlying practical difficulty of the objective which I think we achieve as far as it's practicable to achieve it by the principle of confidence, and that's what worries me about Tony's approach.

Tony Benn identifies a key difference between his and Enoch Powell's approaches to the question in historical terms: 'For me it's the sovereignty of the people, for you, the sovereignty of the House of Commons. I'm really a Cromwellian, you're a 1688 man. But that isn't to say that we don't come together on the tyranny of Brussels, where we're governed by a re-creation of the Holy Roman Empire over which we had no real say.'

But to return from the Holy Roman Empire to our own former Empire and our present Queen, what would be the implications of the fundamental change in the ground rules suggested by Tony Benn? Would his proposals jeopardize the utility and therefore the survivability of the British monarchy?

In Enoch Powell's view it is central to the monarch's role that his or her powers are not constrained:

> The utility of the monarchy, and its necessity in the sense of our parliamentary institutions, is that it is the unlimited, because unwritten, powers of the monarchy which are, as it were, in commission with Parliament. If the monarchy was a creature – as monarchies in most other countries are – of a written constitution, then those powers and therefore the powers of Parliament controlling the monarchy would be circumscribed, and what they were would have to be decided by a court sitting in judgement upon the constitutional foundation.

Thus the judges would get drawn in in lieu of the monarchy? Tony Benn does not accept this; and he goes on to draw a distinction between the person occupying the throne and the monarchy as an institution: 'Edward VIII was removed to save the monarchy. You see, the monarch and the monarchy have got nothing to do with one another. In the end Buckingham Palace thought: if we keep Edward VIII it'll ruin the monarchy and the empire.'

Does this mean that we have a kind of court system, that the monarch is truly a figurehead? That it is a group of courtiers that decides on the health of the British constitution?

> I have no doubt whatever that the court wanted to preserve the monarchy and not the monarch, and that could happen again. But when you introduce a Bill like the one you've referred to, you have to get the Queen's consent, even for it to have a second reading. So I always send these Bills – I've done another one amending the Coronation Oath – to the Home Secretary to send to Buckingham Palace, and I have a letter from the Home Secretary saying: the Queen has put her privileges at the disposal of the House for the purpose of discussing this Bill. And then he puts a little footnote to the effect that – I'm not quoting him precisely – Her Majesty's present advisers would strongly advise against the enactment of the Bill. So the Crown is in a difficulty about Bills of this kind. If it says you can't discuss it, then it is vetoing even parliamentary debate, to which Enoch attaches importance. If it says it doesn't mind it being debated, it must be putting its powers in commission to Parliament. I think there are aspects of this that are worth exploring. The Crown can only be made safe in Britain, in my opinion, by liberating it totally from any form of power, either exercised by itself, or commissioned by itself in others – by the disestablishment of the Crown, rather as it is in the British Commonwealth. India as a republic recognizes the Queen as Head of the Commonwealth. I want us to be a republic or commonwealth recognizing

the Queen as Head of the Commonwealth. Now, if you do that, the Crown is safe. If you don't do that it is inevitably involved, directly or indirectly, in matters of high political argument.

This sounds rather like privatizing the monarchy to save it, though Tony Benn demurs at the term. Is this a prospect that appeals to Enoch Powell?

I wouldn't disagree that the effectiveness of ultimate parliamentary and popular control is a necessary condition of the survival and continued acceptance of and affection for a monarchy. To that extent I agree. My disagreement, I think, with Tony is that I believe that control is as pervasive and efficient as we desire it to be; that by covering virtually every act of a Crown, every exercise of a prerogative with parliamentary advice, everything is earthed in the House of Commons. If the House of Commons doesn't take it up, well, that's the business of the House of Commons. If the House of Commons lets governments get away with it, as the opposition in the late 1980s allowed the government in office to get away with it, then that's the fault of those who man the House of Commons and we can't remedy that by any constitutional change.

In the end, though, if all these powers are transferred to statute powers under the House of Commons, and the government has a majority in the House of Commons, is the government not still going to get its way, and still going to be quite capable of behaving at times in what Tony Benn might see as an arbitrary and over-mighty manner? He concedes the point in theory, but adds:

We're moving – not only in Parliament, but in political parties – towards everything becoming a vote of confidence in the leader, either the Prime Minister or the party leader; and when you do this, you can destroy democracy in the name of entrenching it. You say, 'we could always change the leader,' but people don't want to change the leader, they want to change the policy. To take one example, which I find quite interesting: the decision to entrench the Security Services in statute involves moving services that previously operated under the prerogative into statute. This was by popular pressure because of Peter Wright and *Spycatcher* and other abuses, and I can see the progressive development of my Bill because many of the powers that were previously prerogative powers were transferred to statutory powers. I happen to have put the whole lot down. I've put pardons down. I don't really think the House should debate whether a man should live or die. But I do think there should be some provision whereby a judicial committee of the House might examine the basis on which pardons were granted – so that you could intervene from a parliamentary point of view up to the extent that you think it right, and to that extent the judgement and the wisdom of a House of Commons could be brought to bear sensitively on some matters. You have to go to war if you're attacked; so I don't think it follows that this would turn everything into one vast steering committee on the *QE2* as it crossed the Atlantic in the middle of a storm.

Enoch Powell sees a risk here of the House of Commons being cast in a role for which it is not appropriate:

> There is a major practical issue here in the idea of a judicial committee of the House of Commons. If there's anything that's abominable, it's a House of Commons which sets itself up directly or indirectly as a court of law. And when we propose to render the exercise of a prerogative of mercy an exercise which is carried out by the House of Commons, then we are putting on to the plate of the House of Commons business which it is not capable of digesting, not capable of justly or fairly or equitably handling.

In response to Enoch Powell's point that the main business of the opposition in Parliament is to be vital, strong and effective, and that this isn't happening – and that this is the key to the whole constitutional health of the system – Tony Benn acknowledges the need for a flourishing opposition, but doubts whether that of itself is enough:

> Even if you have a very, very strong opposition, you would still have made absolutely no progress and could not make progress on what the minister of this or that agreed to when he went to Brussels next week, because those are entrenched in the Prerogative. You could not have questioned the appointment of a judge, the appointment of a secretary of state or anything of that kind. Parliament *has* sub-contracted some of these functions. To give an example very personal to me, when I was re-elected as a disqualified peer, I was sent to an election court. Now, that election court was only advisory to the Commons, whereas in the nineteenth and eighteenth century, there were election committees of the House which operated politically. So, Parliament can do what it likes with the powers, but it must have the ultimate power in its own hands, otherwise it's handing them over to people who can never be held to account for what they've done.

There remains, of course, the matter of the 'personal prerogatives' that still attach to the monarch, those seemingly ultimate powers at his or her disposal. This subject is of far more than academic interest – indeed, there have been a number of occasions in this century when it has been of acute and direct concern: in 1910, when George V was going to give Asquith a dissolution before he packed the House of Lords to get through the Parliament Bill, and in 1913, when there was speculation that he was going to veto the Irish Home Rule Bill; in 1923–4 with the first Labour government coming into office; in 1931, with the Labour government crumbling and a National Government emerging after discussion with the party leadership; in 1950, when Attlee was returned with a majority of only six and the question arose whether, if it failed to work, Churchill wouldn't be sent for; and more recently – an episode in which Tony Benn played an active role – in 1974, when Harold Wilson came back in a minority government after Ted Heath had tried over a weekend to cobble together a coalition with the Liberals. This kind of fluid uncertainty could become more acute, even, almost, routine, if we were to move into a three-party system where coalition was a distinct possibility.

Tony Benn thinks that the power of the monarch to dissolve Parliament and to send for a Prime Minister remains a matter of real concern in terms of democracy and accountability.

The classic case is Gough Whitlam in Australia, who had a majority in the House of Representatives and was dismissed by the Governor-General, Kerr, using royal powers – though actually, when Gough Whitlam complained to the Palace, they said, 'these powers have been sub-contracted to the Governor-General, who you yourself recommended should be appointed.' But I think the power of asking somebody to form a government where a genuine matter of judgement may arise is important. There is also the influence of this on the way a party leader is chosen. In 1963 when Macmillan retired and Home emerged, Enoch and Macleod wouldn't serve under Home, and this led – so it always seemed to me subsequently – to the election process in which Enoch stood and got some votes and then Heath was elected. And I remember that during the argument about the electoral college in the Labour Party, a Labour lawyer who had held high office said, 'you can't elect the leader through an electoral college because the right to choose the Prime Minister is personal to the sovereign.' Now, when the sovereign is used to get Lord Home into Number Ten and to deny the right of a party member to choose the leader in the Labour Party, you're beginning to see that influence spreading much more widely than just in the more technical questions.

The idea of a constitutional monarchy is that the sovereign should be above the political fray; is the reality that he or she does get brought into the political arena by the exercise of these powers? Tony Benn thinks so; Enoch Powell disagrees:

> I don't think it can be disputed that the granting of a dissolution or the commissioning of a person to form a government is a deeply political act, which is why I would be opposed to Tony's proposal that the Speaker should be entrusted with something which is so inherently political. But that is a political decision which is always covered, admittedly after the event, but still is covered by a majority in the House of Commons and, if necessary, a majority in the country. When a dissolution is granted, when the Prime Minister seeks a dissolution, then the consequence of that is carried by the Prime Minister who sought the dissolution. There is no party bias in the decision because the decision is then thrown back to the House of Commons or to the electorate. In the case of choosing a Prime Minister, the Crown is looking for someone who can command a majority in the House of Commons. Unless that person commands a majority – if in the Labour Party, for example, a Labour leader had proved not to be able to command a majority in the House – then that person could not have been the Crown's chief minister. These are decisions which, although they are deeply political, are covered by the authority of the House of Commons. They're covered by a majority in that very place.

Let's look at a specific example. In 1969 Harold Wilson was in deep trouble in the Cabinet over his industrial relations legislation, the White Paper *In Place of Strife*. There was discussion as to the possibility of Wilson falling and the Queen being able to send, if she so chose, for Jim Callaghan, who could have commanded a majority in the House; if that had happened, that would surely have been bringing the monarchy directly into internal Labour Party politics? Tony Benn was involved in this episode:

> The position then was that Wilson was half threatening to resign to force people to support him, and Douglas Houghton, the chairman of the parliamentary party, said, 'we'll send somebody in a taxi to Buckingham Palace to say that we could find a leader who could command because he had a majority of a hundred.' The same situation could arise now. Supposing the flagship of the Conservative policy were to be defeated; the Prime Minister could threaten to resign, but somebody could say, 'well, look, so-and-so could create a parliamentary majority.' So I think the question of dissolution is one thing; but take the question of the choice of a leader, and imagine a situation where all three parties have got exactly the same number of Members of Parliament – it's the clearest way

of looking at it. Whoever was entrusted with the right to try to form a government would have the initiative for three or four weeks before Parliament met, and it doesn't have to meet in a great hurry – in the case of Home, it couldn't meet until he'd been elected, and I think we had to wait about two months. So during that period, the initiative could be taken, proposals could be brought forward. All I'm saying about the Speaker is that, assuming no other change, all the powers of the Crown have been sub-contracted or put to the Prime Minister, except these powers, the Speaker should have the mandatory right to 'advise' with a capital A on these two questions.

Challenged by Powell as to whether the Speaker would carry the political responsibility for the advice that he has tendered, Benn adds that it would still have to be endorsed in both cases by the House; to which Powell retorts; 'Well then, you're back in the present position.' Benn persists:

No, not really, because you would be taking a highly political but constitu-tional decision out of the Crown's hands, so the Crown couldn't be blamed if they recommended a dissolution that went wrong on the Crown. But it would be the Speaker, who knows uniquely how the House works, who could advise whether there could be a re-created majority without an election, and, if there was a hung Parliament, which leader was most likely to command a majority.

But – though Enoch Powell doubts that it would be, as he puts it, 'fruitful' for the Crown to consult the Speaker on who had the best prospect of securing a majority for the government in the House of Commons – the Queen can take advice on this point from whom she chooses, as Tony Benn recalls from personal experience:

I asked the Queen once whether she did consult the Speaker, and she said, 'I can consult who I like.'[5] But take the case of whether there has to be a dissolution: in January 1974 I happened to have lunch at the Iranian Embassy with the Shadow Cabinet and the Queen's Private Secretary was there. I sat next to him, and I said, 'If Mr Heath asks for a dissolution, can the Queen refuse it?' and he said to me, 'It's funny you should ask that, because we've been discussing all morning what we would do.' So I went away and wrote my election address because I knew they expected Heath to ask for a dissolution – which he did; therefore, in a sense, the machine was in motion.[6] And this is very, very political. Is the Queen's Private Secretary better qualified than the Speaker? What if the Queen herself were drawn into something which, it if went wrong, might lead to the re-election of a Parliament with a bigger majority than she'd dissolved? Supposing there was a Labour government with a fairly big majority, a reasonable majority, that became very unpopular indeed, and the Crown were to dissolve, and then that Labour government were to be re-elected; the Crown would be utterly repudiated by the electorate. They would say to the Crown: 'You shouldn't have dissolved that Parliament we elected. We're giving you another strong one.' So it was a political decision.

In Powell's view, the monarchy is not 'drawn in' in this way: 'When the Crown has dissolved Parliament, then the Crown is not a partisan in the result of the election . . . I don't envisage the Crown, without advice, dissolving Parliament.'

What, then, of the monarch as a kind of constitutional buffer, taking the strain of a system in crisis? The idea, as it were, that you can look to the Queen, taking advice from whomsoever she sees fit, if the system is grinding to a halt and there seems to be a wide range of possible Prime Ministers on offer? If, in 1974, Ted Heath had managed to put together a deal with the Liberals over that weekend of the end of February/beginning of March, and it hadn't worked, wouldn't the Queen have been perfectly within her rights to say, 'I'm going to send for Harold Wilson to see what he can do?' Again, Enoch Powell lays emphasis on the legitimating role of the House of Commons:

At an earlier point it was necessary for the Prime Minister of the day to provide a speech at the opening of Parliament and an address to the Crown in response to be presented. That is to say, there would be an opportunity to see where the majority in the House of Commons lay. And upon that, Heath, if he hadn't got his majority, would have had to resign.

Tony Benn, in contrast, focuses on the decision-making power of the Queen:

Supposing, to take that case, which is historically on the record, Heath had got Thorpe to join him, which I think Thorpe wanted to do, he'd presented a Queen's Speech and it had been rejected, Heath would have said to the Queen: 'I want another dissolution.' And the Queen would have had to decide whether to give the Prime Minister she'd appointed a dissolution or not. If she said, 'I won't give a dissolution, Mr Heath, I'm going to call for Mr Wilson,' it would have been very political.

Whereas, under his preferred arrangements, 'the House of Commons would have to resolve, in those circumstances, whether in addition to rejecting the

Heath/Thorpe coalition, it wanted a Wilson government with Thorpe, as it were, or not.' He offers another example:

> Imagine circumstances where Labour was the biggest party after a general election, but perhaps not with an overall majority – it's a theoretical consideration – and the Labour leader becomes Prime Minister. He presents the Queen's Speech – it might get through on the grounds that members on the whole don't want another election, it would be very exhausting – but about six months later he's brought down, perhaps because he's refused proportional representation to the Liberal Democrats: *then* the question is, can he say to the Queen, 'I want to go back to the electorate on my programme and not allow PR to wreck my programme'? And the Queen would have to decide whether to do it, or whether to ask the leader of the Conservative Party whether he or she could do a deal with the Liberal Democrats. These are very political questions.

Powell points out that the Queen has to find advisers who can deliver a majority in the House of Commons, to which Benn's response is that 'the only people to do that are the House of Commons; they know, and the Speaker knows, the Commons better than anyone.' Powell continues:

> And if that dissolution is refused, it must be refused on advice. And it is refused by commissioning the Conservative leader – in the example we are considering – to form a government, and he does so successfully and he has a majority in the House of Commons. And he takes responsibility from thence onwards for the fact that it is that government and not the Labour government by which the country is ruled.

Tony Benn takes the example a stage further.

> Supposing that the Conservative leader is asked to form a government in those circumstances. He comes with a Queen's Speech and it is defeated. Is he given the dissolution just refused to the Labour leader? These are inevitably very, very political questions. My starting point is the right of the people to elect their representatives. Their representatives have got to sort out how they handle who is to be asked to form a government.

A detached observer reading these expressions of two strongly contrasting viewpoints might consider that the political system in Britain functions in an extraordinarily bizarre fashion, if two gentlemen who have been in Parliament between them a very long time can discuss and disagree

on the crucial questions of forming a government and selecting a Prime
Minister, in the process making the system seem so opaque as to be beyond
the comprehension of even the smartest constitutional monarch. Isn't the
answer to do what Bagehot said we should do as recently as 1867, which is to
write it down? Enoch Powell voices a note of caution.

> I wonder what Bagehot would have written down in order to ensure that
> you always secured a House of Commons in which there was a stable
> majority for one political party; or for one particular coalition. We are
> dealing with a House of Commons produced by the electorate of such a
> composition that there's an open doubt, maybe a continuing doubt, as to
> the command of a majority in that House. No constitutional device which
> won't have the most damaging side consequences in reducing the power
> of the electorate can avoid that.

Tony Benn is equally cautious, but more enthusiastic about the idea of
writing something down.

> It would have to be looked at very, very carefully. I do not think that the
> Bill of Rights – there should be rights – should be interpreted by the
> courts, but should be referred back to the ombudsman in the House of
> Commons. So, when there's a breach of human rights, the House has to
> deal with it, not leave it to the judges whose political bias is well known.
> On the question of whether people have behaved within the law, the
> judges already have the right, don't they? Already the judges have a role,
> and I think in the interpretation of the law of the constitution you do have
> to have judges, but then I would have the judges confirmed by the House
> of Commons before they're appointed. I think it is possible to contem-
> plate a new constitution for Britain. And I think a lot of people would
> welcome it.

A Government of Britain Bill? How would Enoch Powell view this?

> Tony wants a Bill – and this was the context in which the subject came up
> – which lays down rules for how the House of Commons is to proceed in
> the event of a certain outcome of a parliamentary election. That is how we
> got here, that is how we came to be discussing this. Now, he wants that to
> be formulated so that it can be decided by judges. He wants judges to
> apply their mind to the situation resulting from a general election and say
> how the rules apply to that situation. I misunderstood him.

But Tony Benn doesn't accept this interpretation of his views.

If you had a Government of Britain Bill it would provide that the House of Commons would resolve itself the matters of dissolution within a Parliament – I would like a four-year, or maybe a three-year Parliament, but that's another matter. But within that, the Commons would be sovereign in the handling of these two central questions. One is whether it is to be dissolved; the other is who is to be asked to form a government. And that would not be giving the judges the power to decide when you dissolved, but the Constitution giving the Commons the right instead of leaving it to the Crown with her capacity to consult anybody she wishes. It's only a rough description of the concept, but I think it's one that has been tested and tried in other democratic countries.

Mention of the United States in this context prompts Powell to remark that that country has 'a written constitution, judge-ruled, with the consequence that the judges have a political flavour, a political character which is created by a succession of administrations'. Benn counters that the US Constitution is 'much, much more democratic in its political, constitutional sense' and that the judges all have to be confirmed by the Senate; and he continues:

The President has got to carry the Congress with him, not just in general, but in detail. Indeed, he doesn't have to carry them with him in general because he's elected. But in detail he has to. Now, the Prime Minister has to carry the Commons with him in general, i.e. so that they don't overthrow the Prime Minister, but in detail she or he can do what they like. And every Prime Minister – don't think this is a recent situation only – every Prime Minister has grossly abused the powers of the Crown. Attlee invited the Americans here, built the bomb without telling Parliament. This isn't unique to the present era; it goes right back within my lifetime and probably even further.

Powell points out that this is a case of the House of Commons being proved after the event 'not to have done the job which it ought to have done; not to have asked the questions which it ought to have done, not to have censured those whom it ought to have censured, and I don't think there's any construction that you can make which will ensure that the House of Commons will do its job properly if the people in it aren't doing that job.' Benn agrees that the House may have fallen down on its job, but goes on to offer an explanation of why this may be so:

Patronage corrupts the Commons. You may come in with strong ideas; within a week or two you realize that if you're going to get on, you've got to please your leader. Therefore, the leader makes you either a minister, if you're in office, or a shadow minister. As you get older, if you want to be in the House of Lords, which is a lovely pensionable job, you've got to please your leader. And we do have a craven House of Commons, and that craven House of Commons is craven not just because it isn't doing its job, but because the patronage of the Crown has spread like a virus into the party system.

Powell, again, is sceptical:

You think that corruption would be less severe if the House of Commons itself made the appointments? That a House of Commons which has the conferment of these goodies in its own hands is not going to behave like a House of Commons which had in its hands the fixing of its own salaries and freebies? And you don't think that the party system is going to be just as effective in a House of Commons which votes upon who's to have a peerage?

Tony Benn points out that, while he would not be in favour of a peerage,

the House already does create peers in former Speakers, where it moves a humble address to the Crown, praying that a single mark of royal favour be conferred upon the Speaker. But I think you would have to accompany it with democratic changes within each party. In the Labour Party, I don't believe that there should be any patronage by the leader on the Shadow Cabinet or the front bench. But that's a matter personal to my party. How the Conservative Party or other parties would handle it would be for them to decide.

Enoch Powell is not known as a man who has particularly pleased the leaders of the parties to which he has belonged. Does he think that successive Prime Ministers *have* abused Crown powers which they exercise in the monarch's name?

Successive Prime Ministers have been able to get away unquestioned with things which I would have preferred to see questioned. I think there are a good many examples in the handling of Northern Ireland, the motives which lay behind it. And on the Rock of Gibraltar, where questions were up for being asked in the House of Commons and statements were being made unchallenged in the House of Commons, and not effectively challenged, by which I mean effectively challenged in searching debate, which ought to have been. And I don't think there's any legislation conferring further commitments upon the House of

Commons, further duties upon the House of Commons, which is going to alter that.

Tony Benn finds an echo here of his own thoughts.

I agree with Enoch about questioning, and I think it's a criticism I've made in speeches in the House. It is a craven Commons, spectators of their own decline and fate and almost willing spectators. But having said that, you can't question what you don't know about. Take the cases of Oliver North and Peter Wright. They both committed, so we understand, an offence. Oliver North was covered by the Thirty Minute Rule under which he appeared before the Congress. Peter Wright was pursued all over the world because he revealed what had happened. And now lifelong confidentiality to the Crown is to guarantee, under the prerogative to the Crown, secrecy till you die, and that must apply to ministers, because after all Enoch and I are servants of the Crown.

Does he think, then, that the American system is superior to ours in this respect as well?

You can't question what you don't know, and the prerogative is the power that surrounds everything with barbed wire and klieg lights and mines the area. So the Commons, even if it wanted to question, could not know what it wanted to question because of the prerogative. So a Freedom of Information Act, which would have to be a parliamentary statute, would be another way of opening up the abuse of Crown powers by Prime Ministers.

Enoch Powell doubts the wisdom of expanding the remit of the House of Commons and points to what he sees as the great strength of the existing system:

Without being drawn on to the question of secrecy and freedom of information, which is a big subject in its own right, I'm fascinated to find that Tony is prepared to trust a craven House of Commons which he won't trust even to keep tabs on the administration in its present form, to do all these additional things. That's what worries me about it. I don't think the House of Commons is a fit means of taking these individual decisions.

The British Constitution has the device of confidence, which is not available in a constitution like the American Constitution with a fixed term of office for the President and the Executive. I think it's one of our major political discoveries, because it enables us to combine the effective exercise of government functions, where that exercise depends upon an alteration in the position from day to day and from hour to hour, with the final supremacy and power of decision of the electorate through the House of Commons. I think Tony underestimates confidence.

The whole thrust of Tony Benn's Bill was to suggest – in fact, it was worded to say this directly – that we really couldn't call ourselves a proper democracy as long as these secret powers remained in the hands of ministers, exercised on behalf of the monarch. He put the thesis very simply: unless the real powers *in toto* go to the House of Commons, we're not a proper democracy. In fact, he would go further:

> Well, to the electorate really. The House is only a mirror of the nation, and my belief is in the power and right of the electorate. And if Parliament isn't allowed to know what the Crown is doing through its ministers, the public doesn't know. If the public doesn't know, they can't reflect their view in elections. So it would also transform the relationship, not just between the Crown and the Commons, but between the executive and the people. And I think that unless that is done, you're leaving all these huge powers to people to operate in secret. And that is a most terrifying form of tyranny.

Powell does not accept the suggestion that the government is working in secret; but he picks up the point about representation, referring to

> the other act of genius of a British people in the development of a feudal constitution into the modern British democracy, namely the nature of representation; the underlying sense of a British people, as to what they're prepared to put up with and what they're not prepared to put up with, which they have this curious habit of conveying through the ballot box and through the elective process in the House of Commons. I think our security lies upon this combination of representation. In the end, it is about the electorate, it's about the people out of doors. Those are the people, ultimately, who are our masters. Those are the people, ultimately, to whom we report and refer. Representation *and* the confidence of the House, these are the two pillars on which – and I'm prepared to call it democracy just to keep in with the Americans – our system rests.

Enoch Powell once said that 'the common precious and hereditary jewel of every British subject' was the Crown, the hereditary monarchy. He presented it as one of the great glories of the common people. What of that role now?

Until 1972 I thought we had inherited, all of us, the poorest of us, the right to be governed only by laws and to pay only those taxes which were voted in the House of Commons. That has been taken away from us by treaty; by treaty, but by a treaty which could not have been made unless a craven House of Commons had voted for it. To heap on to this craven House of Commons more functions, more duties, more individual decisions, more invigilation, is not practicable. I think it would just pull down the House of Commons as well.

Tony Benn refers back to the argument advanced when he put his case about the peerage:

They said to me, 'If you undermine the Lords, you'll undermine the Crown.' I thought very carefully, and I realized they were using the Crown to prop up the Lords. Privilege justifies itself because it preserves the Crown, and when you look at it, the Crown is used to preserve privilege, political privilege. Until people think this out and connect it to the homes they live in and the jobs they have, and the schools and hospitals and pensions and peace, until they connect their daily experience with how we're governed, we're never going to make sense of these – what may seem very remote and erudite – questions.

A cynic reading this might say: here are two elderly romantic gentlemen, with a long parliamentary tradition to which they're devoted, together with a third person who's equally obsessed by fine constitutional matters, worrying away about what in reality, in everyday existence for ordinary people, doesn't amount to a row of beans. How would Powell respond to such a cynic?

'Beware of telling the people that the things which are most valuable to them are not endangered if their representatives in Parliament do not function efficiently.'

And Benn?

Callaghan said that the reforms of the Labour Party were arid, constitutional struggles; and he said it publicly. But all real progress is made when you change the structure of power. We've been considering power: not how it's exercised in detail, but who has it, where they got it, to whom they're accountable and how they can be removed. Until you turn your mind to that, you're frolicking on the margins of politics.

And both Tony Benn and Enoch Powell believe that they get that power from the same place, by persuading their fellow countrymen; and that is the business of their lifetimes.

2

The Back of the Envelope

Hung Parliaments, the Queen and the Constitution

Over a hundred and twenty-five years ago, Walter Bagehot said that anyone looking up the word 'prerogative' in a reference book would 'find the Queen has a hundred such powers which waver between reality and desuetude, and which would cause a protracted and very interesting legal argument if she tried to exercise them'. He continued: 'Some good lawyer ought to write a careful book to say which of these powers are really useable, and which are obsolete. There is no authentic explicit information as to what the Queen can do, any more than of what she does.'[1]

Constitutional matters have resolved themselves a good deal since the days of Walter Bagehot and Queen Victoria. Convention has it that only two prerogative powers remain personal to the Sovereign in the monarchy of Elizabeth II: the dissolution of Parliament and the appointment of a Prime Minister.[2] But Bagehot's strictures still apply to the exercise of these far from peripheral responsibilities. There is even now, in the 1990s as in the 1860s, 'no authentic explicit information as to what the Queen can do'.

The last time anyone in authority made anything approaching a definitive statement on the subject was in 1950, shortly after the Attlee government had been returned with what was then regarded as a slender majority of six. Under the pseudonym 'Senex',[3] Sir Alan Lascelles, Private Secretary to King George VI, wrote to *The Times* arguing that

> It is surely indisputable (and commonsense) that a Prime Minister may ask – not demand – that his Sovereign will grant him a dissolution of Parliament; and that the Sovereign, if he so chooses, may refuse to grant this request. The problem of such a choice is entirely personal to the Sovereign, though he is, of course, free to ask informal advice from anybody whom he thinks fit to consult. Insofar as this matter can be publicly discussed, it can be properly assumed that no wise Sovereign – that is, one who has at heart the true interest of the country, the constitution, and the Monarchy – would deny a dissolution to his Prime Minister unless he was satisfied that: (1) the existing Parliament was still vital,

viable and capable of doing its job; (2) a General Election would be detrimental to the national economy; (3) he could rely on finding another Prime Minister who could carry out his Government, for a reasonable period, with a working majority in the House of Commons.[4]

At the beginning of the 1990s this forty-year-old wisdom seemed but a partial guide to what promised to be a politically volatile decade, with at least the possibility of a multi-party system developing. There was a whiff in the air, the scent of political uncertainty that, for veterans of the 1970s, recalled painful, poignant memories of hung parliaments, minority governments, Lib/Lab pacts and tiny majorities melting like snow in April. Double-digit leads in the opinion polls can be misleading: the longer the pre-election period runs, the stronger those unsettling odours become. If we found ourselves once more in an age of political fragility, what wisdom could be distilled from the Seventies' experience about the management of government in such circumstances? Have the lessons been learned? At what point would past experience cease to be a guide and serious constitutional trouble begin?

None of these questions is news in Buckingham Palace, Number Ten Downing Street or the Cabinet Office, where the official guardians of the Constitution will reach for the files. For it is from precedents that the Queen's advisers will fashion their counsel if the electorate produces an inconclusive result and her personal prerogative powers – to appoint a Prime Minister and, perhaps, to dissolve Parliament a second time – come into play.

The most relevant document in the file deals with the events of February/March 1974. The day after the election the Queen returned to London from Australia to find the Conservatives, led by Edward Heath, marginally ahead of Labour in share of the vote, just behind in seats won. Neither party was near an absolute majority. The result opened up a kaleidoscope of possibilities for Her Majesty and her advisers – and for the politicians themselves.

Lord Callaghan was then Chairman of the Labour Party, and Mr Harold Wilson's foreign affairs spokesman. When the Shadow Cabinet and the party's tacticians met, once the final result was known, what conclusion did they reach?

We decided that we would not challenge Mr Heath; we would allow him to carry on and to try to make any arrangement that he could. We did this because we were fairly satisfied that he wouldn't be able to make such an arrangement. But if he had seemed likely to, then I think I would have taken a very different view about the situation because, in some ways, Mr Heath was acting in a way that I think was rather prejudicial. The country had expressed its lack of confidence in the Conservative government. They'd had a majority; that majority had been lost. They were now the second largest party. And in my view, although I won't say it was improper of Mr Heath because there are no conventions on these matters, I think it was stretching the thing a bit for him, as a defeated Prime Minister, then to try to make an arrangement which would have circumvented the will of the electorate, which was not to have a Conservative majority. I remember I took the bold step of saying we should allow Ted Heath – it was a rather cruel phrase – 'to swing slowly in the wind'.

Mr Heath, however, had no intention of 'swinging in the wind'. While Lord Callaghan could stress the number of seats gained – Labour's 301 to the Conservatives' 297 – Mr Heath could counter with share of the poll – 37.8 per cent for the Tories, 37.1 per cent for Labour. Under our parliamentary system, seats normally prevail. But Lord Callaghan is right: the conventions offered Mr Heath no conclusive guidance. So the Conservative leader invited the Liberal leader, Jeremy Thorpe (whose party won nearly 20 per cent of the votes but a mere fourteen seats) to a meeting in Number Ten the next day.

But isn't Lord Callaghan also right in suggesting that Mr Heath, in not resigning at once, 'stretched' the constitution? It is, after all, a key ingredient in the folklore – then as now – surrounding how a Premier treats the Sovereign that embarrassment-avoidance is all. Did his staying on in Downing Street over the weekend not place the Queen in a potentially embarrassing position? Sir Edward himself thinks not: 'I don't believe that's the case at all. After an election, even though defeated, a Prime Minister and his party have the right to face the House of Commons and be defeated in the House of Commons. That doesn't cause any embarrassment to the Sovereign.' He is adamant that there was no sense of potential embarrassment from the Palace; the Private Secretaries just informed each other, and no signal was given to him either way.

On day two of that bleak weekend in Ted Heath's political life, Jeremy Thorpe prepared to hear what the Conservatives had to offer the Liberals:

The Prime Minister said that he had the largest number of votes of any political party in the House of Commons, and therefore had a duty, indeed a right, to form an administration, and were we interested in coming in on a coalition? And I said, 'Well, the first thing we must consider is that, as we sit here, I have more than half your vote behind me and six million people have got fourteen MPs.' And, secondly, I said, 'The arithmetic doesn't add up.' And he said, 'You mean you want electoral reform?' I said, 'Yes.' 'Well, we have no view on that.' And he went away and came back on the second occasion offering a Speaker's

Conference – again, having no view on it; but it was quite clear that the Tory Party would oppose it.

So coalition was on offer. But to make that happen in 1974, it was electoral reform or nothing; and Mr Heath couldn't promise to carry his party on the issue.

There was also another, highly delicate, factor. Mr Thorpe raised the possibility of the Liberals reaching an agreement with a different Tory leader, who might be able to command a majority in the Commons. There are indications that Mr Thorpe suggested to Mr Heath that it might be easier for the Liberals, given the recent confrontation with the miners and everything associated with that, if it were another Conservative figure who was asking for a deal with them. Heath himself is blunter:

'Well, he didn't put it quite like that. The basic fact was that they said, "No, if you're there, we can't do anything."'

'He didn't put it quite like that': Mr Thorpe may have been overplaying his hand, although his hint about an alternative Conservative Prime Minister wasn't unconstitutional. In any event, he got a dusty answer, as Heath recalls:

'My colleagues took the view very, very strongly that they weren't going to give way, in this respect, to anything which either the Liberals or anybody else might say.'

Even with fourteen Liberals, Mr Heath, or any other Tory leader, would have been seven short of an absolute majority; and, contrary to folklore, he didn't contemplate a deal with the Ulster Unionists, still outraged at the power-sharing executive in Northern Ireland created by the Sunningdale Agreement three months earlier.* No Prime Minister since Baldwin in 1924 has met Parliament after an inconclusive election. Mr Heath went to the Palace on the Monday and resigned. The Queen sent for Mr Wilson, who formed a minority government.

One other person was with Edward Heath during the bargaining with Jeremy Thorpe, and that same person accompanied him to the Palace when he resigned: his Principal Private Secretary, now Lord Armstrong of Ilminster, better known as Sir Robert Armstrong in his later incarnation as Cabinet Secretary. For the first time in forty years, Lord Armstrong, as an official of the inner circle, is prepared to place carefully on the record the constitutional principles which would apply if the electorate came up with a 'don't know'.

---

* Recent scholarship suggests that approaches were made to some, but not all, of the 'loyalist' Ulster MPs. See Vernon Bogdanor, *The Monarchy and the Constitution* (Clarendon Press, 1995), p. 149; John Ramsden, *The Winds of Change: Macmillan to Heath 1957–1975* (Longman, 1996), pp. 387–9.

The first point to note is that, after a general election, so long as there is a Prime Minister in office, and the Prime Minister hasn't tendered his resignation, the Sovereign is not called upon to take any action about appointing another Prime Minister. The initiative rests with the incumbent Prime Minister. In the sort of situation we're presupposing, the hung Parliament situation, the Sovereign and the Sovereign's advisers – and, one would hope, the politicians concerned – would have as primary objectives to ensure that the government of the country was carried on, and that everything possible was done to avoid the Sovereign being put into a position where action had to be taken which might bring the Crown into the area of political controversy.

When the officials in Buckingham Palace and Whitehall who are concerned with such matters sit down and consider the contingencies that might arise in the event of a hung Parliament, what is the range of possibilities that they have to consider?

In theory, the incumbent Prime Minister could, whatever the result of the election, decide to continue in office and present a speech from the Throne, and resign only if and when he lost the vote in the debate on the Address, in reply to the Gracious Speech. In practice, I think it's unlikely that this option would be exercised nowadays by any Prime Minister whose party had not won either an overall majority or a larger number of seats than any other party in the House of Commons – unless, of course, he had been able to enter into a coalition, or a pact, with another party which assured him of a majority in the debate on the Queen's speech.

From this passage we can see how smoothly the precedent of March 1974 has been threaded into the warp and woof of the Constitution. The official files have been in good repair ever since.

A Prime Minister's own free choice of an election date is made in the expectation of a conclusive and favourable result. Had Edward Heath contemplated any other outcome in 1974?

'Had I considered it in advance? Not in detail, no. You must remember that everybody then expected we were going to win the election with a large majority.'

By the time of the 1979 election, which was forced upon him, Mr Callaghan had lived for nearly two and a half years without a majority. Did *he* prepare accordingly?

There was no contingency planning of any kind. We went straight into the election, the assumption always being that there would be a clear verdict – my assumption being, of course, that we would win, although I knew very well we were going to lose. For me there was no prospect of there being a hung Parliament at that time. I thought the Conservatives would win easily because of the 'Winter of Discontent'. And, indeed, they did.

Isn't this prime ministerial aversion to contingency planning in conflict with Lord Armstrong's key constitutional principles – that the Queen's government must *always* be carried on and that Her Majesty must not be drawn into political controversy? With the benefit of the 1970s experience to draw on, could our current government and opposition leaders run the risk of improvising on the day? Vernon Bogdanor, Reader in Government at Oxford University, sets the question in a broader context:

This is the point at which you have to ask whether the conventions of the Constitution might not be simply conventions of a two-party system. If you take the view that we're in a period of transition, from a two-party system to a new multi-party system, then the conventions themselves will alter. And the most difficult period is this period of transition when you're not clear which conventions apply, and that's in part a political question because, of course, the Conservative and Labour Parties would say 'We are still in a two-party situation,' whereas the Liberal Democrats – and, no doubt, Scottish Nationalists, Ulster Unionists and perhaps others – would say, 'Well, no, we're moving into a very different situation, a multi-party situation.' And that really will cause strains for the British Constitution. What appears to be a constitutional question is, in part, a political question as well because the British Constitution is a very deeply political constitution.

Questions like these are not just the obstacles in an adventure playground for scholars; they are the very stuff of the party political battle. The ground rules of that battle at moments of political uncertainty are opaque, but they are crucial: they determine for whom the Queen sends, who is given the chance to form a government and to present a legislative programme to Parliament.

The umpires of those rules, then, are central to the political process. So who are they, the continuity men of the British Constitution? Paradoxically, the three people who count are a trio of non-political officials: the Queen's Principal Private Secretary; the Principal Private Secretary to the Prime Minister; and the Secretary of the Cabinet. But *should* they be the people who count in such intensely political circumstances? Philip Ziegler, the Palace-approved biographer of King Edward VIII and official biographer of Harold Wilson, thinks the alternatives are limited:

By and large it always is going to be this little group of insiders who are going to worry about what might go wrong and, to some extent, prepare for it. And the heart of those insiders is bound to be the three people you've mentioned just because they represent the different blocks of power, of influence, within the whole governmental circle. I can't think of a better way. Given that the problem is inevitably going to be unpredictable, it doesn't seem to me that it is possible to produce clear-cut stereotyped answers, in advance, which will suit it. The very best you can do is speculate a bit, throw up a few ideas, get a vague plan of action ready at the back of your mind – and then just hope for the best!

'Vague plan of action', 'just hope for the best': Ziegler's evocation of the British way is charming and alarming in equal measure. Why does he think we're so addicted to doing things on backs of envelopes in this country?

'I suppose it's a national characteristic. We always have, haven't we? I think that, as a nation, we do seem to be empiricists, extremely cautious about principles, strong on pragmatism – we just *are* a back-of-envelope type race!'

At the moment, the working assumption of those with access to the crucial envelopes is that the past will be an adequate guide to whatever minor adjustments might need to be made to the Constitution in the hours after a hung result. The heart of that assumption is that a government with a wafer-thin majority or no majority at all (the experiences, respectively, of October 1964 and March 1974) would, after a decent interval, be granted a second dissolution by the Queen, and that the resulting general election would produce a government with a majority. To assume more, insiders say, would imply acceptance by the Queen's advisers of the highly controversial and deeply political suggestion that we are already in the foothills of a multi-party system.

In 1987, however, the inside trio of the day were presented with a set of circumstances which made them contemplate that very possibility. How much thought did the old SDP/Liberal Alliance leaders give to the opportunities afforded by what they liked to call a 'balanced Parliament'? Sir David Steel, former leader of the Liberal Party, recalls that

There was a lot of detailed planning. In particular, David Owen and I drew up a document on precisely the steps that would be taken in the event of a balanced Parliament. We had no difficulty about this; I'd had my experience from the Lib/Lab pact and he'd had experience from within the Labour Cabinet. So we were both fairly well versed in these matters, and didn't have much difficulty in drawing up a detailed document. We then took it to Robert Armstrong, as the Secretary to the

Cabinet, and he agreed with the steps that we had outlined in it as being technically correct. There was no doubt what might or might not happen if there were a balanced Parliament after 1987.

Those steps were much the same as those David Steel had been ready to take with James Callaghan in May 1979, if the Labour premier had found himself back in Number Ten without an overall majority: first, a coalition government with Liberals and Social Democrats; second, preferably a Bill on proportional representation, but, as the bottom line, PR for the European Parliament, a Scottish Assembly, and a referendum on PR for the country as a whole.

In 1987, as in 1979, David Steel had firm views on what would be needed to make such a deal stick.

The endorsement of the two parliamentary parties, that is the Parliamentary Labour Party and the Alliance Members of Parliament, would have been essential – so that you got, not just an agreement among leaders or among possible Cabinets, but an actual Parliamentary agreement which would commit individuals to see the whole thing through for a four-year period; indeed, with a specific end to that Parliament as well.

This immediately raises a problem. Negotiating a deal of that magnitude with one or other of the major parties – in effect, signing away, perhaps for ever, its chance of forming a majority government alone – is more than the work of a few hours. Yet, as recently declassified documents show,[5] there is a firm timetable, fixed from the moment the Queen agrees to a Prime Minister's request for a dissolution of Parliament and continuing through the election, the choice of a Speaker, the swearing-in of new MPs, the State Opening of Parliament and the debate on the Queen's Speech. Does Sir David really believe that a Conservative or Labour leader is likely to put the Constitution on hold purely for the convenience of the Liberal Democrats?

There is a set timetable, but – the great glory of the British Constitution being that it is unwritten – there is nothing that says, 'because you have appointed 3 November as the date for the State Opening, you have to stick to it.' There is nothing whatever that prevents the Prime Minister and the Palace agreeing that, in view of the political situation, you can put it off for a week, ten days, two weeks. On the continent, governments sometimes take four, five, six weeks to get formed after an election, so why should we try to do the whole thing in two or three days?

But wouldn't such a change require the Queen's acquiescence? And wouldn't she have to give her royal seal of approval to whatever political settlement emerged out of the chaos? What if the incumbent Prime Minister, disdainful of Liberal Democrat demands for an instant whip of a new constitution, said to the Queen either 'I suggest you send for the Leader of the Opposition' or, more dramatically, 'The only way to sort out this mess is to call another election'? Can she really say 'no'? Lord Armstrong, former Cabinet Secretary, addresses this ticklish question with some circumspection:

> An outgoing Prime Minister advises the Sovereign whom to send for; and the expectation must be that, in all but the most exceptional circumstances, the Sovereign would act on that advice. But the Sovereign is entitled at least to say that he or she would like to reflect and, perhaps, to consult, before deciding whether to act on that advice, and must, therefore, be entitled, in the last resort, not to act on it. Obviously the Sovereign wouldn't be called upon to do that if the Prime Minister concerned was acting responsibly and in accordance with the principle of not putting the Sovereign in a position of having to act in a manner which brings the Crown into controversy. And in such a situation the Sovereign would be not exercising political judgement but seeking to identify and enable the course of action which would be most likely to command the widest possible degree of political and public acceptance in the interests of the integrity of the Constitution and the best interests of the country.

What, then, would these 'exceptional circumstances' be in which the Queen would be entitled to consult before granting a request or advice for a dissolution?

> There aren't any recent precedents on the basis of which it would be possible to express a definitive opinion on this, I think. There are some authorities who believe that the Sovereign's right to withhold consent to a request for a dissolution should be regarded as having lapsed, and that such a request must now be treated as tantamount to advice upon which the Sovereign is obliged to act. On another view, while it must be very rare for the Sovereign to withhold consent from a Prime Minister's request for a dissolution, it is still a request and not a demand, nor tantamount to advice on which the Sovereign is bound to act. I personally – and this is obviously a personal view because the precedents don't really guide us – would prefer that second view. It seems to me that it's not just theoretically correct, but common sense that the Sovereign should have the right to withhold consent to a request for a dissolution, if only as a check upon

the irresponsible exercise of the Prime Minister's right to request one, however improbable such a contingency may seem to be.

'The precedents don't really guide us'; 'common sense' suggesting that the Queen could and should act 'as a check' on an 'irresponsible' Prime Minister: here lies real uncertainty. If Lord Armstrong doesn't know, nobody knows. In such circumstances it will be no easy task for the Queen's advisers to reach a judgement on which combination of parties and individuals is best placed to deliver viable government. Next time, will the Liberal Democrats settle for a rerun of the past? Would Sir David Steel?

> If a minority government were allowed to take office and to start off on its programme in the House, then we would be back in the situation that Harold Wilson was in in 1964, when he ran another election in 1966; and, perhaps more accurately, in 1974, when he was able to run another one six months later. That's what would happen, and in those circumstances what you get is the government putting all its sugar candies in the shop window in the first few months and then calling a quick election and getting a majority.

This suggests that the Liberal Democrats should, rather, go for broke next time the opportunity comes around; and indeed Sir David says 'You have to take the chance when it comes.' This is fighting talk. But, next time, will it be that easy to derail the British Constitution? Vernon Bogdanor, a member of that scholarly penumbra likely to be consulted discreetly if someone finds themselves in a position to try, thinks not.

> There is much more of a groundswell of opinion behind proportional representation in the 1990s than there was in 1974, and much more scepticism towards the British Constitution; so from that point of view Paddy Ashdown would have a better chance now than Jeremy Thorpe had two decades ago. However, it remains the case that in each of the three hung Parliaments we've had since 1918, the Liberals, who appeared superficially to be in a strong position, really came out with nothing. On each occasion a seemingly strong bargaining position was dissipated. So the Liberal Democrats will have to break with precedent if they're to achieve anything in a new hung Parliament.

It seems clear enough that a hung Parliament will be no instant nirvana for the Liberal Democrats. It is easy to see why Sir David Steel – perhaps still sensitive to charges that he may have demanded too little from James Callaghan in 1977–8 in return for the Lib/Lab pact – talks up the possibilities for a dramatic reshaping of our political system. But there are plenty of experienced politicians who saw that pact from the Labour side. As a Cabinet minister at that time, Stan Orme opposed it. Before the 1992 election, he was chairman of the Parliamentary Labour Party when Paddy Ashdown, the Liberal Democrat leader, was saying that if a hung Parliament was the outcome he would wait for the other parties to ring him. In Stan Orme's view, this meant a silent weekend in prospect:

> If Labour is the largest party, we will not negotiate with anyone else. We will put forward Labour's policy in a Queen's Speech, put it to the House of Commons, and if the House of Commons then defeat us, then it will be a question of another general election. I don't see any chance at all, or possibility, of the Labour Party negotiating on this issue.

Clearly it will take more than a long weekend to force Labour to shed the mind-sets of a lifetime. Yet there were already signs of flexibility. Only twice between 1945 and 1995 did Labour win a majority that reached double figures; and the last time was thirty years ago. The 1990 Labour Party conference instructed Neil Kinnock to establish a commission of inquiry into voting systems. Yet Labour opinion remains strongly opposed to peacetime coalitions. The spectre of Ramsay MacDonald's National Government of 1931 and the more recent experience of living, in Commons terms, from hand to mouth, don't exactly glow in the memory. What was it like for James Callaghan? Wasn't it a tremendous misfortune to lose his parliamentary majority seven months after becoming Prime Minister in 1976?

> It's never a misfortune to become Prime Minister; it's always the greatest thing in your life. It's absolute heaven – I enjoyed every minute of it until those last few months of the 'Winter of Discontent'. But when you lose your majority it's jolly inconvenient, because you have to look at every piece of legislation, every piece of business that's coming up in the following week, to see whose support you're going to get, whether you're going to be able to carry on the Queen's government or not. This wastes time; or, at least, you have to spend a lot of time on it. It doesn't make for good government. Those who believe that PR is going to improve our form of government are, I think, very much mistaken.

It's not hard to sense the change of mood here as Lord Callaghan glides from the pleasures of being Prime Minister at all to the pains of being one without a majority. Senior Labour figures will at least talk openly about the possibility of a hung result bringing about constitutional change, however unpalatable they personally find it. The same cannot be said of their Conservative counterparts.

The Liberal Democrats, of course, have no such inhibitions. If I were Mr Ashdown, I would draw heavily on the advice of his sole colleague with recent inside experience of Number Ten as a majority-free zone. Tom McNally was Lord Callaghan's political adviser in Downing Street. In the event of a hung Parliament, how would he convert his Labour experience into advice for the Liberal Democrats?

It will be a moment of great hysteria, and individuals and organizations will have a spotlight trained on them with an intensity they've never experienced before. I'm quite sure there will be a good deal of pontificating and, perhaps, a little breaking ranks. My wider advice to the Liberal Democrats is to shut up during this period. It will call for a very cool nerve.

This stress on the need for cool nerves seems well placed in view of what happened after the 1987 election, when what began to fracture, within hours of the result, was not the mould of the political system as a whole but the politics of the Alliance.

Mr Ashdown had another reservoir of inside experience to tap before the 1992 election in the form of the leader of the Liberal Democrat peers and former Labour Cabinet minister, Lord Jenkins of Hillhead. He too counselled a cool head:

There are all sorts of possibilities as to what the *exact* relationship of the parties would be, but I would advise him to have a pretty clear bargaining position with both of the parties; and not to get over-excited. There's a great deal to be said for letting your opponent, or your opponents, play their hand first – shoot their bolt first – in a hung Parliament. I wouldn't advise him to be too eagerly telephoning other people. I'd wait for them to telephone him. And I'd keep in mind the fact that we are moving, to an extent incomparably different from the position thirty years ago, into a three-party system. If you go back to that extraordinary election of 1951 – and 1950 was almost exactly the same – you had a position in which 97 per cent of those who voted, voted either Labour or Conservative. Now this is utterly different from the present time. The number voting Labour and Conservative combined is in the low seventies. We are moving towards triangular politics.

But doesn't even the image of *triangular* politics begin to seem a little out of date? When James Callaghan found himself governing without a majority, he bought valuable time by meeting a long-standing Unionist demand for more Ulster seats; and, as the Lib/Lab pact crumbled, he contemplated a deal with the Welsh and Scottish Nationalists. If John Major found himself where Ted Heath had been a generation ago, might his thoughts not stray northwards, too?

In the 1970s Jim Sillars was a Labour MP; since then he has taken the Glasgow Govan seat for the Scottish National Party. His view on the SNP's response should the phone ring in Glasgow with Mr Major on the line was uncompromising:

> We'd put the phone down. There is no possibility of any deal with the Tories whatsoever. We are bitterly and utterly opposed to Tory policy in Scotland. We're a left-of-centre party so it would be absolutely ludicrous for us even to think of doing a deal with the Conservative Party. Mrs Thatcher was well to the right of us, but so is John Major. So, in reality, if you're talking about Westminster without a single majority party there, it's got to be the Labour Party.

And if it were Labour on the line, what would be the opening bargaining position? Mr Sillars was reluctant to be specific, but definite about the broad thrust:

> It will come as a surprise to many people to say that it is not constitutional. We would certainly not be saying to the Labour Party, 'You must bring in your Scottish assembly package, or else.' Their constitutional package is a devolution setting within the United Kingdom, which is not the policy of this party. So we believe that would be their prime responsibility and their sole responsibility as far as we're concerned. We would be looking in the field of social and economic policy for delivery to Scotland from a minority Labour government which relied on us for electoral support and voting support in the lobbies of the House of Commons.

And what would be in that social and economic package? Mr Sillars offers an example.

> One of the things that we would certainly consider would be a demand that the Labour government write off the capital housing debt of the Scottish local authorities, particularly my own authority in Glasgow, because that capital debt is requiring huge charges on rental income to meet interest payments. And I think it's important that people realize tactically that you should ask a Labour government for something that they couldn't deny.

No joy for the Conservatives north of the border, then; and surprisingly modest demands from a party standing for really dramatic constitutional change, namely Scottish independence. Labour might have more scope, always assuming they were prepared to bargain on a political patch where there is little love lost between the huge cohort of Scottish Labour MPs and the handful of SNP members.

But what possibilities lie across the Irish Sea? In March 1974 the memory of the Sunningdale power-sharing experiment was still fresh. Again in the 1990s, thin and disappearing majorities looked like giving the Unionists the kind of parliamentary leverage they enjoyed in the late 1970s when yet another party changeling, the former Conservative Cabinet minister Enoch Powell, was one of their number. Mr Powell has robust views on the conduct to be expected of elected members in pursuit of office:

> When an election has taken place, it really is no longer within the power of those who have stood at that election to say, 'Well, as a matter of fact, we stood on this policy, but now that we haven't got the majority we're going to change our policy.' They break faith with the electorate. And the minority party, just as the larger parties, cannot break faith with its electorate. It cannot come back from the hustings and say, 'Well, that's what we said when the issue was open, but we're saying something different now because we have an opportunity of supporting and, perhaps, participating in a government.' I don't think you can honourably do that.
>
> Because the working of a system, the confidence system, the system of the Crown governing on the advice of ministers, is qualified, is sustained, by a sense of what is decent and honourable on the part of public men. That they cannot do, in order to gain office, that which they haven't done when office was not tendered.

Thus what the Ulster Unionists would require from a potential government that was seeking their support in the House of Commons is a pledge that severance of Northern Ireland from the United Kingdom was not an option.

With or without the Ulster factor, the prospects look bleak for Mr Major should he finish up after an election as leader of the largest single party but with no certainty of getting a Queen's Speech through the new Commons unaided. Would there be any point in his contacting the Liberal Democrats? Or would they take a similar line to the SNP – that Tories are not fit and proper persons for left-of-centre parties to deal with? Sir David Steel, contemplating the situation before the 1992 election, thought not.

> I think that John Major would have one advantage and one disadvantage. The advantage is that he was not a long incumbent Prime Minister who had, like Ted Heath, gone to the country over an issue and lost. He's had

to go to the country because he's come to the end of the government's term in office. He's a very new and relatively untried Prime Minister. The electorate has decided they're not quite sure which they prefer and therefore there's an inconclusive result. And he is, therefore, not suffering from the disadvantages of being Mrs Thatcher, having been in office for thirteen years and having been turfed out. So I think that he has that advantage of a relatively clean slate and a willingness to listen to others in a way that she didn't have, and a readiness, as he's already shown, to jettison certain policies and perhaps adapt certain other ones. That's on their plus side. I think the biggest negative he would have would be the feeling in the Conservative Party, because I think the mood of the party would be pretty fragile. They've been in power a very long time and there might be many siren voices in their ranks saying, 'Oh, well, we've blown that one, let's regroup in opposition and possibly change the leader and get someone more charismatic.'

The second point might well still apply in 1996; by this time, however, the 'benefit of the doubt' element has long since evaporated. But it is worth noting the contrast between Sir David's assessment of the position in 1991 and that in 1987, when, if Mrs Thatcher had found herself without a majority, he would have insisted on another Conservative leader before even starting to talk. As for the deal itself, Sir David insists that the terms would be exactly the same whether they were talking to a Conservative or a Labour leader.

Even the possibility of talking to the Conservatives represents a change of mind for David Steel between the 1987 and 1992 elections. What kind of strategy could lie behind the shift? That a Labour minority government is the more likely bringer of proportional representation? That to push the Stan Ormes of this world through the last barrier of resistance, to convince the Labour leadership that Downing Street is worth a single transferable vote, would take one more Labour failure, even a narrow one? If so, keeping the Conservatives in place, perhaps even without a new constitutional settlement, would make sense.

But isn't all this wishful thinking on a grand scale on the part of the Liberal Democrats? In such circumstances, a minority government formed by one or other of the major parties is the most likely outcome; and doesn't past experience show that minority governments can prove surprisingly robust and durable? Jim Sillars sat through the last one as a Labour MP:

The minority government is not necessarily over a barrel, in the hands of the minority parties whom it's seeking to do a deal with. If you look at the Standing Orders of the House of Commons – many, many people overlook the Standing Orders of the House of Commons, perhaps the most important constitutional document in our unwritten Constitution – they give the whole initiative to the government of the day. The government of the day sets the agenda in the House of Commons. Its business has priority over everyone else. Now if the government is a minority government, everyone knows there's a timescale within which they are operating and it's a very short timescale. They're looking for nine, twelve, eighteen months until they can work themselves into a position of getting a dissolution, going for an election to get a majority. Therefore, in that short timescale, anyone bargaining with them, knowing that they've got the initiative, has actually got to have, in arithmetical terms, a relatively modest shopping list to put to them; and something that they know can be got on to the statute book, or into administrative action, in a very short space of time. I think the Liberals would make a mistake by saying, 'It's PR or nothing – or out you go.' Because it's perfectly possible for that minority government to bring forward a Queen's Speech and then challenge the Liberals to bring them down.

Mr Sillars is right. Real powers of patronage and agenda control flow into the hands even of a majority-less Prime Minister and his or her business managers in Parliament. The possibilities are limitless – and not only for the government trying to hang on, as Tom McNally, Labour tactician turned Liberal Democrat adviser, points out:

If you've got a hung Parliament you are dealing with a Rubik cube and the twists and turns are extremely difficult to contemplate. In the end a government that is trying to survive at any price dies anyway. And public opinion would kill it off for the cynicism of the whole exercise. But I think it would also be incumbent on the politicians returned to that Parliament to see their responsibilities for the carrying on of the Queen's government, and unless they're in the business of anarchy it may well be that a minority administration would carry on for a period and would be as strong, in terms of the day-to-day governance of Britain, as many minority administrations around the world.

Tom McNally, rightly, is more phlegmatic than David Steel about the instant possibility of deals. And there's another factor working against the would-be mould-breakers: the 'good chap' theory, the belief very strongly held in Whitehall and Palace circles, that, in the end, all the party leaders could be prevailed upon not to embarrass the Sovereign by pushing their claims too far – an attempt which in any case, as Philip Ziegler points out, would be unlikely to succeed.

The Queen is a woman of enormous experience and common sense. And she has no intention whatsoever of being backed into a corner and finding herself put on the spot like that. Her Private Secretary is a man of infinite cunning who will be a master at skating round tricky problems and will see, in advance, the likely crisis and defuse it. No member of any political party that I can see has any wish to embarrass the Queen or would benefit from doing so. And with all the main figures concerned determined not to manoeuvre the monarch into a position where she *has* to take some step which some people would think unconstitutional, I just don't believe it will happen. What the constitutional position is, is *infinitely* more diffi-cult to answer. The whole relationship of monarchy and government has worked on an extremely fluid base of instantly invented precedents.

Yet for all those 'instantly invented precedents' which have allowed us to muddle through in the past, there is a foreseeable contingency where real trouble is possible. Wouldn't a *second* hung Parliament hard on the heels of a first cause a breakdown of the 'good chap' theory as the Liberal Democrats – and others – sensed a once-in-a-century chance to change the constitutional ground rules? Wouldn't this be the moment where the past ceased to be a guide and the golden trio in the Palace, the Cabinet Office and Number Ten found naught for their comfort in those top secret files? How would Lord Armstrong view this situation?

This is a very hypothetical question. Not only I, but none of us, has any experience or precedent to guide us, and so I can't say I know the answer. It would be possible, having held an election, to set aside the date for the opening of Parliament, but it would clearly be difficult and there would be a great desire not to do that unless it's unavoidable. In a sense it's a confession of failure if you have to do that.

There is a sense of a clock ticking in the background:

It's a very strong sense that everybody has; and that's not a bad thing, because a ticking clock and a deadline, the time when the bomb goes off, as you might say, sharpens people's minds very considerably. My own view is that in the sort of circumstances we're talking about, everyone will expect the politicians to accept the implications of the fact that there had been two elections in succession – neither producing a decisive result – and to acknowledge that yet another election was out of the question and that it was up to them to agree among themselves upon an arrangement which would enable the government to be carried on without another election. Such an arrangement, again, could take one of a number of forms: a coalition, or an inter-party pact, or a national government, or a 'government of all the talents'.

There's drama in that list, for all Lord Armstrong's professional poise. Doesn't this suggest that the 'This Is Britain' syndrome, the belief that out of chaos will come certainty, without jeopardizing the Queen's position, is a cherished national myth with which all soothe themselves? Lord Callaghan takes a pragmatic view.

Well, it works, doesn't it? So I think that's the answer, even if it is on the back of an envelope and not a written constitution with every comma and every semicolon in place – indeed, sometimes they can make for difficulties that common sense can overcome. I would say that as far as the Sovereign is concerned, she has to be extremely prudent when she intervenes, especially now that the party leader, who will become the Prime Minister, is elected on a very wide franchise – that is to say, either the Members of Parliament or even, in the case of the Labour Party, rank and file members. And I think it is the path of prudence and wisdom for her to intervene only with the greatest reluctance. I think we are fortunate in being served by a monarch who understands the constitutional position extremely well – quite as well as any Prime Minister does – who is served by very good Private Secretaries and by party leaders who accept the conventions and know that it is their job not to embarrass the monarch with their own party political fortunes in these matters. And so I think it will always work out here.

But will it? Wouldn't two hung Parliaments within, say, twelve months finally show that envelopes are not enough? Precise formulations cannot be captured in a written code to which all can subscribe in advance. But surely those advisers on the golden triangle should plan where the two major parties fear to dream. At the very least, other precedents that might come in handy should be exhumed from the files. Those from October 1963, for example, when Lord Home asked Her Majesty for time to see if a Cabinet could be pieced together in the confusion following the Macmillan resignation.* If he could have a day, why couldn't the clock be halted for a week, or even two, as happens on the continent? To be sure, the State Opening of Parliament might have to be postponed; and some unfortunate incumbent Prime Minister might have to swing in the wind for rather longer than Mr Heath's weekend.

---

* In fact, Macmillan suggested to the Queen that she might give Home time to try to form an administration: Harold Macmillan, diary entry for 18 October 1963, quoted in Harold Macmillan, *At the End of the Day, 1961–63* (Macmillan, 1973), p. 516.

For, whisper it who dares at the Downing Street or the Palace end of St
James's Park: it *could* happen here. And in the absence of careful forethought,
the confusion would be perilous to behold the day they changed the rules at
Buckingham Palace.

Part Two

The Uneasy Fusion

The fact that Ministers sit in Parliament ... catches the eye. This undoubtedly institutionalizes ministerial intimacy with and, most of the time, ensures ministerial control over Parliament. Yet we must not exaggerate the degree of fusion. Only one in six MPs has any direct connection with the government; up to 50 per cent of the House's membership have been sent there to oppose the government with every fibre of their being; even the government's own backbench lobby fodder frequently has to be cajoled or menaced into supporting it. As seen from inside the bureaucracy, Parliament is a hostile, incomprehensible and alien place. This attitude soon comes to infect Ministers as well as officials

Ferdinand Mount, former Head of the Downing Street Policy Unit, 1992[1]

The British Civil Service is a great national asset. Since the 1870s it has been the permanent and impartial instrument of administrations. Governments have always seen it as their duty to preserve its efficiency and honesty for their successors.

House of Commons Treasury and Civil Service Committee, 1994[2]

One of the distinguishing features of the British system of central government is the fusion of the executive and the legislature. Since the 1830s, by convention ministers have been drawn from one or other of the Houses of Parliament.[3] Once appointed to office, they have since the 1870s inherited a permanent, career and politically neutral Civil Service,[4] thereby forsaking the emotional pulls of parliamentary life for the executive embrace. In Whitehall they encounter people who are interested in politics, but rarely in a crudely partisan fashion – men and women who have risen to the top of the Civil Service hierarchy by applying effectively, one likes to think, their powers of reason and analysis rather than by mobilizing prejudice, which is the motor of political advancement, more successfully than their competitors.

The tensions and cross-currents of executive and legislative processes and priorities, and the human factors and personal relationships that are inseparable from them, have been a constant and fascinating element in modern British government, each generation coping with them and playing them out in different ways. This section of the book eavesdrops on these often private and sometimes peculiar practices at three points in late postwar government.

The first part of this section is based on a lecture delivered at the Civil Service College in Sunningdale in June 1995 to mark the twenty-fifth anniversary of the College's foundation.[5] It was prepared at a time when, after sixteen years of unbroken Conservative government, questions were being raised about the durability of a politically neutral public service should the administration change.

The second part, based on the Radio Four *Analysis* audit of the effective-ness of the post-1979 House of Commons select committee system, was created in the winter of 1991 during the run-up to an election in which the possibility of a change of government existed. But it was evident to my producer, Frank Smith, and me that, even if power did change hands, there was no guarantee that the executive bias, or the limited aspirations of Parliament, which had characterized twentieth-century British governance, would be altered in any substantial measure.

The third and final part of this section concentrates on one of those rare, perhaps defining, episodes in which all the tensions of our unhappy marriage between the executive and the legislature, including the sometimes uneasy relationship between ministers and officials, came to the surface thanks to Sir Richard Scott's inquiry into arms for Iraq, whose findings were published in early 1996. Steered by my producers Nichola Meyrick and Simon Coates, I sat down within a few hours of the report's release to try to illuminate the deeper questions it raised with a studio-full of insiders and commentators.

3

Permanent Ballast in the Constitution

No lesson seems to be so deeply inculcated by the experience of life, as that you should never trust experts. If you believe the doctors, nothing is wholesome. If you believe the theologians, nothing is innocent. If you believe the soldiers, nothing is safe. They all require to have strong wine diluted by a very large admixture of insipid common sense.

Lord Salisbury to Lord Lytton, 15 June 1877[1]

My opening text is taken from a letter written by a minister to a viceroy about what a pain and an inconvenience experts are. It has, I hope, a certain resonance for those who have lived through, or witnessed, our two great governing professions, politicians and civil servants, coexisting in a highly necessary, but occasionally fraught, symbiosis. Every ministerial generation has produced senior figures who have echoed Lord Salisbury, that shrewdest of pessimists who was himself to become Prime Minister, especially at moments of frustration with their senior officials. Often the whingeing has come from ministers possessing pretty impressive intellectual equipment of their own, as when Hugh Dalton likened his Treasury advisers to 'congenital snag hunters'[2] and Mrs Thatcher dismissed the output of the Central Policy Review Staff as 'guffy stuff like PhD theses',[3] which made me, as an academic, wonder how long it was since she had actually read a thesis. The problem will be with us as long as our governmental system is driven by this fusion of two callings, in one of which you rise to the top by 'mobilizing prejudice'[4] more successfully than your political rival, while in the other you glide towards Permanent Secretaryism – in theory at least – on the basis of deploying evidence and reason to greater effect than your peers.

It is with this latter phenomenon, the deployment of evidence and reason, in mind that I turn to the Civil Service College. Its purpose over the first quarter-century of its life has been to provide both the technology and the fuel for that reason-driven career path at several levels of the Civil Service, not just its upper reaches. It should not be a kind of leafy adventure playground for tired minds in need of a touch of rest and recreation before returning to the real heavy duty business of government. It is, and must remain, in Ian Bancroft's words, an 'integral part of both the "hardware" and "software" of the state, the systems and the people of government',[5] and therefore part of the state's in-house capacity rather than a contracted-out fringe item.

I have had a relationship with the Civil Service College, first as a journalist and latterly as an academic, for twenty-two years, ever since I came to Sunningdale in 1973 to prepare a profile of the College for the *Times Higher Education Supplement*. On that occasion I had the pleasure of witnessing a very robust former Governor of Wormwood Scrubs stopping a seminar in its tracks by explaining that the then new and promising management technique of Programme Analysis and Review would be of no value to the Prison Service because it would turn out fitter and better villains, which was not the object of the exercise![6]

For twenty years now I have been a contributor to courses at the College, and this has produced in me a powerful, if singular, admiration for it, not just as an institution, but as part of a Civil Service so tolerant and open-minded that it would ask a critic like me down to speak and then afterwards instruct the Paymaster-General's Office to send me a cheque. In return for the cheque I would deliver words that were not always admiring of the current set of public service managers, elected or appointed. Cynics would call this 'repressive tolerance';[7] I would simply remove the adjective and leave the noun. Tolerance it was and tolerance it remains.

I have always gone to the College when asked to do so if I possibly could. A very long time ago Maurice Peston told me that ever since he was first invited to talk to assistant principals at the old Centre for Administrative Studies, the precursor of the College, he had always looked forward to going back because they were the brightest audience he would ever teach in the British Isles. But it's not just the intellectual pull of administration trainee-level courses or that glowing, if semi-detached, phenomenon, the Top Management Programme, that has formed the attraction for me. Some of the best sessions I ever had there were with the senior executive officers, especially Customs officers. They had a directness and a sharpness that always left me personally relieved that I have never been into contraband. The SPATS course is another.[8] It has a special sparkle, bringing together participants from such a wide range of professional and technical backgrounds.

Like SPATS, the College was the progeny of the Fulton Report, and its establishment marked the first real surge of deliberately engineered change in the Civil Service since the Second World War, creating what we would now call the 'culture' of the Civil Service.[9] In 1968 the Fulton Committee produced what its Secretary, Richard Wilding, called 'the last of the great Fabian documents',[10] bringing together an enhanced policy-making capacity with an improved management process to be carried through by a better trained and motivated labour force. Hence the College.

Ever since Sir Edward Heath opened it in June 1970 the College has, as far as I have observed it, been reshaping itself in response to the times and to their needs and demands. For it has, in its way, been a microcosm of a great profession which, like so much else to do with British central government, seems to change almost beyond recognition while curiously staying the same. For me it is like George Orwell's notion of English civilization: 'It has a flavour of its own. Moreover it is continuous, it stretches into the future and the past, there is something in it that persists, as in a living creature.'[11] In the case of the Civil Service, this was a phenomenon recognized in the White Paper *Continuity and Change*,[12] which set forth the latest in the successive waves of fads and acronyms that have washed over the Civil Service College. In 1970 there was the last wave of O&M (Organization and Methods); then PAR (Programme Analysis and Review), then Raynerism, then the FMI (Financial Management Initiative), Ibbsism, (Citizen's) Charterism, and now Market Testing. The College has absorbed each new line, promulgating it to its people and training them to cope with it, as is right and proper in a disciplined service under ministerial control. How much more difficult it would have been for those reforms to take place if the College had not existed.

Training came late to what Lord Radcliffe once described as a standing army of power at the heart of central government.[13] It was not something that the grand designers of the profession thought about. Jowett of Balliol had a profound influence upon the making of the great Northcote and Trevelyan Report of 1854, but it was almost as if Northcote and Trevelyan thought that Jowett's home patch of Oxford University had pretty well provided all the training the 'competition wallahs', as they were called, would need. Thereafter, well-groomed minds would pick up all the practicalities they required once launched upon state service. This was to prove a besetting problem for a profession powerfully 'organized by history', to borrow a phrase that Harold Wilson once used about the premiership.[14] It made the achievement of an effective fit between Ian Bancroft's 'hardware and software of state' that much more difficult.

I owe the title of this article to another phrase of Ian Bancroft's, in this case delivered over a cup of tea in the House of Lords. When I asked him to produce, off the top of his head, a description of the purpose of the Civil Service, he described it as acting as 'a permanent piece of ballast in the Constitution'. His line of thinking was that you can have a very volatile legislature and an equally volatile ministerial executive; sometimes, therefore, you need a degree of balance and permanence, someone who can say: 'Oi – we've been here before.'[15] 'Permanent ballast in the Constitution': there, surely, is a phrase worthy of Mr Gladstone. Something that goes beyond mere functionalism in a system of government without a written constitution, yet laden with 'tacit understandings',[16] which themselves produce what Douglas Hurd described as 'a rich variety of nuances and ironies'.[17]

Continuity and Change, and the recent reports from the Treasury and Civil Service Select Committee,[18] which have been considerably shaped by cross-party influence, reflect the peculiar way in which understanding about the proper recruitment and operation of our public service has developed over the century and a half since Northcote and Trevelyan placed their findings before Mr Gladstone. The crucial initial specks of DNA, as it were, that still mercifully fashion the service today – recruitment and promotion on merit inside a permanent, politically neutral, career public service – have not had an easy ride since Gladstone and Lowe implemented them inside the Home Civil Service in 1870. The shades of Horace Wilson (Neville Chamberlain's *éminence grise* in Number Ten in the late 1930s) are still with us, and his name was associated with a tiny number of Downing Street people as recently as the late 1980s. But even in the high consensus years, long before Mrs Thatcher arrived in Number Ten, the suspicion of politicization reared its head. Churchill, on returning to the premiership in 1951, growled that he had no desire to be served by 'Attlee's leavings'.[19] There were touches of it, too, in 1964. One new Labour secretary of state, who should have known better, was unwilling for a day or two to talk to anyone above the rank of principal because he thought the senior figures bore the taint of Toryism after thirteen years.[20] More recently, even a politician as intelligent as Jack Cunningham seemed to believe that Terry Heiser, then Permanent Secretary at the Department of the Environment, was a kind of Thatcherite.[21] The problem could be a real one if and when the government changes, despite the most welcome and carefully crafted Code of Conduct for the Civil Service that has been brokered between the select committee, the Cabinet Office and the Cabinet itself, with Lord Nolan subsequently suggesting a stiffening here and there.[22]

The new Civil Service Code skilfully sweeps up all the specks of DNA that matter, scattered as they were across a range of procedural guidelines and memoranda. It does not change the constitutional position of the Civil Service one iota, but it gives it a much more focused constitutional personality. Above all, the Gladstonian, the Northcote–Trevelyan-inspired nostrums of 1870 come shining through. So what might be the problem if and when the government changes? Is not the politicization scare a thing of the past, a relic of the 1980s, an artefact of *the* great command premiership of recent history? Is the permanent ballast safe for the twentieth century?

Not quite. The problem, I believe, is not a political one; it's a human one – of two sets of people, possibly destined to work together in intense professional intimacy within days of an election, now hardly knowing each other.

This lack of familiarity is without parallel since 1924 and it can be only partially eased by the Major/Kinnock refinement of the Douglas-Home rules, effective from January 1996, enabling permanent secretaries to meet with opposition spokespeople to discuss the implications for the machinery of government of any changes they may wish to make if elected.[23] There is also an element of policy of unfamiliarity. For example, you have to be in the late forties or older, as an official in, say, the Department of Environment, to remember a time when local government was seen as part of a possible solution rather than a key element in a vexing and important problem. Two long-time practitioners of the two professions of politics and civil service have made acute observations recently on this unfamiliarity aspect. The first, Tony Benn, told my undergraduates that 'the Civil Service is a bit like a rusty weathercock – it moves with opinion and then it stays there until another wind moves it in a different direction.'[24] The second, Ian Beesley, chief of staff in the Efficiency Unit during Mrs Thatcher's premiership, was much taken with this metaphor when talking to my MA students: 'I recognize the weathercock symbol,' he said; 'the Civil Service is dedicated to the status quo. It only changes with a tremendous breath of air; a war, probably the Thatcher period. It's not politicization in the party sense – it's thought colonization.'[25] That's an interesting phrase, 'thought colonization'. I think the two of them were on to something, and it will require forbearance and highmindedness on all sides to surmount the unfamiliarity problem successfully if and when the government changes.

That problem must be surmounted, and the key to it is the crucial strand of the 1870 DNA. The duty of the Civil Service is to speak truth unto power, and to base that truth on evidence, reason and knowledge. Edward Heath as Prime Minister not only recognized this essential element of the Civil Service ethic, he strove mightily to enhance it. He remains the only premier fully to address the fundamental points implicit and explicit in the Haldane Report of 1918,[26] that analysis and careful thought must be the precursors to decision. Sir Edward's 1970 White Paper, *The Reorganization of Central Government*,[27] would repay close study by any incumbent of or aspirant to Number Ten.

To fulfil this part of the Civil Service job requirement takes more than a code. It needs the following:

- a capacity to attract and retain a reasonable proportion of the very best output of the British university system;
- the sustenance and maintenance of the culture of British public service, reason and candour inside the Civil Service;
- protection against book-cooking or the promulgation of falsehoods, for whatever reason and at whoever's behest;

- the frequent accumulation of new expertise and the regular refreshment of the old.

These, I think, are essentials, not optional extras. Why? Because public policy, public business and public money are involved, and because the job of being a state servant is especially demanding, for a number of reasons. First, because the state is a kind of sump into which all the intractable problems that cannot or should not be coped with elsewhere fall. Statutes keep governments involved with them in many cases, paying benefits, running the employment service, raising revenue – the kind of activities they cannot get out of. Second, because of accountability of Parliament. The 'Westminster shareholders' meeting' is in almost constant session. 'Sacked directors' do not take off to the home counties comforted by golden goodbyes, but hang around and watch and complain, even if their party still retains possession of the board/Cabinet room, while between a third and a half of the remaining shareholders are itching to mount a hostile takeover. No company has to face that; when you sack them, they go! Finally, there is the constant media attention, which, thanks to a combination of electronic newsgathering and the final collapse of deference and restraint, has produced what John Birt rightly called a 'feeding frenzy'.[28] It makes that side of government far harder than it was twenty years ago when I was briefly a lobby correspondent.

The Civil Service College, I think, is not a bystander here. It is central to building and maintaining the kind of human 'software' capacity that can more than cope in a tough climate. This is a capacity that the business schools, good though they are in the main, simply cannot provide because very few of their clients have to work in an ecology as demanding as the one I have just described. For several years now I have been pushing for a more ambitious scope for the Civil Service College, one that would serve the public sector as a whole, and recently I came across past support for this view that I had not detected before. One of my students has found and brought into the semi-public domain a paper prepared by Tommy Balogh for Harold Wilson in 1963, out of which came the blueprint for what emerged as the Department of Economic Affairs, and in which training offered by a 'National College for Administration' featured very strongly.[29] From his obituary in May 1995, too, I discovered that that remarkable ex-MI6 officer John Bruce Lockhart had been pressing for something similar based on the model of the Royal College of Defence Studies.[30]

The Top Management Programme has shown just how fruitful not only wider public-sector involvement but a strong private-sector input can be for the purposes of improving the human capital of the state. What is involved here has little to do with political parties and everything to do with the capability of the state. That is a notion with which the British, unlike the

French, have always been uneasy, to our loss and France's gain. It should be possible to move with bipartisan consultation towards developing such a College in time for the twenty-first century, especially as at long last British politics seems almost to have rid itself of its neurosis about the divide between the public and private sectors.

An approaching end of century is always a moment for stocktaking, for running through the life cycles recently past as a preliminary to thinking of those yet to come. The Civil Service has experienced a variety of waves since Churchill stood on the balcony of what is now the Treasury and saluted the crowds on VE Day. The first of them, I think, was what one might call war and post-war state-building, to cope with greater governmental intervention in the economy and social provision. Far too little attention was given at that stage to either the 'hardware' or the 'software' of the state.[31] The Fulton Inquiry, which I have always regarded as a belated examination that should have happened in 1946 rather than 1966, failed to link the 'hardware' and the 'software' properly, partly because its terms of reference, carefully crafted by Harold Wilson, militated against that.[32] The 1970 White Paper I have mentioned above. Its examination of the size and workload of Cabinet, the size and scope of departments and the advice and managerial systems available to ministers has the great virtue of recognizing that policy-making and implementation are part of a seamless garment and that in government the short-term would always be the enemy of the medium- and long-term, unless very determined steps were taken to avoid that. Since 1979 there has been a constant flow of interlocking managerial reforms – Raynerism, FMI Next Steps, Market Testing, Citizen's Charter. More recently there has been the surge of ethical sensitivity to which I have already referred, with the Nolan Committee's report, and the new Civil Service Code so effectively designed by the all-party Treasury and Civil Service Select Committee.[33]

Taken together, this represents a rich compost of experience from which to draw. Future advance is possible, I am quite sure, on a bipartisan basis without the paraphernalia of a Royal Commission. But, for me, the big gap is that no Prime Minister since Edward Heath's time has addressed what the select committee recently called the 'workload and advice system' available to ministers;[34] the refusal to examine this in the most recent White Paper was by far the single greatest failure in *Taking Forward Continuity and Change*.[35] I was alarmed, too, to discover that when criteria were being drawn up for performance-related pay for permanent secretaries recently, policy advice was added rather as an afterthought towards the end of the process.[36] Here, in an area that was once regarded as a core activity of senior officials, there exists an opportunity, I am convinced, for bipartisan advance. The development of Next Steps and the work of the Treasury and Civil Service Select Committee have shown that such progress is possible and how fruitful its future possibilities could be. Indeed, it is crucial. It's very much easier to give a clear lead to the Civil Service on reform if that reform has all-party support.[37]

Despite a welter of distractions – Europe; the future of the Prime Minister; the scent of a general election not too far over the horizon – the condition of the central state, its instruments and its services is a first-order question that must not be neglected. Considerable improvements are still there for the taking, and any well-constructed scheme for their achievement would put at centre stage the Civil Service College, part shaper and part intellectual stimulator of that crucial and permanent ballast at the heart of the Constitution.

4

Teething the Watchdogs

Parliament, Government and Accountability

You don't have to worry about the reform of Parliament because Parliament, or the House of Commons, keeps on reforming . . . Its procedure, its conventions and so on are a living, changing body from generation to generation.

Enoch Powell, 1979[1]

Today is, I believe, a crucial day in the life of the House of Commons. After years of discussion and debate, we are embarking upon a series of changes that could constitute the most important parliamentary reforms of the century . . . The proposals that the government are placing before the House of Commons are intended to redress the balance of power to enable the House of Commons to do more effectively the job it has been elected to do.

Norman St John–Stevas, 1979[2]

Whatever Mr Powell may say, the pace of substantial parliamentary reform in the United Kingdom is glacial. It took exactly sixty years for the House of Commons Select Committee on Procedure to pick up the recommendation of the 1918 Haldane Committee that Parliament should establish committees to shadow the subject matter of government departments[3] – though, to be fair, it had had several tentative stabs at it in the previous decade with Richard Crossman's experimental specialist select committees in the 1960s and the creation in 1971 of the Expenditure Committee which spawned a family of sub-groups.[4] But it was not until the election of a Conservative government in May 1979 and the appointment of a reform-minded Leader of the House in Norman St John–Stevas (now Lord St John of Fawsley) that anything approximating to a Haldanian system was established down the Committee Corridor in the Palace of Westminster.

The principle of scrutiny, of course, was already well established in the form of the parliamentary select committees, the all-party watchdogs whose job it is to keep powerful Whitehall figures – both ministerial and official – on their toes in the long years of policy-making and public spending between elections. Theirs was the role of reasoned, cross-party opposition, as distinct from the adversarial, partisan opposition of the contesting parties in the chamber. But the St John-Stevas changes of 1979, in establishing separate committees to shadow every department, constituted by far the most conspicuous parliamentary reform of recent times. Considerable claims were made for them, not least by Mr St John-Stevas himself. After a decade of feeling their way, and sensing their power, the fourteen new select committees were themselves the subject of an inquiry by the Procedure Committee; and, according to Sir Peter Emery, Conservative MP for Honiton and Chairman of the Procedure Committee, they emerged from their own scrutiny with flying colours:

> Basically it gave them a clean bill of health. We made a number of sugges-
> tions about additions and subtractions and we considered complaints that
> had been made, whether they needed more powers and whether in fact
> they were effective. And the judgement – which was unanimous – of the
> Committee was that they were effective; ministers considered they were
> effective and they had now become an integral part of the working of
> Parliament.[5]

That unanimity was not achieved, however, before one of the Committee's members, Graham Allen, the Labour member for Nottingham North, had pressed his colleagues to push for more powers, more staff support and more analysis – more teeth for the watchdogs.[6] He feels that an opportunity was missed:

> St John-Stevas in 1979 performed a miraculous feat in establishing
> departmental select committees. It was the right thing to do and a marvel-
> lous step forward for our democracy. Ten years later, having seen them
> established and on a sound footing, they should have been taken on
> a further step; I think the Procedure Committee missed the chance and
> perhaps didn't have the courage to propose the very necessary steps
> forward to build upon the St John-Stevas experiment.

What should the Procedure Committee have bid for? How much bite can the select committees acquire in a Westminster Parliament so powerfully dominated by the executive, whose ministers are always chosen from its ranks? Is the United States – the world citadel of committee power – a relevant model, with its governmental functions carefully separated by its written constitution into an executive, a legislature and a judiciary? The Congress is a genuine law-*maker*, not just a statute-approving production line like our House of Commons much of the time.

In 1979, when Mr St John-Stevas cajoled a reluctant Prime Minister and a somewhat sceptical Cabinet into allowing a blossoming of new life along the Committee Room Corridor, there was suddenly a whiff of Capitol Hill about the Palace of Westminster. Briefly, it appeared that, at last, the ecology of Parliament would change, that the mighty in Whitehall might tremble when summoned before the committees to give evidence. Did it turn out like that? Robert Hazell, Director of the Nuffield Foundation and a former senior civil servant, recalls a somewhat less pugnacious atmosphere:

> I've seen senior officials from my old department, the Home Office, putting up very effective and courteous stone-walling performances in front of the Home Affairs Select Committee. If it is courteously done I think the select committee genuinely accepts that the officials are playing within the rules and it doesn't press them too hard for information.

This sounds more like evasion-as-usual. How different is it for an official in Washington, where interrogation by committee is not an occasional invitation to a gentlemanly bout of verbal fencing but a regular part of life? According to Bill Diefenderfer, formerly Deputy Director of the President's Office of Management and Budget, very different indeed:

> It is a little frightening. Congress has great powers and it is peopled by folks who have fairly prodigious intellects in many instances. When you're going to be called up to testify, particularly in a job like mine, Office of Management and Budget, where our purview is the whole of the United States government, they could literally ask you any question in a trillion two hundred billion dollar budget, and it's hard to keep all those facts and figures perfectly aligned in your mind. And that is if there is just a normal inquiry process. If there's something partisan going on, if it's Republican against Democrat, hard politics . . . politics in Washington is very much a blood sport and they would not hesitate to go in for the kill. I think that's very different from the way it's practised in England. Here you've got to anticipate that they will go in for the kill and protect yourself from the outset.

Note the linguistic difference between Westminster man and Washington man. Robert Hazell talks of MPs 'playing within the rules', not pressing officials 'too hard' for information. Bill Diefenderfer's is the language of the bull ring.

The one moment when select committee power at Westminster did seem poised for the kill came in 1986 with the Westland Affair. The Defence Committee's inquiry had the Thatcher administration on the run.[7] Yet it failed to deliver the *coup de grâce*. The government's supporters on the committee made sure its report, brimming with damaging findings, was published the day before Parliament rose for the summer recess. Somehow it's hard to imagine a congressional committee letting a US administration off the hook in such an accommodating way.

It takes more than a rehearsal of constitutional differences to explain this. Could it be a matter of political culture – or of raw power? Of Congress, unlike Parliament, knowing that, as President Lyndon Johnson is reported to have said in another context, that 'When you've got them by the balls, their hearts and minds will follow'? Peter Riddell, *Times* political columnist and former US editor of the *Financial Times*, has spent a great deal of time over the years in the committee rooms of both Westminster and Capitol Hill, and notes in particular the discipline applied in the form of confirmation by the Senate:

> It's much more difficult for an administration official in Washington to pull the wool over eyes or hope that, after two hours of gentle parrying of the *Yes, Minister* variety, he can go back to his department with relief, saying 'Well, I've got through that!' One reason is, of course, that if you're an Assistant Secretary or above, you're confirmed by the Senate and one of the things you always have to say in confirmation is that of course you'll always come up to the Hill and very fully testify – and that discipline's a very important one, because they hold them to that. And it's not just a once-for-all thing, because if you go on to a new post in the administration, if you move up from Assistant Secretary to Under Secretary, or if you become an ambassador or something like that, you have to be reconfirmed, and therefore it's a constant discipline. There are very few people who've gone more than, say, three or four years without having to be reconfirmed in a new post.

We should not, however, be misled by the memory of the arc-lit agony of Judge Clarence Thomas, a Bush nominee to the Supreme Court, whose alleged sexual appetites were dissected on the television screens not just of America but of the rest of the world as well. Confirmation hearings are an accepted weekly commonplace on Capitol Hill, provided for by Article 2 of the Constitution since the foundation of the Republic. It's all too easy for Westminster traditionalists to wheel out the unfortunate judge to frighten reformers who suggest that there might just be something worth importing from America.

Far more crucial to the question of the transferability of Washington-style techniques is that separation of powers which truly distinguishes the American political system from the mush of convention, tradition and procedure that passes for a constitution over here. Professor John Griffith, Emeritus Professor of Public Law at the University of London, briskly summarizes the existing Westminster system of mutual support between majority party and government:

> The whole structure of the Constitution, the way in which Parliament works, is that it is a party machine, and that means that the majority party and the government have a common interest and they are interdependent. The government majority backbenchers have an interest in making sure the government does its job, but also that it manages to put into effect the policies of a government. Therefore it must support the policies of the government; and equally, of course, the government depends on its majority in order to get things through. So there's a relationship and it's very close. Now, unless you can crack that detailed connection between the two, then you're not going to get anywhere in the end. It's very difficult to see how you can break this connection without changing fundamentally the whole system so that you brought it into line, if you like, with the way the Americans do it. You'd have to have it quite clear that the government and the executive were directly elected, so you'd have to go back to something like a presidential system. I think you'd also probably have to take ministers out of the House of Commons and put them, as in the American constitution, in a separate body – a genuine separation of powers.

Lord St John of Fawsley, by contrast, is opposed to a formal separation of powers:

> I think the great strength of the British Constitution is its flexibility. Because it's flexible, it's able to adapt and to grow. Its weakness is that it has allowed the executive to gain excessive power. The legislature has been weakened. We've made one step in the right direction; we should now take another great leap forward. I think that there are tinges of the United States in every proposal that is made, but I think we should make it clear that what we are proposing is the improvement of a domestic product and not the importation of a transatlantic transplant.

'Steps' and 'leaps forward'; 'tinges of America': Are we talking about real reform, or – if we follow Professor Griffith – mere tinkering?

We should perhaps ask whether reform in the past has been worth the reformists' efforts; for if it has not, it will scarcely be so in the future. Dr David Judge, Reader in Government at Strathclyde University, examines just what, in real, practical terms, post-1979 parliaments have achieved which their predecessors did not, thanks to the departmental select committees.

> The committees have collected literally yards of information, providing access for interest groups, and something like half of all the information collected by committees now comes from outside organizations. They've also compelled the attendance of civil servants and parliamentarians, which wasn't there before. That's the positive side. The negative side is that government departments have shown fairly frequently a marked reluctance to give committees information – often to the ludicrous extent where committees have been required to go to the United States and use the provisions of the Freedom of Information Act to obtain information which the government here has refused to give to committees. So the whole secrecy of government, the whole executive mentality of government, has been a restraint upon the collection of information.
>
> If you move to the analysis of information once it's collected, again on the positive side, MPs have been given the opportunity to spend some time to develop their own specializations and expertise on committee. Generally committees have been allowed to become the collective memory of the House. The negative side is that the main problem in analysing information has been the political sensitivity of policies under consideration, and a recurring problem has been that on partisan, sensitive issues, that is, those with a high ideological content, committees have had a habit of either ducking those issues or, if they have considered them, of fracturing along party lines when it comes to the report.[8]

A mixed audit, then, in which the pluses outweigh the minuses. Masses of extra material on the shelves, but relative deprivation in those instances where knowledge really is power. The hot breath of the government warms its supporters' necks on any seriously contentious issue – and we do well to recall that the government enjoys a majority on every select committee, another great difference from contemporary Washington, where one party may hold the White House while the other rules on the Hill.

David Judge's verdict could be summed up as 'could do better', in perceptible contrast to Sir Peter Emery's committee with its 'clean bill of health' report. To which of these positions would the architect of the post-1979 system gravitate? Lord St John of Fawsley thinks the Procedure Committee took a rather rosy view: 'It certainly was an extraordinarily complacent report. It could have been written by Candide: everything was for the best in the best of all possible worlds. And none of the changes that were recommended by various people giving evidence were really seriously addressed, much less adopted.'

Graham Allen, no disciple of Candide, who did address them seriously, did so from the perspective of a separation-of-powers man: a rare species in Westminster. In a written question to the Prime Minister in November 1991 he asked if he would 'bring forward proposals to ensure a constitutional separation of powers and to enhance the powers of the elected representatives *vis-à-vis* those of the government'. 'No,' replied Mr Major. And that was that.[9] Part of Mr Allen is with Professor Griffith in believing that no *fundamental* change is possible without digging up the constitutional foundations and rebuilding along Washington lines. But would he say, then, that the 1979 reforms mark the end of the road, that further steps are marginal or pointless?

> My own agenda for change would have involved, most modestly, making sure that the committees were staffed properly. I've been a member of the Public Accounts Committee, and much as I would like to say it's an effective committee because of the quality of its members, which is undoubtedly true, I have to be frank and say much of the reason that the Public Accounts Committee is feared is because it is backed up by 900 accountants in the National Audit Office. I'm not suggesting 900 members of staff for every departmental select committee, but certainly a unit answerable directly and only to each departmental select committee would immensely strengthen the hand of the legislature against the executive.

'Immensely strengthen'? Again, only by British standards. We've a long way to go before Americanization sets in here, with all its vices as well as its virtues. The difference can be quickly illustrated by a glance at the Capitol while Congress is in session. Tom Mann of the Brookings Institution in Washington described the view as of 1991, when Congress was under Democratic control:

> The number of full committees is not large – sixteen in the Senate, twenty-two in the House – but if you include not just committees but the subcommittees, which are mostly responsible for the oversight of executive agencies, then you have a total of 119 in the Senate and 177 in the House. What this means is that every senator, every Democratic senator, chairs at least one committee or subcommittee and over half of the Democrats in the House chair a committee or subcommittee. As far as staff members are concerned, there are about 2,000 staff members in the House who work directly for the committees and over 1,000 in the Senate who work for committees. But you realize there are also a large number of personal staff members – in the House, over 7,000, in the Senate, almost 4,000.

By British standards, the numbers are mind-boggling. Even Graham Allen's modest increase in departmental committee back-up – one or two more specialists to supplement the non-specialist House of Commons clerks, and a handful of experts brought in *ad hoc* – would move us nowhere near to Washington's democratic surplus. Even allowing for the separation of powers and the institutionalized importance of the Congress which flows from that, and even acknowledging, too, America's relative wealth, the support systems of Westminster's 650 MPs, compared to those of Washington's 100 Senators and 435 Representatives, are extraordinarily meagre – all the more so considering how centralized a nation we are compared to the United States, and how few are our checks and balances compared to theirs.

Nevertheless, scratch a servant of Congress and you often find an admirer of Westminster. Bob Reischauer, Director of the Congressional Budget Office, for example: 'You look across the Atlantic with envy at the great staff support that our legislative body has. I tend to look across the Atlantic and say, if only we had a system that was as effective as a parliamentary system at making decisions and making policies stick.'

Is there an element of touching Anglophilia here? Where Bob Reischauer applauds our ability to have effective decisions implemented swiftly, many British critics of the system lament a virtually argument-free zone in which the majority government can just ram its measures through. The phrase 'elective dictatorship' has been used. Reischauer, however, contemplates the downside of democracy as exemplified in the Washington of 1991:

> The hallmark here is democracy, and democracy can produce effective policies or chaos. We unfortunately have been wallowing in chaos, because we've had a government which has been split, with the Republican Party controlling the White House and the Democrats, by and large, controlling the Congress, and therefore a stand-off in policy. But also, even worse than a stand-off, a lack of accountability or responsibility. We in a sense have no-fault policy-making here. Both the Republicans and the Democrats, the Congress and the executive, can blame the other if something goes wrong, and so we spend our hours hurling blame back and forth against each other and not adopting policies to meet the pressing needs that this country has.

Not for nothing has our Prime Minister's Question Time acquired a cult following on cable television in Washington.

The paralysis identified by Reischauer is partly institutional (the founding fathers, after all, were driven by the need for check and balance) and partly the product of more recent history. When President Reagan arrived in the White House in 1980, a great deal of bipartisanship went out of the Congress. Jim Jones, Chairman of the American Stock Exchange in New York, worked as a special assistant in Lyndon Johnson's White House before becoming a big baron on Capitol Hill as the Democratic Chairman of the House Budget Committee. In his view the Congress needs to reform its own internal structure.

> I do think that there is too much overlapping jurisdiction. In that move to democratize the House and the Senate that occurred post-Watergate in the mid-Seventies, there grew up a plethora of new subcommittees that shared jurisdiction with other subcommittees and there was an attempt to increase the staff on Capitol Hill in order to give Congress a more equal relationship, in terms of research and so on, with the executive branch, and so now you have a good-sized staff with overlapping jurisdictions, and as a result, I think, there's no centrally organized way for Congress to scrutinize the executive branch.

So you can have too much of a good thing, even when real scrutiny powers go with the grain of the political system. But doesn't the constant restatement of the entrenched constitutional difference between Washington and Westminster clutter as much as clarify? *All* governments, with or without divided powers, need continual and effective scrutiny. Given our executive fixation – our bias towards government – surely there are practical experiences in Washington from which the British can learn? Bob Reischauer returns to the question of staffing.

> There are some lessons and the single most important one is that, while the support agencies on the western side of the Atlantic may not be transferable in a whole to the British situation, I think it's undoubtedly true that Parliament could use a larger and more capable staff. Governance is not a matter for amateurs any more, and politicians have a lot of other demands on their time and a limited amount of expertise; providing them with some capable staff, I think, can only help overall progress. I think, by and large, in parliamentary systems the parliament has been starved of capable staff. In the United States, it might be drowned by capable staff – but that's a separate issue.

Perhaps there might be a halfway house, a kind of island of solidity and common sense, between the American and British systems. If so, the people to design and build a British halfway house are the Westminster counterparts of Capitol Hill's barons. Are they in the market for lessons from America?

Would Sir Peter Emery like to see his Procedure Committee casting an eye over the Atlantic?

> No, we looked at that. What we don't wish to see is the sort of inquiries, of which the worst illustration is that concerning poor Judge Thomas, much led by officials behind the scenes. It is that sort of thing which we don't think ought to happen in Britain, and we want to try and ensure that it is the Members who stay in charge of these inquiries, that they do not get led by some people working behind the scenes who are trying to make reputations for themselves.

No powers please, we're British. Note, too, how Sir Peter seizes on the Clarence Thomas case – that spectacular rarity – to discredit a multi-faceted scrutiny process. As to the possibility of advisers taking over the MPs they assist, this must be a remote danger in thinly staffed Westminster – with perhaps one exception: the Public Accounts Committee. As we've already noted, the PAC is the only select committee with real back-up, a unique feature it has enjoyed since Gladstone's time. Inevitably, envious eyes have been cast by members of other select committees at the 900 professionals of the National Audit Office at the disposal of the PAC. Accountants for the most part, they concentrate on the past in a kind of perpetual inquest on Whitehall inefficiency and profligacy. Wouldn't it make sense to open up the market for their services to the departmental select committees looking at current and future policy? Robert Sheldon, Labour MP for Ashton-under-Lyne, former Treasury minister and chairman of the PAC, thinks not – in no uncertain terms:

> I think that would be a disaster. We see it in America, where you have the General Accounting Office, which is looking at questions of policy because they're instructed by Congress: they look at the implications of government decisions as to how you can make changes of policy, and it's used as a tool by one political party against another political party. In other words, it's brought the General Accounting Office into the areas of political decision-making. Now, the National Audit Office is very different from that, and much more powerful because of it. Nothing to do with policy – and the last thing I would ever dream of is getting, allowing, or seeing the National Audit Office answering questions on policy. That would be a major setback because, once it became involved, or ever was thought to be involved, in political matters, its power and its independence would be immeasurably weakened. We have a unique instrument of great value over a long period of time. If we try to broaden it into other areas, it will fail in those areas where it has been so successful.

Notice again the powerful image of Washington, this time not as inspiration but as horror story. Leave future policy to the amateurs, assisted by the occasional expert. What we're good at is what's been and gone. That's very revealing of Westminster. You wouldn't think that our Parliament already has a competitor of growing importance in Strasbourg, and the real possibility of another one in Edinburgh before the end of the century.

But we shouldn't swallow the transatlantic folklore whole. Are those cautionary tales of political takeover on Capitol Hill entirely justified? Chuck Bowsher was a businessman before he became Comptroller General of the United States. Was his 5,000-strong General Accounting Office a tool of the Democratic Party in opposition? Or did its operations merely reflect that ever-present fundamental, the separation of powers?

> The split government, as it's sometimes called, makes it more difficult, I think, because if you had one party controlling all three branches there would be more unanimity of policy and so on. But that's part of our system – in other words, we can have split government, we have separations of power. So we just have to deal with that. We take a request from the ranking minorities of the committees, equally with the chairman of the committee, but when your party controls the White House and the executive branch, sometimes they're not as anxious to send in the auditors, to find out how the programme is working. I think that's a fair statement. So we did end up doing more for the Democrats, and some of the Republicans raised that issue in Congress. And we said we'd be more than willing to do the work if they would just ask us. We weren't anxious to have more work being done for one party than the other.

This sounds a little like the argument that breaks out here every time one party wins a couple of elections in succession: has the Civil Service gone native? It's often circumstances that create the impression of politicization.

Just as Mr Sheldon took his committee to Washington to be underwhelmed by American practices, so Mr Bowsher came to Westminster with comparison in mind. What did he find strange about the British way of scrutiny and accountability?

> Your people tend to rely more on the MPs' personal knowledge and ability, they don't have the large staffs and everything like that; but I think in this world, as it gets more and more technical, as you get into some of these issues that you have in the defence area and even in agriculture and health care today, you've got to have people who are technically trained and experienced to review the programmes, really to understand them. I think the legislators and parliamentarians, if they don't have expertise on

their side, can be overwhelmed by people in the government ministries with facts and studies and so on. I think you need this kind of independence on the parliament side, and I think the National Audit Office is moving in that direction.

But is it? Only in the British Parliament is professional knowledge thought to be slightly out of place in a business best left to the eloquent amateur, able to see the broader picture, to resist the distorting special pleading of the experts and that much-feared capture by the informed. The 'this is Britain' syndrome is fall-back number one for defenders of the status quo who cherish our singularity. Fall-back number two is related to it: those highly polished constitutional differences. Fall-back number three is finance. Experts cost money. Arming the watchdogs with the knowledge weapon might break the bank.

How far is this the case? Sir John Bourn, a former senior civil servant at the Ministry of Defence, now works for Parliament as Comptroller and Auditor General. If MPs at Westminster asked his National Audit Office to do more for them, along the lines of what Chuck Bowsher's people did for the legislators on Capitol Hill, what would he say?

I don't think I could do it with my present staff, because we are fully engaged in our current remits and the current kind of work that we do for the Public Accounts Committee. Of course, if other work were required, I think that I could do it; but it would require some expansion of resources in order to fulfil this. What you're talking about would involve a sea change in the whole range of attitudes and approaches. But if all those things were to come about and I were to be required to operate in this way, I would take on some extra people in a number of other subjects – it's hard to say how much bigger the office would have to be. I don't think it would have to be 50 per cent bigger or even 25 per cent bigger. I think that for 10 or 15 per cent bigger, it could do good work in the area that you describe.

That's about a hundred extra people, which would bring the NAO total up to a thousand, and another £5 million a year, on top of nearly £40 million in the existing budget. Cheap at the price, you might think, if it meant that MPs – *our* representatives in Parliament – got more of a handle on the hundreds of *billions* of pounds which pour from central government each year. It's all so easily achievable without MPs on select committees succumbing to Sir John Bourn's analytical Svengalis. Now that the NAO works for Parliament and not for the Treasury, the power to extend its remit and its budget rests with the members themselves – with the legislature, not the executive. This shift in ownership of the NAO from Whitehall to

Westminster was achieved by Norman St John-Stevas's Private Member's Bill in the mid-1980s. He describes how this came about, and his own view on what its role should now be.

> I feel very strongly about the National Audit Office, of course, because that was in my original set of reforms which I put before the Cabinet; and then I was strongly opposed by the Treasury and it was taken out. But then, when I went back to the back benches, by a sort of poetic justice, an operation of Divine Providence, I drew second place in the ballot for Private Members' Bills, and I was therefore able to set up the National Audit Office as a part of Parliament, subjecting the Comptroller and Auditor General to parliamentary appointment. He became a parliamentary officer as opposed to a Treasury officer. That was a very important change; and certainly the services of that department should be available to all of the select committees. It's ridiculous that it should be confined to the Public Accounts Committee. It's there to serve the general wellbeing.

A minute concession in this direction was made in response to the 1990 Procedure Committee inquiry. Some existing unpublished NAO reports, commissioned by the PAC, can now be made available to other committees pursuing investigations in the same or a related field.[10] But there is no question of their being able to commission new ones. Is this really going to boost the flow of knowledge down the Westminster Committee Corridor? Robert Sheldon is fiercely protective of the PAC's priority:

> If we're producing a report we really must have the right to produce that report, and if you can't have two reports, I would have thought our report is the most important because it strikes at the very probity and efficiency of government operations. It has been agreed – this was said in the procedure debate by the Chairman of the Procedure Committee – that effectively we'd have a veto on other uses being made that conflict with ours. I don't think there's any doubt about that, and that's sensible. Whether you call it a veto or whether you call it just common sense is another matter. But what we'd have to do is to make sure that the government accounts are held properly.

Vetoes; *we're* the most important; you wouldn't think the PAC and the departmental committees were on the same side – which, incidentally, is meant to be our, the taxpayers', side too. If this *amour propre*, this rivalry, were to dissipate in a future Parliament refreshed, perhaps by new MPs with less atavistic impulses – and the National Audit Office's staff were restocked and redirected as a result – how might this new instrument of parliamentary accountability be best deployed?

Perhaps the greatest weakness of recent Parliaments has been their inability to scrutinize complicated government bills *before* they turn into law. Pre-legislative hearings, thorough and searching, are routine in Congress. The executive in Washington has to broker every piece of law through the legislature. Here, specially constituted standing committees on Bills are all too often a showground for the crudest partisanship and a platform for those whose opinions are as strong as they are inexpert – the province, in other words, of adversarial rather than reasoned opposition. Does it have to be so? Robert Hazell was the Home Office's man on the officials' bench as the Public Order Bill passed through the House of Commons in the 1980s, and he thinks that the select committees might have a useful role to play in this context.

> One of the disadvantages of standing committees, as presently consti-
> tuted, is that the members of a standing committee brought together to
> consider a Bill generally have no interest in it, or knowledge of the subject
> matter of the legislation. They are dragooned into serving on the
> committee by the whips, who have a different set of selection criteria.
> They push MPs on to standing committees, either for punishment or for
> preferment, and the MPs on the standing committee frequently show
> very little interest in the proceedings, signing letters and doing other
> constituency business. A select committee does have considerable exper-
> tise in the department's business, and it is much better briefed by its own
> experts and outside consultants than is the normal standing committee.

Lord St John of Fawsley agrees that there is a need for a form of pre-legislative committee and points out that there is provision for this. He also points out that it was one of the reforms with which he had most difficulty in the Cabinet.[11]

> It was strongly opposed by a whole series of Cabinet ministers; in the end
> I got it through by agreeing that there should be an experiment with three
> or four Bills, which would be considered by a select committee to begin
> with, which would then turn itself into a standing committee subse-
> quently. But that was really never followed through. I think this is a
> sphere where there could be quite radical reform.

As Lord St John notes, the standing orders of the Commons already allow for this. It's rational; it's achievable; it's a way of bringing the best of Washington to Westminster without cracking open the constitution. If such committees had been in operation isn't there just a chance that, say, the original poll tax legislation might have looked rather different? And yet it doesn't happen. Why not? Could it be that British parliamentarians suffer from a poverty of aspiration as well as a lack of analytical back-up? It's almost as if they want to be marginalized and starved of information. Recall David Judge's comments on select committees having to use the American Freedom of Information Act in pursuit of their enquiries. And consider the *Memorandum of Guidance* for civil servants appearing before select committees – the Osmotherly Rules, so called after the Whitehall official under whose name they were originally circulated once the St John-Stevas reforms had been enshrined in Parliament's Standing Orders. They amount to twenty-five pages of how to say, 'I'm sorry, Chairman, I can't answer that question. May I refer you to my minister?'[12]* They wouldn't last a millisecond on Capitol Hill – not that anyone in the administration would try to do an Osmotherly. Yet the 1990 Procedure Committee, while noting that they were *Whitehall* rules, not House of Commons ones, declined to seek their liberalization for fear that the government would come up with something worse. Lord St John does not think much of this pusillanimity.

> It was extremely feeble of them to bow down and worship the Osmotherly Rules as though they were the tablets of the law. What they should have said was: these rules are out of date, they came into existence in an entirely different situation, they could be swept away entirely and we should start again, appointing a special committee to go into this question alone and come up with a model set of rules and present these to the executive. That would have been a splendid thing to do.

Furthermore, Lord St John would have wanted that committee to have changed the whole basis of the process, so that the onus would be on the government to justify why a civil servant couldn't say something, rather than the other way round: 'The whole instinct of the Civil Service, admirable beings though they are, is to conceal information, not to impart information, and to slow things down rather than quicken things up. There was a real chance, there, of altering the balance of power in the relationship between the civil service and the legislature.'

For the deeper explanation of such surpassing supineness we return to Graham Allen, the one member of the Procedure Committee who set out his stall for greater committee clout:

---

* The 'Osmotherlys' were updated in 1994 to reflect the more liberal information climate created by the Open Government White Paper of 1993. See Peter Hennessy, *The Hidden Wiring: Unearthing the British Constitution* (Gollancz, 1995), pp. 158–9.

As a parliamentarian and someone who believes in the separation of powers, I have to say quite frankly that if I go into the executive, if I'm a minister, then the very last thing that I will do is to seek to build up the people who will stop me from getting on with the job that I feel I've been elected to do. That is the permanent contradiction that we have to live with as Members of Parliament, under a system which does not have a separation of powers. As a democrat, my view is very strongly that we need to change that system. However, as a member of an incoming Labour government, I would take the view that we had years of Conservatism to put right and want to get on with that job.

This can't be an easy dilemma to live with. Imagine a newly elected Labour government including Graham Allen, the one person who had stood up, against his own Labour colleagues as well as Conservatives, for putting real teeth into the watchdogs, now shimmering around as a minister with a mission, having sloughed off all that concern for effective scrutiny. Mr Allen acknowledges its existence, but sees no way around it: 'That is the dilemma which every practising politician who believes in democracy has to live with, until we can resolve the problem of the executive controlling our Parliament.'

Here we have it: the real balance of power in our system. The pull of the executive is paramount, even on a Graham Allen, even before an election is called, let alone won. Nothing is more calculated to dry up the independence glands at Westminster, often before they've started secreting at all. This suggests a depressing conclusion that no would-be reformer could contemplate without discomfort: that even if our watchdogs used their existing powers to vote themselves better analytical support, it might not make that much difference.

Lord St John of Fawsley has described the House of Commons, Westminster, as the most conservative body in the world; why does he think it is so difficult to interest MPs in serious parliamentary reform?

You need two things. You need a reforming mood in the House of Commons and you need a reforming Leader of the House. Sometimes you have one, sometimes you have the other. It's rare that they actually come together.

One of the great characteristics of British life in the past has been deference, which you see at all levels of British society. It's lessened as our society has become less hierarchical. But deference has grown within the political system and deference in the House of Commons is now at a historical high; despite all the noise, despite all the appearances of rebellion, the deference to those holding office, the deference to civil servants, has grown, is growing and I think could profitably be diminished.

The death of deference would be the greatest advance of all. Without it, nothing substantial will happen save a touch of tinkering here, the sharing of an odd NAO report there. What is at issue here is not the rough trade of prejudice-driven adversarial confrontation, but reasoned, thoughtful, cross-party opposition. But even in the select committee context, what distinguishes our Parliament from the US Congress is a lack of fire and passion, of any burning desire to make the powerful account for themselves fully and regularly. Forget the constitutional differences. Forget the hapless Judge Thomas. If Westminster wanted Whitehall to walk in necessary fear, it already has the technical and financial means at its disposal. It's the *will* that's lacking on the part of our MPs. No changing of the rules, no beefing-up of the NAO alone, will alter that. The remedy lies within themselves.

5

No End of a Lesson?

The Scott Report on the arms to Iraq affair was published in February 1996; the fight for the dominant interpretation of it began instantly and ferociously. Sir Richard Scott brought grief and relief alike to both sides. For the government, there were mistakes to be acknowledged but no guilty men in high office. There was no conspiracy to stand by while innocent men went to gaol. Heads need not roll. For the opposition, the judge's findings that, while ministers were not duplicitous, Parliament had been misled consistently and persistently, thanks to an endemic culture of Whitehall secrecy, confirmed their long-proclaimed charges against the government.

The difficulty at moments of high political frenzy such as this is how to winnow out the substantial argument from the transient impression, the revealing insight from the misleading, neon-lit headline. What does the Report tell us about ministerial power and accountability to Parliament, the proper relationship between the courts and the executive, the role and functions of the intelligence services, and the whole process of this most secret kind of government overlain by constant stress?

More immediately, was political blood going to be spilt? Would heads roll? Peter Riddell, associate editor of *The Times*, contemplating those in the deepest shadow of the scaffold shortly after the Report appeared, thought their prospects were fairly good:

> I don't think the heads, or particularly the two heads of William Waldegrave and Sir Nicholas Lyell, will be chopped off. John Major committed himself pretty firmly to them after the Report appeared. I think the reason for that is the way in which it was defined by the government, by Ian Lang in his Commons statement. He defined it as a matter of honour and propriety and was able to quote from the Scott Report that Mr Waldegrave and Sir Nicholas had acted in good faith; that perhaps their actions had been wrong – indeed, he found their actions had been wrong in many cases – but there was no suggestion of dishonesty. They acted sincerely at all times. And by defining it in those terms, Ian Lang and indeed other Tory ministers were able to say there's absolutely no reason for them to go because they behaved totally properly. It's rather

similar to what happened with the Franks Report into the circumstances leading to the invasion of the Falklands by Argentina, where again it was shown that, despite all the intelligence failings which had led up to the invasion, every minister had behaved entirely properly and therefore they were exonerated. So I don't think we'll see heads rolling.

But could that line be held? And indeed, should it be held? Giles Radice, Labour Member of Parliament and chairman of the House of Commons Select Committee on Public Service, thought the government's interpretation inadequate:

According to old-fashioned views about ministerial responsibility, our ministers are meant to be responsible if things go wrong, and it's quite clear from this Report that a lot of things went very wrong indeed; that Parliament was consistently misled about the changes in the guidelines, that there does seem to have been at the very least a tremendous cock-up over the Matrix Churchill trial – and in those circumstances, I think it's not just a matter of honesty or whether Mr Waldegrave is an honourable man or whether Mr Lyell is an honourable man; the fact is that they have been shown to have fallen down in their job and I think they should go.

Tom King, former Secretary of State for Defence in the Conservative government, did not agree with this at all. For one thing, he stressed that Sir Nicholas Lyell 'acted on the advice of senior Treasury counsel in the action that he took'; for another, he took the view that the ensuing period would see 'a sort of marshalling of the different legal experts who quite clearly have quite different views'. And his own view?

My own view was that one of the central issues is whether innocent men could have gone to gaol because of so-called 'gagging orders', because people were trying to suppress evidence. Now, I have signed Public Interest Immunity certificates myself in the interests of national security; I was required to do so. But I always knew that a judge could look at the documents and if he thought it would prejudice somebody's fair trial he could require them to be disclosed. The central issue here is whether there was a conspiracy that would have allowed innocent men to go to gaol and was deliberately planned. That's one of the hearts of public concern on this, and Sir Richard Scott has said that it was 'not well founded'.

A cock-up, then, not a conspiracy? We will return to the question of Public Interest Immunity certificates, which, as Mr King rightly observes, lies at the heart of much of the concern. But we should pause first on the question of ministerial responsibility. It seems to take a great deal these days to get a minister to walk. Sir Percy Cradock, former Foreign Policy Adviser to the Prime Minister, has observed ministers at close quarters over many years as an official; does he not think that now – perhaps in contrast to former times – they exhibit what one might call limpet-like qualities when it comes to being criticized?

There has been, I think, a rather worrying tendency to blur the lines of responsibility between ministers and officials. Officials, of course, privately can argue and recommend and push for various policies, but it's for the minister to decide, and he carries the responsibility. If you have a situation where the official tends to be pushed forward when things go not so well, then I think that's rather worrying. I think it would require a situation then in which officials – serving officials – were able to speak up and argue for their particular lines of recommendation and that would be a fairly chaotic situation.

The issue of Public Interest Immunity certificates is, as Tom King remarked, the one that probably exercises most people because it is the most easily understood. Innocent men would have gone to prison while ministers stood idly by: that was the accusation. Anthony Scrivener QC is a former chairman of the Bar Council; did he think that in the particular instance of the Matrix Churchill trial the way the PII certificate system was used was that of normal custom and practice? And even if it was, was it satisfactory?

The starting point here is that Scott found that this prosecution should never have been brought. So the question is, how was it that it came to be brought? And Scott is quite clear about it. If you read the Report very carefully, you will see he says that the Attorney-General did not conduct the case properly; he did not inform prosecuting counsel as to what the facts were, he kept them largely in the dark, so prosecuting counsel had no idea what was in these documents that were being held back. He also said that wrong advice was given to ministers about the PII certificates. Now, no one will hold it against Sir Nicholas if he makes an error on law or takes a different view on the law, but it was not just a question of that. What Scott said is that the class claim should not have been made at all, the category B documents were not entitled to be claimed, and none of the ministers were told that they could in fact stop and hold back these documents because it was a criminal case. That ought to come into account. And I can't help thinking it's a very poor reflection on public life that we have to rejoice because a minister has only been found grossly negligent.

Sir Percy Cradock was in that part of the Whitehall world where Public Interest Immunity was most often cited in intelligence. He has seen it operating over many years, but of course the public doesn't see it; it's the sort of thing that remains completely out of sight until an aberrational case like this one arises. Did Sir Percy think, from his knowledge of the way Sir Nicholas handled it in the Matrix Churchill case, that there was anything unusual about this case, or was it business as usual?

I don't think there was anything unusual about it; and indeed, we have testimony, including that of the judge and of two of the defence counsel, that the PIIC system worked perfectly well in a lawful, proper way in this case. And that seems to me to be fairly decisive. The hard fact is that when you have a court case involving intelligence agents or material, you have to take certain precautions otherwise agents are publicly exposed and their lives put at risk, or sensitive material is open to the public, and of course the value of British intelligence services is negated because no one will trust them with serious and sensitive material any more. So you have to draw the judge's attention to the fact that there is sensitive matter there, but you leave it to him to decide to settle how much of this is necessary for a fair trial.

The problem highlighted by Sir Richard in this case, however, was that, quite apart from those intelligence aspects in relation to which everyone understands the need for confidentiality, too much advice to ministers was lumped together in a class that was of itself going to be exempted, using a kind of blanket procedure of which he was highly critical. Mr Heseltine, in fact, asked specifically that the judge's attention be drawn to his reservations about the imposition of the certificate in such circumstances; but this was not passed on. What was Sir Percy's view of this 'portmanteau' approach to the PII system?

We are talking here about what is called class claims. The judge allowed a contents claim and said that the whole thing had been perfectly proper and there was no question about the defence being prejudiced. You cannot give immunity, of course, to someone who has worked for the intelligence services, and there would be a great outcry if we tried to do that; all you can do if someone who has helped intelligence later gets into trouble with the law is to say that at one time or another he served his country well. That's what happened with Mr Henderson and Mr Gutteridge in the Matrix Churchill case. An SIS agent testified to the fact that Henderson was a very brave man.

But there is a stumbling block here, as Anthony Scrivener pointed out:

The difficulty here was that there's only one person who had the complete view of all the facts in this prosecution, and that was the Attorney-General. And unfortunately he did not pass on that information to prosecuting counsel. Had he done so, prosecuting counsel would either have packed the case in completely, straight away, and refused to prosecute, or else he would have insisted that those documents were made available to the defence.

Does this mean that it is the Attorney who should be in the firing-line, not the head of the Secret Intelligence Service, who some have argued should have gone to the judge privately and said, please leave these chaps alone, they're ours?

No, it's a legal responsibility. And we can't blame Sir Nicholas for taking a different view on the law from other people; we all make errors. He may well be right and Scott may be wrong. But that's not the point. The fact is that he was the only person who had knowledge of all the facts, and you must pass such information on to prosecuting counsel because at the end of the day prosecuting counsel has the authority and the responsibility of either stopping or bringing the case. And, had he known all the facts, prosecuting counsel would have stopped this case.

Was it on this point of the PIIs that the media feeding frenzy, as it is sometimes called, did perhaps get out of hand? Because this was where the blood was thought to lie? Peter Riddell certainly takes this view.

When the case collapsed there was a lot of focus on the PIIs when in fact that wasn't the reason the case collapsed. The case collapsed because what Alan Clark said was inconsistent with his earlier deposition. I think one of the problems was that there was enormous uncertainty about what it meant, and the whole law on PIIs has been changing enormously. In fact, Ian Lang in his statement rather brushed aside what Sir Richard Scott said, and said we don't agree; your criticisms aren't the accepted legal view and we can give you several judges and lawyers who take our view when you quote your view. I think one of the problems relates to the position of the Attorney as a lawyer as well as a politician; the current Attorney, who I think is a very honourable man and does behave decently, is perhaps too much the lawyer and didn't realize the need politically to explain. It does look like a gagging order, and I think the lesson is that for PIIs to work effectively in the future, and quite rightly, to protect intelligence assets and information, it has to be explained what their purpose is;

that it's for the judge to determine. That's all got to be made clearer. Because it's been so rapidly evolving as a section of law, the Report and the response to the Report have shown the need for clarity in the way it works. The need is not for all things to be revealed, but for greater clarity.

Sir Percy Cradock agrees, and adds a further related point:

I think it would have helped everyone a great deal if the press had explained a little more what the real nature of a Public Interest Immunity certificate was. In fact you had nothing of the kind. They were consistently described, up to the very last minute, as 'gagging orders'. They were neither: they were not gags, nor were they orders. And I hope now that, after two years of some really fairly mischievous stories about this in the press, about innocent men being sent to gaol by ministers and officials who wanted to guard their backs, a handsome retraction will be published – though of course it would be a matter of interest if it were.

One thing that forcibly strikes many who have read the Scott Report is the stress factor, the overload on everybody involved. It was all done in a terrible rush. A thousand and one other things were going on. Wherever you look, civil servants and ministers are under stress, they are flat out. The decisions are taken, quite often, by middle-ranking people or on the advice of middle-ranking people. There's a lack of coordination. Tom King moves in this world and has personal experience of its unrelenting demands. Does he not think that one of the lessons that comes roaring out of this Report is the detrimental effect of the stress on government at all levels? He prefers a different emphasis.

What does come through – just to talk about the export licensing aspect – is the extraordinary thoroughness and endless agonizing that went on at every level. And to make one completely separate point, while I don't want in any way to be complacent about some of the issues that arise, I haven't found in the Report any evidence whatsoever of any minister or any official being accused of corruption in any respect. We get a lot of flak in the public administration and the Civil Service here. I think it's worth just putting that on record.

It is striking how many of the decisions and discussions took place at a very low level. For much of this period Sir Percy Cradock was chairing the Joint Intelligence Committee – the high table of British intelligence. It doesn't seem to have reached him, it doesn't seem to have reached a Cabinet committee, it doesn't seem to have reached the full Cabinet. Mrs Thatcher was busy on other things. Here we have the greatest furore since the Franks Inquiry into the Falklands War, and all the business was done at that kind of middle-ranking level, among both ministers and civil servants. What does that tell us about the system? Why was Sir Percy not getting regular reports and putting himself in a position where he could bang heads together and coordinate?

> The intelligence services are tasked services. They are given certain jobs to do, certain areas of priority – by the Joint Intelligence Committee – but their actual operations are for the agencies themselves. The intelligence services in this matter were told that we wanted information about Iraq's weapons of mass destruction, the big things, the nuclear weapons, the chemical and biological weapons, the Supergun, and they got that. They did the job extremely well. They were not given any such priority orders for the sort of thing that came up in the Matrix Churchill case. But I think that the intelligence services performed perfectly well. You have here a case where the activities of a particular firm ran into the official machine at two very separate points. First of all, Mr Henderson provided some intelligence about Iraq. He was used; he was then let go. Later, as an entirely separate episode, his firm was charged with falsifying, or attempting to falsify, export licence applications and action was taken by the Customs, who operate very independently. No one would suggest that we should not bring an action in a case of illegality like this simply because a particular firm had helped intelligence at an earlier time. So you had two different operations going on. It would be wrong to say that they were entirely independent and neither knew what the other was doing because SIS and Customs did put their heads together, but you can't stop the legal action. All you can do, as I said earlier, is to point out that the firm in question, Matrix Churchill, and Henderson, did some work for the country at one time. And that can be used in mitigation. And that was provided in this case.

But, in Anthony Scrivener's view, it would nevertheless have been possible to inform the Customs and Excise what the true facts were; in which case it is unlikely they would have embarked on the prosecution at all.

Another issue around which much argument has swirled is the Howe guidelines of 1985. Alan Clark has often characterized this as part of the parliamentary game. You deliberately frame guidelines so that they are flexible, so that they can be bent if not broken, and it's up to the parliamentarians to winkle out as much as they can. 'Everyone should be grown-up about this,' he has said. Why should we be so easily shocked, then, to discover that guidelines of the kind that Geoffrey Howe first formulated in 1985 might

have been changed – as Sir Richard Scott thinks they were, in 1988? Giles
Radice thinks that talk of being grown up is a cloak for little better than
hypocrisy:

> That's a highly cynical view. The problem with the British system is this.
> The French would have said: we're going to sell arms to Iraq. And they
> did; and they were open and honest about it. The problem with the
> British is that they want to say they're going on being very very good, and
> ministers will parade themselves in front of Parliament and in front
> of other people saying how tremendously good they're being, and at
> the same time they think: this is a very important industry, the defence
> industry, and we must see that we get our share of the jobs.

Tom King takes great exception to this depiction of the government's
attitude.

> That's simply not true. We did not sell any lethal arms. I saw with my own
> eyes the equipment that the French had sold to the Iraqis during all that
> period. They scooped the pool – and the French defence minister, at the
> start of the Gulf War, was actually the president of the Franco-Iraqi
> Friendship Society. It was a symbol to the closeness of their relationship.

Nevertheless, does it not worry him – as a parliamentarian, not as somebody
who is in the business of selling as much defence equipment abroad, legally,
as possible – that people on the opposition benches, in the all-party select
committees, got nowhere near any of this until a succession of contingencies
– cock-ups, perhaps – brought it to the public attention? The Select
Committee on Trade and Industry looked at the Supergun and got nowhere.
Isn't there a point to be considered about how little Parliament is told, particularly in these areas? Should ministers not pay more attention to the House
from which they are sprung?

> The Foreign Office and DTI administering guidelines that had been set
> up were broad guidelines for what we were going to do. One of the guide-
> lines which was never touched is that we did absolutely refuse to sell
> lethal equipment to Iraq. Year after year, the Iraqis were flying Mirage
> jets, they had Exocet missiles, all supplied by the French. We deliberately
> turned our back on that trade. What we said was that we will sell non-
> lethal equipment. You ask why this was dealt with at a lower level. The
> truth is that this has now become a hypnotic subject which has fascinated
> the media and everybody else. If you go back to the years when this
> started, this was actually pretty second-order business. What was actually

going on in the world? The Cold War was ending, the Berlin Wall was coming down, the Soviet Union was collapsing. There were huge changes going on in the world and, to be blunt, at that time Iraq and Iran was a bit of a sideshow.

Surely not. Sir Percy Cradock and his colleagues knew that where sand met oil met weaponry met warfare the Middle East was potentially explosive. This can't have been marginal; wasn't it, rather, the kind of thing he worried about night and day?

'We worried quite a bit about the Iran–Iraq war. After that we worried about the potential of Iraq, and we were right to do so. And we got some fairly fearsome intelligence about its military capabilities.' But, he stresses, Britain did not in any way contribute to Iraqi military capabilities: 'It was played absolutely straight, and, as Tom King has often said, to our great commercial detriment.'

But the question of ministerial roles and responsibilities remains. We have ministers to take a wider view; surely they should be given time to do it, not have to act on technical advice from the Attorney, as on the PII certificates? We all remember the description of Tristan Garel-Jones reading his fourth box at two in the morning with a note saying 'you must sign this by 9 a.m.' and so on. Again, isn't the lesson of this that somehow the executive mentality, the executive-mindedness of a system that does run flat out and under stress, means that people – honourable people but stretched people – simply do not do the jobs that the Constitution assigns to them, ministers in particular? Peter Riddell concurs with this, and links it to the perception among parliamentarians that this was not, in fact, a priority area of concern at the time:

I think one of the reasons why so much has been thrown up by the Scott Report about answers not being given frankly, guidelines being modified and then people saying they haven't been modified, the twenty-seven answers to MPs and so on, actually comes back to this – that they were, to some extent, second-order problems. The answers weren't frank, they weren't entirely truthful, devious things were said. And some of that is a result of that type of pressure. Ministers clearly didn't have time to read those things fully, they didn't really have time fully to explain them in that way. And for the MPs concerned at the time, it wasn't remotely at the forefront of affairs. It was one of those things the Middle East buffs were interested in, or perhaps that those people linked with arms manufacture were interested in; not actually central political things. It wasn't at that stage anything that was particularly to the forefront of the political debate. That doesn't alter the fact that questions should be answered candidly, and I think this relates to the point about honesty and hypocrisy. If there had been more candour, more readiness to say yes, this is the way the world works on arms sales, we would have had less fuss and people would have felt less need to behave as cynically as the Scott Report shows they did.

This leads on to another element of the system of checks and balances that didn't work: the select committees, Parliament's watchdogs – watchdogs that didn't bark. The Trade and Industry Select Committee tried with the Supergun, and yet it is surely a fairly damning indictment of the executive that if it had not been for Judge Smedley in the Matrix Churchill trial allowing the discovery of documents by the defence, none of the subsequent events would have happened, because the Trade and Industry Select Committee was fobbed off with consummate ease by one witness after another. Peter Riddell suggests that the select committees may not be very good at this kind of investigation:

Select committees are very good at investigating systems or processes; they're not very good at investigating particular cases and scandals. That, I think, is partly a reflection of their party basis, because it's clear the governing party is going to suffer. Giles Radice was involved before the current Public Service Committee was set up in investigations which led to the Civil Service Code and the report on the Bank of England. They're very good ones, because they're to do with processes and structures. But when it comes to cases, the interest and the disciplines of MPs aren't really up to doing it, I think – apart from something like the Public Accounts Committee, which has a big staff; the other departmental committees just aren't very good at it.

Does Giles Radice, as the chairman of a select committee, accept that criticism?

Not entirely. I think there are times when we are on the ball. I think there is a difficulty about the fact that, drawing on all this period, the governing party has had a majority on all these select committees and it has not been, frankly, to the interest of the governing party to have some juicy scandal going on in a select committee and being investigated by it – particularly in the run-up to a general election. It's a matter of considerable embarrassment. And that in a sense does limit the effectiveness of a select committee. It is true that it's easier to get that sort of camaraderie as parliamentarians together when you're looking at a more general issue, for example, should civil servants have a code to protect them against ministers and people who are asking them to do things that they shouldn't. That's easier to get a consensus on. It's more difficult if you're going to nail a government minister or a top civil servant for doing something which is clearly not right.

Sir Percy was not surprised that the Trade and Industry Select Committee got nowhere in particular – and perhaps, as an official, he was not terribly upset either?

> We come back to the point that it is all done at breakneck speed. There is a certain artificiality about the Scott Report in that you have one consider-able legal mind applied to one facet of foreign policy. The clock has been stopped for the benefit of Sir Richard Scott. It was never stopped for the rest of us. And we were busy with a hundred other things, many of which seemed at the time to be more important. It may be that one of the results of this episode will be the need to strengthen the machinery of select committees. But I think we should beware of setting up some vast super-visory system which is engaged all the time with plucking at the govern-ment's sleeve and insisting that it dig up and explain what it's doing because then half the government's energies will be used in defending themselves rather than getting on with promoting sales, protecting British jobs, looking after British security.

Giles Radice dismisses this as 'a Civil Service answer' and considers it 'extremely unfair to Sir Richard Scott, who was actually asked by the government to inquire into this affair; it wasn't just because he was interested in the subject, he was asked by the Prime Minister.' But Tom King thinks that it reflects the reality, that 'Sir Richard shone a very bright light on one partic-ular part of the endless passage of business that goes through, and for a moment the frame is stopped and it is examined. It's not a criticism of Sir Richard.' And he endorses Peter Riddell's point that 'select committees aren't very good at what I call almost the criminal investigation work. They can't do it and they're not equipped to do it; and they try to do it, and that is a problem.'

One of the problems for the House of Commons is that the clock has stopped for it too, in the sense that everybody's been waiting for Scott for three and a half years, and since the humiliation of the Trade and Industry Select Committee on this issue there has been no sign – with the one very significant exception of Giles Radice and his colleagues getting the Civil Service Code in place – of the select committee system having raised its game as a tool of scrutiny. It has not been shamed into improving its performance. Everybody seems to have been traditionally supine.

Peter Riddell thinks this is not an entirely fair assessment.

There are two key new committees: one is Giles Radice's, looking at public services, which is going to be kept pretty busy, and the other is the one Tom King chairs on intelligence oversight, which is critically involved in this area. So there is a change. I think there is also a particular factor relating to the actual area covered by Scott. In a sense it was frozen because Scott was going on. But I think the select committees – apart from the Public Accounts Committee – are weak in looking at particular examples, and that has remained true. In some respects they have got worse. There are also career factors in Parliament, with so many MPs being ministers or shadows; the chairmen of the committees are good, but in many cases a number of other members of the committees aren't that good, and are therefore less good at following up these issues. I think that has been a problem. But I think, too, that one aspect of Scott which is very valuable is its discussion of ministerial accountability. And I think that one of the things which will apply both to civil servants and to the select committees, both Tom King's and Giles Radice's committees, is the very interesting discussion of the questions raised about actual accountability and particularly the definitions given by Sir Robin Butler, the Cabinet Secretary, of the distinction between responsibility and accountability, made in the middle of the report.

Anthony Scrivener pinpoints one finding by Sir Richard that bears crucially on the potential of the select committees: 'Scott found that the minister had misled Parliament. It may have been done incompetently, he may not have intended it, but that was the impact of it. And select committees are never going to get anywhere if ministers mislead them. It doesn't matter how good they are, you'll never penetrate that.'

Perhaps the lesson of that is that it does take a person like Sir Richard Scott, with a special remit, to get at the truth of something like this? And that you need a judge, following quasi-legal procedures, actually to get behind the arras, as it were? Judge Smedley got the documents discovered. Parliament itself never seems to be able to do this. Anthony Scrivener thinks this is so.

This was an inquisitorial investigation, and I think that was very necessary in the circumstances. It did require an inquiring, objective mind, coming from the outside, to look at these facts. And as he said – I heard his interview – he was quite surprised at what he found. He hadn't realized, being an ordinary member of the public in that sense, what went on. And yes, I think he was quite shocked – not shocked, he said, in the sense of watching a road traffic accident, but definitely surprised at what he found.

One of the problems remains what one might call the compartmentalization of parliamentary scrutiny. The Intelligence and Security Committee looks at one thing, the Treasury Select Committee looks at another, the Public Service Select Committee looks at public service in the round, and so on. But this issue falls across, roughly speaking, four or five select committees. It's rather like the parliamentary equivalent of the problem of creeping departmentalism in Whitehall. How do you get a grip on an issue like this which slithers down the crevices? Tom King acknowledges that there may be a need for further coordination and some work on structure to this end, but he also believes that progress has already been made: he refers to the joint inquiries that have taken place – though these have been very rare – and against those who perceive 'an incipient increase in secrecy' cites the Intelligence and Security Committee as a 'very major step forward in greater openness'.

One way in which the Public Service Select Committee must surely raise its game in the aftermath of the Scott Report is to break with precedent and insist that the Prime Minister appear before it to give evidence. Prime Ministers don't go before select committees. The Cabinet Secretary makes an appearance now and again. But the premier is head of the Civil Service and head of the government; the buck stops in Number Ten. This matter crosses all the issues; this is high policy, high strategy, and the committee must claim some stature. Parliament must not fall prey to what Ernest Bevin called 'the poverty of aspirations'. But would it succeed, if it tried to do this? As Giles Radice notes, 'the only weapon of select committees is to send for persons and papers, and that is theoretically an unlimited power – except you have to get the support of the House of Commons, the floor of the House of Commons and the majority party'. Here's the rub. For in the end, if someone doesn't want to go before a select committee you have to get an Order of the House, which means a vote on the floor of the House, which means the whips come on, which means that – even with a somewhat fragile majority – the government would almost certainly prevail. That, ultimately, is the problem with parliamentary scrutiny. If it ever comes to a showdown between the House of Commons and the executive, the executive wheels the whips out and people do not turn up. Can this be a satisfactory position for the House of Commons to be in?

Tom King thinks this is too bleak a view. 'There are a lot of stages in between, and there are a lot of people who fight very hard on issues about parliamentary sovereignty and the responsibility of Parliament. It isn't just a question of a three-line whip and you've got to do what you're told. It doesn't work like that. We've actually had a few rebels occasionally in our party.' As Giles Radice points out, it's not a matter that has been put to the test recently.

Persons and papers: Anthony Scrivener reiterates the importance of the papers, the documents, in the success of an investigation such as this:

> Scott was successful because he got hold of the original documents. That's what happened to Clark. Clark blew up at the trial because he was suddenly confronted with documents which he thought were hidden by a certificate, and his own statement was a page and a half long and referred to one lot of minutes which were in his favour. That's why he collapsed. It's the documents.

Sir Percy Cradock is not a great believer in open covenants openly arrived at in this sort of world, in terms of select committee scrutiny of any kind.

> You cannot conduct a successful foreign policy on the basis of moral outrage or perpetual public scrutiny. You have to have realism and you have to have confidentiality. You have to deal with the world as you find it. Most of the countries we deal with would never pass an elementary examination in human rights or democracy; but we have to deal with them because that's the way to protect British interests, to protect British jobs and to look after security. The decisions that ministers and senior officials face all the time are never between pure black and pure white. They are degrees of grey, a lesser or greater evil. And that's the way it has to be done. But I would like to make the point that despite the demonstration of errors shown by Sir Richard Scott's inquiry, you have in this country an extremely dedicated and skilled public service and a very effective intelligence service who do the state, and all of us, a good deal of service. I do wish the press would say something to that effect occasionally instead of constantly presenting Whitehall as a den of iniquity. I'm afraid there will be a tendency, after this report, for that note to be accentuated, and I think that would be a very bad thing.

Would he say, perhaps, that Sir Richard Scott, for all his evident decency and good intentions, was naïve about the necessarily tricky and nasty ways of the world in which business had to be done?

> I have immense respect for Chancery judges of all kinds; but there is a great difference between that world and the world of foreign policy and intelligence. Reading some of the Report, I found from time to time an air of unreality. As, for example, when he said that the head of the SIS should have done his research himself for the letter that he sent me at one point. It just isn't the real world, the one in which we have to work.

Is the judiciary not qualified, then, for this sort of task? Anthony Scrivener offers a different light on the interface between the legal and political worlds: 'I think that Scott had a principle in mind which may not go down too well among politicians. He was looking for the truth. And he could not understand why it was necessary to make false statements to Parliament. It seems quite an elementary principle.'

And is openness such a threat to the system? Giles Radice thinks not.

What I think has been valuable about all this is that Scott has opened up the workings of government, the mysteries that people like Sir Percy Cradock are involved with. He's opened it up to the general public, and I don't see anything wrong in that. That's actually what democracy is meant to be about. It's not something terrible. Government isn't going to break down just because that happens. The other thing it has shown is that our civil servants, who are very skilled people, were living in a particular time: it was the last years of Mrs Thatcher and it was actually quite difficult for ministers to say 'no' about things and indeed for civil servants to say 'no'. It wasn't that kind of culture. And there are times when civil servants do have to say 'no'; not just 'Yes, Minister', but 'No, Minister.'

The huge multi-volume performance, a very subtle and elegant performance, of the Scott Report, offers wonderful searchlight beams into this very arcane world for its scholars, observers and participants; but what about the wider audience? Is it possible for Peter Riddell to convey the essence of this report, through the many ramifications, subtleties and nuances, to his *Times* readers?

I think there are real dangers here – in part because of the circumstances of its release, the hurry; there's a maximum you can do with a first glimpse of history. Getting proper proportion and balance is terribly difficult. One tries over a period of a few days to get the proper balance. The standard of our public service is on the whole high, but the trouble was that people were reluctant to admit the nature of what was involved in arms sales, that it is a slightly devious business some of the time. It would have been much better to have been franker about that, and then a lot of the problems wouldn't have occurred. We wouldn't necessarily have run into the problem of the trial, the answers to Parliament. I'm sure we behaved much better than a lot of other countries do. But to convey that I think is difficult because inevitably the media focus is on the ministerial heads of Waldegrave and Lyell and on issues like that.

Political debate in Britain has a pronounced tendency to throb for a week or two before everybody turns to the next sensation. Thereafter, only the odd phrase clings to the mind while scandals, real or imagined, sink into the obscurity of collective memory. One wonders whether memory of the Scott Report will go the way of the Franks Report, which now seems a generation or more distant and whose lessons hardly anyone can remember. If this is not to happen, several political players will have to raise their game to a level we have probably not seen in our lifetimes – not just the press or the opposition in Parliament but, perhaps most of all, those watchdogs: the Commons select committees. If Parliament itself is not to revert to the easily dismissed and casually misled legislature its critics decry, it must genuinely hold ministers to account. This is the central finding of the Scott Report. But beyond that, it must also peer persistently and professionally into those arcane areas where weaponry, trade, diplomacy and intelligence jostle inside an overloaded system of government. It has also got to ensure that the deficiencies identified by Sir Richard Scott are put right and are seen to be put right. As an approaching general election refracts every issue, including this one, through its partisan prism, this looks a very tall order.

Part Three

Where in the World?

Even though the material strength of the United Kingdom would decline relatively, we should still have other assets which would enable us to play a significant part in world affairs. The best periods of our history had by no means been those, such as the nineteenth century, when we had a preponderance of wealth or power, and for the future we must be ready to consider how we could continue to exercise influence in the world other than through material means alone.

> Harold Macmillan as Prime Minister in 1960,
> contemplating Britain's place in the world by 1970[1]

Perhaps we are the itch after the amputation.

> Senior officer of the Secret Intelligence Service, MI6, contemplating
> his service's contribution to the UK's continuing desire
> to exercise influence in the world, 1995[2]

So far, every set of ministers that has filled the Cabinet room since VE Day has wished their country to carry more clout in the world than a tough appreciation of their current resources (financial, industrial, military, human) would have allowed. The long march of high policy-making since 1945 has been punctuated by a series of undeniable traumas, especially (and most regularly) in the world's money markets. And yet the impulse to punch heavier than our weight in the world has continued unabated, though frequently redefined.

This section of the book deals with aspects of that compulsion and its associated beliefs that others 'may have all the moneybags, but we have all the brains',[3] that 'skilful play can squeeze more out of any particular hand',[4] and that 'when you need credit' it is a good idea to 'wear your best suit' in terms of diplomatic effort and overseas representation.[5] The second part deals with *the* defining moment of the postwar period, the Suez crisis, once described to me by that great figure in the early postwar state, Lord Franks, as 'a flash of lightning on a dark night' that illuminated a political, diplomatic and military landscape that had long been changing.[6] The documentary on which it is based was pieced together at high speed by Mark Laity and myself when the bulk of the Suez archive was declassified at the Public Record Office in January 1987. Straddling the Suez episode, the first part deals with a continuous element in the UK's great power impulse: the desire to become, and remain, a nuclear power. Nearly two years on from the winter night when the first Royal Navy Trident submarine, HMS *Vanguard*, slipped out of the Gareloch and into the Firth of Clyde on its first deterrent patrol,[7] it is a good moment to pick up the trail that began in Whitehall's most secret committee rooms and laboratories in the 1940s and follow it through the squadrons of V-bombers that speckled the Lincolnshire landscape in the 1950s, on to the Polaris submarines that carried the British bomb after it was transferred to the 'Silent Service' in the 1960s, and back into the secret suites of government where the decision was made to carry the UK's nuclear weapon deep into the twenty-first century aboard the Trident boats. Caroline Anstey, Mark Laity and I put a two-part documentary together in the spring of 1988 to mark the fortieth anniversary of Parliament's being told that research into atomic weapons was under way.

The section finishes with a look taken at the great power impulse in 1992 in a polity destabilized and made anxious both by continuing economic difficulties and by the question of Britain's place in Europe. Zareer Masani and I conveyed our questions and equipment around the British political and administrative classes at an especially revealing moment in their postwar journey – though the shocks of 'Black Wednesday' and Maastricht were then still to assault the body politic as a whole.

6

'A Bloody Union Jack on Top of It'

We have got to have this thing whatever it costs. We've got to have the bloody Union Jack on top of it.

Ernest Bevin, 1946[1]

On 12 May 1948 A. V. Alexander, Minister of Defence in Mr Attlee's postwar Labour Cabinet, rose in the House of Commons to announce that Britain was making its own atomic bomb. It's an awesome moment for *any* country when its government decides to become a nuclear power. Great responsibilities fall upon its political leaders and defence chiefs. The cost and technical complications involved have a profound impact on its industrial capacity and research establishments. Its relationships with other nations change. Yet on that spring day at Westminster, not one voice was raised in praise or blame of the decision. The reason? Nobody was surprised. In 1948 it was, as a senior official later put it, an 'of course' decision. Sir Frank Cooper, who was to spend nearly thirty years on the inside of defence policy-making, had just joined the Air Ministry when Alexander made his statement on the atomic bomb; as he says,

> I don't think it really ever occurred to anybody that we shouldn't have it. We were a great power. We were a great scientific nation. We were a great industrial nation. Quite natural that you should have a nuclear weapon. And all this sort of analysis, philosophy, and so on, which we tend to apply to these things I just don't think came into the equation at all.

The story of the genesis of the British nuclear weapons programme and the pattern of its development over four decades begins long before Parliament was brought into play, and in circumstances far removed from the Chamber of the House of Commons. Several of the world's leading scientists, including the eminent Dane, Niels Bohr, had pondered the potential of atomic energy during the interwar years; but the crucial theoretical breakthrough was made in 1940, in a Birmingham University laboratory, by a pair of refugees from Nazi Germany, Otto Frisch and Rudolph Peierls. Sir Rudolph describes the background to their discovery.

Nobody had really thought hard about how much separated uranium would be required to make an explosion, what was a critical size, and then one day it occurred to us to ask what would happen if you had a large quantity of separated isotope, and to our surprise if you worked this out on the back of an envelope, the amount came out quite small. Then we asked ourselves, if you could make such an explosion, what would happen? And again, on the back of another envelope, it came out that while you couldn't predict the exact power, the effects would be enormous. We also then pointed out the consequences of this weapon, including the fallout, including the fact that it would probably be very difficult to use it without killing a lot of civilians, and we added for that reason it might never be a suitable weapon for use by this country.

The magnitude of their discovery was not lost on the scientists: 'We were elated in some sense, but also frightened.'

The British government, at that time standing alone and locked in total war with Germany, had no idea that the two men had produced, in outline at least, the kind of breakthrough in weaponry that the world has not seen before or since. Frisch and Peierls were aware of the implications and alerted Whitehall. The official reaction was not all they would have wished.

The immediate response was to acknowledge this, be grateful for this information, and to warn us that we wouldn't hear any more about it. The work would now be continued by other people, which we didn't think was very sensible. I complained. I wrote a letter to point out that we were interested in getting this continued as quickly as possible, and that as we had some thoughts which hadn't occurred to other people, we might be able to do so again. And in fact, within weeks, the rules were changed. A new committee was set up, the so-called Maud Committee, in two tiers. There was a Policy Committee, and a Technical Committee; we were not put on the Policy Committee, and that we didn't mind, but we were on the Technical Committee, and therefore were able to continue working on this.

By July 1941, the Maud Report on the feasibility of an atomic bomb was in the hands of Winston Churchill and the handful of ministers and officials admitted to the secret. In research terms, it placed Britain ahead of the United States, where investigations were also under way. The Maud Report was passed to the Americans; they were not yet in the war, but it was imperative that if an atomic bomb was going to be made, Hitler should not be the first to do so. The Americans were impressed, but the British were reluctant to go into partnership with them. Lord Sherfield, who as Sir Roger Makins was engaged in Anglo–American diplomacy for most of the 1940s, explains why – and the consequences of this reticence:

> I think it was partly psychological. We thought that we had all the information, we could probably get on pretty well on our own, and we could be willing to exchange information with the Americans, but not really go into a joint project. The result of that was that the Americans were not very much impressed with the British attitude, so they decided to go ahead on their own, and of course when Americans decide that they are really going to have to do something, they really get on with it, and so by the time collaboration was really established in 1944, the Americans had gone miles ahead.

That collaboration, which involved a small team of British scientists travelling to North America, resulted from an agreement struck between Churchill and Roosevelt at Quebec in 1943. The two leaders also pledged their respective governments not to use the bomb without the consent of the other, and Britain undertook not to proceed with a civil nuclear power programme without American agreement.

In the following year, a note of another conversation between the two men at Roosevelt's country estate at Hyde Park in New York State pledged the continuation of Anglo–American atomic collaboration in peacetime. But, given wartime secrecy, no hint of either the Quebec or the Hyde Park agreements reached the United States Congress or the British Parliament – a factor of great significance in the early months of peace. For no sooner had the bombs been dropped on Hiroshima and Nagasaki and the British scientists returned home than to all intents and purposes collaboration ceased. The Anglo–American atomic partnership had always had an on-and-off air about it; now, with Germany and Japan defeated, the Americans regarded the bomb as their exclusive property.

British negotiators in Washington attempting to restore the collaboration had to contend with bureaucratic bungling as well as American suspicions, as Lord Sherfield recalls:

> The trouble with the Hyde Park Agreement was that the American copy of the agreement was lost. I had the rather invidious task of taking a copy down to the State Department because they couldn't find it, and what had happened in fact was that the President's secretary, or whoever was with him in Hyde Park, had passed it down the line and whoever got it in the administration looked at it, saw the codename 'Tube Alloys' and thought, 'Well, "Tube Alloys", that must be something to do with naval engineering.' So they sent it over to the Navy Department.

To make matters even worse, as these difficult negotiations proceeded Senator McMahon, Chairman of the Senate Committee on Atomic Energy, in complete ignorance of the Quebec and Hyde Park agreements, was busy pushing legislation through Congress prohibiting cooperation with *any* country on nuclear matters. Lord Sherfield, however, did have copies to brandish in front of his American counterparts.

> Of course we made the most of it, but in fact they were very weak documents, and they had no legislative backing. They were not capable of being ratified, or even produced to the parliaments. So it wasn't really a very strong hand. However, we did in fact make a draft, and submitted it to the Combined Policy Committee in April, I think, and the Americans just threw it out. By that time the McMahon Act had either been passed or was in the process, and they said, 'We can't sign this. It's impossible, we can't have an agreement.' Mr Attlee sent a long message to the President, rehearsing the whole background of our collaboration in the war, and so on, and saying that this really was an intolerable situation. A very strong document. He never got an answer.

Senator McMahon told Winston Churchill in 1952 that had he known about the Quebec Agreement he wouldn't have put the Act through Congress. Would Congress, for its part, have passed such a measure if it had known about the Quebec Agreement? Lord Sherfield thinks that 'they would have been taken aback by it. I think they would have thought that it was a document which probably never ought to have been written. I don't think it would have made the slightest difference.'

The barren result of these negotiations made a great difference, however, to a Britain exhausted by six years of war. This difference was not so acute on the theoretical side, for several British scientists had been involved in the minutiae of the uranium and plutonium bombs dropped on Japan; William Penney, for example, the British expert on blast effects, carried home the details of the Nagasaki bomb in his head, from where not even the McMahon Act could expunge them. Where its effect was very keenly felt, however, was in respect of the vast industrial infrastructure needed to produce fissile material for the warhead, where the Americans had so much to offer their former partner. A British bomb would have been a far easier proposition if collaboration had continued, particularly on the industrial side. Yet in 1946 there was no doubt that Britain would have to go it alone.

Ironically, at this stage ministers had still to take a formal decision to make the British bomb. As early as December 1945 a small, highly secret Cabinet committee had authorized the construction of an atomic pile at Windscale to produce plutonium. In October 1946, however, there was a political hiccup in the Cabinet committee when ministers were asked for money to build a gaseous diffusion plant in addition to the plutonium pile to improve the supply of fissile material. Sir Michael Perrin was assistant to Lord Portal, the leader of the bomb project, and recalled the occasion in an interview for BBC2's *Timewatch* programme.

When the meeting started, the Foreign Secretary, Bevin, had not turned up. Two of the other ministers, Dalton, the Chancellor of the Exchequer, and Sir Stafford Cripps, were very much against this, because, they said, we haven't got the money to do it; we haven't got the materials; we want building materials for the present crisis in the country, and all the rest of it. The Minister of Supply was there, and I was there with Lord Portal, sitting between the two of them. He said to me, 'Look, I think we'd better withdraw this paper,' and Portal said, 'Go on talking,' and he did go on talking, and at that stage Mr Bevin came in, and apologized for being late, and the Prime Minister summed up very much on the lines of what Dalton and Cripps had been saying, that the country couldn't stand the money or the materials, and Bevin turned up and said, 'No, Prime Minister, that won't do at all. We've *got* to have this.' And one of the reasons he gave was a very striking one. Quite bluntly, he said, 'I don't mind for myself, but I don't want any other Foreign Secretary of this country to be talked at, or to, by the Secretary of State in the United States as I just have, in my discussions with Mr Byrnes. We've got to have this thing over here, whatever it costs,' and I think I'm right in remembering, he ended up with saying, 'We've got to have the bloody Union Jack on top of it.' And that swung the meeting right round.

There was a great deal more to the animus against America than Bevin's resentment at the way his opposite number in Washington had behaved. The Truman administration had cut off Lend-Lease in the first days of peace, and had done nothing to thwart McMahon's measure, despite Britain's gift of precious atomic know-how and brilliant scientists to the wartime partnership. There were doubts, too, about America's maturity as a great power and fears of renewed isolationism. All these feelings were involved when the Union Jack was finally placed upon the bomb on 8 January 1947 in yet another secret Cabinet committee from which, significantly, Attlee had removed Dalton and Cripps. Attlee chose not to take the bomb decision to the full Cabinet, though there's no doubt it would have received approval from the majority if he had. Cripps' and Dalton's dissent was based on cost. Only a couple of scientists, Patrick Blackett and Henry Tizard, cast doubt on the decision in principle. Tizard, Chief Scientific Adviser at the Ministry of Defence, drafted a minute which argued, to the horror of his colleagues, that

Britain was not a great power, and never would be again. 'We are a great nation,' wrote Tizard, 'but if we continue to behave like a great power, we shall soon cease to be a great nation.'

Was the 1947 decision based on an illusion? Sir Frank Cooper would not go so far as that.

> I'm not at all sure about that. I think if one had started to do the bomb ten years later, yes. But it came simply as part of many other illusions. We thought it was a natural process. We were entitled to it. We'd been in there. Let's have it. It made a lot of sense. It didn't seem terribly expensive at the time. It wasn't some great analytical, heavily thought out decision, which you read about in textbooks. As with most things, it was taken out of one's guts rather than out of one's head.

However strong the conviction of Attlee and Bevin about the need for a British weapon, they never ceased trying to restore American aid. Their cause was hampered by the exposure of a string of spies, the atomic scientists Allan Nunn May and Klaus Fuchs in 1946 and 1950, and the diplomat Donald Maclean, who defected in 1951. But three years earlier a *modus vivendi* had been reached. In return for Britain giving up its veto under the Quebec Agreement on American use of the bomb, America relinquished its right to veto Britain's civil nuclear power programme and the British continued to have access to American intelligence on what the Russians were actually up to – though there was a good deal of surprise, especially among the politicians, when the Soviet Union successfully carried out an atomic test in 1949. Lord Sherfield negotiated the *modus vivendi*; did he not think he had given away too much for a comparatively meagre return?

> My own view is that a great power cannot allow another country to prevent it doing whatever it needs, or thinks it needs, for national security, and that therefore that provision was really, in practice, not enforceable. And that the other provision, about the President controlling our civil programme, was totally unacceptable on our side, and that therefore by cancelling those two provisions out, nothing was lost. Something, indeed, was gained. I think we gained more, really.

Part of the restored collaboration took the form of the pooling of information, on intelligence matters, monitoring other people's atomic explosions. This, as Lord Sherfield points out, turned out to be a valuable provision. 'If you're monitoring other people's explosions of atomic weapons, you can't help learning a great deal about what atomic weapons are about, how they're made, so I suspect that we got a great deal of information through that channel, which of course was never broken.'

By the time Labour lost office in October 1951, the project was well advanced. The returning Churchill was amazed that so much had been achieved so secretly for so long, and at Attlee's skill in concealing the £100 million cost from Parliament. Three scientists, known as the 'atomic knights' (Sir William Penney, Sir John Cockcroft and Sir Christopher Hinton), created what Churchill once called 'the art and the article' of the British bomb; Lord Plowden, first Chairman of the Atomic Energy Authority, worked closely with all three and gained insight into their distinctive qualities:

> Cockcroft was the scientist, the research man *par excellence*, who was always extending his researches at Harwell further and further. Bill Penney was an extremely nice man, and with great ability, great knowledge of nuclear weapons, because he'd spent all the war, or a large part of the war, in Los Alamos in America. He was very good at leading his team, and yet keeping them disciplined. Cockcroft allowed them to wander off into discovering new worlds. Bill Penney didn't. He kept them directed down the line that had been adopted. Hinton was an extremely able engineer, a great driving force, determined always to have his way, and very often – perhaps usually – his way was the right one. But if it wasn't, it was very difficult to persuade him that it wasn't.

By the late summer of 1951, Hinton had produced enough plutonium for a test. In the early autumn, Penney took his device to the Monte Bello Islands off the north-west coast of Australia. Churchill had two telegrams drafted ready for despatch: 'Thank you, Dr Penney,' if it failed; 'Well done, Sir William,' if it worked. Penney got his knighthood.

But the pace of nuclear technology was relentless. Within a few weeks of the Monte Bello test the Americans exploded a thermonuclear device demonstrating that an immensely more powerful hydrogen bomb was feasible. In 1953 the Soviet Union followed suit. Although the Royal Air Force had yet to put atomic squadrons into operation – that didn't happen until 1957 – British ministers felt the need to follow where America and Russia had led. Lord Plowden was briefed to investigate the possibility, and was present when Churchill committed himself.

> I got a minute from the Prime Minister, from Churchill, saying to let him know what it would cost, what effort would be necessary to develop and manufacture hydrogen bombs. And under the direction of Bill Penney, and the collaboration of Hinton and Cockcroft, I was given the answer to his question, and I went to see Churchill in his room in the House of

Commons after lunch, and when I'd explained what the effort necessary would be, he paused for a time, and nodded his head, and said in that well-known voice of his, 'We must do it. It's the price we pay to sit at the top table.' And having said that, he got up and tied a little black ribbon round his eyes, and lay down on his bed in his room, and went to sleep.

Churchill was a stickler for the priorities of Cabinet government. Unlike Attlee, who had kept the bomb hidden in the undergrowth of Cabinet committees, Churchill took the H-bomb decision to full Cabinet – three times – in the summer of 1954. The scientific advice suggested that a British H-bomb was possible, but it was an assessment fraught with risk. It could well have been beyond British resources in terms of manufacturing costs, if not in terms of design. Observing fall-out from Russia in 1955 – as permitted under the *modus vivendi* – gave the scientists the reassurance they needed, as Victor Macklen, who worked on the British H-bomb in the 1950s, explains: 'It helped to give us the information that we could produce a thermonuclear device which would give a very large yield, without an enormous additional cost. There was of course a very large amount of additional scientific complexity, but there wasn't an order of magnitude increase in cost.'

Analysis of debris from the Russian tests showed British scientists that most of the fall-out came from the fission of natural uranium by the fast neutrons of fusion. Natural uranium is taken from ores dug up from the ground and does not require the expensive reprocessing of enriched uranium. The Russians in the 1950s had unwittingly made some tiny compensation for the British and American secrets purloined by their spies in the 1940s.

But the builders of the British hydrogen bomb had their eyes on the Americans as well as the Russians. Victor Macklen explains why the politicians pressed the scientists so hard.

There were two reasons, I think. First, they were obviously attracted by the fact that if you could produce a megaton, then this was a more powerful political weapon than a kiloton. But I think also, and perhaps more strongly, because the British governments of the time wished to re-establish the close cooperation with the Americans on this subject which had continued until 1946. The only way this could be done was by the British being able to demonstrate that they had the capability of producing these very large explosions.

From 1955, so great was the confidence in those future large explosions that ministers and civil servants began a fundamental reshaping of defence policy around the hydrogen bomb. The result was unveiled in a White

Paper in 1957. Sir Richard Powell, Permanent Secretary at the Ministry of Defence, was deeply involved in drafting it.

It was thought of as something cheaper than having to provide the enormous conventional forces that would have been required to consti- tute a deterrent, or an adequate defence of Western Europe, had the need arisen. In fact, I think you could say really that it was an impossibility for an alliance to produce forces of that size. So, in that sense, it was a cheaper way of achieving the objective. There's no doubt about that.

A number of people have now said in effect that the stockpile of weapons we had in the mid-1950s was small, and deliberately so. The theory was extended to envisage the construction of British defence policy henceforth on the foundation of this very small stockpile, albeit with enormous destruc- tive force. The nuclear capability was in fact quite a limited capability – limited but, as Sir Richard points out, adequate: 'Provided the vehicle is accurate, and you have enough, you could do sufficient damage with ten bombs, I would have said.'

But ministers were beginning to think bigger than this. The declassified papers for 1957 show that Macmillan's Defence Committee was planning for some hundred hydrogen bombs for fitment to the V-bombers now rolling off the production line in considerable numbers. Lord Plowden was asked to produce still more fissile material from a new plant costing £134 million. He told ministers it might be possible to provide what was needed without new plant if further tests were successful – or if technical information was forth- coming from America. Macmillan, he recalls, was determined to grasp the prize that had eluded every Prime Minister since 1946.

We were quite convinced that it was right to do everything we could to persuade the Americans to restore the collaboration, because their nuclear effort was enormously greater than our own, and they had covered a lot of ground which we might have been able to, but it would have taken us a tremendous effort to do, and in the end there were tremendous economies as a result of the restoration of collaboration.

The Americans were the spectre at the feast in every top-level discussion on the bomb. From Attlee and Bevin onwards, British ministers were adamant that Britain needed a deterrent of its own, that America should not be the only nuclear-armed state in the West, that she was an uncertain ally. Yet, at the same time, they hoped that a demonstration of British capability would persuade the Americans that we were, once more, worthy of partnership. Monte Bello failed to achieve this. But the explosion of a hydrogen device at Christmas

Island in May 1957* gave Macmillan his chance to convince his old wartime colleague, President Eisenhower, that the moment had come. Victor Macklen describes the crucial scientific negotiations in which he took part.

> The first set of meetings, which were combined political and technical level meetings, took place in Washington, first of all to see whether there was any basis on which cooperation could take place. These began in a very difficult atmosphere, with neither side wishing to reveal anything of its technical progress, except the barest outlines. The meetings were obviously on a very friendly basis, but the first day's meetings were not more than just barely satisfactory, and it didn't look as though any progress would be made. That night, the leader on the British side, who was Sir Frederick Brundrett, had a discussion with Bill Penney and Bill Cook and the Aldermaston scientists, and decided that they would offer to present to the Americans one of our designs, and it was done on the basis that it was in fact the best design that we had, but we were not going to tell the Americans that particular point. This took place the next morning. We offered the Americans this presentation and they agreed, and the Aldermaston staff presented the design, as one of the designs that they were working on and had tested. After the presentation, the Americans asked for a recess. They came back about ten minutes later, and it was at that point that Edward Teller said that after twelve years of separation, it was obvious that the laws of physics operated on both sides of the Atlantic and the British, in scientific terms, knew as much about the matter as did their American colleagues. And from that time on the negotiations for the exchange took place quite quickly.

Eisenhower agreed with Teller. Within a year his administration had squared Congress, the McMahon Act was amended and a new agreement was concluded in 1958 which has been the basis of nuclear collaboration ever since.

But almost immediately a new set of problems confronted those responsible for maintaining the effectiveness of the all-British deterrent of V-bomber and hydrogen bomb. Professor Peter Nailor taught at the Royal Naval Staff College; an earlier part of his career was spent working on the deterrent in the Ministry of Defence. He remembers the anxieties of British policy-makers in the late 1950s.

---

*It is now known that the first fully genuine UK thermonuclear explosion took place on Christmas Island in November 1957. See Katherine Pyne, 'Art or Article? The Need for and Nature of the British Hydrogen Bomb, 1954–58', *Contemporary Record*, vol. 9, no. 3, Winter 1995, p. 579.

The first was the very rapid acquisition and development by both the United States and the Soviet Union of enormously more sophisticated thermonuclear capabilities. This was the period in which the superpower armouries began to grow very quickly. So this raised the question of what Britain should do in order to maintain a credible minimum deterrent, and this might affect not merely the weapon systems themselves, but the whole size of the programme. The second issue was the enormous enhancement of the pace of change from the middle 1950s on. I think one of the facts that tends to be obscured in this period is the step change that occurred with the successful testing and deployment of thermonuclear weapons. These are on an entirely different scale, in both military and political influence, from the Hiroshima-type bomb. This effectively occurred in the 1952–5 period, and immediately afterwards you got quite unexpectedly fast technical breakthroughs in reliable solid fuel rocket motors, the development of miniaturized components, both for warheads and for guidance and instrumental systems. And the pace of change was accelerating to an extent where a country like Britain was being forced to make technical choices with bewildering rapidity. The V-bomber free-fall [bomb] combination was a jolly good combination, but it was already becoming obsolescent almost before squadron service capability had been reached, and the question, the specific question for British defence planners, was: what came next? Could we, in fact, find something that would enhance and prolong the service life of the V-bombers, or would we have to make the switch straight away to something like land- or sea-based missiles? That was an option which, I suppose, as late as 1954–5 nobody thought would be an immediate problem. By 1957–8 it was already knocking on the door.

Naturally, a home-grown answer was sought first; but, as Professor Nailor explains, it was not sufficient.

They attempted to provide for a transition which in the first place was based upon the maintenance and development of an indigenous missile industry. This was the plan to develop the Blue Streak missile, which technically was a very good vehicle, but in political and military terms was very quickly overtaken by technology, because it was liquid-fuelled and the advent of solid-fuelled motors meant that you could get an enormously enhanced state of readiness, which would in fact make the Blue Streak missiles on pads, or on silos in East Anglia, very vulnerable to attack.

Blue Streak was cancelled. Going it alone – even with American know-how – was no longer possible; a deeper reliance on the United States seemed inevitable. The new hope was an American missile – Skybolt – which, if it worked, could be fired from the V-bombers hundreds of miles from the rapidly improving Soviet air defences. The Americans were also developing an advanced missile system to be launched from submarines – Polaris. Thus, by 1960 Macmillan *had* to turn to the Americans for the latest technology. Sir Philip de Zulueta was the Downing Street Private Secretary who accompanied the Prime Minister to Camp David, the President's mountain retreat, to ask for Skybolt; not, he recalls, a very pleasant mission.

> It was not at all agreeable to have to do that, but there was really no alternative, and he fortunately managed to succeed in doing it. Curiously enough, when he was asking for Skybolt at that Camp David meeting, the Americans in the background were talking about Polaris. I remember Eisenhower's naval aide, who was a charming man, had got a model of the Polaris there. Of course, he was the Navy lobby, and was trying to persuade one to go ahead with Polaris. I discussed it with Sir Norman Brook, and he said, 'For goodness sake, let's hope they don't raise that question; we must have an airborne missile, because we want to use our bombers.'

Sir Norman, the Cabinet Secretary, had genuine cause for concern. The Vulcan bombers were in mid-production and would be coming off the line for another three years; so the idea of putting the deterrent underwater on Polaris submarines was deeply unattractive.

So Skybolt it was, even if, metaphorically speaking, there would be a Stars and Stripes on the British version as well. In the early 1960s there was also a prospect, albeit fleeting, of there being a Tricolour on it too, for Macmillan had another grand design to set alongside Britain's special relationship with America: a diplomatic approach to the French which, it was hoped, would lead to our joining the European Economic Community. A tall figure by the name of Charles de Gaulle stood in the way.

The French have long believed that Macmillan, as part of this plan, trailed the possibility of an Anglo-French nuclear partnership at a pair of meetings with de Gaulle at Champs in June 1962 and at Rambouillet the following December. Sir Philip de Zulueta, who was present at the first of these meetings, thinks that no specific suggestions were made then: 'There were some conversations which took place with just the two of them alone, but I doubt whether Macmillan went quite as far as that. I think he made gestures in the direction of the French, but not more than that.' By the time of the follow-up meeting at Rambouillet there were rumours that Skybolt was in technical trouble and de Gaulle proved resistant to Macmillan's diplomatic charms. Sir Philip offers an explanation of the link:

> President de Gaulle went on as he did at the Rambouillet meeting

because, my own feeling is, he'd been advised by the French Ambassador in Washington, M. Alphand, that if Skybolt was cancelled, which he must have guessed correctly it would be, we would not be given anything else. He had been listening, I suspect, to the anti-Polaris British school of thought, and I suspect – this is a subjective view – that de Gaulle didn't expect us to get what Macmillan persuaded Kennedy to give, and therefore thought we should be left with nothing, no Skybolt and no alternative.

There was another, deeper, factor too. Skybolt or not, de Gaulle was never convinced that the British would forsake their 'special' Atlantic relationship for a genuine European partnership.

At the time that relationship didn't always seem very special. Macmillan came home from Paris to discover that Skybolt was indeed on the rocks. Why had he been left unprepared for this outcome – particularly as the British Ambassador in Washington, Sir David Ormsby-Gore, was a close friend of President Kennedy? Sir Philip anatomizes the limits of the 'special relationship' at this juncture:

> There were two lobbies in America, the naval lobby and the Air Force lobby, and we, rightly or wrongly, were paying attention to what the Air Force lobby were saying; they, of course, were in favour of Skybolt, and David Ormsby-Gore didn't actually realize that the argument had swung the other way, against Skybolt. The first that we really officially knew of it was when McNamara made an announcement, I think it was at London airport, which of course was a great shock, because apart from anything else the Prime Minister had thought that the President would be in touch with him if he was going to cancel Skybolt, before he'd cancel Skybolt, because of the agreement having been made between the Prime Minister and the President in the first place. And Kennedy didn't appreciate this.

Lord Home, Macmillan's Foreign Secretary when Skybolt was cancelled, remembered the news as 'a pretty good shock. We'd set a lot of store by its success, and the success had been advertised and it was widely known that the government set a lot of store by it; so it was a shock, undoubtedly.'

It's hard to appreciate nowadays just how vulnerable Macmillan and his team felt as they set out to salvage what they could – and this time they hoped to do a deal on Polaris, whatever the effect on the V-bombers – at a meeting with President Kennedy at Nassau just before Christmas 1962. Lord Home recalled their apprehensions:

'I didn't think we would be successful when we set out. Jack Kennedy, and indeed the State Department and the Pentagon, were not at all keen on this deal, clearly, and from their point of view there was a lot to be said for keeping all the nuclear power in American hands, of course.'

And if that negotiation had failed, 'we would have been in a very, very nasty position politically. I think that the government would probably have been beaten. It might well have been a case for an election, I would have thought.'

The hard men in the Pentagon and the State Department may have cared little for the electoral prospects of an elderly gentleman from Britain compared to the inconvenience, as they saw it, of mini–deterrents in Europe cluttering up the field between the two superpowers. But in such matters it is presidents who decide. Sir Philip de Zulueta describes how Macmillan played on the younger man's feelings at Nassau.

> He made a most moving and emotional speech, about the great losses and the great struggles for freedom and so on, and Britain was a resolute and determined ally, who was going to stand firm, and that it was very un-reasonable for the United States not to assist her to do so, in a nutshell. And it was very well done indeed and very effective, and there wasn't a dry eye in the house. Splendid.

Lord Home, who as Prime Minister himself after Macmillan had his own finger on the British nuclear button, thought there was a personal sub-stratum to Kennedy's Anglophilia that worked in Macmillan's favour on this occasion:

> Jack Kennedy, I always think, felt fairly lonely in carrying this responsi-bility and being the only man who could put his finger on the button, and of course he and Macmillan had hit up an extraordinary friendship, the much older man with the younger man. Kennedy trusted Macmillan absolutely, and feeling as I think he did, I think he was relieved to feel that somebody else was in on the act.

The terms of the Polaris deal were genuinely advantageous to Britain. America carried the bulk of the research and development costs, and Britain's right to use its own Polaris force when 'supreme national interests' were at stake was recognized. Notwithstanding such generosity, Macmillan shared the ambivalence of all postwar British premiers about the special nuclear relationship. Sir Philip de Zulueta tells a pertinent anecdote.

> As far as the relationship with the Americans went, Macmillan was primarily concerned, as I think people still are today, that we should have enough nuclear power to prevent some foolish decisions being made to

our detriment on the other side of the Atlantic, and indeed at one point I think he said to the Americans, 'Of course, if necessary, I shall use it against you.'

This remark, Sir Philip thinks, was addressed to McNamara, who was – not surprisingly, perhaps – 'rather taken aback'.

But what would have happened if the fears of ministers on the outward flight to Nassau had been realized and the Americans had refused to help? Sir Frank Cooper does not think the options in that event were ever seriously addressed, 'except in what you might call a fairly low-level kind of way. The choices would have been to have got out of the business, which I don't think would have happened, or to go on with some probably air-launched missile, which I think is probably the most likely outcome; to go on with a British rocket of one kind or another.'* Cooperation with the French, in Sir Frank's view, was a long way down the list: 'probably least likely to go in with the French, because at that time, which is a long time ago, I don't know that the British had a great deal of respect for French science and technology.'

Within a month of Macmillan's success at Nassau in the face of doubters from the State Department and the Pentagon, uncertainty appeared closer to home in the shape of Harold Wilson, chosen to lead the Labour Party on the death of Hugh Gaitskell. Wilson lost few opportunities to decry Polaris, arguing that it would not be British, nor would it be independent, nor would it deter. Peter Nailor, a member of the Polaris Executive, recalls the immobilizing effect this new political element had on the programme.

The question that presented itself to us in the summer of 1964 was a particularly difficult one, because we had by then been going about a year, and this was the stage at which a number of important contracts came up for negotiation. We had taken very nearly a year to determine what it was that needed to be done and how it should be done, and my recollection

---

* Papers released at the Public Record Office in 1993 and 1994 show that Harold Macmillan, while consulting the full Cabinet on two occasions about the purchase of Polaris, kept his private doubts about the durability of the Nassau Agreement (and those investigations of an all-British alternative Sir Frank Cooper mentioned) to a small group of ministers, diplomats and civil servants. For the Cabinet meetings see Public Record Office (PRO), CAB 128/36, CC(62), 76th conclusions, 21 December 1962 and PRO, CAB 128/37, CC(63), 2nd conclusions, 3 January 1963; for Macmillan's private doubts, see PRO, PREM 11/4412, 'Polaris', Macmillan to Thorneycroft, 26 December 1962 and PREM 11/4147, 'Record of a meeting at Admiralty House, 31 December 1962'. For the all-British alternatives to a Polaris purchase, a list of which Macmillan instructed to be drawn up, see PREM 11/4148, Amery to Thorneycroft, 15 January 1963.

is that the most significant effect was that we found it really quite difficult to get those contracts concluded until after the election programme. Government administrators are not supposed to play two ends against the middle, but it certainly was a problem then of maintaining momentum until everybody, not merely Whitehall, but everybody knew whether or not the programme was going to continue.

Nineteen sixty-four was *the* nuclear deterrent election. Keeping it was one of the main planks of the Conservative campaign; renegotiating the Nassau Agreement of 1962, whereby the United States undertook to supply the Royal Navy with Polaris missiles, was a key element in Labour's manifesto. By the time the election took place, work had already begun on the British Polaris submarines: some £40 million had already been spent and a further £270 million was committed. But the net cost of cancellation, at between £35 million and £40 million, would have been far from prohibitive.

Lord Home lost the election, narrowly, to Harold Wilson. Did he expect Wilson to cancel Polaris in his first days in Downing Street?

I had always found, in dealing with Harold Wilson on security matters, that he was reliable in terms of the national interest. And so in spite of the manifesto, in spite of what he said during the election campaign, I didn't think he'd be able to bring himself to cancel it when he understood the facts. There are quite a lot of facts the leader of the opposition doesn't have. When he got into government I thought he would carry on the programme, so it didn't worry me unduly.

Wilson's new Defence Secretary was Denis Healey. During his first weekend in post, he discussed the future of Polaris with Lord Mountbatten, the Chief of the Defence Staff, and Lord Zuckerman, the ministry's Chief Scientist. Lord Zuckerman recalls the meeting at his house that Sunday evening:

We told them there would be major opposition; I'm fairly certain we didn't say, 'OK, carry on with your pre-election propaganda about elimi-nating these things.' We just said what the consequences would be of trying to eliminate them – that we'd carry on with our V force and as a presumed independent nuclear power, but with a vulnerable air force. And Harold Wilson, almost straight away, decided to carry on.

Why? Before recommending to the Cabinet that the Polaris programme should continue, the Prime Minister consulted two colleagues. One of them was Denis Healey:

The basic reason was that the deal which Macmillan had got out of Kennedy was a very good one. It was a very cheap system for the capability it offered. We'd already got one boat nearly complete and another was on the stocks. So the saving from cancellation would have been minimal, and given the uncertainties – the Cuban Missile Crisis was only a year or two behind us, the memory of Hungary was still in our minds, Khrushchev had been deposed the day before the British poll, the Chinese had just exploded their bomb the same day – we felt, on the whole, it was wise to continue with it.

Wilson's nuclear group did trim the programme, however, cutting the Polaris fleet from five to four boats. When that recommendation went to the Cabinet at a special session at Chequers a few weeks later, the Chancellor of the Exchequer, James Callaghan, tried to cut it back still further – and gained support from a surprising quarter, as Denis Healey recalls:

Jim wanted it down to three, just to save money, of course. But George Brown wanted it down to three on the grounds that with three boats we couldn't be sure always of having one on patrol, and therefore it couldn't be regarded as capable of being used independently. I remember Michael Stewart saying at the time that it reminded him very much of when he was on the committee of the Fulham Co-op in the 1930s and they were discussing, being good Methodists all, whether, for the first time, they should stock wine. And they finally decided they would stock wine, but only very poor wine.*

---

* The sequence of ministerial meetings dealing with Polaris can now be reconstructed from the declassified files. MISC 16, a Cabinet committee consisting of Wilson, Gordon Walker and Healey, met on 11 November 1964 and decided to proceed with at least three Polaris submarines which 'would represent the minimum force which would be acceptable to us in the event of the dissolution of the NATO Alliance'. MISC 17, a larger group consisting of Wilson and ten other ministers (Michael Stewart was not one of them, though George Brown was) gathered at Chequers on 22 November 1964 to discuss the continuation of Polaris. The full Cabinet met on 26 November 1964 and discussed the minimum number of Polaris boats needed to sustain the force. Both Brown and Stewart were present, so it was probably on this occasion that the 'Fulham Co-op' exchange took place. The Cabinet's Defence and Overseas Policy Committee met on 29 January 1965 and took the decision to proceed with four Polaris submarines. Brown, Callaghan, Healey and Stewart were all present, so the 'Co-op wine' may have flowed through this meeting rather than on 26 November 1964. For MISC 16 see PRO, CAB 130/212; for MISC 17 see CAB 130/213; for the full Cabinet see CAB 128/39, CC(64), 11th conclusions; for the Defence and Overseas Policy Committee see CAB 148/19, ODP(65), 5th meeting.

That took care of George Brown. Four boats it was, sufficient to guarantee at least one submarine on patrol all the time.

Polaris, as a deal, lived up to expectations. When it took over the deterrent role from the V-bombers in the summer of 1969, it was on time *and* 13 per cent below the anticipated cost. But there was another motive behind Labour's decision to keep it, as Lord Wilson acknowledged in a radio interview in 1985. I reminded him that he had gone to enormous pains to keep the independent deterrent going over those years – and that it had cost a great deal of money. He was very clear about the reasons why:

> I never believed we had a really independent deterrent. On the other hand, I didn't want to be in the position of having to subordinate ourselves to the Americans when they, at a certain point, would say, 'We're going to use it,' or something of that kind – though in fact, I doubt if anyone expected it ever to be used. It wasn't that we wanted to get into a nuclear club, or anything of that kind. We wanted to learn a lot about the nuclear thing, and so on. We might need to restrain the Americans, if we learnt about new things that could happen of a devastating character.

Denis Healey made a similar case for keeping Polaris:

> Cost was not a major factor one way or the other. The real question was whether it was worth continuing with a programme whose real value lay in the ability to have a handle on the Americans, rather than anybody else, and I'm bound to say that one factor which strengthened my support for keeping the thing going was that McNamara, and some other Americans, were so anxious we should get rid of it.

Did the independence factor, then, in his view pale into insignificance beside the importance of having some kind of leverage with the United States? What did this 'handle on the Americans' amount to?

> There were two factors. First of all, the cooperation in the nuclear field which had been established really for the first time by Macmillan, before the Nassau Agreement, gave us the ability to make an input into the discussions between the Americans and the Russians on disarmament, and Macmillan used that in getting the first Test Ban Treaty. Secondly, it gave us knowledge of what the Americans and Russians were doing at a time when the certainty of American support in various parts of the world could not be assumed, and equally there was the possibility the Americans would do some things with which we would not want to be associated.

Here one sees again the ambivalence, the reservation at the heart of the special nuclear relationship.

It was business as usual in another sense, too. Even before the Royal Navy's Polaris boats began their patrols, the nuclear community in Whitehall and at Aldermaston began to worry about Soviet advances in defence which might set Polaris on the slope to obsolescence. The Russians were known to be developing an anti-ballistic missile capability. The Americans – moving on from Polaris to Poseidon, with its more sophisticated multiple warheads capable of scattering and defeating the Soviet radar to hit a multiplicity of targets – were confident they could beat the new defences. The single-warhead Polaris A3 missile with the Union Jack on it couldn't be viewed with such confidence, and by 1967 Wilson's inner group on nuclear matters were once more faced with a technical dilemma. They could resolve it by following the Americans and buying Poseidon; or they could seek a British-designed improvement of Polaris which would involve packing decoys into the nose-cone (a miniature spacecraft, in essence) to confuse Russian radar. The warheads themselves would be hardened as well.

There is still debate among Whitehall insiders as to whether or not Poseidon was, in fact, on offer. Victor Macklen, who as assistant Chief Scientist at the Defence Ministry took part in the discussions, believes it was.

The Americans had had Polaris in service for some years and were looking forward to introducing their next-generation system, Poseidon, into service. They had offered to sell us Poseidon in 1967 but the British government of the day decided that they did not wish to buy a second-generation system. So we had, in a sense, to go it alone to improve the Polaris system. The Americans had offered some development work they had done on the improvement of Polaris, but this would not have been sufficient for our small force. But it was a very useful beginning for our own programme.

That programme was codenamed 'Super Antelope' and took the form of a study of future needs. Knowledge of it was confined to a handful of Labour ministers, among them the Minister for the Navy, Dr David Owen.

There was very little cost in the 'Antelope' programme. I believe that the key ministers did know about the cost. Certainly the Chancellor knew, the Foreign Secretary at the time knew, the Defence Secretary knew and I, as the Minister for the Navy, knew. So it wasn't totally closed, but it was kept on a need-to-know basis. I think that is wholly legitimate. I've always held very open views about government and freedom of information, but I think there are some things which it's wholly legitimate to keep private and secret, and I think what is on the front end of a British nuclear deterrent is an entirely legitimate, confidential secret. And I do not think you should go to the whole Cabinet.

The scientists involved in 'Antelope' were, naturally, cocooned in secrecy, as Victor Macklen recalls: 'They placed very strict restrictions on us. In the period of 1968–70, we were not allowed to place contracts with industrial firms on this work. We were not even allowed to discuss the research work with the Navy.'

When Labour lost office in 1970 the Polaris Improvement Programme was under way but incomplete. Victor Macklen summarizes it thus: 'A good deal of research had taken place. There were the beginnings of a design of a new re-entry system but it hadn't really gone beyond the very first development stage. The warhead side was much more advanced than the decoy side.' An incoming government naturally reviews the nuclear inheritance bequeathed by the outgoing administration; in 1970 the Heath government looked first at the existing Polaris fleet and considered commissioning a fifth submarine before ruling this out on grounds of cost. Instead – with Russian work on its anti-ballistic defences, the so-called 'Galosh' system, advancing all the time – they re-opened the question of improving Polaris, changing the codename of the work from 'Super Antelope' to 'Chevaline'.

Sir Hermann Bondi joined the Ministry of Defence as its Chief Scientific Adviser in 1971. What did he see as the key issues at that time?

Question one was for how long would Polaris do us? And would the then existing soft Polaris, which was distinctly vulnerable to the 'Galosh' defences, as we imagined them to be, be sufficient or not? How long could we maintain an American missile if the Americans retired it? What if anything should be done about either hardening Polaris or replacing it?

Once more the American Poseidon missile was considered as an answer to Britain's needs. Poseidon was tipped with what the nuclear jargon called 'multiple independently targeted re-entry vehicles' – MIRVS for short. It was considerably more sophisticated than both the British Polaris warhead and the improved designs which resulted from the Super Antelope research. However, in the early 1970s it was far from clear whether President Nixon would offer Poseidon to Britain if Prime Minister Heath asked him to. Sir Frank Cooper, then Permanent Secretary at the Ministry of Defence, believes that there was never any serious prospect of this in the mid-Seventies, and explains why:

The Americans were going through one of those in-and-out periods.

They were still suffering from euphoria that their technology was so much in advance of the Soviet Union, that the Soviet Union would never, ever, catch up with them in any area. Therefore they were being pretty tight-lipped about any new invention, and they regarded MIRVS, for example, as something nobody else was ever going to invent. It was an 'it's only invented here' syndrome, rather than a 'not invented here' syndrome. I think some of the senior Americans at that time were not sure what kind of relationship there ought to be with Britain in the nuclear field. Discussion was getting more and more into arms control and so on. But I think it was the technology, in the end, which was the dominant factor.

In 1972 Poseidon had its backers in the Whitehall nuclear weapons community as it had in 1967, when fears about new Russian defences began to crystallize. Equally, there were those who persistently argued against the need to improve Polaris, even if the Russians put a protective anti-missile screen around Moscow. Prominent among the latter was Lord Zuckerman, by now the government's Chief Scientific Adviser in the Cabinet Office.

At that time I didn't believe that if an ABM [Anti Ballistic Missile] treaty was going to be concluded we needed to do anything about our warheads because, even if you assumed that the Moscow system worked, which our intelligence did not say it did, there were other targets – the whole of the USSR was still open. My second argument was that, whatever else, we must wait to discover what the conclusion of the negotiations for an ABM treaty was. Instead of which Aldermaston and the nuclear enthusiasts wanted to go on. I can understand their wanting to and it's their job. But it was merely copying what was already being done by everybody else.

And in fact, in 1972, the Soviets and Americans did conclude an Anti-Ballistic Missile Treaty which put paid to the prospects of an effective ballistic missile defence on a large scale, though a 'Galosh' system was installed to protect Moscow.

Lord Zuckerman was not alone in his scepticism about the need to be able to destroy the heart of Soviet government – the so-called Moscow Criteria – as Sir Hermann Bondi recalls:

He was by no means the only one. It is, I suggest, very much a matter of political judgement. Are the Moscow Criteria necessary or not? We argued about this, but in the end it is a question of the impression you make at home, the impression you make on your allies – and eventually, no doubt, the impression you make on the Russians. And this is strictly a political decision. Now, Lord Zuckerman, who is an old friend, firmly believes that we argued too strongly for doing something, and clearly he is a man for whose opinion I have the highest respect. My own impression, from the odd conversation, particularly with our friends and allies, was that they would have seen an unwillingness to do something to Polaris as not that different from giving up the independent deterrent.

There was another factor in the minds of Conservative ministers – including Sir Hermann's boss at the Ministry of Defence, Lord Carrington – which tilted their thinking away from Poseidon and towards Chevaline. There were also factors working in the opposite direction. Sir Hermann sets out the conflicting strands in thinking at this juncture:

The Wilson administration had very firmly said that they were not going to buy a new missile. Now, it was very clear to everybody, Lord Carrington especially, that the kind of things we were discussing stretched over decades and you could not expect one party to be in power all the time. So, while he was not in any way seeking Labour Party agreement, there was in all our minds that to do something which was totally against their declared policy might not be wise. Yet, at the same time, there were advantages in staying with the Americans. With any immensely complex piece of apparatus, operational experience is very, very useful and all the modifications that come along are, of course, incorporated – the Nassau Agreement gave us the right to update the information – and what the Americans experienced in their *much* larger enterprise was, therefore, of direct use to us. So, anybody operationally responsible – and that essentially meant my Navy colleagues – was directly interested in having something as like what the Americans had as possible. On the other hand, those who had some interest in British technology, who appreciated the likelihood of government changes, who appreciated the desirability of being different, were pulling in the opposite direction.

In the end, Conservative ministers were persuaded of the need to keep the British deterrent capable of striking Moscow. They also kept in mind the need to avoid provoking the Labour Party into a rerun of the 1964 election campaign. In December 1973, notwithstanding Mr Heath's troubles with the winter crisis which was eventually to bring his government down, a small group of Conservative ministers gave the go-ahead to Chevaline. Once more it fell to an incoming Labour government in the spring of 1974 to decide whether or not to cancel it. Lord Carrington's political sensitivity paid off; a small Cabinet committee approved Chevaline, and the following November Wilson persuaded the full Cabinet to endorse that decision.

James Callaghan, as Foreign Secretary, was present at both meetings.

> I recall that we were told that this was an updating of the weapon and that it would cost only a relatively small amount. Of course, I think the decision had already been taken. It wasn't for us to take. We could retake it, obviously. But our predecessors, the Conservative government, had taken the decision on Chevaline, and I think, in the press of government business that day, it came forward and I don't know that there was a great discussion about it. I don't remember a great discussion. When I came to office as Prime Minister, I could then have said, 'Well, all right, we'd better cancel it.' But it's awfully difficult, unless you have the virtue of hindsight, when something is going on, has been going on for three or four years, and you're told, 'Oh, it's going to be pretty soon now, can we have another hundred million, or fifty million?', to say, 'No, put it all on one side,' to be so certain you're right that it's not going to succeed. In fact, it did succeed; but it did cost a lot more than everybody expected. And every time they called for a new tranche, I used to write 'agree' on the minute, or whatever it was, because one always thought it was just around the corner.

Minutes changing the estimated cost of Chevaline were a familiar feature of the secret nuclear world in the Seventies. The 1972 estimate was £175 million; by 1976, when James Callaghan had become Prime Minister, it had spiralled to £595 million (the equivalent, allowing for inflation, of £388 million at 1972 prices). In 1977 it was revised upwards once more to £810 million (£494 million at 1972 prices). By the time the existence of Chevaline was disclosed in 1980, the price tag had risen to £1 billion – £530 million in 1972 prices and thus over three times the original estimate. The contrast with Polaris was stark.

As Chancellor of the Exchequer while Chevaline was totting up the millions, Denis Healey has still to forgive himself for not stopping it; but he was rather preoccupied at the time:

> People often forget we won the election in March. I decided I had to produce a Budget within three weeks, and the physical effort of getting that done, I think, wiped pretty well everything else out of my mind. Actually I regard myself as having failed in my duty as Chancellor, especially with the knowledge I'd gained as Defence Secretary, in not subjecting the whole Chevaline programme to severe scrutiny, right from the word go.

In 1981, Chevaline *was* investigated, by the all-party House of Commons

Public Accounts Committee. Its report was highly criticial – not just of its cost, but of the quality of its project management as well. Victor Macklen, assistant Chief Scientist at the Ministry of Defence throughout the Seventies, thinks that some of this criticism was misdirected by the politicians.

> I think anyone who has to manage a programme which is only funded on a six-month basis and then, for a period, only on a three-monthly basis, must realize that they are not going to be able to make the most efficient use of resources. Most of the time was spent in preparing papers and briefs as to why the programme should continue, rather than getting on with the work. Also, for a period, we were not allowed to deal directly with the Navy and this also cost us a great deal of additional wasted time because the Navy Department acted as the direct link with the American navy on the Polaris weapon system, as opposed to the warheads. The figures that were given to the Labour government, when they came into power in 1974, were the best figures that we had available at the time. It has to be remembered that the period from 1974 to 1980 was a period of really roaring inflation in this country. If you take inflation into account, the figures are not so badly out as many of the ex-Labour ministers have wished to suggest.

In fact, Chevaline's management team was changed, and control tightened, in the mid-1970s – and in mid-project. Sir Hermann Bondi recalls the problem and the remedy:

> We then had a major task of space engineering in hand. Of course, much of this was new – very new to British technology. Naturally, the new team took quite some time to gain sufficient knowledge to make its own estimates, but I can tell you that I was a very worried man about having stuck my neck out and said this could be done – until the new team was firmly in place. After that I slept very well.

In the end, after several delays, Chevaline did work. It was fully operational and at sea by the autumn of 1982. Back in the mid-1970s, however, the now tranquil Sir Hermann was succeeded as Chief Defence Scientist by Sir Ronald Mason. He was new to the nuclear world and the Chevaline file was a key part of his early reading. He makes no bones about its impact on him:

> It left an indelible mark on my own mind, and that is the tremendous resources that you have to call into play if you develop a major strategic programme unilaterally. I think that probably – consciously, rather than subconsciously – played a very considerable part in my approach to the

government's request to look at strategic successor systems to Polaris. My feeling was that all opportunities for commonality – particularly, of course, with the United States – ought to be seen through before one really faced up again to an independent national programme.

The request to examine the possibility of replacing Polaris with an entirely new system was a very sensitive one in political terms. In its manifesto for the second of the 1974 general elections, Labour had pledged itself not to proceed to a new generation of nuclear weapons. Did James Callaghan consider following the manifesto and letting the deterrent die out once Polaris had reached the end of its life?

No, I never considered that. I considered that we ought certainly not to let it die out; that would have been ducking our responsibilities. I considered that we ought to have all the options in front of us and take a decision on them. The option might have been, of course, not to go ahead with it – but that wouldn't have been a case of letting it die out, that would have been a case of taking a positive decision.

So, in January 1978 the Prime Minister commissioned studies of the options for replacing Polaris. Why, with a general election in the offing, did he take the initiative on so sensitive a subject?

It was believed, on expert advice, that the date at which the submarines would start to become obsolescent would be about 1990 to 1992. It was also believed that it would take about ten years to build them – as, indeed, proved to be the case. And so, in 1978, I took a decision that we'd better start examining this, knowing that we wouldn't have to take a decision in the lifetime of the government of which I was head, but expecting to have a decision, one way or the other, after a general election.

Thus, after consultations with a secret group of three colleagues – Denis Healey, the Chancellor; David Owen, the Foreign Secretary; and Fred Mulley, the Defence Secretary – Mr Callaghan commissioned two studies: one on the political and military aspects of a deterrent for the 1990s and beyond, from a committee chaired by the diplomat Sir Antony Duff; the other on the technical choices, from a group led by the Chief Scientist, Sir Ronald Mason. The second, as Sir Ronald explains, was dependent on the first:

The Foreign Office and the Cabinet Office, with their particular preoccupations and expertise, were in the lead on establishing the concepts of deterrence, in establishing, basically, what criteria had to be met to sustain deterrence for the kind of future that we'd been talking about – twenty-five, thirty-five years on. The Ministry of Defence were the contractors in the sense that, if criteria for deterrence have been laid down, in what one would hope to be an independent and rational way, then the contractor says, 'If those are the criteria, then technically how are they going to be met?' That was the way in which we had this dyad approach. The Ministry of Defence lead was subsequential.

Even today, Sir Ronald cannot go into details about these criteria; in general terms he describes them as 'those criteria of what constitutes deterrence, of an equation of long-lasting deterrence with a retaliatory capability – and a retaliatory capability that was focused on political, military, industrial assets of the Soviet Union, rather than more general assets'.

Here, rearing its head again, was the question of striking at the heart of the Soviet system – the Moscow Criteria. There was considerable scepticism inside Mr Callaghan's nuclear group on the need for it, not least on the part of Denis Healey, this time round less distracted by matters financial:

> David Owen and I both felt that the Chevaline programme was too expensive. We didn't need to be able to hit Moscow. But again, I think, the thing slipped through, after this very perfunctory and almost meaningless paper had been produced by the Chief Scientist. This is not, after all, to do with technology; this is to do with how likely you think a certain contingency is and, in that contingency, how you think the other side will react to their knowledge that you have certain capabilities. That's what it's all about. It's nothing whatever to do with scientists or, with respect, with generals.

So averse was David Owen to the Moscow Criteria that he turned his personal Foreign Office Policy Unit to the task of demolishing the proposal and finding a cheaper solution than Trident to the problem of replacing Polaris. He turned for help to the Cabinet Office and Lord Zuckerman, who was still there as a consultant and who was well primed on the development of sea-launched cruise missile technology in the United States. Dr Owen believed ministers should make the running in the British system, and resented the deployment of his own diplomats on the official committees to which the work was devolved. But wasn't this slightly unusual – an individual Cabinet minister mobilizing a kind of private army, with the venerable Lord Zuckerman as its talisman, to tackle what the Foreign Secretary saw as a misguided Whitehall orthodoxy? Why did he do it?

My own justification for that is, if they want to take it out of the system and Sir Antony Duff becomes no longer my man, I'm entitled to have somebody else there. I think Jim Callaghan knew perfectly well this was going on – and all credit to him; he thought it was a good idea to have a debate, he didn't resent this at all. He believed it was a major decision, and I think he would say 'Well, young David's doing his thing.' That was one of his skills as Prime Minister. And he didn't want to feel that the whole thing was a closed and shut case. I think he was probably a bit surprised when this socking great paper arrived.

That paper came into play in December 1978, when Mr Callaghan summoned a gathering of his nuclear ministers before his trip to meet the American President, Jimmy Carter, at the Guadeloupe summit scheduled for the following month. Dr Owen had his alternative strategy prepared:

'We were all meeting at, I think, something like seventy-two hours' notice. So I just said, press the button – and out went the photostats. I think it was something like a fifty-six-page paper, and, in my judgement, our paper totally demolished the Moscow Criteria. It was a detailed, very serious paper.'

This paper, produced by Owen, his unit and Zuckerman, also benefited from 'a good deal of American input':

We tapped in to US expertise. And, of course, what we discovered was that the US cruise programme was very far advanced but that the navy was shutting up about it because Trident was in trouble with the Senate and the Congress, and so they were keeping it very much under wraps because they wanted to get the Trident programme through, and only when Trident was uncancellable would they then unveil the next element in their defence, which was an extensive cruise missile programme, both on submarines and on surface ships. And people wouldn't believe that in Britain.

In 1978 the United States was not Britain's only potential nuclear partner. The French had made great strides with their own deterrent since Macmillan had briefly flirted with de Gaulle at Rambouillet sixteen years earlier. Did James Callaghan's committee regard going in with the French as a serious option? David Owen thinks not:

Not very, at that stage. Probably we should have done. It was certainly something which I was talking to the French about. I opened a dialogue, with Jim Callaghan's full agreement, with my opposite number, Monsieur de Guiringaud, and we began to discuss nuclear questions. And there was a little bit of a dialogue between the two ministries of defence. It was a glint in my eye, then, yes, but not fully developed. Their weapon system, at that stage, too, hadn't really become as effective as it has done since.

In real terms, then, the choice boiled down to which system Britain would buy from America – cruise or Trident; and that depended largely on whether it was required to be able to hit Moscow or not. Dr Owen may have thought that the Moscow Criteria were in ruins, but the Prime Minister was keeping an open mind and postponing all decisions until after the general election. What Callaghan did need was an assurance from the Americans that Trident *would* be available under an extension of the Nassau Agreement *if* the British Cabinet decided to ask for it. In Guadeloupe, one Caribbean afternoon in 1979, he made his nuclear approach to President Carter.

He was lying on his bed in his swimming trunks when I walked in – we all had grass huts or something equivalent, and I just walked across ten yards of grass, with the blue sea shimmering almost beneath our feet, and woke him up and said, 'Jimmy, before we resume tonight, on our next session, I want to have a word with you about the possible replacement of Polaris.' And then I went on to explain that we hadn't taken any decision, that I was trying to find out all the information I could before we had to get to a decision. He was very forthcoming straight away. He said he had no difficulty about transferring the technology, if we decided that we wanted it. I said we would need to bargain about a price, and he said yes, he fully understood that. He thought it would be advantageous to them to let us have it because we would then be able to share in the costs of research and development that they would be undertaking. It was really a much easier interview than it might have been. I must stress, in view of what has been alleged elsewhere, that I made it absolutely clear to him that we had taken no decision on this and would not take any decision on it for some time to come.

The winter crisis to which Mr Callaghan returned so preoccupied ministers that he had little chance to do more than report to his nuclear colleagues the gist of his conversation with the President before they were plunged into an election campaign. But, as one of his last acts as Prime Minister, he broke the usual convention that new governments don't see the papers of their immediate predecessors by instructing his officials to pass the Polaris replacement file intact to Mrs Thatcher. Why?

Because it was a matter of national importance. I think it is very important that succeeding ministers and succeeding governments and administrations should not know about the political decisions of their predecessors – that is a principle I adhere to. But if one administration, or the Prime Minister, wishes to leave a note for his successor about a matter of the greatest national importance, then I think he is entitled to do so.

Those who worked closely with James Callaghan take the view that he, too, would have recommended Trident to the Cabinet had Labour won the 1979 election – and he suspects they may be right. 'It would have been my instinct. But it cost an awful lot, and it is, I think, of only marginal importance to Britain; I don't think it is of supreme importance. I probably would have come down that way. But I'm certainly not disposed to brush all the alternative arguments on one side.'

For Mrs Thatcher, by contrast, Trident was an 'of course' decision with no caveats or lengthy debates about the Moscow Criteria. She quickly commissioned a Cabinet committee on Polaris replacement, and by the summer of 1980 a decision had been taken to purchase Trident 1, the so-called C4 missile. Within two years of that decision, however, advancing technology persuaded the Prime Minister and her colleagues to follow the Americans and go for the bigger and still more sophisticated Trident 2, or D5 missile, even though this would boost the estimated cost, at 1982 prices, from £5 billion to £7.5 billion – an estimate that by 1988 had risen to just over £9 billion.*

In respect of her style of dealing with Cabinet on the bomb, Mrs Thatcher came somewhere between Attlee and Churchill. The original decision to purchase Trident 1 reached the agenda of the full Cabinet only on the morning of 15 July 1980 – a few hours before it was announced in Parliament. There was a last-minute rush because of rumours that the story was about to break in America. However, the full Cabinet was involved in plenty of time to consider the decision to proceed to Trident 2. Which approach is the wiser? Sir Frank Cooper, Permanent Secretary at the Ministry of Defence at this period, takes a pragmatic view:

I don't think the full Cabinet is brought into a lot of things until before various announcements are made. I think people worry increasingly about leaks. If they're taking some kind of decision which is likely to cause political problems, they tend to plot a path where a great deal of work is done in a small group, a Cabinet committee or something of that kind. Then they move ahead through the various stages, quite quickly, to avoid some bowdlerized account coming out from some unknown source.

---

* By the time HMS *Vanguard* put to sea the cost of the programme was put at £12 billion: *Statement on the Defence Estimates 1996*, Cm 3223 (HMSO, 1996), p. 56. See also Christopher Bellamy, *The Independent*, 26 November 1994.

Even that second Trident decision, to go for the bigger, more sophisticated D5 missile, which was preceded by a full Cabinet presentation, with the scientists, the Chief of the Defence Staff and others explaining the whys and wherefores to ministers, was in Sir Frank's view not all it might seem: 'The basic decision, in principle, had been taken. You were then dealing with whether you should do A or B or C.'

Sir Ronald Mason was one of those who took part in that presentation, and he recommended the improved D5 missile. Why was this?

It was a very, very straightforward decision. My commitment was to maintain commonality with the strategic programmes of the United States. And that had no more grand objective than minimizing the national cost. And, therefore, although there are perfectly fair criticisms along the lines that the Trident 2 programme was beyond the necessary capabilities of the United Kingdom, if we had stuck with Trident 1 we would have been casting ourselves into precisely the situation that bothered me in 1970 and 1971 – that is, come about 2005, what are we going to do to the Trident 1 to maintain its capability? My advice was entirely determined by the need for continuing commonality with current strategic programmes in the United States.

Whatever else might happen, there was to be no more going it alone, no more Chevalines. There will be a Union Jack on top of the deterrent well into the 2020s, some eighty years after Bevin's outburst in Attlee's Cabinet committee about the need to go it alone. Since 1960, however, the Union Jack has faded into the background somewhat with the increasing reliance on American technology. Indeed, in the short term, dependence on the United States has been near total since Polaris came on station in 1969. Sir Hermann Bondi encapsulates the situation bluntly:

'If the Americans were to tell us at one stage, "We will go on for another twelve years but not a day longer," we can adapt. If the Americans say tomorrow, "All we do now for you will stop," then it won't be many months before we don't have a weapon.'

A British deterrent so vulnerable to American whim was not at all what Ernest Bevin had in mind in 1947. At the Cabinet committee meeting which formally authorized the first British bomb, he said Britain 'could not afford to acquiesce in an American monopoly of this new development'. And a scintilla of suspicion persisted among several of those who came after Bevin, with Macmillan's reservations at Nassau, and Wilson's and Healey's explanations of why Labour kept the deterrent going in the 1960s as a restraining influence on the United States. Indeed, what strikes the observer of the history of the British bomb is the degree to which the United States and US policy have dominated the decision-making process in Whitehall. It is noticeable, too, that while nuclear partnership was in abeyance for ten years after the war, when Anglo-American relations were built on economics and politics, over the course of the subsequent decades intelligence and nuclear links seem to have assumed the greater part of the special relationship.

Official secrecy prevents a precise costing of the British nuclear weapons programme since the late 1940s, but it's probably in the area of £40–50 billion all told.* In the end its purpose can be expressed very simply: the placing of a nuclear button beneath the finger of a British Prime Minister should hostile forces – until 1990, Soviet forces – threaten. This button has been potentially under the digit of seven Prime Ministers since 1957. Lord Home was one of them, and he believed that the Soviet Union could never bank on a British premier not pressing that button – not if there were 'great hordes marching right across Europe and demolishing European civilization as we know it'.

This seems to imply that retaliation might have been launched before the 'hordes' reached the Channel ports. Lord Home admitted the possibility.

'Terrible, isn't it, the thought; but reason, cold reason doesn't operate in those circumstances, quite often. And I'm not sure what cold reason would tell you, either, if they were on the march.'

Lord Callaghan was Prime Minister for three years and, like all to whom the ultimate responsibility falls, had to practise launch procedures. But would he – could he – in the direst of circumstances have fired a Polaris missile?

> If that had become necessary and vital it would have meant that the deterrent had failed, because the value of the nuclear weapon is, frankly, only as a deterrent. But if we had got to that point, where I felt it was necessary to do it, then I would have done it. I've had terrible doubts, of course, about this. And if I had lived after having pressed that button, I could never, never have forgiven myself.

---

* This was a late 1980s estimate.

7

A Canal Too Far

To the guardians of British power and the British Empire, Colonel Nasser's seizure of the Anglo-French Suez Canal Company in July 1956 seemed to threaten the end of their world. 'If Nasser wins, or even appears to win,' the Colonial Secretary, Alan Lennox-Boyd, wrote to the Prime Minister, Sir Anthony Eden, 'we might as well as a government (and indeed as a country) go out of business.' The Prime Minister felt, if anything, even more passionately that the Canal had to be retaken and the flow of Middle East oil, the lifeblood of our economy, protected against disruption. But it was Eden who was toppled, not Nasser. Britain survived the loss of the Canal; and, with hindsight, Suez may have been a comma, not a full stop, in our postwar history.

How did a seasoned international figure like Anthony Eden come to think as he did in the summer of 1956? Sir Guy Millard, his Private Secretary and confidant in Number Ten, was privy to all the secrets of Suez; and for the thirty years thereafter during which the official papers – which include his own internal account of the affair, written in 1957 and filed under the rubric 'For UK Eyes Only' – remained under wraps in the Public Record Office, he kept them. The passage of that period allowed him for the first time to muse in public about his master.

It was his mistake, of course, and a tragic and disastrous mistake for him. I think that he overestimated the importance of Nasser, the importance of Egypt, the importance of the Canal, the importance of the Middle East itself, even – and to a certain extent this was a hangover from the war. You must remember that we'd recently emerged from a war in which he'd been one of our leaders, second only to Churchill in eminence, and the Middle East at that time had been considered more or less the strategic centre of the world. It's an example of the fact that in strategic terms we're always thinking of the last war. But that, as I say, was his mistake.

Another figure on the inside track in 1956 was the Commonwealth Secretary, Lord Home, who became Eden's successor's successor in Downing Street. He sat in Eden's inner Cabinet, the so-called Egypt

Committee, which handled the Suez crisis, and shared Eden's apocalyptic view of Nasser:

> I was immensely concerned with Nasser's designs upon the Middle East. To have the Russians in Egypt and in Syria and, should a war start, in the Middle East; and should it be Nasser's design, which it seemed to be, to throw the West, the democracies of the West, out of that area – ourselves and the French, and possibly the Americans later – then that would have been a very serious position indeed. Mind you, there was no cushion of North Sea oil at that time.

What was distinctive about Eden's view of Nasser and of the problem created by the nationalization of the canal? Lord Home, like Sir Guy Millard, saw a connection with the recent conflict: 'Eden really had been one of the leading opponents of Hitler's Germany, and he really disliked dictators and disliked above all people who cheated. And he thought that Nasser, again beginning with the process of the breaking of treaties, was a public menace and that his influence on the Middle East ought to be broken.' This was a view Lord Home shared; Nasser, in his eyes, was 'a danger, a real danger to British interests; and you had to put the vital British interests first.'

What Lord Home did not share with the Prime Minister was the strength of Eden's personal animosity towards the Egyptian leader, founded, he believes, in that perception of Nasser as someone 'who cheated in public affairs. That was really what it was. It was a blatant cheat, it was, and he was a nasty bombastic fellow. If you look back at those broadcasts, the Radio Cairo broadcasts, they were really vitriolic.' Eden's loathing of Nasser was a constant factor in the whole affair; indeed, it had already overflowed even before the seizure of the canal. He saw the hand of his *bête noire* in a crisis in Jordan in the spring of 1956. Sir Anthony Nutting, a minister of state at the Foreign Office who was to resign over Suez, recalls trying to dislodge the Prime Minister's attention from his *idée fixe* and turn it to wider Middle Eastern matters:

> The telephone rang and a voice down the other end said, 'It's me.' I didn't quite realize who 'me' was for a moment; however, he gave the show away very quickly by starting to scream at me. 'What is all this poppycock you've sent me about isolating Nasser and neutralizing Nasser? Why can't you get it into your head I want the man destroyed?' I said, 'OK. You get rid of Nasser, what are you going to put in his place?' 'I don't want anybody,' he said. I said, 'Well, there'll be anarchy and chaos in Egypt.' 'I don't care if there's anarchy and chaos in Egypt. Let there be anarchy and chaos in Egypt. I just want to get rid of Nasser.' But the real consequences

of getting rid of Nasser were never really thought out and never really investigated by the Cabinet or by anybody else.

Nasser's nationalization of the Canal only deepened Eden's hatred of the Egyptian leader. Publicly, the British government's response to this move turned on the need to extract the Canal from Nasser's possession, to make it a safe and open international waterway. So what was the overriding purpose of British policy-makers? To retake the Canal? To remove Nasser? Or both? The question was never resolved, and the resulting confusion bedevilled the British throughout the three months that elapsed between Nasser's seizure of the Canal and the Anglo–French invasion. It was a failure that Lord Home still regretted thirty years later.

'There was a wider ambition, and I dare say that with hindsight we ought to have included this from the start; that was to depose Nasser. Because he was the origin of the trouble. I think the minds of most of the Cabinet hadn't gone as far as that, and didn't think that was a necessary objective.'

The inner group of ministers on the Egypt Committee was very clearly aware that the aim was to topple Nasser as well as to take the Canal. However, in Lord Home's view the priority of most was 'to take the Canal, believing that if that was done Nasser's authority in Egypt would go.' Eden's priority was different: 'Eden's priority was to topple Nasser.'

Lord Home was a member of that inner ring of ministers, the Egypt Committee, throughout the whole episode. What did he remember of their meetings, and of how Eden conducted them?

They were fairly restless. We were under extreme pressure. And the pressure, of course, was not lessened because the Prime Minister was not, indubitably, well. I don't think it clouded his judgement – that will be for historians to tell us later on – but it was restless, and therefore I think the meetings were not as methodically conducted as they would have been in times of lesser stress.

The Egypt Committee put pressure on the Chiefs of Staff to produce a plan for the speedy recapture of the Canal, so as to capitalize on the prevailing mood of resentment at Nasser's unilateral act. Marshal of the Royal Air Force Sir Dermot Boyle was then Chief of the Air Staff, and remembers Eden's relentless urgency.

I remember a feeling that we couldn't get on quick enough. 'Can't you do it quicker?' And I suppose that's a very natural political desire to get the thing over quickly because the more it hangs around the more difficult it is to hold the ring. I'd say that's the only sort of thing I saw him getting edgy about. 'Why can't you do it quicker? You always say you want more ships, you want more this, you want more that, and they can't be found' – that sort of thing, which is very understandable.

Did this have to be so? Was the need for a capability of this sort not almost self-evident – again, with hindsight – for what was still an imperial power with global responsibilities? Sir Dermot points to the way the wind was blowing:

> It may be very nice to have the capability, but all the thinking was moving towards a major war with Russia. That was the trouble. And that meant a NATO war, and it meant that if we had the things we wanted for NATO we would inevitably not have the things we wanted for these little operations all round the world.

Britain's military might, though still substantial, had declined dramatically since the Second World War. Considerable armed forces were stationed in what was still an imperial network around the globe, and there remained a set of imperial assumptions to match them. There were no plans for a limited war, and therefore there was little of the airborne and amphibious capability essential to independent action. Sir Richard Powell, then Permanent Secretary at the Ministry of Defence, takes Sir Dermot's point about the shift in geopolitical focus further, to the concomitant gradual shift in assumptions:

> There was a feeling that the nuclear deterrent was so powerful, the deterrent from global war so strong, that people would be deterred from undertaking even limited operations for fear that they would escalate into a situation in which the nuclear deterrent would come into play and there would be a global conflict. It was only over a period of considerable time that thinking moved on this from the feeling that the nuclear deterrent wiped out any risk of any kind of war to the realization that round the fringes of the Central Front in Europe it was possible to have conflicts without an unacceptable risk of their escalation into a global conflict. These things only emerge over long periods of time. Thinking doesn't shift that rapidly unless you've got some very radical, very far-sighted thinkers, and they're very rare.

And yet Britain had substantial numbers of troops in Libya, contiguous to Egypt. Why was it not possible to use them in the Suez operation? And if we couldn't use them, what was the point of their being there? Sir Richard Powell answers the first question in terms of the political risks attached to using forces based in one Arab country against another Arab country. The second question carries its own answer within it: there wasn't one. Why did we keep them, then?

'A hangover from the past, I think. We were still thinking, or predominant opinion was still thinking, in terms of Britain as world power with interests all over the world and with a need for bases all over the world.'

And yet if we had had the capability for a quick operation, the Suez affair might have been not a fiasco, but a triumph: 'Had it been possible to compress the operation into two or three days the world would have been faced with a fait accompli and would have settled down to accept it.'

In the longer term it was the memory of that inability to grasp the fleeting opportunity which led to the creation of assault forces still available when they were needed in the Falklands in the early 1980s. But in 1956 the necessary instrument was not available to ministers like Lord Home, chafing at military caution and thirsting for a quick win:

> That was very desirable, that we should act fast. But there were all sorts of difficulties. We had certainly plenty of warnings from the Chiefs of Staff as to how difficult the military operation was likely to be. I think most of us had the feeling that there were too many excuses for delay. At the end of the day it's very difficult for the – so to speak – layman to question this.

One of the strongest criticisms of the British military, expressed by their French counterparts as well as by their own political masters, was that they grossly overestimated the fighting capability of the Egyptians. Air Chief Marshal Sir David Lee was Secretary to the Chiefs of Staff Committee and recalls the view of the Chief of the General Staff, General Templar: 'His opinion was undoubtedly pretty low, and of course he was an experienced soldier and he knew the Egyptians. But I don't think that even he would have felt that an operation on a very light scale was militarily sound because of the sheer size and numbers of the Egyptian army and air force.'

But even allowing for the size of the Egyptian forces and the quality of their equipment, weren't the Chiefs over-cautious? Sir Richard Powell is fairly cautious himself in responding to this charge: 'I think I would say that they certainly did not underestimate them. As is natural, you have to assess to the best of your ability the opposition you're likely to come up against and demand forces of sufficient strength to deal with that opposition. It's not for them to take gambles in that way when they're giving advice to ministers.'

Another element in the criticism was that the military were refighting the Second World War and seeing the Egyptians as Germans. Sir Richard points out with some fairness that 'if you've been through a war of the kind that they'd all been through, the shadows are bound to cast themselves forward over all thinking of that kind.'

But it wasn't just the Egypt Committee pressing for speed. From start to finish the French were a pressure group for military acts rather than diplomatic words – for their own specific reasons. Lord Gladwyn was British Ambassador in Paris and had a ringside view of the French attitude:

I represented to the government that the French felt very passionately about this and that they connected Nasser very much with the revolution in Algiers, which at that stage they still thought they could contain perfectly well. They believed that Nasser was the real enemy at that time and that anything which enfeebled him or did him in was a very good thing from a French point of view. It was as simple as that. And therefore they were disposed, if necessary, to consider using force in order to humiliate Nasser; also, of course, I suppose, to reverse his decision on the nationalization of the Suez Canal. But that was their simple view, that it was almost a question of life and death to suppress a rebellion in Algeria, and that was the only point of view that mattered to them.

With this ulterior motive, Paris never wanted a peaceful settlement. But the pressure from Washington, the most crucial capital of all, was powerfully directed in favour of a different outcome. Lord Sherfield was British Ambassador to the United States; and, like Lord Gladwyn in Paris, Sir Humphrey Trevelyan in Cairo and Sir Pierson Dixon at the United Nations, he was kept in the dark about his own government's intentions. This seems a curious way for the government to treat its principal representative in Washington and a very senior diplomat. Lord Sherfield himself infers a knowledge, or suspicion, that if he had been more fully informed he would have been 'on the first plane home in order to protest'.

And would he? If he had been brought into the complete picture, that is to say of the deception that was being practised on the United States, how would he have felt, given his close relationships with Dulles and the President?

'I can't say. All I can say is that I would have been in an almost impossible position because I was on close terms of friendship with Dulles, I was an old friend of the President and I don't think I could have been a party to the deception that was being practised upon them. But I can't say how, in the position that I was, I would have played it at the time.'

The little he did know was enough to cause him some anxiety: 'My knowledge was fragmentary. But from what I did know I was very concerned about the way things were going, as indeed were the President and Dulles. So I knew enough to send some pretty sharp warnings to the Foreign Office about the danger of proceeding without full American moral and material support.'

Why was it, then, that Eden was so deceived – or so deceived himself –

about American intentions? Again, in Lord Sherfield's view, we have to look back at the recent world war:

> I think they had a feeling that because Ike and the American establishment had been so friendly during the war, that friendship would be sufficient to condone whatever actions they took, and of course that was a fundamental misunderstanding because Eisenhower was a very much stronger and more dominant President than people have given him credit for. He was the man who ran American foreign policy, not Dulles.

It's clear British ministers deluded themselves about the attitude of the US administration. Trying to gain American support, the British government allowed Eisenhower's Secretary of State, John Foster Dulles, to persuade them to convene an international conference in London in August. Out of that came the plan for the Suez Canal Users' Association, SCUA – a SCUA without a point, as a French negotiator put it. Among other things, SCUA was intended to collect Canal dues to deprive Nasser of his revenue. But the American agenda was at odds with the British, as Sir Guy Millard recalls:

> What I think people didn't anticipate was the extent to which the Americans were putting obstacles in our path and the extent to which, in a way, they were deceiving us over things like, for example, the Suez Canal Users' Association, on which they gave us certain quite specific assurances: that they would deny any dues to Nasser, and that if Nasser didn't accept this they would take whatever steps were necessary to assert their rights, which implied the use of force in the last resort. But all this was simply designed to be an obstacle to the use of force by Britain and France.

Dulles, who it was thought had considerable scope independent of Eisenhower, was a thorn in British ministerial flesh, particularly in that of his opposite number in London, Selwyn Lloyd. Sir Donald Logan was Lloyd's private secretary and witnessed the works of Foster Dulles at first hand. He describes the attendant frustrations:

> He was extremely ingenious in thinking up new ideas and new approaches from one meeting to another. You went away and worked on those ideas, but by the next time round you found he was working on a quite different hypothesis and plan, and Selwyn found this very frustrating. He tried, I think, quite genuinely and honestly, to put flesh on the outlines of the plans that Dulles was producing, but you could

never pin Dulles down. He was always coming up with something new.

Another great and constant uncertainty, even at this stage, was money. As early as August the Treasury warned its hawkish Chancellor, Harold Macmillan, that sterling might be under pressure in the autumn even if there were no war. If there was a war, everything would depend on whether Britain was alone or had America as an ally prepared to cushion the financial shock. In late September Macmillan, in Washington for talks, was sent an even starker warning that confidence in the pound was unlikely to be restored even if Nasser fell. Looking back, Lord Home felt that it should have been a different man doing the talking in the US capital:

> Mr Dulles had really not conveyed to us, I think, the depth of the feeling of President Eisenhower. The only thing that might have been done, and I think probably ought to have been done, would have been for Sir Anthony Eden to have gone to see the President, and then he couldn't have failed to realize the strength of the personal feeling of the President himself. And, of course, this was on the eve of an American election.

But in September the restless Eden was preoccupied with military worries, not money worries. The original plan, codenamed 'Musketeer' – involving a full-scale assault on Alexandria and an advance through Cairo to the Canal – could be postponed no longer. The more limited alternative recommended by the Chiefs of Staff, however – a direct assault on the Canal at Port Said, which they called 'Musketeer Revise' – could be kept on hold. It was indicative of the growing uncertainty about an invasion that a key element in the revised plan was a relentless aerial bombardment to force Egypt to surrender without the need for a seaborne assault. The task force commanders were very unhappy with this new plan, feeling that 'the whole timing was too cumbersome', as Air Chief Marshal Sir Denis Barnett, the air force task commander, put it. For Sir Denis, already confused about the aim of the operation, it gave cause for grave concern in respect of both its aims and its likelihood of success:

> With the first plan, against Alexandria, one could perceive what would be the likely political aim underlying it. But with 'Musketeer Revise', and an assault on Port Said and just going down the Canal, it was extremely diffi-cult to detect exactly what the political aim would be and how it would contribute to toppling Nasser. In this area of psychological type of opera-tion, my feeling is that it will only succeed if it is done with overwhelming force. You need obliterative attacks, the sort of thing that Hitler did against Rotterdam.

And it was entirely clear that under no circumstances would the commanders be given the political go-ahead to launch air strikes of such brutality against Egypt.

As he went about his task of planning, did Sir Denis think the operation was actually going to happen? His sense of dissipating impetus is palpable: 'As the planning went on for so long, and as the months passed into September/October, one noticed more and more how world opinion – as well as public opinion at home – was inclined to be anti. I could not see, really, that there would be a compelling political reason for doing it.'

The slowness of the new plan would cost the operation dear later, when speed was once more of the essence. To make matters worse, there was disagreement among the military at the highest level about the justification for the enterprise as a whole, whichever plan was followed. The Chiefs were split. Lord Mountbatten, the First Sea Lord, as the Chiefs of Staff papers show, was a consistent doubter, and his fellow Chiefs were very much aware of his dissent. Sir Dermot Boyle recalls the tensions:

> He was always really doubtful. Now, it's understandable, I think, that Mountbatten was in a slightly different category. He could regard himself as an elder statesman, and he'd been Viceroy of India and all that. But on the other hand, Gerald Templar had done that wonderful job out in Malaya, and therefore I took a lot of encouragement from his attitude, which was 'Dermot, this is a military business, don't let your mind be wasted on swanning around on what might or might not be the political implications.'

But international politics could not be excluded from the Chiefs of Staff's meetings. Britain's tapestry of treaties with Middle East countries threatened entanglement with every possible move. Sir David Lee took the minutes as the Chiefs grappled with the sticky threads:

> Lord Mountbatten was the strongest opponent of the operation, but I think the other Chiefs of Staff, if not quite so vociferous about it, were very anxious that it was an operation which might lead us into very considerable difficulties, and, for example, get us bogged down again in Egypt, a country which we'd only left six months beforehand. We had a number of what I can only describe as conflicting treaties. So really, we were the meat in the sandwich, as it were.

That problem was demonstrated starkly as late as the middle of October, when Israeli raids into Jordan raised a genuine fear that Britain might find herself allied to Egypt in a war against Israel. The Royal Air Force was warned that it might have to destroy the Israeli air force on the ground at short notice. Lord Home explained how this possibility came about, and its nightmarish implications:

> We had a treaty with Jordan which legally bound us to support Jordan if Jordan was attacked. Israel was getting very restive and the chances were that she would attack Jordan, the weakest of the Arab countries, and if she had done that we would have found ourselves fighting with Jordan against Israel, and a lot of other Arab countries would come in on the side of Jordan, including Egypt. One couldn't conceivably imagine a worse scenario.

By mid-October 1956, the prospect was bleaker than could have been imagined less than three months earlier when Eden and his colleagues first set out to reverse Nasser's acquisition. The initial impetus had gone. The operation seemed to be running into the sand. Several Cabinet ministers were uneasy. The Chiefs of Staff were split. Parliament and British public opinion were split. The United Nations was increasingly unsympathetic as Foreign Secretary Selwyn Lloyd tried to negotiate a settlement. The United States continued to act as a brake on any decisive action. The Treasury feared for the currency. Even the Commonwealth was mostly unhappy. Eden was boxed in on all sides.

Suddenly, on 14 October, the beleaguered Prime Minister was presented with a way out. That weekend, two French emissaries came to Chequers. They brought a plan to use the Israelis to force matters to a head by attacking Egypt. The British and French would intervene as international peace-keepers, taking the Suez Canal in the process. Sir Guy Millard was with Eden as the emissaries explained the plan. What were his feelings as it unfolded before him? And what were Eden's – was he excited by the prospect?

> It was surprising, certainly. It was a total surprise to us. We knew nothing of it in advance. I was worried about it, naturally, but the Prime Minister's reaction was to recall the Secretary of State, Selwyn Lloyd, from New York and that seemed to me a fairly sensible step to take. Eden was intrigued. I think he was clutching at a straw in a sense; he was looking for a pretext. The problem was that the operation, which had been planned for a long time, had either to go ahead or be scrapped altogether. The reservists had been called up, the shipping had been mobilized and so on. You couldn't disperse all that without abandoning the whole idea of the use of force. Therefore you might say that this plan, originally worked out by the French with the Israelis, came at a convenient moment and he saw it as a handy pretext.

The French initiative came just as Selwyn Lloyd was at last inching towards a peaceful settlement in New York. This was based on the so-called 'Six Principles', the most important of which were free international transit through the Canal and its insulation from the politics of any country. Sir Donald Logan, his private secretary, was with Lloyd in New York as these plans neared fruition, only to be swept away by the new military scheme. He stresses the Foreign Secretary's commitment to a peaceful, international, resolution:

> He attached a great deal of importance to the work that he was doing in New York to try to work out, under United Nations auspices, the basis for a peaceful solution to the problem. He didn't get full support from the French, but he certainly hoped that he had laid the basis for development of a peaceful solution. He returned to London in the hope that there was something there which could be developed. I think it was that development over the weekend of 14–16 October that as it were foreclosed the peaceful approach. Selwyn Lloyd and the delegation with him were recalled from New York a day or two early in order to come back and deal with that situation.

And the French proposal?

> I don't think he ever liked it from the start. It was not in his nature to be the sort of person in charge of this kind of operation. He had been Minister of Defence, it's true, and indeed in his youth he enjoyed playing with toy soldiers, he was a great reworker of military campaigns; but he was not the kind of person you would ever describe as belligerent.

But Lloyd the peacemaker was no match for his belligerent boss, as Sir Harold Beeley, one of the Foreign Office's Middle Eastern experts, recalls: 'Selwyn Lloyd was a modest man and was not very confident in his own judgement, I think. Eden, of course, had a great reputation as an expert in foreign policy and I think Selwyn felt that he ought not to challenge Eden's judgement.'

The 'Six Principles' are one of history's great 'if onlys'. They might have given Britain peace with honour. But instead their architect, the hapless Selwyn Lloyd, was sent to Paris for a secret meeting with the French and the Israelis on 22 October at a suburban villa in Sèvres – an 'extraordinary experience', as Sir Donald Logan, who travelled with Lloyd, described it: 'A Foreign Secretary and one of his staff negotiating on a very important matter in Paris with nobody else knowing anything about it.' The Foreign Secretary's lack of sympathy with the enterprise could not but come through. 'He did his best to put the British case, but I agree with the Israeli accounts of the conversations that his heart wasn't in it. He did his best, but I'm not surprised that they felt that he was not enthusiastic about the project.'

As for the essential nature of the agreement made at Sèvres, Sir Donald explains how the declared objective of coordination came to be implicated in accusations of collusion:

> It had been known for some time, and indeed discussed in the British Cabinet from about the beginning of August, that it was quite possible that the Israelis would make a move against the Egyptians, and the purpose of our talks in Paris was to coordinate what actions the British and the French would take when the Israelis did move. Later all this came to be regarded as collusion, largely, I think, because of the insistence of the Prime Minister, Sir Anthony Eden, that the role of the British and French should be that of intervening to separate the combatants. But our own discussions in Paris were rather designed to coordinate what actions each would take in those agreed circumstances.

Did Sir Donald get the feeling at this meeting that the Israelis did not trust the British?

> The Israelis hated being put in the position of being called upon to stop something which they knew perfectly well was convenient, at least, to the British and the French. They didn't like the idea at all. But they had to be persuaded to go along with the Eden formula and I think the reason which made them accept this was that at the time – and this was very much a point which Ben Gurion insisted on in our conversations at Sèvres – they conceived that the intervention of the RAF was essential if immediate Egyptian retaliation against Tel Aviv was to be prevented.

How much of this was known to ministers outside Eden's inner circle? Much more than has been supposed, as the papers show. The full Cabinet met on 23 October, the day after Lloyd and Logan had travelled to Sèvres. The confidential annex to the Cabinet minutes for that day, which contains a fuller account of the discussion than the standard, more widely circulated minutes, contains the following very significant passage: 'From secret conversations which had been held in Paris with representatives of the Israeli government, it now appeared that the Israelis would not alone launch a full-scale attack against Egypt.' So the Cabinet at least knew about those ultra-secret talks. Lord Home, who was present at that crucial meeting, acknowledged that 'the full Cabinet knew that there had been meetings,' but added that 'the plan was still in a fairly embryo stage at that point.' He was adamant, however, that he was not under instruction from the Prime Minister to limit what he told his fellow Cabinet ministers.

The secret plan was finally arranged the day after the Cabinet had been informed of the first meeting. But while the Cabinet may have known what was afoot, the Foreign Office – the experts – were kept almost entirely in the dark on Eden's specific orders. Sir Anthony Nutting's instructions from the Prime Minister were 'only to consult two people in the Foreign Office. When I said, what about the legal adviser? he said "Oh, for God's sake don't ask him" – this was "Fitz" Fitzmaurice – "Fitz is always against us doing anything." He knew that the more Foreign Office voices I consulted, the more horror would be exclaimed against going ahead with this conspiracy.'

Harold Beeley was equally disapproving of the exclusion of the FO's Arab experts. 'I thought it was foolish not to allow any of the people who were dealing with the Middle East, who had been following events in the Middle East in the Office, to become involved in the preparations for a policy of this kind.' Indeed, his disapproval went further, when he realized what the policy actually was: 'I thought the whole think was pretty silly. I thought it was crazy. For one thing, one question that didn't seem to have been asked was what we were going to do in Egypt after we'd occupied the Canal. As far as I'm aware, to this day there is no evidence that the sequence of events after the immediate attack on the Canal had been properly thought out.'

As for Eden's view that the Foreign Office was very pro-Arab, that it saw life through sand-coloured spectacles, Sir Harold points out that it was not alone in this tendency: 'I think the Foreign Office on the whole was traditionally, and continued to be in 1956, more sympathetic to the Arab cause than to the cause of Israel. But I think Eden himself had similar views until 1956 when he found it convenient to make use of Israel.'

In fact, it was hard to find an enthusiast in Whitehall for Eden's Suez policy, even among civil servants taken fully into his confidence. Yet it was on these doubting insiders that the Prime Minister, under relentless strain, relied for advice and reassurance. Sir Richard Powell at the Ministry of Defence was one of them:

> He was very jumpy, very nervy, very wrought up, there's no doubt about it. He regarded almost the destiny of the world as resting on his shoulders, I think. There's no doubt about that. And he was very anxious, very communicative of his views to everybody. For example, I had to have a scrambler telephone installed in my flat so that he could ring me up and talk about these things.

Powell was in a privileged position. He knew the Prime Minister's mind and the plan to involve the Israelis – which is more than all but a handful of the military knew. But truth will out, and out it came, in the office of the Commander-in-Chief of the Anglo-French force, Sir Charles Keightley, to land at the feet of Sir Denis Barnett, the air commander:

> As he went out the door opened, a gust of air came in and it unsettled a piece of paper that was on his desk in front of him and planted it absolutely straight between my feet, so that as I picked it up I couldn't help – although it was not my business, it might have been private – I couldn't help seeing what it said. In his own handwriting were a couple of notes that I couldn't help noticing. One was 'Israeli D-Day is such and such, our D-Day is such and such.' I couldn't believe that it could be so. I didn't think we would behave like that. I was appalled that political entanglement of that sort could lie at the root of this operation that we were trying to do.

General Sir Kenneth Darling was Chief of Staff to the Army task force commander, Sir Hugh Stockwell. Two days after the Sèvres agreement was made, they stopped off en route from London to Malta at Villacoubley airfield near Paris, on a routine visit for Stockwell to consult his French number two, General Beaufré. Sir Kenneth describes the far from routine outcome.

> The scene was really almost like a James Bond sort of set-up. There were two or three rather dilapidated wartime huts, I think there were one or two odd gendarmes standing about, sucking their teeth, and General Stockwell was then taken by the arm by General Beaufré into one of these huts. Meanwhile I and the other officers of General Stockwell's staff sort of hung about kicking our heels. Eventually he came out of the hut and took me to one side and told me what he had learnt from General Beaufré, which was, in a nutshell, that it was likely that the Israelis were going to attack Egypt and that we would undoubtedly get involved. And it was, therefore, quite obvious that we'd been living in a fool's paradise up to that particular moment.

From that point on there was to be no paradise at all – and no postponement. Events moved very fast. As agreed, the Israelis launched their assault against Egypt on 29 October. The following day Britain and France delivered an ultimatum to Israel and Egypt to halt the fighting. On 31 October the Royal Air Force and the Fleet Air Arm attacked Egypt's airfields and destroyed its air force to fulfil the British part of the bargain with the Israelis.

If that bargain were to remain secret, the Anglo–French armada could not move before the ultimatum expired. So the bombers took off to satisfy the Israelis' overriding requirement while the task force was still six days' sailing from Port Said. Sir Denis Barnett, who gave the order, was aware that there was some discomfort about this: 'The root of their worries lay in the fact that we had to start the air operation, which was the beginning of the entire operation, so long ahead of the time at which the convoy could arrive from Malta. This made the whole plan, the timing of it, much too cumbersome, in my view.'

Just as at the start of the crisis, military action had to be swift to be successful. But the long-winded plan and the need to maintain the cover story made this impossible. As the task force steamed towards Egypt, there was uproar day after day at Westminster, leading General Stockwell to write in his inquest report when it was all over that 'Her Majesty's Opposition had rocked the landing craft.' But there was private dissent even closer at hand. On 2 November, in an unprecedented move for a serving officer, Mountbatten wrote to Eden begging him 'to turn back the assault convoy before it is too late, as I feel that the actual landing of troops can only spread the war with untold misery and world-wide repercussions'.

The First Sea Lord's action has lodged in the consciousness of the military, not least in the mind of his fellow Chief of Staff, Sir Dermot Boyle: 'I think it was a great pity to do it two days after the thing had sailed. If you were going to do it, the only object in doing it would be to stop the operation, and we were so committed then that it would have been practically impossible to stop it. By then we had taken out the air force. How do you stop on that basis?' The Suez invasion had, as military operations can do, acquired a momentum of its own.

Lord Home continued to justify the collusion thirty years later. He believed that eventually Israel was likely to attack some other country, and that being the case it might as well be Britain's enemy – Egypt – rather than her ally, Jordan. But he had no illusions about the dangers of the situation.

What struck me all the time was the horror of the situation we were in and how on earth we could deal with this in order to limit the fight if it occurred. The plan that Israel and Egypt should be invited – if war started – to stop short of the Canal, twenty miles or whatever it was, recommended itself to quite an extent. It would stop the main fight between Egypt and Israel which was going to start off the whole boiling of the Middle East at war. No plan was good. Any plan was absolutely full of worries. But at least that had a chance to stop the war and a chance to renationalize the Canal, reinternationalize the Canal again.

And so, he believed, a case could still be made for Sir Anthony Eden's solution in October/November 1956; but it was not a solution that anyone embraced with any enthusiasm.

A case can be made. I didn't like it. I didn't like it then; none of us liked it. Various accounts have been given about the attitude of the various members of the Cabinet, but none of us liked the operation at all. It was a horrible situation to be in, the worst I've been in. The Americans at the time of Cuba was a particularly nasty one too, but you could hardly invent anything so completely unpleasant as that scenario when we had to decide what to do with Egypt on the move like that and Israel very, very restive, and going to break out somewhere.

Lord Sherfield, the Ambassador to Washington, returned to London in time to witness the last stages of the crisis as the newly appointed Permanent Secretary to the Treasury.

I discovered that there was something up in Whitehall, if only for the reason that nobody wanted to see the returning Ambassador from Washington at the height of a crisis. That made me suspicious and so I made it my business to find out what was going on, which, being an old Whitehall warrior, I very quickly did. And I was appalled. I couldn't say anything about it. I merely prepared myself for what I knew would be the consequences: in other words, some very serious economic and financial problems. And I would be one of the officials most responsible for dealing with these problems.

The declassified papers from the Treasury's overseas finance division show that Bridges, Lord Sherfield's predecessor as Permanent Secretary, warned Macmillan in August about the likely repercussions of a war for sterling; at the end of September Leslie Rowan added another warning, very specifically, about the consequences even if the action were successful. The Cabinet minutes for 30 October, the day the British government issued its ultimatum to Israel and Egypt, show that further explicit warnings on the position of the currency were given to ministers. They were ignored. But on 6 November the events they predicted happened. Faced with the imminent collapse of the pound, the Cabinet capitulated and halted the invasion.

Why did ministers ignore this succession of increasingly precise warnings? Lord Sherfield thinks that in August and September 'Macmillan, with the inner group of ministers who were running this, at that time were still running in blinkers'. Lord Home detected a degree of scepticism towards warnings in general:

> A warning is a different thing from it happening, isn't it? You often get
> warnings of this sort and then the results are different. I think what really
> turned the scale and made the Chancellor of the Exchequer that day so
> terribly anxious was the American action in putting the Sixth Fleet along-
> side us in the Mediterranean, for all the world to see, and therefore
> announcing in effect that America was totally against us. The effect on
> sterling as a result of that was catastrophic. It was the actual effect on
> sterling, rather than the warnings, I think. Perhaps we ought to have taken
> the warnings more seriously.

Macmillan, he said, was 'very fussed and upset by the fall':

> But what he had to deal with was the actual situation as to whether the fall
> in the pound sterling justified us in curtailing our action. And on the
> whole he persuaded the Cabinet that we had to do that. It might have
> taken two days to get to the other end of the Canal; it might have taken
> longer, and that was a consideration in Cabinet's mind at that time. And
> time was the essence of the matter, as it had been from the start.

Eden, though, wanted to go on. Lord Home agreed with him that it would
have been better to have got to the other end of the Canal; while he felt the
force of the argument for getting out at that point, 'there was the compen-
sating feeling that we had got into a position where the United Nations could
put a force in'.

As ever, the military got their information second-hand. General Sir
Kenneth Darling heard it on the radio.

> It was the BBC news bulletin, it might have been six or it might have been
> seven p.m., I can't remember when it was exactly, when suddenly we
> heard on the tannoy echoing round the ship the news that there would be
> a ceasefire at midnight GMT, which was 0200 hours on the 7th, local
> time. We were just astounded. It came straight out of the clear blue sky.
> The whole thing was brought to a halt and it had hardly started.

For the invasion force, the ceasefire was particularly difficult to take as
victory was within their grasp: another day, two days at most and they would
have reached the other end of the Canal.

At the highest military level in the Ministry of Defence the impact of the
ceasefire fell with equal force. For Sir Dermot Boyle, as a professional
military man, stopping at that point was the worst of all worlds.

We were shocked, very shocked. And we felt terribly for the poor men on the ground who had done everything we wanted of them, done it extremely efficiently, and some of them had got killed, and yet they were being stopped when victory was, from their point of view, imminent. I think, certainly, with hindsight, that it was unwise to launch the operation. Certainly unwise if you're not going to go ahead with it.

The American role in the collapse must have been an additional factor in the shock for Sir Dermot and others like him who had been the closest of allies with the United States in the Second World War and in the early Cold War. The working assumption was that Britain and America stood together on all these occasions. But while Sir Dermot concedes that it was 'an awful blow', he remarks judiciously that 'maybe a little of it was our fault in that maybe we assumed that they would never be anything other than our best friends'.

Sir Dermot has seen other Prime Ministers in operation at close quarters in peace and war – most notably Sir Winston Churchill. Churchill's style of running events, as he observed it, was different from Eden's: 'I think if he'd been doing the Suez thing I'm sure he would have gone to the Americans and got them on our side – or maybe got a flat "no" from them. What he'd have done then I don't know, but he wouldn't have waited for the flat "no" to come in the middle of the operation.'

It's difficult to overestimate the sense of shock felt by Eden and his Cabinet supporters about their treatment at the hands of the Americans. Even after the ceasefire, the United States continued to turn the financial screw until the Cabinet announced that the last British soldier would be withdrawn from the Canal Zone. Begging telegrams went out from the Treasury to Washington as ministers and officials contemplated the collapse of sterling. It was utter humiliation, particularly for Eden – and, in the view of Sir Guy Millard, who was with Eden throughout, intended as such: 'He didn't realize quite how vindictively, in a way, the Americans would behave after the operation. They didn't really need to. They didn't need to block our drawing rights from the International Monetary Fund; they didn't need to deny us oil in a crisis; but they decided to do so and they went ahead.'

As for opinion at home, Eden apparently thought he could get away with concealing the collusion with Israel, pretend it hadn't happened, and that the public would believe him. Sir Guy thinks that his political judgement in this was sound – had there only been a success to carry him through:

I think he thought that the end justified the means. He was an intuitive politician. He had an instinctive feel for public opinion which was usually correct. I think that he felt that provided the operation was a success, that's to say if we were able to seize the whole Canal and if Nasser was overthrown, then the general public would be so relieved and delighted that most of them wouldn't worry too much about the means by which it was achieved. And I think that judgement was almost certainly correct.

And yet, after the awful consequences for himself, for his party and for British policy were matters of actuality, he still persistently maintained that there had been no agreement with Israel. Sir Guy thinks that it was difficult for him to admit it; but did this not put him in a difficult position, as a public servant who knew his minister was lying to the House of Commons? Sir Guy preserves a mandarin-like detachment: 'I didn't feel the need to strike a political or moral attitude. I don't somehow see that as the function of a civil servant.' But presumably he was distressed by his boss lying to the House of Commons? 'Not unduly.'

Surprisingly, given the scale of the catastrophe at the time, the long-term effects on Britain in the Middle East were small. Sir Anthony Nutting, whose career was wrecked by Suez, was taken aback by the speed of the recovery.

In the Arab world we were forgiven remarkably quickly. I remember Nuri Said, who was then Prime Minister of Iraq, saying to me afterwards that it was rather like the children finding that the governess had been pocketing their pocket money. That for so long nanny, or the governess, had been telling the Arabs that they must be truthful, and they must not tell lies, and they must be honest, and they must not steal and do things like that, and then suddenly nanny was found with her hand in the till. He spoke of it really very light-heartedly and said, now, come on, you know, all is forgotten. And this was only a few months after Suez.

The unfortunate Nuri, however, perished in a coup the following year.

Closer to home, the collapse of the venture was not so quickly forgotten, and there was less light-heartedness in Paris, where Lord Gladwyn was Ambassador. 'They had no moral feelings, I think, about the use of force, and it didn't occur to them that it might have been against the whole principle of the United Nations. That didn't seem to occur to them at all. They were just extremely annoyed.'

Could it have been the case that this French fury at their betrayal – as they saw it – by Britain was what kept us out of the Common Market in the early 1960s? Lord Gladwyn is in no doubt about this.

In the long run, yes, it did have an effect on that. Certainly it did. That was the main unfavourable result of Suez as a whole, that the French then turned instinctively to Germany; and then when de Gaulle came to power a year and a half later it was all set, the deal with the Germans had then been set, and was acceptable to public opinion in France then. That was the long-term disaster of Suez.

Lord Home, however, ever loyal to Eden, believed that overall, the practical consequences of Suez were slight and that his initial doom-laden assessment was unjustified.

Hindsight tells me that Nasser probably couldn't have dominated the Middle East. Nobody has been able to unite the Arabs and therefore the chances are that perhaps Nasser couldn't have done it. But it was a horrible combination, you know. The Russians were there – and that was new, you have to remember that was new – and they've always wanted the Gulf area. If Anthony Eden's instinct was right that Nasser's operations really were going to cause very great trouble and could lose us our oil, then we had to try something of this kind. Some would say, and I'd be inclined to agree, that we ought to have contemplated a much bigger operation and taken the whole of Cairo, made sure that Nasser fell.

Did the Suez débâcle hasten the end of empire? Lord Home thought not, definitely not: 'It illustrated to people that Britain was no longer a great power and couldn't mobilize sufficient force to subdue a country like Egypt. This was the damaging thing, really. But it was inevitable that the empire should dissolve.' However, it did, he thought, teach future Prime Ministers – including himself – that Britain could never again mount a serious military or economic initiative without the agreement of the United States. And still, after thirty years had passed, he felt less than charitable towards the attitude of the US government in 1956: 'It was unnecessary for them, to put it no more strongly than that. We'd been allies in the war and all that kind of thing, we understood each other and basically all stood for the same things. It was quite unnecessary for them to demonstrate their hostility with the Sixth Fleet movement. That was what stuck in my gullet.'

The effect of Suez on the national psyche was profound. The realization of lost power was brutal and lasting – nowhere more so, as the official papers show, than on those who took part. We never saw ourselves, or the world, in the same light again. For the principal actors, who had lived through war and victory against Hitler, the circumstances of the Suez operation – the Canal too far – still retain their capacity to dismay. Sir Dermot Boyle encapsulates the painful legacy: 'When you compare it with the Second World War, one was proud of everything that happened in the Second World War, and one wasn't proud of everything that happened at Suez. I think that's about the summing up of the situation.'

8

Out of the Midday Sun?

Britain and the Great Power Impulse

*We have no eternal allies, and we have no perpetual enemies. Our interests
are eternal and perpetual, and those interests it is our duty to follow.*

Lord Palmerston, 1848[1]

*It seems such a shame when the English claim the earth
That they give rise to such hilarity and mirth*

Noel Coward, 1932[2]

'The UK,' according to Geoffrey Smith, journalist, commentator and
chronicler of the 'special relationship' between Margaret Thatcher and
Ronald Reagan, 'is a diplomatic trading nation as well as an economic trading
nation.'[3] This has been so throughout the lives of those in today's political or
public arenas – an assumption sustained throughout the vicissitudes of the
postwar period. What does this tell us about the image the British have of
themselves? Does the rest of the world expect us to carry on as a player in the
'great game' of international affairs? Even if it does, can we afford to?

These questions have been pertinent ones ever since British troops
halted their advance down the Suez Canal in November 1956. Not even the
end of the Cold War has seen them answered in a clear or fundamental
fashion. Could it be that Britain and the British have a profound reluctance
to remove themselves out of the midday sun once and for all, whatever the
condition of their currency and their domestic economy? As the twenty-
first century approaches, it is time to take a long, hard look at the diplomatic
and defence effort of a long faded superpower, its empire a distant memory
and the Cold War, that great post-1945 justification for a Rolls-Royce
foreign service, now over. In 1992 Britain ranked eighteenth among the
advanced industrial nations in terms of gross domestic product per head,
yet devoted nearly £25 billion a year to its defence budget and spent over
£1 billion a year on the various forms of political, cultural and broadcasting
diplomacy funded by the Foreign and Commonwealth Office. Is this
sensible? Is it possible?

Launching the government's defence White Paper in July 1992, the then Defence Secretary Malcolm Rifkind admitted: 'We are not a global power, nor do we have any aspirations to be a global power. We are primarily a middle-ranking European power.'[4] But has the great power impulse really gone at last? Lord Healey wrestled with the armed forces' budget both as Defence Secretary in the 1960s and as Chancellor of the Exchequer in the 1970s. In 1992, for him, Mr Rifkind's declaration rang more than a little hollow.

If we are really a medium-sized European power, why the dickens are we spending £25 billion a year, when the threat to our own security has disappeared, in order, as the White Paper says, to have the capability for intervening anywhere in the world with military force? I find it very difficult indeed to reconcile what Rifkind said in his press conference with the whole climate of the White Paper. By common consent we're doing worse economically than any other big country in Europe. And yet we're cutting our defence forces, which are already larger in relation to our economy than those of any other West European country, by far less than they are.

How are we to explain these contradictions? Could it be that the vested interests of Whitehall, the whole institutionalized apparatus of overseas and defence policy, is still marching to the old drumbeats? Lord Healey plants the responsibility firmly elsewhere.

I think the problem is entirely that the government is frightened to confront these choices, partly because it would put at risk their reputation among their own followers for being a defender of Britain as a great power.

But can it be just the reluctance of ministers that prevents us from confronting the paradoxes of the 'great game'? As Permanent Secretary at the Ministry of Defence until his retirement in the spring of 1992 Sir Michael Quinlan was chief of one of those great Whitehall vested interests which Lord Healey exonerated, perhaps too blithely, from his strictures. He looks to history for part, at least, of the explanation.

We have a certain sense of ourselves, born of history, which does mean that we view what we might do rather differently from some of our partners. If you compare ourselves and Italy, we are about the same size, about the same wealth, about the same population. We are not in a more obviously threatened strategic position, yet we are spending rising twice what Italy spends on defence. That, I think, can in the end be explained only by having a different view of what kind of contributor we are in the world. I don't think it's necessarily something that's wrong or unwise. I think we have influence which redounds to our advantage.

Why are we so different from Italy? What are these special factors that drive us still to play the role, as the former Foreign Secretary Douglas Hurd put it, of 'a main contributor to the creation of a safer and more decent world'? Until May 1992 Sir Percy Cradock was Foreign Affairs Adviser to the Prime Minister in Downing Street. Chairman for nearly ten years of the Cabinet Office's Joint Intelligence Committee, which sits at the apex of Whitehall's secret world and is the eyes and ears of ministers, Sir Percy was regarded as our greatest modern practitioner of *realpolitik*. He too draws on history, but in a more specific and perhaps more calculating fashion.

We exercise disproportionate influence for a medium-rank power. So we are still a very influential player. We come to the table with certain cards having been dealt, and the skill in the game is making use of those cards and playing them as well, as forcefully, as cleverly as we can. For example, because of our position in the world in 1945, because of our conduct in the Second World War, we were given a position on the Security Council as a permanent member. Now that, of course, is an immense asset and not something we're going to cast away. For similar reasons we enjoy very close relations and links in Washington. That again is of immense importance. These are things that are given to us and, I suppose, in theory it would be possible for us to cast them aside, but no government is going to do that. They're going to use these cards and play them as best they can. We don't make the choice in a void. We have these cards, we try to use them in order to impose our vision, our pattern, on events. If we weren't to do so there would be others who would impose their views along lines that could be inimical to British interests.

One can imagine that the Sir Michaels and Sir Percys of Whitehall could be a formidable in-house pressure group were a more modest role ever to be contemplated.

Sir Anthony Parsons, former Ambassador to the United Nations and an old Middle East hand, is regarded as something of a radical by his Foreign Office generation. Yet even he believes that Britain, along with France, is a special case.

We are the only two non-superpowers which, for historical reasons, have to deploy a worldwide foreign policy. Both of us still have dependent territories dotted across the world, and we're going to have them indefinitely in the Caribbean and elsewhere. Most of the conflict situations in the world derive from decolonization and self-determination, and principally decolonization and self-determination in the British and French empires. That means that the people concerned in the countries concerned still regard us as something special because we were the creators of their problems and expect more of us than they do of, say, any other run-of-the-mill middle-sized power.

Is history a prison? Can't we say at some point, with the Empire long gone and the Cold War over at last: you may want us, you may think we're a bit special, but we've got to stop sometime? Sir Anthony doesn't think we can cut the links unilaterally.

This is a two-sided business and the other side has something to say about it. Take South Africa as an example. We haven't really exercised power in South Africa since 1910. But neither the Boers nor the English-descent South Africans, nor the black South Africans, will allow us to forget about the past. Whether we want to break the tie or not, they're not going to let us. And I think this is the same if you take another example, the Middle East. Nobody in the Middle East is going to let us forget that we and France were responsible for the post-First World War settlement in the Middle East which has really been at the source of instability, militarism, expansionism ever since. You're never going to persuade a Palestinian to regard us, the British, in the same light as he would regard, say, the Italians or the Belgians or the Scandinavians. I would love it if we could become like Norway, where you can pick and choose. You can do good round the world if you feel you've got the money and if you run out of money you don't need to do anything. Nobody expects anything of you. But it's going to be a very, very long time before people stop expecting something extra of us. We are now paying the price in these terms for our history – for having ruled a quarter of the world's population right up to 1945. That's a very short time ago, and you cannot simply wish that away in a matter of half a century.

On the other hand, do the British players of the great game – any more than the British public – really wish they were with Norway as a kind of part-time team in the lower divisions? It seems unlikely. Historian Keith Robbins is the author of a standard work entitled *The Eclipse of a Great Power*.[5] Could it be that, half a century after that eclipse, the guardians of British foreign policy still have some old imperial habits to unlearn? Professor Robbins, like Sir Anthony Parsons, sees long memories at work.

Such habits are very difficult to unlearn quickly, and when you've had an empire which has had so conspicuous a part in British life in terms of overseas settlement, in terms of family networks and connections and so on, there has been a reality which you can't simply wipe away and say 'it was a sort of aberration, now Britain is really just an offshore island from the European mainland.' Recall Eden's comment about letters pouring in from all over the globe to villages in obscure parts of these islands, whereas the amount of postal traffic coming in from continental Europe by comparison was tiny. I suspect that's changed quite significantly. But I'm not surprised. It takes a very long time for this to work its way through.

But what is it about those formidable Whitehall knights – the Sir Percy Cradocks, the Sir Michael Quinlans and the Sir Anthony Parsonses – that makes them all, without exception, want to carry on as players in the great game? Professor Robbins suggests a mixture of motives:

I suspect it is the excitement of it; and men of talent and ability are clearly anxious still to portray themselves on a world scale. Also, I think they genuinely see the British role as an intelligent role – perhaps not quite with the arrogance of the notion that the British were the Greeks to the Americans as the Romans, where the British had all the wisdom,[6] but I think a genuine sense that there is a peculiar British way of dealing with things, a residue of experience across the globe which is still somehow or other carried in the blood, which other European countries, for example, don't possess.

Mr Gladstone said in our heyday that he wanted us to devote the absolute minimum resources to being a great power commensurate with our being a great power. Are we, these days, devoting the maximum resources commensurate with being a medium-sized regional power? Professor Robbins thinks we are, because 'we still have this incubus from the past which makes us feel that if we are a medium-sized power, we have to be, as it were, the best medium-sized power, the most active, the most reliable, the most energetic medium-sized power.' But shouldn't it be possible to retain an appetite for excellence without undue gluttony in terms of public resources? After all, not every member of the postwar Diplomatic Service craved what old Empire men called 'a place in the sun'.

Sir Leslie Fielding, former Director-General of the European Commission's External Affairs Directorate, left Whitehall for Brussels the day Britain joined the Community in 1973. Does he think that there are still many people at the Foreign Office who really don't want us, even now, to be out of the midday sun? His own recommendation is that we undertake a kind of historical leapfrogging, back over the Empire:

> Our right approach is to go back to an earlier British tradition before imperialism, that of the seventeenth and eighteenth centuries, when we were the masters of diplomacy and clever constructors of alliances of people with similar interests. I don't want us to be out of the midday sun either, but I don't think that we can claim a place in the midday sun where we don't have the credentials. We've got to get as close to it as possible. It seems to me that people in the Foreign Office well understand it. The problem which they face is a public and parliamentary opinion, most of it anchored in realities which have long since gone.

Are there echoes here of Lord Healey? It's not the realistic professionals who are unwilling to scale down their ambitions; it's the politicians and the public who elects them. It is they who expect the UK, as a victor in 1945, to remain a permanent member of the United Nations Security Council even though the defeated military powers turned economic superpowers, Germany and Japan, have no seat at that most exalted of top tables. As Foreign Secretary in the 1980s, could Lord Howe justify our occupation of that coveted place?

> We have been able to make the most of it by giving to our position there a very high degree of diplomatic expertise and strong inputs of political leadership as well. To offer an example, when Shevardnadze began shaping Soviet foreign policy through Mr Gorbachev, they identified the United Nations as a place where they could perform differently. It was the British permanent representative at New York who began the informal meetings of the five ambassadors and the five permanent members at his own apartment, as a means of beginning to restore the dynamo at the heart of the United Nations. He continued sharing those meetings for years thereafter. It was skilful exercise by a succession of extremely high-quality ambassadors at the UN which enabled us to take the lead in doing something that the world needed done.

Is this also, perhaps, a good example of the kind of pre-imperial diplomatic skill that Sir Leslie Fielding would like to see revived?

What is just as significant as the polished performance of our men at the UN is that not only did the rest of the Big Five permanent members of the Security Council expect them to take such a leading role, they acquiesced in it – even the United States, which, since it bailed the British war economy out with Lend-Lease over fifty years ago, has undeniably been in the driving-seat of Western diplomacy. Professor Philip Zelikow, who was Director for

European Security Affairs in the National Security Council in Washington as the Cold War ended, offers an insight into the origins of this forbearance.

> If you conceive of a world in which you have one superpower, the United States, with Russia somewhat debilitated at the moment, and a number of medium powers – Germany, Japan, Britain, France and so forth – then you have to conclude that the United States, unless it wants to pursue unilateralist policies, must form absolutely critical linkages with these medium powers. And in turn the medium powers will want to have a critical linkage with the United States; and the medium powers on which the United States relies the most will be the most influential.

This explains why the United Kingdom needs that kind of relationship with the United States; but given that there are quite a number of medium-sized powers these days, not least in Europe, why does the United States particularly need Britain? Professor Zelikow expands his point to identify Britain's specific qualifications:

> In part because the British share our values and share our broad goals as to how the world ought to evolve. There are not so many powers that share our fundamental objectives so completely that we can afford to dispense with a crucial power that does – especially a crucial power that can enlist so much skill in the pursuit of our common diplomatic objectives. In sheer professionalism and skill, British diplomats have few if any equals throughout the world of diplomacy.

The fabled 'special relationship', nevertheless, rests on something more than just a philosophical construct of this kind. There is a more human and intimate element as well. Sir Anthony Parsons turns to the Gulf War for an illustration of both this connection and the expectations held of Britain in the Middle East.

> In all my dealings with the Americans over many years, particularly in the United Nations, I've always noticed that they very much like to have company in whatever they're doing. They don't like to be out on their own. And we are the obvious company they look for; and we had our own reasons for joining in the Gulf War, both historical and contemporary. So it's not surprising that the coalition formed itself in the way that it did. We joined in as number two in the coalition – number two rather than number three, four or five – really for historical reasons, partly to do with our relationship with the Americans. But it's only twenty years since we withdrew our protection from the states of the southern Gulf. We were

there from 1829 onwards and all the Gulf states would expect Britain to play the number two role to the United States in any protective exercise in their regard. They would have been amazed if we had failed to do so and our national interests – commercial and all the rest – would undoubtedly have suffered if we had stood back and folded our arms while all that was going on.

Sentiment, history, expectations; together, a potent, irresistible cocktail which peps up generation after generation of British diplomats. But is there not a risk that it may lead to a heady exaggeration of British influence? There is a view which has taken on almost the status of the received wisdom that it was Mrs Thatcher's presence at President Bush's side at Aspen, Colorado, which put the beef into US policy as Iraqi tanks invaded Kuwait in August 1990. Sober truth or delusions of vanished grandeur? Philip Zelikow was well placed to observe the intimacies of allied policy as the crisis developed, and he is not inclined to dismiss Mrs Thatcher's part.

There is no doubt that President Bush was quite resolved to take a firm line. But then you do have to confront the fact that on this crucial day, after this very first meeting of the American decision-makers, the President spends hours talking to one single statesperson – Margaret Thatcher. That extraordinary conversation at that critical moment was undoubtedly very important in shaping and forming the policies which then emerged in the succeeding days. Actually turning a conviction of firmness into a specific policy required the crafting of a strategy. What exactly do you do? What do you do in the United Nations? What kind of military measures are appropriate in the initial stage? Those absolutely critical strategic decisions would determine the fate of a policy of firmness and Prime Minister Thatcher played an important role in shaping those policies.

Britain, of course, prides itself on intimate local knowledge where oil meets desert. Historical intimacy can mean enhanced intelligence, a real asset for a declining power like Britain, strapped for cash and weapons. Intelligence is another activity where the Americans don't like to do the work of analysis alone. Could this be the area where the 'special relationship' is least unequal? No one is better placed to consider this question than Sir Percy Cradock.

Our intelligence machine not only helps to preserve our security in the direct sense, it also allows us to look ahead and gives our policy an extra edge and foresight. Our habit with the Americans of collecting intelligence worldwide and of sharing the assessment of that intelligence gives us an entry at the very highest level of US policy-making. I can recall during the Gulf War that we had the very closest liaison possible with the Americans, both at the policy and at the intelligence level. And we do this really for a very small expenditure of resources, certainly compared with what the Americans do.

But the finely honed appraisals of the Joint Intelligence Committee, prized though they may be by their Washington readers, are not, in the end, what buys influence in the White House, the State Department and the Pentagon. If they were, our world role would come cheap. It's weapons that count – modern ones which are costly to buy, expensive to maintain and difficult to project across continents. Wasn't it tanks in the sand that bought kudos and influence in Washington as war in the Gulf approached? Philip Zelikow pays due regard to the value of the British contribution, but is clear-sighted as to its limits:

> If you compare the British contribution to the contribution of any of the other countries in the coalition, I think you'll see that the British military units were in fact the only units that were fully suited to engage in combat with the best Iraqi forces at the same level of capability as their American counterparts. That's a very important capability for General Schwarzkopf to have had access to. But at the same time, I think, one can observe that Britain, after mustering all of its strength, was able to field one division in this very important crisis, and could only do that by cannibalizing equipment from throughout its armed forces and relying crucially on support not only from the United States but from a number of other NATO allies in making up the logistical infrastructure that was needed to support the armoured division's operations. Once you fall below a certain threshold, you simply are not able to field any significant military combat unit to engage in helping resolve the crisis or reinforcing the diplomacy that allows you to play a global partnership role.

Britain, in Zelikow's view, is very close to that threshold. It is an immensely significant one, and the implication of its existence is that if there is to be a sizeable peace dividend in Britain, a repeat in other circumstances of the number two role we assumed in the Gulf may be out of the question, however disappointing that may be to the White House.

However, gratifying Washington is not the overriding purpose of Britain's foreign and defence policy. We cannot let the view from the White House determine how we spend our national wealth; and when it comes to spending, defence hardware is what really counts. Trimming an embassy here, closing down a consulate there will be as nothing on the balance sheet compared to the potential economies in fighters, tanks or submarines. Sir Leslie Fielding thinks that a hard look at priorities is in order.

> The big area for cuts is defence. The 1992 Defence White Paper still shows overstretch, something with which we've been struggling since 1956 and the Suez crisis. What we have to do is to take it seriously when we see ourselves as a medium-sized European power, and not by any means the richest in Europe, and have a defence budget which is more in line with theirs than with what we now have. Because in the long term we can't project power, exercise leadership in Europe or be listened to with respect anywhere in the world if we are economically underdeveloped, if our infrastructure is lousy and we are unable to sustain at home the image of a medium-sized European power which we are so anxious to foster overseas. So I think we have to put the domestic scene first and then, beyond that, do what we can. It's a matter of judgement, without going overboard. Let's be modest for a change.

What would such modesty entail? If Whitehall followed Sir Leslie's advice and slimmed its defence budgets down towards a European norm it would involve reducing its proportion of GDP by between one-quarter and three-quarters to bring it more in line with, variously, France, Germany or Italy. However, the real comparison must be with France, which, like Britain, possesses a nuclear weapons capacity. In 1992, almost in the same breath which consigned us to medium-power status, Defence Secretary Rifkind announced the order of a fourth Trident submarine for the Royal Navy. What price modesty, then? Hasn't possession of the ultimate weapon always been tied up with Britain's notion of itself as a power to rank with few others? Lord Healey's political career spans the eras of the V-bomber and Trident, and he recalls the motives behind the postwar Labour government's decision to acquire the bomb.

> If you look at the arguments which took place in the Attlee government about whether we should have a nuclear bomb, there's absolutely no doubt at all that Attlee himself and, even more explicitly, Ernest Bevin, wanted the nuclear bomb to show we were a world power equal to the United States, irrespective of any particular function it would have in the military field.

As Secretary of State for Defence from 1964 to 1970, Denis Healey had his chance to confirm or cancel the nuclear weapons programme. The left at the time depicted him as a kind of latter-day John Bull because he refused to get rid of it; there was, for example, a considerable fuss when the Secretary of State and his wife went to launch a Polaris submarine at Cammell Laird. Looking back, does Lord Healey think that he could perhaps have bitten more bullets in those six years?

> I think the case of the left was nonsense. They believed that if we gave up our nuclear weapons other countries would give up theirs. On the other hand, I think with hindsight that if I'd known then what I know now, I would have cancelled the programme. If all I knew now is what I knew then, I would go on with it. At that time, when American policy was very uncertain, we had very much more influence on America if we had our own nuclear weapons; and we didn't want to leave de Gaulle as the only nuclear power in Europe. I think there was a marginal case which I accepted for going on with the programme, especially as it was very cheap at that time – the bulk of development expenditure was over. But, with hindsight, if I'd known how the world would turn out I would have cancelled it; and it's a pity in some ways that I didn't, because it's still hanging round us.

The trouble is, of course, that no Defence or Foreign Secretary ever does know how the world will turn out, and so the nuclear weapons bullet remains unbitten, not just in London but in the capital of every other nuclear power – including France, the country to which Britain is most comparable in size and history. It was especially rich of General de Gaulle to veto our application to join the EEC in 1963 on the grounds that we were insufficiently European-minded, given that it is longevity as a state (and the assumptions about sovereignty that go with that) which curbs the appetite in both Britain and France for a wholly integrated Europe. When French diplomats talk of a common European foreign policy, are they really contemplating giving up a distinctive French role? For former French foreign minister Claude Cheysson national identity retains a very prominent place in the scheme of things.

> We are old nations. We are very proud of being what we are, and I think that's very important. I think that part of our role in the future is that we shall insist on keeping our identities, on keeping our nations as nations. Even if we go further and deeper in our Community, for us it is a community of nations – for you as well as for us – and this belongs to our history, it belongs to our past.

On the question whether a common European foreign and defence policy is the best way to proceed for these two ancient sovereign nations he is cautious:

It depends what one calls a common policy. I think that what's done in Maastricht is very reasonable in that respect. It's been agreed that there should first be a decision taken unanimously on the fields, sectors, policies where there should be a common policy. It will not be all fields. We can have a common foreign policy in Central and Eastern Europe. I doubt that we'll have a common foreign policy in the Near East for the time being. The British policy, which is very much like the American policy now in the Near East, has been well defined since the First World War; it's not the same as the French one, and the Germans have decided to take no risk out there. We should have a common foreign policy on some of the most significant problems with regard to the South: raw materials, how much they should be paid, development policies. But common foreign policies will not extend to all fields, will not extend to all parts of the world.

Could Europe be the way forward for a nation like Britain, which clearly wants to be a champion in whatever league it chooses to play in? Could we be a world-class performer (perhaps even unofficial captain) in a European team of increasing combined skill and importance? Lord Howe jibs slightly at the idea of captaincy:

I wouldn't like to endorse the phrase 'team leadership'. I would prefer to take the phrase 'being influential and successful at the heart of Europe', and I think the essence of the position now being adopted by Britain is not revelling, as President Bush said we should revel, at being an anchor to windward of Europe but placing ourselves at the heart of Europe. It's a fuller representation of the point I've made many times, quoting Archimedes: 'Give me a place whereon to stand and I can move the world.' For Britain, Europe is the place whereon to stand for that purpose.

It is very interesting to see here once more the desire to shape the world. It used to be said of Harold Macmillan that he was always looking for a new stage from which to launch exactly this singular British role. Does this tell us a lot about the British political class, the aspirations it has always had – and still has – as a nation? Lord Howe stresses that 'the singular British role is to serve Britain's interest as well as possible. That means maximizing Britain's influence in the world. The reason Macmillan gave for our accession to the Community in 1962 was to avoid losing influence in Europe and in Washington at the same time. And that's why we're there now.'

And so we are still hoping, Archimedes-like, to 'move the world'. Provided we act in concert with our European partners and ministers keep a wary eye out for overstretched ambitions and budgets to match, is this the kind of niche in the world influence market that advocates of greater national modesty would like to see us occupy? After all, the best brains in today's Foreign Office are already deployed on European affairs, for all the emphasis on Britain's world role and keeping our seat on the UN Security Council. Sir Leslie Fielding is keen to distinguish between modesty in respect of role and in respect of abilities.

> At the practical business of multilateral diplomacy we are probably better than the French, the Germans, the Dutch, the Italians or anyone else, and we should use that skill. It goes back to something in our national character which we have displayed for centuries in European affairs. So while we need to be modest about the economic means that we have available, I think we should capitalize on the technical skills which we undoubtedly possess.

He is also emphatic about the need for a properly focused engagement with Europe:

> I'm not talking about a sergeant major shouting at a lot of scruffy recruits. I'm talking about a member of an SAS team in which they all recognize each other and treat each other as equals but where one of them is there to give the impulse. I think we should try to do that. We must be integrated with others and we've got to take Europeans seriously. There are far too many Englishmen who feel more at home with Hausa tribesmen or Malaysian Dyaks than they do with Dutch or Italian colleagues.

The imperial legacy is revealed once again as a less than entirely helpful inheritance.

It is nearly forty years since the British Cabinet formally recognized that the imperial game was up and approved the renaming of 'Empire Day' as 'Commonwealth Day'. Now perhaps even the Commonwealth, let alone the Empire, has metamorphosed from a prime diplomatic instrument into a relic of national heritage – a relic, incidentally, which requires Britain to sit on more international organizations than any other power. Yet Sir Anthony Parsons, as Britain's representative at the UN during the Falklands crisis, did find the Commonwealth link unexpectedly useful:

> A lot of people think the Commonwealth is a lot of nonsense – a kind of intangible, a dinosaurs' club, a bit of nostalgia we can well dispense with and so on. But when the chips fell in 1982 and the Argentines invaded the Falklands and we desperately needed international support, both for

trying to get a resolution condemning what the Argentines had done and demanding their withdrawal, and for military action in the last resort, I suddenly found that we could actually rely more on the Commonwealth than we could, for example, on many of our European partners. I could cite other cases – Rhodesia, for example. The Lancaster House process in 1979 could never have started if it hadn't been for the imprimatur of the Commonwealth. This gave us the green light, as it were, to start an international negotiation which ended up in solving the Southern Rhodesian problem and producing an independent Zimbabwe. The support of the Commonwealth was absolutely vital.

Sir Sonny Ramphal, former Secretary-General of the Commonwealth, identifies himself and Sir Anthony as coming from 'very much the same mould, the same kind of generation'. As a result, he reflects,

we have lived through periods in which we know the value of that Commonwealth link. We have the facility to talk and work with each other in a language that we both speak well – sometimes, increasingly, we speak it better than the British – in an idiom that we understand, against parliamentary traditions that are common form, against an educational background in which we can quote each other's poetry. When all this is put together, you've got something of a club. When I became Secretary-General of the Commonwealth, I was quite sure I was going to do everything to ban the use of the word 'club'. I thought it sent all the wrong signals; this was not the way the Commonwealth should see itself, and so on. Then I came to realize that that was the way the Commonwealth did see itself, and that it wasn't such a bad way after all. It's a good club.

It may be true that this peculiar fifty-member club can be good for the occasional outing into the real world of power and diplomacy. But could it be that now and in the future its most valuable routine function is as an arm of cultural diplomacy – that bunch of influential intangibles which ties together the British Council, the BBC World Service, foreign students coming to Britain for their higher education and British orchestras touring the world? In the 1977 Berrill Report – the last official inquiry into British overseas representation – the Central Policy Review Staff, the famous Cabinet Office 'think tank', cast a notoriously unsentimental eye over these glittering intangibles as part of a wider recommendation that Whitehall's foreign and defence aspirations should shrink to meet the country's resources. Sir Anthony Parsons was Ambassador to Iran at the time, and had little sympathy for the CPRS view.

I thought they'd got it completely wrong, quite honestly. I personally regard the BBC Overseas Services and the British Council as the two most important instruments in projecting Britain abroad – and I'm not talking about projecting Britain just in some kind of airy-fairy sense, Morris dancers in Ulan Bator and so on, I'm thinking of hard-nosed commercial interests, political influence, all that kind of thing.

Sonny Ramphal is equally emphatic in his defence of these areas of activity.

I think it certainly does pay off for Britain. It is one of the reasons why many of us find quite incomprehensible the situation that developed over high overseas students' fees, which was a reversal of this trend, and I remember very well Claude Cheysson talking to me when he was foreign minister in France and saying, what on earth are the British doing? Why are they giving us this inside track? And putting me on notice – I was then Commonwealth Secretary-General – that France, Germany, Japan were all going to occupy the space that Britain was leaving. I would say quite unequivocally that I think it's an enormously important link.

An accountant would say: prove it to me. How would he respond to that challenge?

I think you prove it in contracts. I think you prove it in consultancies. I think you prove it in influence. I think you prove it in relations with virtually every prime minister and president of a Commonwealth country for the last forty years.

Many overseas students now have to pay the going rate in Britain's increasingly cost-conscious universities, but some £89 million still goes on 'putting across a positive image of British society and values', as the official literature likes to describe the role of the British Council. That's nearly a tenth of the entire Foreign Office budget. That think tank report, now nearly a generation ago, urged ministers to consider abolishing the British Council altogether. Baroness Blackstone, now a Labour peer and Master of Birkbeck College, London, was one of the report's authors. Has she changed her mind since?

The option for abolition was one I was never happy with, really, even at the time. I think it was a mistake. But where I think we were right was to suggest that the impact of cultural diplomacy is always going to be limited in a rational world. I don't believe that Japanese businessmen are likely to buy more British goods because they have seen some marvellous performances of the Royal Ballet. I'm in favour of cultural exchange, and a great deal of it, for its own sake. But I think we should be a little sceptical about how much value it has in bringing about a better economic, trading or political atmosphere.

The example is often given of a hypothetical student from the Third World who has a good time at a college of the University of London and goes back home; twenty-five years later he finds himself trade minister and, all other things being equal, would rather place the contract here than elsewhere. Baroness Blackstone is less than convinced that this is the way to foster British exports.

> I don't think we can justify huge numbers of overseas students here paying very low fees simply because they might one day become a minister and buy British goods. I think people buy British goods because they're of high quality, they meet their needs, they're delivered on time. Those are the real things that count.

Like almost everything else to do with cultural diplomacy, the payoff – if there is one – cannot be measured in a manner that will satisfy the professionally hard-hearted monuments to cost–benefit analysis in the Treasury. But what about the exporters themselves? Lord Prior, a former Cabinet minister, is now chairman of GEC and a captain of industry in the front line of the global export business, and robustly confounds the sceptics.

> I have absolutely no doubt that helping with the cultural contacts pays off in the long run with hard British contracts for goods and services. I've had people in this office from places like the Sudan who came over here to work in British factories when they were at university, or even for short courses, and now you find that they're head of the Sudan railway industry or something of that nature and they've never forgotten what they learned over here. I'm certain that that is enormously important. So is the aid and trade programme, because although it's not very large, and ought to be larger, that again helps to establish British industry in those countries. This is something the Treasury simply don't begin to understand, and I am immensely critical of the Treasury for what they've tried to do to stamp this out. When you get east of about Italy, you're dealing with governments, with ministers. You're not dealing with a large private sector. And because you're dealing with governments, you actually need the support of the British government, and the whole cultural side comes into it to a very large extent. In those markets where you are seeking to establish yourself and to maintain a foothold in the developing world, the

government can help a good deal more than perhaps it's doing even at the moment.

If Britain does do more on the cultural side, however, something will have to give. No Chancellor is going to shovel more of the national wealth into the 'great game'. Yet cultural diplomacy is cheap at the price. It was the Coca-Cola can, McDonalds and video recorders as much as, if not more than, Western missiles which turned minds beyond the old Iron Curtain. And the UK can do far better in the cultural balance of trade than fast food and film.

But the real overstretch is not about having too many men in Havana or too many Morris dancers in Ulan Bator. It's about having too many military bases and too much human and manufacturing capital tied up in the weapons business. Does the end of the Cold War really mean that we can pull out of these costly military commitments and perhaps discover a new specialist niche within a more cooperative world order? Lord Healey sees an opportunity to pull back on one level, but also a need for a better-organized international context for a revised role.

This gives us an unlooked-for opportunity to opt out of the attempt to keep up with the Americans; we don't have to keep up with the Russians, and there's no other world power around, so we don't need what you might call an all-round capability, a self-contained capability for intervening outside Europe. The difficult question is, can we create a political framework for security in the very unstable parts of the world which are likely to face wars, including civil wars, to which we could usefully and sensibly contribute? The dreadful muddle in policy now between the roles of the United Nations, NATO, the Western European Union and the Conference on Security and Cooperation in Europe shows how far people are from tackling that. What I think we should do, and urgently – and I'm very disappointed that the British government has rejected this – is to take up the UN Secretary-General's proposal to create a permanent peacekeeping capacity with standby forces, with an effective military staff, through the Military Committee of the United Nations, and should concentrate on this area. But when this was raised the Americans opposed it totally and we fell in behind the Americans, which I think was a dreadful error.

Does a new danger lurk in these altered circumstances, that because of their specialist military skills, the British may become the world's mercenaries?

We were mercenaries in a sense during the Gulf War because we got most of our expenditure paid by other governments, and there is a slight danger of that. But I believe that the attitude which has been taken particularly by the Swedish and Finnish governments, both neutral countries, that it's worth paying some money to maintain a force which can contribute to peacekeeping, is the right one. I think that's very necessary. What worries me very much at the moment, and seems to me to be very self-contradictory, is the desire on the one hand to have the capability for acting all over the world and the refusal on the other to act anywhere where there happens to be trouble at the time, like Yugoslavia.

Lord Healey is right to contrast a defence capacity to project British power globally with a reluctance to use it, in company with allies, on Europe's Balkan doorstep for fear of creating what one British diplomat called 'a Northern Ireland with mountains'. Is it enough to lend the world former British Foreign Secretaries like Lords Carrington and Owen? Or should those prized peacekeeping skills be more readily applied, not just when the United States leads or where an oil-rich former protectorate is involved, as it was in the Gulf?

It is true that history has dealt Britain an unusually rich hand – a mixture of top-flight diplomacy, a first-class intelligence capacity, highly professional armed forces and the kind of moral authority that cultural diplomacy can bring. But if we rely on our history, could we not find ourselves increasingly disregarded by a wider world that does not pine for Britain as superpower? Sir Leslie Fielding labours under no illusions.

The world isn't going to be gravely distressed if Britain opts out. I don't believe that hundreds of nations around the world are yearning as they get up each morning to open their newspapers and read of some new British initiative. There's residual goodwill, a willingness in some parts of the world to work with us, but we are not the gift to the world which some of our leaders think we are.

So Britain may have to devote all its traditional diplomatic guile to keeping even a place in the shade. If our past capital can be drawn on with discrimination in the cause of keeping the peace in the post-Cold War world, it may not match the glories the seasoned Whitehall knights can recall. But it would be a valuable and quite unusual role for a medium-sized power *and* a future worthy of a former great power cleverly adapting to necessarily reduced circumstances.

Part Four

Portraits

Power, power? You may think you are going to get it, but you never do.
H. H. Asquith on being Prime Minister, undated[1]

I was less aware of the Prime Minister's power than the constraints upon his power. When you are in there, you don't feel you can do anything.
Bernard Donoughue, Head of the Downing Street Policy Unit
under Harold Wilson and James Callaghan, 1974–9, 1995[2]

For all Asquith's very human reaction to his frustrations and Bernard Donoughue's trained political scientist's eye brought to bear on the stressed realities of late 1970s premiership, the impact of person and personality on the headship of the British government and the thrust of both policy and politics remains considerable. The premiership is – and has been at least since Peel – an office of great potential. Its reach and its potency are, however, always relative in a Cabinet democracy and, in some circumstances, the potential can remain latent or be seriously diminished. Power always seems more lustrous and robust to those seeking it than to those in possession of it.

Any study of the British premiership must go far beyond a concertina of the biographies of those who held it. But no account of the office of Prime Minister is complete without a careful biographical element – hence the sections that follow. The treatments vary. How I would have loved a staccato fifteen minutes (it would have been folly to have expected more) with Clem Attlee on his Downing Street stewardship 1945–51. If I had been able to talk to Churchill it would, as with Kingsley Amis's Professor Welch in *Lucky Jim*, have been a case of 'history speaking'. Chatting to Eden would have required a supreme feat of the diplomacy in which he was so skilled on his day. Sadly, no such conversations were possible. The next best thing was a series of studio conversations with those who, as ministerial colleagues, had spent hours in their company in real life or who, as biographers, had lived with them for years in the metaphorical sense. The BBC Radio Four *Living*

With . . . series was made possible in 1989 by the energies and insights of Caroline Anstey.

Edward Heath and James Callaghan kindly agreed to revisit their premierships for our microphone when Julian Hale and I came to call in 1989. It is not always pleasant or easy for old statesmen to reflect upon the rockier passages in their periods of office. Both proved to be old troupers in the best sense.

The art of radio obituary is a peculiar one. For a start, such documentaries have to be prepared in advance and updated regularly – a faintly macabre process when the subject matter is still very much human matter. I tackled it first with Harold Macmillan as the PM in question under the seasoned guidance of Anthony Moncrieff. Thereafter I was in the hands of that great connoisseur of politicians and political biography, Simon Coates, as we sought to place Alec Home and Harold Wilson in their historical contexts.

Mrs Thatcher, fittingly, fits with none of the previous approaches. By a bizarre coincidence I found myself at the dais in Georgetown University, Washington DC, delivering a long-planned lecture on 'Mrs Thatcher as History', on the very day she vacated Number Ten for John Major. Would that I could have claimed foresight. In having none, I was not alone. Of the nine postwar Premiers treated here, only one – Anthony Eden – was the clear heir apparent. Holders of the office of British Prime Minister are usually, to some degree, a turn up for the book. Unpredictability adds to the spice of power, and of biography.

9

Living with Clem

When I listened to the Prime Minister's speech last night, in which he gave such a travesty of the policy of the Labour Party, I realized at once what was his object. He wanted the electors to understand how great was the difference between Winston Churchill, the great leader in war of a united nation, and Mr Churchill, the party leader of the Conservatives. He feared lest those who had accepted his leadership in war might be tempted, out of gratitude, to follow him further. I thank him for having disillusioned them so thoroughly. The voice we heard last night was that of Mr Churchill, but the mind was that of Lord Beaverbrook.

That 1945 election broadcast was the making of Clement Attlee. It was one of the most effective party politicals ever recorded – the more so for being entirely unexpected. For, as Prime Ministers go, Attlee was smaller than life: physically unimpressive with a reedy voice and sparse vocabulary. In 1935 he became Labour leader by accident at a time when many of the party's more dominant figures were temporarily out of Parliament because of electoral defeat. But the stopgap became a fixture: Attlee stayed for twenty years. By the time war came he had made little impression as leader of the opposition, and in the coalition government he was inevitably overshadowed by Winston Churchill; yet when he surprised the country, the world and himself by winning the 1945 election with a majority of 146 he quickly proved a highly effective administrator and chairman of Cabinet. He never shrank from lecturing backsliders in his headmasterly fashion; and, if the occasion demanded, he would do the same to the aristocrats of the labour movement, as he did to the London dockers who went on unofficial strike in 1948:

> This strike is not a strike against capitalists or employers. It's a strike against your mates. A strike against the housewife. A strike against the ordinary common people who have difficulties enough now to manage on their shilling's worth of meat and the other rationed commodities. Why should you men strike? You're well paid compared with the old days. You have a guaranteed minimum wage of £4 8s 6d a week whether you work or not. You no longer have to go to the Labour Exchange and stand in the

queue. Whose only obligation is to attend at the proper call times, and, if there is no work, to sign on and get your money. What a contrast with the former days! I lived in dockland for many years. I remember the old horrible conditions. I knew what casual labour meant to the women and children of East London, and to the men too. The British government never again want to see you going home to a wife who, meeting you at the door, would say, 'How have you got on?' And you'd have to look at her and say, 'No work today. No pay.' That has gone for ever under this scheme. We must and we will take steps to discharge the cargoes so that people will not lose their rations. We will not allow these subversive influences to wreck this tremendous social experiment which obliterated from the dockside the curse of casual labour and casual earnings. Your clear duty to yourselves, to your fellow citizens and to your country is to return to work.

Now, for the first time, Labour had a working majority in Parliament. One wonders whether Attlee felt in 1945, as Churchill had done in 1940, that his whole life had been but a preparation for this hour. If he did, he kept it to himself. Lord Jay, who worked as Attlee's assistant in Number Ten, recalls that on hearing the election result 'the first thing he did was to go to the Paddington Hotel and have tea with his daughter. I would infer from that that he was somewhat surprised by the result, but that he kept calm and got over his surprise fairly quickly.'

Once in office, Attlee seemed to have a very clear idea of the essentials of what his government was there to do. Kenneth Harris, his biographer, has seen the documents and set him in perspective. What did he think were the new Labour premier's priorities?

'Nationalization first. That was the big thing – socialism: the banner of the party for years had been public ownership, Clause Four in the 1918 constitution. Then the welfare state.'

Governmental priorities, of course, are not necessarily the same thing as personal priorities; Lord Longford, a personal friend and ministerial colleague of Attlee, recalls that

As far as I was concerned, Attlee didn't care a damn for nationalization. I was Minister of Civil Aviation for three years in his government and I didn't think he was the slightest bit interested, except when I took a decision which caused controversy and he then hauled me over the coals. As far as I was concerned, it was the poverty that really motivated him, all his years in the East End. Nationalization was just a party cause. He was absolutely heart and soul with the Labour Party, and nationalization was their thing. I think he left it to Herbert Morrison.

Kenneth Harris reinforces the point:

> All through the Thirties the party had been working on these immense blueprints for taking everything basic into public ownership, and Attlee, who was not only leader of the party but the expresser of the party's policies, had to give that the top priority. His personal attitude to it was not that of the party as a whole. He was not doctrinaire about nationalization. In fact, there's one quote in the biography in which he says, 'As long as the industry is being run well, it doesn't really matter whether it's nationalized or not.'

The priorities of the new administration were clearly reflected in the way Attlee organized Number Ten and his own workload, and in his own way of conducting business as head of the administration. Sir David Hunt, his private secretary in Downing Street, has very great respect for his former boss.

> I think his way of conducting business was perfectly admirable. He was really a very ordinary, but very efficient and very intelligent man and he carried these qualities to their highest possible degree. This is the way I look at him. I'm always puzzled when people talk about him as though he was mysterious, and his rise was strange. Alan Herbert wrote a poem – not a very good poem – called 'Man of Mystery'; Harold Macmillan said 'in many ways a mysterious character', and Michael Foot said 'as time went on, he got more and more incomprehensible'. To me, simply coming in as an ordinary official, it seemed that he had every capability for the job of Prime Minister. He was immensely assiduous. He always read all the papers. He had no obvious ambitions. He had not the slightest touch of vanity or conceit about himself. He started at the beginning of his day's work and went on till he got to the end and finished it, and he'd say, 'Is there anything more?' and I'd say 'No,' and he'd say, 'Goodnight.' And that, I think, is a very good way of conducting business.

What, then, was the key to this rather strange Victorian personality? Certainly the philanthropic impulse was powerful. Despite coming from an upper-middle-class family, he was what one might call a prototype social worker in the East End in the 1920s. In Lord Longford's view, this experience was central to Attlee's political life.

> I think he was what someone once called the last of the upper-middle-class social workers. Nowadays you don't find that, because on the whole people don't want it. Anybody turning up from the public schools and

trying to run a boys' club is resented, for various reasons; the professionals have taken over. To my eyes, this was what gave him his strength. Others may question that, but compared with Hugh Gaitskell, whom I of course admired enormously, he had been through it all, he had those years in what you could only call the front line of poverty.

He was remarkable, too, in terms of personal style, notably in his great economy in the use of words. As Douglas Jay acknowledges,

He was no orator. As to his use of language, it was marvellously abbreviated; I myself coined the phrase in my year at Number Ten that he never used one syllable when none would do, and I still think that's about the last word. There is a television film of the crowd outside Number Ten when the 1950 election was announced, with a crowd of journalists with a spokesman holding a microphone; Clem came out and the spokesman said, 'Mr Attlee, you've announced a general election. Is there anything you would like to say about the forthcoming general election?' 'No.'

Oratory, however, is not all declamation and efflorescence, as David Hunt reminds us:

I've been reading up a lot of his speeches in *Hansard*, and the vital thing is that oratory is an art indeed, but it is also a science. It has an aim, namely to persuade, to persuade people to do things. Now, in fact, Attlee was extremely persuasive. He was nothing like as sonorous as Churchill and he was indeed waspish, clipped and quick. If you were at a debate, for example, Churchill was admirable at the set speech at opening a debate. Very good, it rolled on and it was capital stuff. Then, normally, it was for Attlee to wind up, and he would wind up, very briefly, in a style which quite conveniently punctured and deflated Churchill and put his own followers into a good mood, and sent them cheerfully into the lobbies at the end of it. This, of course, you don't see in the printed text, but if you'd been there and heard the House of Commons, the way they were behaving, then you would know that it was thoroughly effective oratory.

It's said that he used to type his own speeches with two fingers on a battered typewriter and had little time for the black arts of the journalistic profession. Kenneth Harris recalls an anecdote told by Francis Williams, Attlee's press secretary, concerning the attempt to get a tape machine into Downing Street:

They thought they ought to have a tape machine in Number Ten, but Attlee didn't favour the idea at all. Francis said, 'Well, of course, it's a very versatile machine, you know, you can get the cricket results on it, for instance.' Attlee sucked his pipe for a moment, and silence meant consent, so they brought the thing in and it worked. But a few days later Attlee walked into Francis's room, rather angrily, and said, 'There's something gone wrong with this machine, all the Stock Exchange prices are coming in and mucking up the cricket results.'

When it came to dealing with Cabinet business, Attlee's personal efficiency came into its own. He was said to be a very good chairman, keeping everyone to the business in hand. Douglas Jay applauds his skill:

He was really, I think, an example to anybody as a chairman. He assumed that everyone there had read the papers. He didn't start by asking the author of the paper to say it all over again. He very often used to ask: 'Is there anyone here who disagrees with this paper?' And if there wasn't, then you could go straight on and adopt the conclusions. Nor did he fall into a bad habit which Harold Wilson got into at Cabinet meetings, commenting on each other member of the Cabinet after their speeches, which intolerably lengthened the proceedings.

If a colleague was not up to the job, moreover, he was quite ruthless in sacking people – though Douglas Jay thinks his reputation as an excellent butcher may have been 'rather exaggerated'. The exception was Frank Longford, who quite often wanted to resign but was talked out of it:

I'd write some rather hysterical letter, saying that my conscience didn't enable me to continue much longer – this was particularly over the dismantling of German industry when I was a minister – and he would write to me, in a very friendly way, 'My dear Frank, I have noted the point you mention. I hope to see you later. Yours ever, Clem.' Leaving one absolutely sunk; you couldn't get any further. I tried it two or three times and failed.

Longford ended up becoming First Lord of the Admiralty. How did Attlee persuade his reluctant colleague to run the King's Navy?

I think I did want to do it really, because I was getting pretty browned off. I'd been in Civil Aviation three years and I didn't know one end of an aeroplane from the other – either at the beginning or the end of the procedure. We'd been quite successful, in fact very, by some standards, and so I was very pleased really when he asked me to be First Lord of the Admiralty, which was rather more interesting than it might be, because I was on the Defence Committee, and that's when you saw him really controlling things, from the inside.

Did he not, then, try to talk the Prime Minister out of making the appointment?

Not really. I was pretty half-hearted. I said, 'I think I'm too eccentric, Prime Minister,' and he said, 'Oh well, the Navy survived Winston and Brendan Bracken, it will probably survive you,' and so that was that.

David Hunt reveals the existence of a file in Number Ten when he arrived which was referred to as 'Lord Pakenham's Conscience', with a special reference to his 'eloquent pieces about occupied Germany'. Lord Longford appreciated his master's forbearance on this subject:

He was marvellous about that. It was only later I discovered how anti-German he was, because he never told me. When he was discussing Germany with me, he never let on the fact that he was really rabidly anti-German. I didn't find out until much later, when I was chairman of the Anglo-German Association, and he was in the Lords. I asked him to be a patron, and then he paused. He didn't want to hurt my feelings, but, he said, 'I think I ought to tell you that I always disliked the Germans. Vi and I once had a German maid we liked very much, but she was an exception.' He really couldn't bear the Germans; a First World War kind of reaction.

Nor did he have any time for Europe, in the sense of the Coal and Steel Community, the precursor of today's European Union. The suggestion in 1950 that we might join it was never really a runner – not least, as Douglas Jay points out, because of the manner in which the opportunity was presented.

'What actually happened in 1950 was that the French delivered an ultimatum to the Cabinet, in which the government were asked to say they were in favour of the plan, without knowing the details, by eight o'clock the following morning.' Nevertheless, even if the Cabinet had had plenty of time, surely the decision would have been the same? 'There was no discussion of the merits because nobody knew what the merits were, and the discussion at Cabinet level never really got beyond that. But generally speaking, he had after all had the experience of two great wars, and I think he was naturally rather cautious as a result of that.'

Some people have drawn a contrast between Attlee's attitude to Europe and the institution-building which he, with Bevin, did brilliantly – for example, in the crucial role they played in the foundation of NATO, and indeed in starting the independence process in India, Burma and Ceylon. Why was there this mismatch of vision, as it were, with NATO and Empire on one side, and Europe on the other? Kenneth Harris attributes it to 'historical experience':

> One of the many committees which Attlee chaired during the war was concerned with postwar defence, defence of Europe and defence of the Anglo-American alliance. It was in that committee that what we came to know as NATO was worked out; and it was worked out much more by Attlee, who of course was obsessed by what the Germans might do if they could not be contained and controlled, than by Ernest Bevin, who, bless his heart, was fully engaged in winning the war on the home front. Bevin came into NATO only after a tremendous amount of thinking had been done by both parties during the war. For Attlee, having excogitated and to a great extent implemented NATO with the total backing of the United States, that was his ambition. Europe was really a secondary matter. He'd done the really big thing, and then, having done that, he wondered about whether he wanted to get too close to the Europeans, because he wasn't terribly keen on them.

Douglas Jay makes the further point that the two kinds of institution were not the same: 'Attlee was strongly in favour of international organizations. He was not in favour of supranational organizations. That was consistent throughout.'

Together, Clem Attlee and Ernest Bevin were the rock of the postwar government. With the big, tough trade union leader Bevin alongside the retiring figure of Attlee, and Stafford Cripps coming in as well, as Chancellor, the line could be held in Cabinet whatever the external circumstances, however severe the crises. It was a remarkably united government by any standards – not just Labour government standards. David Hunt recalls the strength of the duumvirate at its heart.

> Normally speaking, when any submission comes from a department, most ministers and prime ministers that I worked for have a nice way of delaying things by saying, 'Oh, we'll get a second opinion on that. Ask so and so. Ask the First Lord of the Admiralty, for example.' But if ever Attlee thought it necessary to ask for a second opinion, he'd say, 'Well, I'll have a word with the Foreign Secretary on that.' I don't think he ever thought about anyone else. And there is, of course, the famous story of the plot against him in 1947, when Stafford Cripps did indeed go to see him and said that he thought it would be a much better idea if Bevin became

Prime Minister, and Attlee picked up the telephone and said, 'I'll ask him.' He said, 'I've got Stafford here. He says you want my job.' Long pause. 'Thought so.' Put the phone down. 'He says, "No, he doesn't."'

Nevertheless, crises and disagreements there were, and these had to be managed. For example, a substantial proportion of the parliamentary party didn't like the government's foreign policy, the drive towards NATO; they wanted a third force between East and West. How did Attlee handle the dissenters on the back benches? Douglas Jay recalls examples of his tactics, which were not confined to the deployment of the speech-making skills described by David Hunt:

When it came to Dick Crossman, of whom he was not very fond, he did indulge in one sentence which you could call rhetoric, which I've always remembered. He said, 'I'm not much impressed by these critics of Mr Bevin, whose service to the labour movement is dust in the balance compared with his,' and that was never forgotten. There was another less well known one, a reply to a letter from Zilliacus, which I think was eighteen pages long, about all the sins of Mr Bevin, and all his mistakes, to which he replied, 'My dear Zilly, thank you for sending me your memorandum, which is based on an astonishing misunderstanding of the facts. Yours ever, Clem.'

As well as the crises Attlee had to weather on the foreign affairs side – the withdrawal from Empire, the Korean War and so on – there were others of an economic nature, and here the Prime Minister's own grasp was less sure. He did not seem to have a particularly good grasp of economics when trouble descended with a convertibility crisis in 1947 and a devaluation in 1949. Douglas Jay identifies his speech in August 1947, after the convertibility crisis, as 'one weak point in the whole record':

He was very tired, the subject was one he didn't like, and his speech didn't come off. Stafford Cripps, who spoke after him, winding up the debate, spoke with extraordinary effect. Generally speaking, Clem's attitude to economics was rather that it was a subject like medicine, which he didn't understand – and he knew he didn't understand it, which was very refreshing, unlike some people nowadays; he consulted people whose opinion he respected, and if necessary took a second or even a third opinion. In the case of the 1949 devaluation, when I was in very close touch with him, along with a few others, over about a fortnight, his attitude was that the gold was all running out; this was the only suggestion put forward for stopping it disappearing altogether before Christmas; and if nobody else among the experts had any alternative suggestion, then we'd better accept that one. And that, I think, was common sense.

Turning to the longer-term perspective on Attlee and his 1945–51 government, it is the welfare state that stands out for many as its greatest achievement. The National Health Service, the 'jewel in the crown', takes pride of place, perhaps, but there was much more too: family allowances; workmen's compensation, adequate for the first time; and many other measures, a whole range from cradle to grave, implementing the Beveridge Report. Yet there are many who say, with forty years and more of hindsight, that while it was a noble vision, we were simply too broke, not only at the time but subsequently, to sustain it. Kenneth Harris is of the opinion that these detractors demean the record of the pioneering postwar government.

It was a prodigious achievement to establish the welfare state, not only in terms of the opposition to it, particularly the opposition of the doctors, which was very considerable, and the opposition of a very large section of the Conservative Party – but not all the Conservative Party, by any means – and to structure it in the way they did. A tremendous amount was owed, of course, to Aneurin Bevan. It was a tremendous achievement and for thirty years it was the envy of the world – and to a very great extent it still is. And though we hear a great deal about what Mrs Thatcher has done to demean the welfare state, to criticize it, and to reshape and diminish it, the amount of damage that has been done to it is relatively small. Why? Because, whether people like it philosophically or not, they dare not do too much to it, because they know that even the Conservative Party, when polled, make it quite clear that they want it to go on, and it does go on and will go on.

Is this the key to Attlee's legacy, the anti-poverty impulse? In political terms, Lord Longford agrees, it is. He adds a sidelight on the relationship between Attlee and Beveridge which is perhaps telling as an illustration of the contingency of political life:

There was a moment when Arthur Jenkins, father of Roy, tried to bring Beveridge [who was a Liberal] into the Labour Party. There was a dinner arranged at the Oxford and Cambridge Club. Unfortunately these two great men, who'd known each other for many years, didn't hit it off altogether, because first of all Attlee fell asleep – he was very tired, he was Deputy Prime Minister – and when he woke up, Beveridge fell asleep. So there was hardly a moment, in my recollection, when both of them were awake. So this effort to bring him into the Labour Party didn't really get off the ground. We walked along Pall Mall and Arthur Jenkins, the eternal optimist, said to me, 'I think it went pretty well, don't you?' Actually, I can't imagine anything having gone worse.

It has been alleged that the creation of the welfare state was economically damaging to the country. Douglas Jay has no truck with this.

To suggest that the foundation of the welfare state somehow impaired the economy of the country would be absolute economic nonsense. All it did was to redistribute our internal income rather more fairly. Also, I think that some people forget that, not only was the welfare state in a number of respects established in those years, but this country, after all the wartime losses, actually had a balance of payments surplus in 1948 and 1950; and if you take the years from 1945 to 1950, in two out of three of those years we had a surplus in our balance of payments, and we had full employment throughout, and actually the rise in real income of the UK as a whole in those twenty-five years was higher than it's been in any twenty-five years since 1850, before or since that period.

Is this to say that the mixed-economy welfare state that Attlee put into place was responsible for those years of unparalleled prosperity? Douglas Jay does not go so far.

I don't say that it was responsible for it; many other things were responsible for it – sensible economic policies – but it was compatible with it. And compared with a balance of payments surplus in 1948, in 1988 we had a deficit of £15 billion. The deficit we have now is absolutely nothing to do with what we did in the first ten years after the war; it's to do with mistakes made since 1970. But that's another story.

Attlee's critics focus on another aspect of the economy as well as – as they would put it – the 'welfare burden': public ownership. There are very few people now who would defend the model of public ownership, the so-called Morrisonian model, on which those great 'commanding heights of industry', as they were called then, were brought into the state sector. Looking back, was this not a rather elephantine way of proceeding, in fact replacing one kind of autocracy, the private ownership autocracy, with another, the bureaucratic autocracy? Again, Douglas Jay would not accept this analysis wholesale.

All this is a matter of opinion, but I believe the truth is that public ownership is a suitable instrument for natural monopolies and for public utilities, but is not a suitable instrument for manufacturing industry. I think the trouble began when the attempt was made to extend it to manufacturing industry. But as far as the natural monopolies and the public utilities went, if you're going to have public ownership I think probably the Morrisonian instrument was as good as any; and if you look, for instance, at the record of the gas industry and the electricity industry over the thirty years when they were under that type of organization, their record is very remarkable both for expansion and for efficiency.

Kenneth Harris concurs, and doubts whether there was in any event a workable alternative.

There's another way of looking at it which to my mind illustrates the foolishness and lack of realism of many of the people who criticized the development of nationalization, at the time and in retrospect. Let's suppose that the Labour Party, or whichever party was in power or came to power in 1945, said, 'Let us go back to private enterprise,' even if it's a reformed private enterprise. How the devil could you have done it after six years of war, and after the slump of the mid-1930s? The country had moved into public ownership. We've been told that the greatest perpetrator of socialism was a submarine blockade during the war. The country was under siege. It would have been impossible, as a practical matter, whatever people wanted, to move rapidly away from the development into public ownership and reverse the process.

Many people would say that, for all Attlee's profound realism and lack of grandeur, he, as much as Ernest Bevin, was deluded by the feeling that we were only temporarily disrupted as a superpower, that once the economy had recovered, we would be back with the other superpowers, with pretty much of our Empire intact – not the Indian sub-continent bit, but certainly the African bit – and we were up there with the great power players for the foreseeable future and had to have all the associated trappings, including our own atomic bomb. David Hunt was the foreign affairs and defence private secretary in Number Ten. In his view, those assumptions which numerous critics now disparage as over-grand were almost universally shared at that time.

If that is a correct expression of what the policy was at the time, it is, I think, one which was accepted by public opinion, with no question of party differences at all. You could perhaps say that the Tory Party had slightly more reminiscences of greatness, and aspirations to continued greatness, that Attlee was more realist. But both he and his Cabinet, and the rest of them, did proceed, roughly speaking, on those lines – and they would have been very strange if they hadn't, in that they were representing the opinion of practically everyone. There were, of course, always people who would say, 'Ah, I'm afraid we're well past our prime,' but then you heard that in 1887, for example. I am not sure that Attlee was committed to the preservation of the Empire in Africa; I know, for example, that he was quite prepared to dispose of our special position in the Middle East. After all, the colonies in Africa were only a confounded nuisance. They were acquired simply; Africa was nothing but a nuisance bit of land that got in the way of the route out to India. That's why Egypt on the one hand, and the Cape on the other, were vital. We had to hang on to them. The rest was all nonsense. I believe myself that Attlee, although he would no doubt have agreed with the general opinion in the Colonial Office at the time that the African states were not yet ready for independence, that they would take a little more time to bring on, would certainly have contemplated the forthcoming deliverance from *all* these imperial ties, which after all were at that time costing us a very great deal of money.

Douglas Jay takes issue with the terminology of 'decline' from 'superpower' status, and applies some contextual perspective:

It seems to me that much nonsense is talked now about this being a superpower, and abandoning being a superpower. After all, the fact is that in the nineteenth century all the European powers, roughly speaking, acquired colonies. That epoch came to an end because of development within the colonies. It became impossible. We went through the same process as France and Belgium, Portugal and Spain, of granting independence. We did it rather better than the others did. You can call that declining from being a superpower; but what it really meant was the end of the old nineteenth-century imperialism, which everybody shared with us.

But this leaves out America. When the Cabinet Defence Committee had to find what aircraft they could to break the Berlin blockade in 1948, or when the Korean War started, they must have been aware that Britain was very much the junior partner in the Western Alliance. We still had a big navy, but the United States was what mattered. The defence ministers must have known, surely, that the game was up for Britain as a great power? Not at all, according to Lord Longford.

It didn't occur to me in that way at all. I've always said that after the war Attlee and Bevin created the Atlantic Pact. They took the initiative. America was relatively supine, really; when Marshall made his offer, Bevin grasped it, but there was tremendous initiative coming from here.

If we were the junior partner, we felt we were the more effective partner. So I don't think the idea of our being in some sort of mysterious way inferior, in the Attlee period at least, ever crossed my mind, and I don't know whether he ever said to himself, 'we've ceased to be important nowadays.'

Making the British bomb and not telling the Cabinet, though: that did seem to some to be hubristic. Or is this being ahistorical, reading back from where we stand now? Kenneth Harris thinks there is a danger of this.

It is wrong to create the idea that in 1945–50 the Labour government had no idea of how our power was running down outside the country in all kinds of ways and was pushing on with the same foreign policy that we'd had under Queen Victoria. That wasn't going on at all. The Attlee government was being criticized far more at the time, and not only by the Conservatives and public opinion, for pulling out than for staying in. Take, for instance, a notable example, the development of the Truman Doctrine. The Americans went into Greece and Turkey in 1947 because we told them we couldn't afford to stay there. Dalton, the Chancellor of the Exchequer, was saying all the time that we couldn't afford it, and we couldn't. In some cases, of course, we knew perfectly well that we would have to get out. We wanted to get out. But we couldn't just say it and do it because there would have been chaos. There was the oil issue, for instance, in Iran. We couldn't just say, 'Well, you can't hold these people down any more. You've got to get out.' What was going to happen to the oil? Similar considerations, of course, fouled up our policy towards Israel, or Palestine as it was then. The government of the day was perfectly well aware of what it was up against, and wanted to do something about it, to get out, not to stay in. India, of course, is the outstanding example.

British dependence on the United States became increasingly apparent, not only in the grant of base facilities for their B29 bombers on request in 1948, but particularly when the Korean War started. There was a Commonwealth brigade in Korea, but would it not be true to say that it was an American show, and that this set the pattern for all time thereafter? David Hunt emphasizes the role of – and Attlee's support for – the United Nations:

It was an American show in that the great bulk of the forces employed by the United Nations in Korea was, of course, American and South Korean – the South Korean forces were rather larger than the American. But Attlee was quite determined – he took the decision inside the day – that they should support the United Nations, and also, of course, but incidentally, the United States, by standing by them in their attempt to defend the Republic of South Korea. It was with this in mind that he concurred before any Commonwealth brigade arrived.

David Hunt went to Washington with Attlee in December 1950, when the Prime Minister had to restrain the US President after a slip at a press conference which gave rise to a public misapprehension that Truman had threatened to use the atomic bomb. But what of substance did the British premier achieve? David Hunt is in no doubt as to the impact of his presence.

First of all, he strengthened Truman's nerve; not merely in the war, but also against MacArthur, towards a proper way of treating generals who behaved as though they were proconsuls or satraps. Attlee's visit to Washington at that time was, I am quite sure, the first nail in the coffin of MacArthur, who was sacked later. I think that it also, very importantly, rallied United States public opinion.

But in British terms, in straight British power terms, Attlee failed in his attempt in December 1950 to reclaim the British veto over an American use of the atomic weapon, which we had had under the 1943 Quebec Agreement. Sir David thinks that in fact this was never on the cards.

It wasn't likely that he would get that. Dean Acheson was on the lookout, and when he had in fact pushed Truman that far, he was able to persuade the President that he couldn't go quite as far as that. Nevertheless, Attlee got something very close to a veto, a virtual veto; he announced as much to the House of Commons when he came back, and it was accepted as such, and was accepted as such by Churchill.

Musing further on the description of Britain as a 'junior partner' to the United States, Douglas Jay notes that not all the facts support the image of subordination:

When the Korean War started, there were more British warships in Japanese and Korean waters than there were United States warships. I happened to be sitting next to Attlee when he made this statement in the House of Commons. Winston was clearly astonished and thought it must be a mistake. I happen to know it wasn't, because I'd just had a letter from my brother who was commanding one of the British warships, and he had mentioned this remarkable fact that we had more of a navy there than the United States. That was only one instance; but on the general issue of being subservient to the United States and being a junior partner, the fact was that in 1946 and 1947 the real income of the United States was 50 per cent of the real income of the whole world. In recognizing that, Attlee wasn't being subservient, he and Bevin were simply recognizing the real facts of the situation, and to have acted otherwise would have been extremely foolish. As a matter of fact, if you count our so-called decline since then economically, on the fall in our percentage share of world trade and world production, the same applies to the United States. This isn't often mentioned.

The Korean War is one of the many hammer blows which afflicted Attlee's government in its last eighteen months. By now its once handsome majority had shrunk to six. How will Attlee, the understated man who nevertheless dominated his party for twenty years, be remembered? Could we ever see his like again? David Hunt thinks he would have done very well in the television age.

I think that's exactly the kind of thing that the television age would lap up. Because he was such an excellent man. He looked so honest – as a matter of fact, he *was* so honest. He spoke so sensibly, and he used the same kind of language that they like to use and, in my opinion, he was almost the ideal Englishman, in that he was the slave of duty; he was thoroughly methodical; he was a great believer in doing the day's work in the day. He dominated the Labour Party easily, because he was so much better than the others. And yet he wasn't the slightest bit conceited. It always surprised me. I used to say to myself, 'He *must* know he's both better and cleverer than all the rest of them, and why is it then that he's so modest?'

Frank Longford remembers him as 'an ethical giant'.

This moral sense came through very strongly. I'm bound to say that, in my opinion, he would never have fought his way to the top. It's possible to discuss the place of accident in the life of all these top people but as a man of fifty he hardly gets a mention in the Webbs' diaries, and then by the accident of the election of 1931 he found himself at the top and stayed there for twenty years. But he hadn't got the quality which would ever have led him to fight his way there and that was, in a sense, linked with the fact that he was morally superior.

Kenneth Harris agrees on both counts.

I think that if we found him at the top today, or near the top, he would have a very big impact. The times call for people like him. But whether he would be able to make the ascent to the top today, since the 1960s, is a very different matter. He owed a very great deal to the support of the trade union movement, which today is in the doghouse and has been there for nearly fifteen years. Attlee came up as a welfare worker, a man of great compassion, a man of caring, a man who went into the East End.

That wouldn't have gone down very well in the age of the yuppies, certainly. But, as Douglas Jay remarks, that is not to say that the age would not have benefited from his presence:

Michael Foot and, incidentally, Herbert Morrison were quite wrong in saying he was inscrutable and impossible to understand. I think it was quite simple. I happen to have an excuse for that view in that Attlee was in many ways very like my father, who was a Victorian Christian who believed in doing the right thing, doing his duty as Attlee would have said, and he simply stuck to that throughout. Because this type of individual is extinct nowadays, people think it could never have existed. But it *did* exist. I think that's the person he was, and I think if he appeared at the top now, he would be received with enormous relief by a great number of people.

10

Living with Winston

His Majesty's present Government intend, if we can, to bring election-eering to a full stop. These are not the times for party brawling. Of course, we shall answer attacks made upon us and give back as good as we get; but we shall do what we believe is right and necessary for the country in its present crisis, according to our convictions, without being dominated by the idea of winning or losing votes. We do not seek to be judged by promises but by results. We seek to be judged by deeds rather than by words. After six years, we have a right to have a fair try. Not for the sake of any class or party, but to surmount the perils and problems which now beset us.

Thus spoke Winston Churchill in a party political broadcast on BBC radio a few weeks after the electorate had put him in Downing Street once again in 1951. His words on ending strife were not the customary cant of routine political exchange. In his 'Indian Summer' premiership of 1951–5 he behaved as an elder statesman, almost above party. He made no attempt to dismantle the welfare state, or – steel and road transport apart – to undo the nationalizations of the Attlee government. Churchill's personal preoccupation was with foreign policy. He had foreshadowed the Cold War with his famous 'Iron Curtain' speech in 1946. But with Stalin gone in 1953, the ageing Churchill hung on at Number Ten for two more years in the hope of bringing it to a close, as he made plain on a trip to Washington in 1954:

I am of opinion that we ought to have a try for peaceful coexistence. A real good try for it, although anyone can see that it doesn't solve all the problems. But it may be that time, if it is accompanied by vigilance, will enable peaceful coexistence for a period of years to create a very different situation to the one so full of peril, so doom-laden as the present one, under which we live.

Closer to home, Churchill said his priorities were red meat and not getting scuppered, which one might translate as getting meat off the rations, getting the standard of living up, and not being ruined by the economic

crisis. Lord Boyd-Carpenter was Financial Secretary to the Treasury in the
new Conservative government of 1951. How did he remember the priorities
of the administration from his watchtower at the Treasury?

I think that was a fairly accurate summary. Of course, he was very
amusing when he sent for me to his house at Hyde Park Gate and offered
me Financial Secretary to the Treasury. I accepted and got up to go. 'Sit
down, my boy. Sit down.' And he talked for about half an hour, with
anxious people waiting about outside in the queue, and was very interesting. He said, 'Rab Butler' – who was the new Chancellor – 'and you
will have a lot of difficulties with the economy.' He said, 'I don't understand it.' He said, 'I was Chancellor of the Exchequer, you know, for five
years, and, you know, I never understood it.'

Policy priorities were one aspect of this premiership; another was the
question of personal style. Everybody has a grand impression of the great
sweeps of history, but what was it actually like in Number Ten? Anthony
Montague Browne, Churchill's Foreign Affairs Private Secretary from 1952
and later his constant companion, was in a position to observe the Prime
Minister's working patterns at close quarters. Did he run the country from
his bed, as has often been thought?

Not entirely, no. I think he tried to mirror that administration on what
he'd done during the war. It was more management, I think, perhaps,
than political government, in that sense. He liked to have his 'Overlords'
and the people he knew well and trusted, such as Lord Cherwell, to advise
him. His lifestyle was fairly relaxed. He'd always worked in bed in the
morning; he got up if there was a Cabinet, otherwise he'd work in bed.
But he was working. There were queues of people coming to see him, and
his budgerigar, Toby, sitting on his head and Rufus, the poodle, sitting on
his feet. And he would work until shortly before lunch. He'd have a long
working lunch, go to the House or not, and in the late afternoon he'd have
another rest. He took a good deal of rest.

Others sometimes got less rest. Lord Boyd-Carpenter recalled an occasion
which bore witness to the Prime Minister's timekeeping at the other end of
the day: 'I was winding up for the Government, so he sent for me to give me
my riding orders. The hour of my summons was eleven o'clock at night. I
finally got out of Number Ten just before three. My driver thought he'd
eaten me. But it was all enormous fun. My only regret was that I hadn't got a
tape.'

In some ways it seemed that Churchill wanted to recreate the war: not in terms of fighting it, but having his own people around him. His system of 'Overlords', the supervising ministers standing above the departments, represented in many ways another version of the War Cabinet. They were both cronies and trusted friends. And Lord Ismay, who had been with him throughout the war, came back. Did that experiment work? Or could you not, in fact, run British government in peacetime on that basis? Dr Paul Addison of Edinburgh University ponders on Churchill as a Cabinet man.

He had extensive experience of peacetime Cabinets as well, of course. And one thing which he practised extensively during that government was genuine Cabinet government – which is something that has fallen into disuse, I think, since. But he had memories of genuine Cabinet government under Asquith and that, I think, was his favourite government of all time, when all ministers had felt capable of discussing all issues. The 'Overlords' were an interesting experiment, in trying to coordinate areas of policy in which he perhaps didn't feel entirely confident himself.

Churchill certainly took a romantic view of Cabinet – and, as Lord Boyd-Carpenter stressed, thoroughly enjoyed it: 'as he generally lunched about half-past one, even though the business really might well have practically been worked through by half-past twelve and ministers were looking anxiously at their watches, thinking about their lunch engagements and so on, he would carry on the Cabinet until his lunchtime at half-past one. And we jolly well had to wait.'

He has, however, been regarded as terribly inefficient, compared to Attlee who would never let ministers use one syllable in Cabinet where none would do. Anthony Montague Browne disagrees:

I don't know if that's inefficient, libertarian or just a liking of oratory but no, I wouldn't have said he was inefficient at all. He loved discourse. He was a great historian, of course, and he used to draw parallels and I think this had its own style. The Private Office didn't go into the Cabinet unless they were summoned. So I've never sat in a Cabinet; but I used to dodge in and out and occasionally deliver messages; one always had bits and pieces. Indeed, I remember a scene of some confusion. I went in. I happened to have been copying out Walter Raleigh's last letter to his wife which hadn't been widely published. I had it in my hand as I went in and he said, 'What have you got in your paw?' And I said, 'Raleigh's last letter to his wife.' 'Let me see.' None of the Cabinet could hear this. He read very slowly and then tears poured down his cheeks and in a broken voice he said, 'That bloody James the First.' And the Cabinet were, indeed, utterly astounded. They couldn't think what tidings I'd brought him. But I think it was a discursive style which he enjoyed. And I don't think it was a monologue; I think he was perfectly prepared for people to answer him.

Lord Boyd-Carpenter agrees.

Indeed, he was; and not only at Cabinet. One of his great habits was to get the morning papers at midnight and look at them, and alarm departmental ministers – I was Minister of Transport – by ringing you up at home, about eight o'clock in the morning, before you had breakfast. 'What is this in your department? What are you doing about this?' One hadn't got to the office; one hadn't even seen the papers; one didn't know anything about it, and had to make some sort of noises to suggest one was dealing with it. But I thought he kept ministers very much on their toes and when people said he was failing I could only say that my life would have been much easier if he had been failing. He seemed to me too alert.

Churchill turned Cabinet meetings into great occasions. People felt that the sweep of history was going on beneath them, as it were, and they looked forward to Cabinets, which probably hasn't been the case all that often since. But there is also a constitutional significance to his approach. For example, he is the only Prime Minister we know of who has brought a key nuclear weapons question – whether or not to go ahead with the H-bomb in 1954 – to the Cabinet for full discussion before a decision was taken.* Subsequent Prime Ministers of both parties, Macmillan apart, have taken these questions away from full Cabinet, again limiting its role to that of giving the nod at the last minute. But Churchill conducted no fewer than three full discussions on the H-bomb, in part because ministers had asked for more. Paul Addison identifies two contributory factors in Churchill's handling of this episode. First, a specific historical and political contingency:

If you look back at why the Attlee government had kept the decision to a small circle of people, it may have been because within that Attlee Cabinet it might have been very difficult to work that decision through. Churchill may have had more confidence in a Conservative Cabinet that they would have been united on that issue.

But secondly, a consistent preference for openness:

---

* Macmillan almost deserves a similar place in the history of Cabinets and the bomb. But he kept his private doubts about the robustness of the Nassau Agreement away from the full Cabinet (see section 6 above).

Throughout his life I think one of the hallmarks of Churchill was that he was not afraid of disclosure. He believed in disclosure. His war memoirs, for example, which were being published at this period, put masses of wartime documents into the hands of thousands of readers all the way around the world. Now, I don't think any British politician has ever liberated so much material from the Public Record Office so quickly as Churchill. And I think it's part of his aristocratic style that he felt that he could confront issues and carry people with him, and that he needn't keep many things secret.

And, as Lord Boyd-Carpenter says, all historians have reason to be grateful to him for that.

For their part, Cabinet ministers were certainly ready to assert their position. Take the minutes of the meetings that took place in the Cabinet in 1954 when Churchill had come back from the United States on one of the Cunarders and engaged in personal diplomacy with Molotov, sending the Russians a telegram asking for a summit: the Cabinet was enraged – particularly Lord Salisbury – and it looked as if some ministers might resign. They upbraided the grand figure of Churchill and said he must not do it again. And he took it from them. This suggests that Conservative ministers in that era were great figures in their own right; Churchill might be a legendary world figure, but they were going to make sure that he observed the niceties of Cabinet government. As Lord Boyd-Carpenter points out, 'he had a very high-grade Cabinet, with a lot of very senior people with very distinguished careers already behind them who were not afraid and weren't worried too much if they were sacked. And, of course, Lord Salisbury resigned about once a week.'

Anthony Montague Browne identifies another factor: 'He had an heir apparent in the shape of Anthony Eden, and that is an act of self-castration. And you're not nearly as powerful and people are not so frightened of you, if your heir is sitting there and it's quite visible you're not going to be there all that long.'

Churchill in Parliament, of course, was a great set-piece. He loved the House of Commons and the great parliamentary occasions. But did he still dominate the House in these years, despite his growing physical frailty? Lord Boyd-Carpenter is in no doubt:

Oh yes. Particularly in answers to Parliamentary Questions. In those days, Prime Minister's Questions began at question number forty-five, and therefore, if the other ones went slowly, it was possible that he wouldn't be reached. And, when that situation appeared to be developing, he got very jumpy indeed. I remember once I was sitting beside him and Arthur

Salter was answering Treasury questions with me, and giving, as he generally did, very long answers. The old man got very agitated. Gaitskell got up and asked a question and he said, 'Don't answer him. Don't answer him,' patted me on the knee and said, 'You wouldn't make a long answer like that, my boy, would you?' Coward that I am, I said I wouldn't.

Anthony Montague Browne knew how much preparation had to go into the Prime Minister's appearances at the Despatch Box, but also what the great parliamentarian could still achieve off the cuff:

> He required a lot of preparation always. And he had a most able man who did it for him called Peter Oates who worked very, very hard on these questions. But he still had the great impromptu in his very old age. Woodrow Wyatt got up and said, 'Will the Prime Minister say something about the empty chair policy?' – that is, going ahead without France. Woodrow Wyatt had just been disavowed by his constituency, and the Prime Minister – it was almost the last question he answered in his life – got up and said, 'I think the Honourable Member would be more inter-ested in the empty seat policy.' He had a very sharp repartee. He could retort, but he could be knocked off his perch, as we saw.

Lord Boyd-Carpenter recalls another instance of this quick-fire wit: 'There was the splendid one with Mr Paling. Mr Paling, who was a Labour Member, was so angry at some answer Winston had given that he shouted at him, "Dirty dog," which was quite outside the rules. The old man swung slowly round towards Mr Paling and said, "The Honourable Member knows what dirty dogs do to palings."'

When Churchill returned to office in 1951, he famously looked around Attlee's private secretaries and said 'Drenched with socialism' – which was monstrously unfair. But he did seem to become very heavily dependent, very quickly, upon the Civil Service, particularly on the Cabinet Secretary, Norman Brook, Jock Colville in Number Ten, and Christopher Soames, his Parliamentary Private Secretary. Anthony Montague Browne describes it as a 'selective' dependence:

> I don't think he knew the Civil Service very far down, but Norman Brook was absolutely the *sanspareil* of advisers and he sought his advice on every possible subject. He used to say of him, 'He has a very good mental muscle.' And Norman Brook would sigh, whatever he was asked to do, and say, 'I will take it on board,' and did. Beyond that, I don't think he had the same relationship with Edward Bridges, the Head of the Treasury, who had a wonderfully austere, first-class brain, but was a very different

sort of figure. Norman Brook was a very executive figure. I don't think the Prime Minister's relationship with the Civil Service went beyond a very few people; you can count them on two hands.

Foreign affairs was his great love, and it was in this field that we might expect his capacity or inclination to meddle to have been particularly evident. He was, for example, a very reluctant decolonizer, and gave Anthony Eden at the Foreign Office terrible trouble over withdrawing from the Suez base – not, according to Lord Boyd-Carpenter, without justification: 'One can argue that, in view of what happened the year after we'd withdrawn from the Suez base, he was right. I've often felt that it would have been much better if his view had prevailed and we might have been spared the whole Suez episode. His instinct was against it, and, oddly enough – or not so oddly, really, because his instinct was very sound – was probably right.'

Churchill was an Empire man. He'd come to manhood at the zenith of the British Empire and it would have seemed inconceivable to him that it could disappear in his lifetime. As he said in 1940, he hadn't become the King's First Minister to preside over the dissolution of the British Empire. Did he really believe at all in the Commonwealth idea as any surrogate for the old Empire? Paul Addison thinks that it was gaining a place in his scheme of things, albeit a different one from that occupied by the old Empire:

> I think that by this time of his career, strange to say, the Commonwealth, in the sense of the white dominions, was actually becoming rather more important in his thought than it had been before. And the reason is, of course, that the old Empire, which he had known and loved when he was a subaltern, when he had fought on the North West Frontier of India and in the reconquest of the Sudan, that was collapsing at this period. But he still thought of Britain as a world power, of course, and, although he didn't like the transition from Empire to Commonwealth, I think, for example, in his dealings with Nehru he took great pains to try to keep on good terms, and flattered him, calling him 'the light of Asia'. Now, this is a sign that Churchill wanted to keep this group of nations together, and he did so, I think, because he thought that in a world of the two superpowers the Commonwealth might have a future. That's something we rather forget now. We tend to think that the Commonwealth was always written off as only a pale imitation of Empire, but people in the mid-fifties still thought that it had a future as a power bloc.

Churchill's great desire, in the last days of his last premiership, was to end the Cold War. Once Stalin had died, he thought the moment had come to try to stop it in its tracks – as it were, reversing his famous Fulton 'Iron Curtain' speech of 1946. Was that the real reason he hung on until the bitter end in 1955? Was this the great priority for Anthony Montague Browne, as his Foreign Affairs Private Secretary?

> Yes. That was his major theme, undoubtedly. He used to say there was a more temperate breeze blowing from Soviet Russia, and that we must grasp these opportunities. He had the 'great man' theory that, if people met at the top, all could be solved – which, of course, was an illusion. I think that he had many other thoughts in his mind at that time, but he was very keen on that. He wanted to be seen as the peacemaker. When he got the Nobel Prize for Literature, I told him that he'd been awarded the Nobel Prize and he was frightfully excited. Sat up. And I added, 'for literature'. And his face fell. He'd wanted the Nobel Peace Prize. He saw that as the greatest opportunity and he got very angry with the Cabinet at the time when he was coming back from America on the *Queen Elizabeth* and took the view that his overtures were being undermined by the Foreign Office – which was totally true. He was rather contemptuous of the Foreign Office.

By this stage, though, after his stroke in 1953, his health was really very perilous indeed. Even before the stroke, he hadn't been the same man as he had been during the war. Nevertheless, Lord Boyd-Carpenter warns against writing him off too soon: 'He was still a very considerable personality and figure. Of course, I wasn't close to him during the war. I was an exceedingly junior officer and never thought of meeting Prime Ministers. So I can't make a fair comparison. But I think it's very easy to exaggerate his decline. He was, I thought, a very considerable figure right to the end.' Still, it is hard to avoid the conclusion that in 1953 his political career was saved by the summer recess. If it hadn't been for that, the doctor's minute could not have been doctored, as it were, and the fact that he had almost died, and was not in full command of his capabilities for at least a couple of months, could not have been disguised. Anthony Montague Browne was actually in Number Ten when Churchill suffered the stroke:

> I think the recess undoubtedly saved him politically. I don't think he was near death. He could still speak and take things in, and he made a whole series of very melancholy remarks. He went down to Chartwell. But the recess did give him the breathing space. And there was another aspect: it wasn't just that he wanted to have a detente with Soviet Russia; it was that he didn't think that his visible successor was going to be up to the job. He made that quite clear.

This 'visible successor', of course, was Anthony Eden. Did Montague Brown think Eden's own ill-health was a factor in Churchill's lack of confidence in him? 'Perhaps. Perhaps because of the effects the ill-health had on his temperament, on his extraordinary petulance and taking decisions at the snap of a finger and flying into a fearful rage. He was becoming increasingly concerned at Anthony Eden's ability to be a Prime Minister – sadly, well justified.'

If we look at Churchill in the long-term perspective, he appears as the last of the grand Victorian political figures, in that he had no time for the black arts of television. There's the famous occasion on which he made a pilot programme, which was terrible; he treated the cameras almost like a public meeting. And he had no time for the ordinary journalist. He was not a man of the modern communications age. And yet, as Lord Boyd-Carpenter reminds us, he could certainly communicate:

> I remember the day he had resigned. He'd been to the Palace and resigned. He summoned a number of ministers whom he hadn't seen earlier in the day, to Number Ten, and gave us a farewell talk. I remember the scene vividly – a stormy spring evening, with rather stormy light coming into the Cabinet Room – and he talked to us for an hour and a half about the future; and his theme, the whole way through, was the need to stay in close friendship with the United States. Indeed, he went so far as to say that if we and the United States remained friendly all would be well in the end and peace would be preserved. And, if we fell apart, then he could see nothing but disaster. It was a most moving thing. It really was, I suppose you could say, his political testament.

That kind of thing could move people in the flesh, as it were, and would still do so today. But if it were filtered through a television camera, or in the knockabout of contemporary elections, it would seem wildly out of place, even more than General de Gaulle's press conferences did in the 1960s. Paul Addison, acknowledging that Churchill's notion of how to communicate with the electorate was 'very antiquated', reminds us that

> after all, we are talking about a man in his early eighties, whose formative political experiences lay fifty years in the past by this time. Now, his view of how people found out about politics was that major political statements were made in the House of Commons, they were reported in the press and people then read about them in the newspapers. He had used the radio during the war but rather reluctantly. And it's interesting that he didn't use it again between 1951 and 1955. He reverted to the idea of parliamentary politics, and he disliked the impact of television because he

thought it was taking over the role which the House of Commons should have as the medium through which people found out about politics. And he would have hated what people are now describing as the 'short attention span' version of politics. He liked people to concentrate upon reasoned argument in a speech which might last anything up to an hour or an hour and a half. And that was his idea of how politics should be conducted.

Lord Boyd-Carpenter believes there might have been possibilities for taking advantage of the new media: 'This scene at Number Ten: we were there the best part of two hours, and it was very exciting and very moving. I've often wondered whether it wouldn't have been a superb television performance, given the background that it was the end of his career.' Usually, however, if Churchill wanted to have an impact on public opinion through the press, he would pick up the phone to a press lord: 'One of his friends . . . he hoped.' And, as Montague Browne recalls, he could be very effective:

He had as close friends Lord Camrose, Max Beaverbrook and so on and so on – . Esmond Rothermere. And they might not do exactly what he said, but he could always talk to them and he was very persuasive. He wasn't always a bully by any means. He could charm a bird off a tree. I've heard him cajole, most persuasively and successfully. As to the television, he had two utterly bad starts with it and they just weren't successful, and he hated the sight of himself on television, which was strange, because on newsreels, when he was making public speeches, he was frightfully good.

In the long-term perspective, with hindsight, what is perhaps most striking of all is how Churchill was thirty years ahead of the game, in many ways, on the Cold War. His brave attempt to bring it to an end before it was more than ten years old, in 1953–5, was in effect an attempt to bring about what has happened in East–West relations since 1985.

Montague Browne does not quite accept this assessment: 'I think that one must realize that the relaxation has come mostly from the other side, from Gorbachev. Whereas in those days we were still confronting an implacably hostile Soviet Russia. I think he had illusions about this. I never took the Foreign Office line at all, which made me exceedingly unpopular, I can assure you.' And this even though, of course, he was himself a Foreign Office man: 'I was most unpopular, particularly with Anthony Eden's private office. But I think he still had the illusion of the friendship of Stalin, and he said something extraordinary to me once. He said, "Stalin never broke his word to me." In technical detail that's probably true. But Stalin's undoubted intention and purpose was to do us in.' And while the big effort on East–West detente came after Stalin had gone to his reward, Montague Browne insists that 'it would have been a mistake to consider his successors to be anything but following the same general pattern of international policy. Perhaps not domestic policy.'

Certainly Churchill had a great animus against the Foreign Office. He used to decry Anthony Eden for becoming 'Foreign Officeissmus'. This too Montague Browne well remembers:

> He used to say, 'I cannot stand the Foreign Office. A cowardly lot of shuffling scuttlers.' And the Treasury were 'all mean swine'. And then he'd gaze round us and say, 'Always excepting my Private Office,' with a grin. He thought the Foreign Office would always come off second best in any negotiation. They would present the foreign country's point of view most admirably, but they would not put ours across; and I think he was right.

Looking at it from the perspective of the entire sweep of postwar history, however, surely the Treasury and the Foreign Office were right, even to the extent to which they doubted our capability of sustaining a great power role. For really, even then – and even with Churchill's enormous personal prestige weighing heavily in the balance – the role of honest broker between East and West was beyond our capacity. Wasn't the attempt the sustaining of a great illusion? Paul Addison sees a logic in Churchill's policy:

> What better way to break out of the predicament of being a power which is overcommitted than to try to put an end to the Cold War? I'm sure that this was part of Churchill's strategy for saving Britain as a great power. And, after all, one of the things that a power in the second rank can do is to seek to act as a broker. It may not be able to determine events, but it can play that role. So it strikes me that that was a remarkable vision Churchill had which would have enabled defence expenditure in Britain to be greatly reduced. And, of course, he added, in a typical Churchillian flourish, that people would be able to work a four-day week; there would be the leisured masses whereas once there had been the leisured classes. And we mustn't build Churchill up so much that we forget that he was always a party politician. While he was ill with his heart attack, Beaverbrook wrote an obituary of Churchill in the summer of 1953 in which he attributed Churchill's bid for detente with Russia partly to party politics. After all, the Labour Party in 1951 had campaigned on the theme that Churchill was a warmonger – a theme which Churchill greatly resented – and I think one of the aims of his final premiership was to prove once and for all that he wasn't a warmonger, and to dish the Labour Party on foreign policy.

That campaign, of course, had included the famous headline 'Whose Finger On The Trigger?', which Lord Boyd-Carpenter believes probably lost a lot of seats.

Party politics aside, Montague Browne stresses that Churchill 'did believe that the great powers should run the world. I remember Evelyn Shuckburgh, who was Anthony Eden's Private Secretary, saying to me, "The Prime Minister's foreign policy is monstrous. It seems to consist of kowtowing to the great powers and bullying the little ones." And I said, "But, Evelyn, have you tried it the other way round?"'

This must have required a high degree of subservience on Churchill's part to his old friend from Algiers days in the war, General Eisenhower. Perhaps 'crawling' is the wrong word – he was too grand a man to crawl – but there were a great many 'My dear friend' letters constantly being drafted and sent across the Atlantic. Montague Browne agrees:

I think that he did have the illusion that American policy would be to some extent dictated by a sentimental regard for old friendships. And, of course, it wasn't. In many ways, American policy was anti-British. I remember annoying him very much by saying that the object of the Secret Service was to spy on our friends, because we knew what our enemies were doing anyway. He disagreed most vehemently. But it was certainly the case that he was making the running in that friendship all the time and, of course, Eisenhower, who was a man of great integrity but limited intelligence, thoroughly resented that sort of gentle, persuasive stuff. He thought it would be far better if he didn't communicate, I'm afraid. Although he was very fond of the old man – indeed, in 1959 I went and stayed in the White House with Winston Churchill, with Eisenhower – and the friendship was very real, it was personal rather than anything that influenced policy.

Did he think that Churchill's getting the atomic bomb, as it were, after the successful test in 1952 – and, even more so, the decision to go ahead with the hydrogen bomb – make him think that really we *were* still a great power? Did this perhaps contribute to the illusion? Montague Browne thinks it may have, 'if illusion it was. Remember, at that time, we still had the second most effective air force in the world and the second most effective navy. And not a bad army at all. We still had conscription. I don't know. I think he looked on it as part of the ironmongery of modern warfare.'

Again with hindsight, it would seem that Churchill was still looking at the wrong target: he was thinking of Empire, keeping as much of the Empire together as he could, forging closer links with the dominions, with the Commonwealth, when in fact it was Europe that was the rising force. What had happened to his vision of Europe on which he had been so eloquent in opposition in the 1940s? When he came back into office it was as if that had never been.

Lord Boyd-Carpenter would not go so far as that: 'I think that's an overstatement. His great concern was relations with the United States. That was really what mattered, from the point of view of world peace and all the rest of it. On Europe, he was apt to be a little irritated, particularly by the French, and unenthusiastic, but realizing we'd got to live with them.'

It strikes one, too, that this era of Churchill's last premiership was that of the key economic moment, when West Germany, above all, surged ahead in the early fifties with the great investment boom and export-led recovery; and we faltered. It does seem that, with Walter Monckton as Minister of Labour being pressed to appease the unions at all costs, and with British industry being allowed to wallow in ever more favourable terms of trade, the great economic opportunity of the postwar period perhaps slipped away. And, as Lord Boyd-Carpenter has said, Churchill had no feel for economics.

Addison makes the point that Churchill was important 'for what he didn't do as well as for what he did do':

One thing we often forget is that he was leader of the Conservative Party from 1940 until April 1955; and, in a sense, I think, the effect of that on the Conservative Party was very far-reaching. Churchill caused a kind of vacuum in domestic policy-making which was never entirely filled up by R. A. Butler or Harold Macmillan or others who attempted to fill it, and I think there was no overall strategy – grand strategy – in domestic policy after 1951. And that had two consequences, of course. On the one hand it meant that the universal welfare state, which Labour had bequeathed in 1951, was by and large taken over with a certain amount of tinkering around the edges, mainly due to desire for economy in the first instance. It also meant that there was no conception of a radical economic policy in 1951, though there were people about in the Conservative Party who were what you might call proto-Thatcherites, like Brendan Bracken, or, indeed, Beaverbrook. Or Oliver Lyttelton, who could have constituted the core of a more economically radical approach. And I suppose, from the Thatcherite point of view, that's a great act of omission by that government.

Boyd-Carpenter thinks this assessment is a little overstated.

Churchill was very concerned when he came in in 1951 because it had been said by the Labour Party that a Conservative government would be devastated by strikes, paralysed by strikes. Therefore, he appointed Walter

Monckton, a great advocate, a great conciliator, with riding orders to see that there wasn't a strike, see that the employers were pushed, if necessary, into making further and further concessions. And this, in the long term, obviously did harm to the economy, though in the short term it bought industrial peace. But as soon as he'd resigned – I remember this because I was Minister of Transport at the time – we had a railway strike which lasted three weeks and they then went back for not a penny more than they'd had before the strike began, and we began to toughen up. Which bears out the idea that he was perhaps a little obsessed with the need to conciliate the unions to an excessive degree.

Churchill in Number Ten was not really terribly interested in domestic or economic affairs. If you look at the minutes from the Number Ten papers, now declassified, if there was a meeting on welfare, at which he would reluctantly have to take the chair, he would use the phrases he'd used as President of the Board of Trade in Asquith's government: 'We must bring the law of averages to the rescue of the millions.' And there were one or two phrases which made him glow. But he was never one to get into the technocracy of an ever more complicated welfare state. Was this a question of lack of ability or lack of inclination? Anthony Montague Browne tends towards the latter interpretation: 'He was capable of going into technicalities. One of his remarks, many years before, was to his advisers at the Board of Trade. He said: "Oh, I understand the figures all right. I just want to put some revivifying ginger into them." And earlier, when he was asked to do some job – probably in Asquith's day – he said that he didn't want to be locked up in a soup kitchen with Beatrice Webb.'

Many people have said he was really an Asquithian Liberal and not a Conservative at all. Paul Addison agrees. 'Yes, he was. In instinct I think he was. But of course, by 1951 he'd been out of touch with social and economic policy since 1929 and it's doubtful whether, even as Chancellor of the Exchequer, he'd fully grasped economic policy. So he had only the phrases left. He had the phrases but no longer the facts.'

Looking again from the long-term perspective, it could be said that his legacy to Anthony Eden was to ruin his chance. Eden was kept waiting for too long. He had a nervous disposition and was in many ways not at his peak, to put it charitably, when he finally did take over in April 1955. Is this a fair judgement? Lord Boyd-Carpenter thinks not:

If you recall the dates, Anthony had this operation in which he suffered so terribly from the mistake by the surgeon – a cruel mistake – who cut the gall bladder; and that was several years back, in 1953. And so he was a sick man, a very sick man, from then on. I don't think there was any question of his being appointed before – and indeed, if he had been, and then had had that operation, it would have been even more disastrous.

Is Lord Boyd–Carpenter hinting perhaps that Eden shouldn't have been the heir apparent? That it should have been Rab Butler, perhaps?

I was very close to Rab Butler, at the time, and so this touches on an area where I have some bias. I think Rab would have been a much better Prime Minister. I remember when Anthony succeeded we were all saying it's a pity he knows nothing about economics or social security or finance, but at least we shall be all right with foreign affairs. That was rather ironic.

Indeed.

Did Churchill perhaps begin to feel increasingly that Eden wasn't the man, and to regret that he was heir apparent? Was this one reason – another reason – why he clung on so long? Anthony Montague Browne is certain that this is so.

I think it was increasingly apparent to him that he wasn't the right man. Whether he would have thought Rab was, I rather doubt. But there weren't very many horses in that particular race. I think he always had some sort of prejudice against Rab. Possibly because of Rab's Munich stand at the time he was Under Secretary at the Foreign Office; I think he was considered a Munichois by Churchill, and was allegedly opposed to his appointment as Prime Minister in 1940. There are many stories. But there's another thing, which was very unfair to Rab because physically he could not have taken any part in the war – he had a disabled arm. But he took a keen account of war records and Anthony Eden, of course, had the Military Cross from the First World War. He was never very cosy with Rab. He didn't feel at ease with him.

From a political historian's point of view, there seems to have been a kind of paralysis in British politics, certainly from 1953 to 1955, in the last two years of the 'Indian Summer' premiership. Paul Addison thinks this was so, but that the context is important:

I think we have to put that in perspective. We're now used to the idea, due to events I think since the 1960s, that politics should take the form of constant strife and constant reorganization of everything and that continuous revolution is the way to success in the modern world. Churchill, partly because of old age, was at this period a genuine Conservative, I think, in the early 1950s. He didn't have the energy to devote to anything except one or two major issues. And you can argue that, after all the reorganization that had taken place between 1940 and 1951, there was room for a period, an interlude, of tranquillity in British politics; and that if there are critical failures, they are critical failures in the late 1950s and 1960s, when the state of Britain's economic decline was much clearer than it was in the early 1950s.

For all Churchill's lack of energy and lack of interest in many of the details of domestic policy, this was the period when Lord Boyd-Carpenter, at Transport, was getting the first motorways programme under way, modernizing British railways, replacing steam engines with diesels, and so on. Did Churchill take any interest in all this?

'Oh, yes. He gave very full support. He gave support with the beginning of the motorway programme, because even though I had come from the Treasury, I had some difficulty in view of the sums involved in extracting the necessary funds. He was extremely helpful. He was interested in transport and very progressive in his views on it.'

The biggest question, obviously, is how will history remember him: this wonderful grand old man who perhaps sustained illusions that we were a great power, which we shed painfully after Suez, and that we were still a formidable economic nation, which our manufacturing decline in the Sixties, Seventies and Eighties throws into a very sharp and depressing relief. Did he perhaps do an unwitting disservice to the nation he loved so much in that being who he was, what he was, he enabled us to delude ourselves for very much longer than most other Prime Ministers could have? Anthony Montague Browne believes not.

I wouldn't say that. I don't think so. I think that the transition from being a really great world power downwards is a very difficult one and one that can hardly be managed. It runs itself. He had a phrase about that sort of thing: 'You cannot ignore the facts for they glare upon you.' I rather liked – and I think the nation liked – the romantic side of his belief, which was a very noble one; he took a very proper pride in our history and the fact that where we had been, people were happier and where our writ ran there was not much murder and look what happened when we cleared out.

How, then, does Montague Browne think history will remember that last premiership?

I think as an anti-climax, of course, to the war, because if it could be said of any single man that he won the war, it would have been said of him. You can't say that, of course. But I think an anti-climax, and it is questionable whether he was right to become Prime Minister for the second time at all. But you must again go back to what were the alternatives.

When the wartime coalition broke up, he was in tears, and he said: 'The light of history will shine upon your helmets.' How does Lord Boyd-Carpenter think the light of history will shine upon his last helmet?

I think very favourably. Obviously, it can't be compared with the war, when he, almost alone, in 1940 took the firm decision not to play ball with Hitler's proposed armistice and discussions but to fight on, when all the advice of experts and everything was that we were in a hopeless position, the Channel coast occupied, and all we could do was settle. He made it quite clear – and he was really the only one at the top level – that we were going to fight on, and that was one of the great decisions of history. No subsequent administration can touch that for importance. But he did see us through quite a difficult time. He inherited a pretty bad economic situation; he inherited a period of a certain amount of disillusion; and he saw us through them. It was a not unsuccessful episode, though plainly less dramatic and less important than the first.

Historians have to be a bit brutal, in a way; they have to put romanticism and personal affection on one side in reaching their judgements. It's a cruel question, but it has to be asked: should Churchill have been allowed an 'Indian Summer' premiership? Does Paul Addison think that he should perhaps have given way to a younger man in the late 1940s?

Had he followed what you might call the ideal course from the point of view of the Conservative Party, he would have resigned at the end of the war as leader of the party and focused on his war memoirs and given the Conservative Party that period of opposition in order to discover a new leadership and a new set of policies. By 1951, I think, there was a vacuum which had been created and it was too late to do very much about it.

Churchill was the last person in the world to underestimate the importance of luck in politics, and he was, in a sense, very lucky in that final administration because many of the brutal postwar decisions had been taken – in India, in Palestine, in domestic affairs, over austerity rationing and so on – these had been taken by a very hard-bitten Labour government, between 1945 and 1951. And, in a sense, what Churchill was able to preside over, very graciously, was the easing of these constraints; and he was able to preside, I think, in his own case through luck rather than through judgement, over a rather more enjoyable society in the early 1950s.

11

Living with Anthony

Ladies and gentlemen, in this field of industrial relations I am particularly anxious to see the growth of what I've often called 'partnership in industry'. And I use the word 'partnership' – as the Minister of Labour did yesterday – in its widest sense. I include in it joint consultation, the giving of full information to employees about the affairs of the companies in which they work, and also profit-sharing in a number of forms, particularly when it offers opportunities for employees to hold shares, and so acquire a real stake in the enterprise in which they work.

That is the forgotten Anthony Eden: Eden the progressive Tory reformer, never happy with the class-ridden basis of old-style politics. But the Eden premiership is remembered for one thing only – Suez, the crisis which brought him down, his promise unfulfilled, less than two years after he entered Number Ten. On the evening of 3 November 1956, after the Royal Air Force had attacked Egyptian airfields, and with British and French troops about to land at Port Said to wrest the Suez Canal from Colonel Nasser, Eden broadcast to the nation.

All my life I've been a man of peace. Working for peace, striving for peace, negotiating for peace. I've been a League of Nations man and a United Nations man and I'm still the same man, with the same convictions, the same devotion to peace. I *couldn't* be other, even if I wished. But I'm *utterly* convinced that the action we have taken is right.

Three days later, American pressure brought the Anglo–French invasion to a halt. Eden wanted to carry on, but his Cabinet colleagues held him back.

It had all looked so different when – at last – Eden had succeeded Churchill as Prime Minister in April 1955. In many ways it was a glowing inheritance. He came from the Foreign Office with a string of triumphs behind him – peace in Indo-China, the withdrawal of British troops from the Canal Zone in Egypt; the economy was vibrant; rationing had ended. Within weeks, Eden won a handsome majority in the general election.

Nevertheless, there were shadows threatening the spring promise. Lord

Carr was the new premier's Parliamentary Private Secretary. Did he think the shadow of the great man, Winston Churchill, was perhaps the darkest of these?

> No, I don't think so. That shadow had been casting itself over him for a long time, and I think it's the length of time it had been there that was the problem, not its presence at that moment. I think that one of the great difficulties he saw from the beginning was that he felt he ought to create his own government, in his own image, and yet he felt that for personal reasons, because of the position of the Chancellor, Rab Butler, he couldn't make the great changes then and delayed for six months. I think that was a shadow, and I know he often told me he felt it got him off on the wrong foot.

Such circumstances were not, perhaps, propitious for relations with his Cabinet colleagues. Were they difficult – prickly – or in fact relatively smooth? There were some rivals who had their own eyes fairly closely on the premiership by then, most notably Harold Macmillan. Did this lead to personality clashes? Robert Rhodes James, Eden's biographer, has examined the documents and seen the strains they reflected.

> There certainly was a considerable difficulty with Harold Macmillan which had gone back a very long way. In Eden's papers there are some notes about Harold Macmillan which I didn't publish in my biography because Harold Macmillan was still alive and which emphasized that the tensions between the two went back a very long way. There was also the relationship with Rab, which went back to the Munich period. Anthony Eden never forgot those who were his friends and those who were not, at the time when he was Foreign Secretary and resigned; these tensions went on and were remembered, I think, perhaps not entirely to his advantage.

Lord Hailsham did not join the government until 1956, but he already knew many of its illustrious members personally. Did he feel any sea change in relationships or in style after April 1955?

> Winston, obviously, was a one-off job and I think the idea at that time was that we were back to normal at last. Anthony had been waiting in the wings as heir apparent, or at any rate heir presumptive, for a very long time indeed; now, we thought, we will make all things new, we'll get back to a real peacetime Prime Minister and a real postwar government. I felt that we had a Prime Minister now who represented contemporary manhood, rather than the pre–First World War generation.

These feelings were mirrored outside Westminster, too; Eden had a considerable public following because of his brave resignation in the 1930s and his success as Foreign Secretary. An Eden premiership must have seemed a very glowing prospect in many ways.

Perhaps the expectations were too high. Certainly, disappointment within the Conservative Party was not long in coming. There was the famous 'We Need the Smack of Firm Government' leader in the *Daily Telegraph*, which seems to have upset Anthony Eden profoundly. It struck a raw nerve. What was at the root of this rapidly emerging dissatisfaction? Lord Carr goes back to the contrast with Churchill and Eden's inability to reshape his government as he wished:

> He was wanting to form his own government and to establish a domestic theme to his premiership, but because of the sad illness of Rab's wife couldn't move him then. Until he could make that change he couldn't move his government, and so there was a hiatus. This is how he saw it; and he also felt – and he wasn't alone in this – that there was some rather bad economic misjudgement in the early autumn, with what was called the 'Pots and Pans Budget'.

The *Daily Telegraph* leader was not the only press comment to get under Eden's skin; he seemed to take far too seriously what the *Daily Express* wrote and said about him. Indeed, he suffered a degree of irritation with Fleet Street in general – and perhaps also a degree of naïveté in respect of dealings with them, as Robert Rhodes James discovered:

> Certainly there was a hypersensitivity at Number Ten to what was written in the press, which certainly reveals itself in Eden's diaries. A very interesting aspect of him was that he was literally astounded to discover that under the Churchill government there was a regular daily meeting to decide which Cabinet papers to leak to the press. He was deeply shocked. He was astonished. That was not his style at all. He was excessively upset by the reactions of the press, not least the *Daily Telegraph*. I think this hypersensitivity to criticism began very early and was a very corroding element in his premiership.

Sir Guy Millard was Eden's Downing Street Private Secretary and saw him every day. He thus had ample opportunity to observe that 'he was too sensitive to criticism in the press, particularly in the popular press and indeed on the BBC as well.' It is part of the job of the Private Secretary, put crudely, to hose down his boss periodically, and Sir Guy had to do a bit of this; but he felt that 'nothing I could do or say really would have made very much difference.'

And yet, as Lord Carr stresses, 'it was immensely important. He *was* too sensitive to this, and he knew it and often said so to me. His urgent need was to have somebody who would calm him down rather than hype him up, and I was appalled that there were a few people around him inclined to come and say, "Have you seen this? Isn't that awful?" instead of the reverse.'

The problems with the economy soon became fairly acute. There was the famous emergency Budget in the autumn of 1955, the 'Pots and Pans Budget', with purchase tax going up. Anthony Eden had not had to grapple with economic affairs in the way that Butler or others had, and he was, Lord Carr recalls, very conscious of this.

People have called him vain, but he also had, perhaps, at times, excessive humility in that, as he often said to me, 'I only feel confident in a subject I really know, and if only in my early days in politics I'd had to be at the Board of Trade and the Ministry of Labour as a junior minister I would have spoken with much more confidence.' He had a very good strategic sense, I think, a broad direction, but not, in economic affairs, when it came to the detailed argument in a tactical way.

The Cabinet papers show that two problems loomed large among those Anthony Eden had to confront at this juncture. One was trade union power; he would get notes periodically from Lord Nuffield pressing for legislation against 'naked trade union power' and the matter was discussed in Cabinet committees. The other was immigration. Lord Hailsham had to deal with both these areas over many years in the course of his own ministerial career – indeed, the Immigration Bill drafted by Eden's administration was rather like the one that Macmillan's Cabinet, in which Lord Hailsham served, came up with in 1962 – and he remembers the problems very acutely.

All the time I was subsequently in the government, there was this problem of immigration which had been caused by the extraordinarily unprescient British Nationality Act of 1948, for which Attlee at the time preened himself enormously. And of course all this was going on and it was bound to cause problems because there was an open door to anybody who wanted to come and a labour shortage here. So it added up to a large influx which was very difficult to digest. The trade union problem had not, at that time, emerged very strongly in my consciousness, but when I became party Chairman it was the factor which was uppermost in the rank and file of the Conservative Party in the country.

It's often said that Anthony Eden was a vacillator, failing to grasp nettles of this sort – what we would now call a 'fudger'. Robert Rhodes James identifies part of the problem with the Minister of Labour, Walter Monckton.

> One of the most interesting aspects, which has always puzzled me, was the reverence given to Walter Monckton, the Minister of Labour, and then unfortunately made Minister of Defence by Eden, who had an extraordinary hold over Churchill and Eden and many other people. I only remember him as a very young man. He made his reputation in the Churchill government by basically conceding, again and again, on whatever the issue was and stoking up a problem; Eden saw this very clearly, which was one of the reasons he moved him from the labour ministry.

Rhodes James applauds Eden's 'extraordinarily good strategic under-standing of what was needed' and his 'vision, which is still with us today'. Because of what happened subsequently, this vision, the Disraelian 'One Nation' side of Eden in respect of home affairs, has been almost entirely forgotten. Lord Carr sums it up in a phrase that became common currency:

> The 'property-owning democracy' – he'd be the first to say he didn't create that phrase, but that was the core of his belief and, of course, it included home ownership and that's why everybody talked about it in the first place. But, above all, it included what we would now call industrial democracy. He wanted to involve people in their jobs, give them a sense of dignity in their jobs, of ownership in their jobs, and he didn't believe in trade union law because he wanted to tackle it the other way round, the positive way round. Also, the trade union leaders at that time were on the whole very responsible people, and he'd been a very close colleague of Ernie Bevin's during and indeed after the war. So he was conditioned very much against doing something that responsible trade union leaders didn't want to do.

Robert Rhodes James stresses the part played in Eden's outlook by his military past.

> We should never forget for a moment that Anthony Eden had been a soldier and was at his happiest among soldiers. His Conservatism really began not only from County Durham but from his platoon in the First World War. He took the view that if a country of all societies, all backgrounds, can fight and die together for a great cause, why can't they do that in times of peace? This was, I would say, the great vision of his life, and he was not alone in it. That particular generation had a faith in the British people, and this, I think, accounted for Anthony Eden's

astonishing and huge popularity. He was one of the most popular and respected politicians of modern times. The 1955 election was a triumph. People loved him; he was talking essentially to his platoon and to the things he really, deeply, believed in.

And yet, for all the strength of this domestic vision, foreign policy was the area where Eden's great gifts were best known and acknowledged. He had a great triumph in nudging the first detente, as it were, through the great powers: the Austrian Treaty, by which the armies of occupation were taken out of Austria. But there were nagging problems – indeed, imperial problems by the score. The Cabinet papers show the huge amount of time the Cabinet had to spend on decolonization, even though the rush had not yet begun; above all, on Cyprus. This was, inevitably, a constant burden on the Prime Minister's time, and that of his private office. Sir Guy Millard thinks that his boss was perhaps *too* absorbed in these problems.

Maybe it would have been better if he'd been able to leave them more to the Foreign Office. I think in that way his previous experience was a kind of handicap in his prime ministership. And, of course, Egypt was a constant problem, a constant irritant to him. He'd met Nasser, but he felt betrayed by him, because he thought Nasser had given him some sort of assurance that once British troops had been withdrawn from the Canal Zone he would stop the anti-British propaganda, and when this proved not to be the case I think he felt betrayed. And of course he felt a special sense of responsibility because of his role in the agreement to withdraw the troops from the Canal Zone.

When Suez erupted, it seemed to do so as a bolt from the blue. Did the nationalization of the Canal Company come as a complete surprise to Number Ten? Sir Guy recalls the moment when the news came through.

It came out of the blue, although of course it was provoked to a very large extent by the Americans withdrawing suddenly their aid for the High Aswan Dam. It was a very dramatic occasion when it occurred, because there was a dinner party going on upstairs for the Iraqis, as I remember. I was on duty downstairs, not at the party, and suddenly this news came across from the Foreign Office, and I was summoned to call a meeting of the Chiefs of Staff, the Cabinet Secretary and so on, whoever else was involved.

Once Nasser had struck his blow with the nationalization, it seems that all the other policy preoccupations of the government were put on the back-burner. For example, when the Hungarian uprising happened, the Cabinet hadn't got time to discuss it on a single occasion. Lord Hailsham was about to become First Lord of the Admiralty as the crisis broke in Egypt. Did he have the impression that everybody, throughout the government, went on a kind of Suez alert?

No, I think it happened rather differently myself, but of course I haven't any documents. Undoubtedly, the nationalization of the Canal – which, according to my way of thinking, was a double breach of an international obligation and therefore a breach of treaty – was a very dramatic event when it occurred. But it was not connected with Israel. It was connected with a false view of what the British Commonwealth could become and of the importance of the Canal to that view. And it was also an act of aggression because it was in breach of international obligations. That's how it was viewed to begin with. Then came Nasser's next move, which was to have staff talks with the Arab neighbours of Israel, coupled with an intention to block the straits which lead to Eilat. Those of us who knew a little about this situation realized that that was the one thing which would force Israel to fight, in the position they were in, and the original offence of nationalizing the Canal disappeared in the crisis which was brought about by the Israeli–Egyptian tension caused by the closure of Eilat.

Or, as Robert Rhodes James puts it: 'Ben Gurion couldn't care less about the Canal, but he cared very deeply about the Straits of Hormuz and the threat to Israel.'

It does seem, looking at the way Whitehall was run, that Cabinet government took on a different form for the duration of the Suez crisis. First of all a Cabinet committee including all the major ministers, the Egypt Committee, made a lot of the running; then, for a fairly long period in October, as the crisis was approaching boiling point, not even the Egypt Committee was in operation. It almost seems that Eden put Cabinet government on ice for the duration. Robert Rhodes James acknowledges this, but draws attention to Eden's honesty with his colleagues at the crucial Cabinet of 23 October, held after the Sèvres meeting to concert British, French and Israeli actions against Egypt, to the minutes of which was attached a confidential annexe giving ministers more than a broad hint as to the nature of the very private undertakings that had been made in Paris.

What we didn't realize at the time was that the French and Israelis were up to certain arrangements of their own. Eden was in effect faced with a *fait accompli*, and I think it was very remarkable that at that famous

Cabinet meeting it was Eden who used the word 'collusion'. And I was very struck, reading the records of that meeting, how honest he was with his colleagues, how he explained exactly what was involved.

It is often said that Eden's health was very shaky pretty early on in the crisis, and remained so. In the opinion of Sir Guy Millard, who saw him several times every day and was thus in as good a position as anyone to know, 'he certainly wasn't well. His health was not as good as it had been and this certainly increased the physical strains of the premiership – and no doubt the psychological strains as well, which are considerable in any case.'

By the time of Suez, Lord Carr was a junior minister in the Home Department. He did not notice a particular change in his old patron then:

It was before then that I noticed the change. He was never the same man after the gall bladder operation that went wrong in 1953. He appeared to be getting very much better, but then within the first six months of his premiership he started getting the fevers again, two or three. The first one was generally written off as flu. Then there was another one. When he actually appointed me to be a junior minister I had to go and see him in his bedroom, where he had a temperature of 102. That was ten months before the crisis of Suez. It was quite clear to me by the end of 1955 that he was a far from well man.

Lord Hailsham became First Lord of the Admiralty as the crisis brewed up. Even then, he remained in the dark about the nature of the planned naval operation for some time.

I didn't, curiously enough, have to mobilize the task force. It had been mobilized before I became First Lord; but it was mobilized for a purpose rather different from that which ultimately emerged as the operation that took place. It wasn't until about three weeks, at a guess, after I had taken office that I asked to be told what the contingency plans might be, and at first I wasn't told. They had to get Eden's special permission to tell me; then they sent a young naval captain who explained it all.

Reticent though he may have been in respect of details of the operation, legend has it that the Prime Minister was for ever on the telephone pestering his subordinate ministers. Lord Hailsham concedes the truth of this.

I'm afraid you have to say 'yes' to that. I put it down to his state of health. On the whole, the other prime ministers for whom I've worked have rather left their senior staff to get on with their own thing and intervened only when they thought things were going wrong. But certainly during the Suez operation, he'd be very much on the phone to ask a number of quite unimportant questions about very minor units of the navy.

In view of Eden's career as a whole it seems very surprising that he chose the people he did, the French and the Israelis, to go into business with, as it were. His past practice, his allegedly pro-Arab sentiments, all seemed to point in the opposite direction. Equally surprising, from this perspective, is his near-total neglect of the area where he had a very sure touch, namely dealing with the Americans. Sir Guy Millard was the foreign affairs specialist in Number Ten; how would he explain this apparent paradox?

It has to be remembered that by the end of October there was an acute dilemma. The operation had been mounted, the expedition had been mounted, the reservists had been called up, the shipping had been commandeered and so on, and was being held, and it couldn't be held for ever. You either had to disband the whole thing and therefore abandon the whole idea of the use of force, which would have meant taking the pressure off Egypt; or else it had to go ahead. This was why, when the French unveiled their plan, he was naturally intrigued, because it offered a way out of this dilemma.

This was the plan to arrange with the Israelis that Israel would attack Egyptian territory and the French and British would go in as the peace-makers between the two. But what about the dog that didn't bark, the 'special relationship'? It seems extraordinary now that any of these steps were taken without Eisenhower and Dulles being carried with them every inch of the way. Sir Guy thinks that more deception was practised west of the Atlantic than on this side.

Eden has often been accused of deceiving the Americans, but the one thing he never deceived them about was his ultimate intention to use force if all else failed. On the other hand, you can certainly say that the Americans deceived him. They deceived him over the thing known as the Suez Canal Users' Association, SCUA. Dulles gave Eden quite specific assurances that they would withhold the dues from Nasser and that if Nasser didn't accept this then they would more or less force their way through; and in the event, of course, both these assurances turned out to be false.

All this planning activity took place against a backdrop of very fierce divisions, both within the country and within the House of Commons. There seems to have been a quite unprecedented ferocity between the two major parties, and in some cases within them as well. Robert Rhodes James, at this time a Clerk of the House of Commons, witnessed the levels to which tensions rose at Westminster.

At the beginning of the Suez crisis, I remember it very well, it was a Friday, the first comparison of Nasser to Hitler and Mussolini was actually made by Hugh Gaitskell, and the Labour Party was at that stage, I think, even more belligerent and shocked than the Tory Party. And then, for various reasons, things changed. It wasn't really until the emergency debate in September that you began to see the division between the parties opening. Then, when the announcement of our ultimatum was actually made, Gaitskell was trying to control the Labour Party. That was a fascinating moment. He was looking at his own benches; he wasn't actually talking to the Speaker. But the thing then degenerated into a really intensely emotional division and there was a lot of noise, but also a genuine passion, on both sides. If it hadn't been for 'Shakes' Morrison, who was then the Speaker of the House, whose handling of the matter was absolutely brilliant, I think there might have been serious disorder. One episode I shall never forget. After 'Shakes' had had to suspend the House, and feelings were running so high, Anthony Eden spoke; he was listened to with silence and respect and at the end of his speech there were cheers. I regard that as the greatest parliamentary performance I've ever heard.

It must have been very galling for a Prime Minister who looked upon Britain, as it were, as a good regiment, to see his country dividing into such hostile camps beneath him as the autumn progressed – though Lord Carr, as a constituency MP, believes the dissenters were in fact fairly few in number:

I got the feeling that the majority of my constituents in semi-industrial suburban London were wholeheartedly behind Anthony Eden. I don't think the country at large, rightly or wrongly, was divided. The minorities in both parties, on both sides, felt passionately one way or the other; but I suspect the great mass of the British people on the whole, wanted it to be done. But, of course they wanted it to be done successfully, and, alas, it was not done successfully.

In one of the military inquests that has now been declassified, there is a very vivid phrase used by one of the task force commanders. He said: 'With the Opposition behaving as it was, and with world opinion divided as it was, there was a hand rocking the landing craft.' Did Lord Hailsham feel at the time that the divisions and uproar behind the scenes – or even in the open, in front of the scenes – compromised what he and the rest of the government were trying to do in the operational sense?

I never thought that. The Navy, which was the principal arm involved, was absolutely rock solid and carried out a totally successful operation and everything, with one qualification, went as it ought to have done. The one qualification, which I felt very deeply when I found it out, as I did only some months, I think, afterwards, was the extent of the civilian casualties. I had hoped and believed that certain changes I'd made would avoid civilian casualties altogether and at the time I thought that it had succeeded.

On 6 November 1956 one of the most important Cabinet meetings of the postwar period was held. The Americans had unleashed the dollar weapon on sterling. The assembled ministers were faced with the task of deciding whether to carry on with the invasion or to stop. Lord Hailsham, though not present at the meeting, was strongly in favour of continuing: 'I sent a message in that I thought we ought to go on, and I was very near resignation when we didn't.'

The Prime Minister also wanted to go on, as did some of his colleagues; but, as Robert Rhodes James relates, they were eventually outnumbered.

This was when Macmillan, of course, changed his side. Some people, like Derrick Heathcoat Amory, were all for stopping. Others were for going on. But the going on vote was very much a minority. The American intervention – or the Macmillan intervention – was critical. The fatal misjudgement of the whole thing had been to listen to Dulles, rather than to Eisenhower. Eisenhower had been totally consistent throughout; the telegrams and telephone conversations between them were absolutely clear. Right from the beginning, he said, 'I'm not going to be involved.' Whereas Dulles had muddied the waters; he wanted Nasser down, he loathed Nasser, and he was in effect encouraging the British, saying, 'When it comes to the crunch, we will look the other way.' And, of course, that didn't happen. And then Macmillan made his intervention, and Eden suddenly found himself in a tiny minority in his own Cabinet.

The atmosphere in Parliament was still very febrile when Eden made his last appearance in December and, some would say, lied about his collusion with the Israelis when asked a direct question by Denis Healey. Lord Carr remembers a 'general fear of uproar' and also 'great unhappiness, which of course, in my case, was magnified by close personal affection for the man whose career and mission I saw broken, because I regarded it not just as a personal tragedy, but as a national political tragedy.'

Robert Rhodes James remembers 'the occasion when Anthony Eden came into the House of Commons and there was total dead silence, and one Conservative got up waving an order paper, looked around him and saw no one else was budging and sat down. I think that was the most poignant, awful moment of them all. It was terrible.'

But how does Anthony Eden's biographer, with his sympathy for his subject, explain how this honourable man could mislead the House of Commons so fully on that day about the nature of the arrangement with the Israelis and the French?

One's got to be realistic. In the national interest ministers have in the past – and no doubt will in the future – not disclosed the full scale of secret arrangements with other countries. This has happened under Labour governments and under Conservative governments and will continue to happen. I think that, looking back at the circumstances of the Sèvres Protocol with all the wisdom of hindsight, things could have been done differently. But the fact is that these things happen. Anthony Eden was a professional diplomat and a realist, and one can criticize the decision itself, but I would always defend the right of any minister of the Crown, in the national interest, not to disclose to the House of Commons or to the press what has been agreed. This has happened on many occasions and it's not dishonourable or a disreputable thing to do. But the trouble was he gave so many hostages in the Sèvres Agreement, and inevitably the truth was going to come out.

Sir Guy, who was listening from the Officials' Box that day, takes a similar view: 'I think that statesmen very often have to do things which in private life might be considered wrong. It's called *raison d'état* and is sometimes justified and sometimes not.'

But it was all over by this stage. Should he not have come clean? Lord Hailsham is one of those people who doesn't believe the House of Commons should be misled; but, not having been faced with such circumstances himself, he declines to pass judgement. In any case, he had reached his own conclusions about what had been going on.

I, who was kept very largely in the dark, had correctly divined from my own sources exactly what the fundamental situation was. Once I thought that Nasser was making a concerted attack on Israel, I realized that the Israelis at that time would mobilize at about 250,000; that they were all bank clerks and that the whole life of Israel would stop. That they had to fight. That they had to secure a quick and decisive victory, which they did, and that we should have to do exactly what, apparently, as I subsequently discovered, was agreed at Sèvres. And I supported it, not because we'd agreed it, but because I thought it was the only possible course.

Having seen Eden in the House of Commons in December, how soon did he think the Prime Minister would go?

I had absolutely no inkling. I was holding a birthday party for one of my then very young children, in Admiralty House – which I didn't normally occupy; I occupied the flat above the Arch. We were sent for, the three service ministers who were not members of the Cabinet: John Hare, Nigel Birch, and me. Each of us had the same idea, that we'd done something wrong, and brought all the controversial files on our positions. When we came into the room, all Anthony said was that he was going to resign. I was absolutely thunderstruck and was aghast, but of course it was a genuine illness and he was genuinely unable to carry on. I thought the government would fall, in the aftermath of having run away when they were within motoring distance of success; but I was wrong about that. This event occurred in a way, and at a moment, when I had no inkling of what was going to take place.

How will Eden be remembered? It is the most difficult question of all. In some ways, as a lost Disraelian, he is a forgotten Prime Minister, as Lord Carr regretfully acknowledges.

This is why, at his downfall, I felt I was seeing not only a great personal tragedy – the life of someone I was attached to – but also a great political tragedy, because of all the political leaders I've known, while I saw in him weaknesses – his oversensitivity to criticisms, his tendency to interfere – which might perhaps not fit him to be the best of all prime ministers, his vision of where Britain was, and what its society needed to be, seemed to me to be clearer and, to me, more appealing than any I've ever heard from anyone else. But I fear this will never really be fully understood and appreciated, what might have been.

Many people now see – maybe with hindsight, again – a great gap in Eden's vision, which is Europe. This was the period in which the Messina discussions were going on that were to lead to the Common Market of the Six with the Treaty of Rome in 1957, and he's seen as the man who took almost no notice of the European tide. Is this an unfair judgement? Robert Rhodes James thinks not.

No, I'm afraid it's very fair, and it's one of the lacunae he had. He had this concept of the 'three pillars' foreign policy. The essential one was the Empire; then the Atlantic Alliance – although he didn't particularly like the Americans, one had to live with them; and then Europe. It was a very interesting order of priorities, because Europe came right at the bottom of the list, and much though I admired him, which I did very much, this was the one area where his normal imagination deserted him. He wasn't the only one who was opposed to the Schuman Plan and Messina, but his hostility to the concept of a united Western Europe was a very deep and real one – and very sad.

Eden in retirement took the view that the real tragedy of 1956, quite apart from his own personal tragedy, was that the forces of decency and order in international affairs had not stood their ground. Was that, in fact, the real principle at issue in Suez? For Sir Guy Millard, while there is force in this view, the lasting scars were more domestic than foreign.

He believed passionately in the lesson which he'd derived from his experiences in the 1930s, namely that the appeasement of military dictators, once they start on a career of aggression, leads to disaster and ultimately to war, and I don't know that he was wrong in that. I don't think he was. You've only got to look at the career of, for example, Galtieri. So, to that extent, I think that probably the failure of Suez did lead to international indiscipline and less international order. But also, I think, the effects of Suez have very often been exaggerated. In fact, the long-term effects were comparatively slight, because within a few years of Suez, our relations with the Middle East were much better than before: obviously with Egypt, after the death of Nasser; with Saudi Arabia, after Nasser's influence had been removed; with King Hussein of Jordan, for the same reason; with the Gulf states, after the independence issue had been settled. The exceptions, of course, were Syria and Libya. And we must remember that, within two years of Suez, we were landing troops in Lebanon in cooperation with the Americans.

One might argue that Anthony Eden was the most tragic of all the postwar Prime Ministers. He over-reacted to Nasser, had a very personal animus against him; he over-estimated British power; and he was destroyed on the field of activity he knew best, foreign affairs, where he was regarded as *sans pareil*. That is a fairly unrelieved picture of tragedy. But Robert Rhodes James prefers a less bleak summation.

I would first say that in my view, with the possible exception of Arthur Balfour, Eden was the most cultivated Prime Minister of this century, whether in terms of art or writing – everything that he touched. He had an extraordinary eye for beauty and he was the most cultivated, civilized, of all modern prime ministers. Looking at his life, I never forget Churchill's phrase about Gallipoli: 'The terrible "ifs" accumulate.' If perhaps he hadn't married too young the first time. If Churchill had resigned in 1945 as his wife and advisers wished him to do. If the operation in 1953, which was so trivial, had not gone so catastrophically wrong – who knows? Obviously history would have been different. I don't personally regard his career or life as a failure. I think he was one of the most courageous, physically and morally, of all modern British politicians. And if he saw in Nasser another Mussolini, who can say that he was wrong?

Eden is the only clear heir apparent to have attained the premiership in the postwar period; he succeeded to Number Ten and then went down in flames within a couple of years. Did it come too late for him? If Churchill had had the wisdom to go in the late 1940s, it might have been an entirely different kind of Prime Minister and an entirely different kind of story.

Lord Hailsham sees tragedy in both the personal and the political outcomes.

I think that it was almost like a Greek tragedy, that this splendid creature, who really was extremely talented, civilized, with a first-class intellect, should have met with complete disaster as a result of an event which I myself do *not* condemn. I am far from saying that he was wrong in thinking that this was a watershed in our affairs. It's quite right that our relations with the Gulf states, with Saudi Arabia and with Jordan are better now than before. But what about Iran? What about Syria, where the Hashemite dynasty was destroyed, and the little boy king was dragged through the streets at the end of a hook, eight years old? What about Iraq? I think it *was* a tragedy.

What of Eden's own wishes in the matter of remembrance? Sir Guy Millard saw Eden in retirement.

I think he would wish to be remembered as an extremely liberal Prime Minister. He was very much on the left wing of the Conservative Party. He really loathed the old guard of the Conservative Party, Chamberlain, Simon, Hoare and so on, the appeasers, whom he regarded as largely responsible for the disasters of the 1930s, leading up to the war; and, to a much lesser extent, Halifax. But I think he would wish to be regarded as somebody who wanted to unite the nation, who wanted to do the best. He was a man not only of tremendous courage, but tremendous patriotism as well. And he would certainly not have done what he did at Suez had he not believed that it was in the interest of his country.

12

The Last Edwardian

'One has to remember about Harold Macmillan that he was the only survivor – survivor in public life, that is – of a generation that had existed before the First World War. There was an element of the dining club, the country house party, about his conduct of Cabinets.' Thus Lord Hailsham, who sat at Harold Macmillan's Cabinet table for six and three-quarter years. There is a danger of over-gilding the Macmillan years in Downing Street. There were resignations and scandals and moments of panic, as in July 1962 when a third of the Cabinet was sacked in an orgy of political brutality; and the timing and manner of his departure produced an unseemly struggle for the succession in full view of the television cameras at party conference time in 1963. But from the moment he replaced Anthony Eden in January 1957 at the head of a government and a party still reeling from Suez, Harold Macmillan presided over an administration with a style that was as unforgettable as it was contrived. He enjoyed being Prime Minister, he said,

> because I found it much the most relaxed of the offices I held. You didn't work so hard. You didn't have to do all the work of the departments. Oh, you had the Cabinet to run and all that. I found I read a lot of books and so on. I rested a lot. It's a great mistake to get yourself into a state of nervous excitement all the time. Nobody should ever overdo it, you know. You can't make good judgements unless you've got . . . you should read Jane Austen, then you'll feel better, and then when they come in with some awful crisis, having read about *Pride and Prejudice* and so on, you'll feel better.

This mannered, elderly literary gentleman dominated his Cabinet and British politics from behind a smokescreen of Edwardian elegance and wit which continued to delight traditional Tories and to discomfort the harder-edged, new breed of Conservative well into the 1980s. A performance in the House of Lords by the Earl of Stockton, as he became at the age of ninety, would be keenly awaited by those with an eye for a great actor, as his grandson Alexander, the new Earl of Stockton, remembers:

I talked, by pure chance, to Lord Olivier just after one speech. He said that technically it was remarkable in one aspect that probably he alone of the peers had noticed, which was that when he started the speech he was standing resolutely parallel to the government front bench, facing the opposition. But as he became more critical he turned to his left so that he was then standing parallel with the cross bench, therefore in a somewhat ambivalent position. Olivier said that whether this was deliberate or not, it was a superb piece of theatre.

In the mid-1980s the voice was frailer, but the kind of performance that delighted Lord Olivier was still being delivered:

And then President Reagan did a very wise thing. He dismissed all the academic economists in Washington. And he said to himself, 'Well, this is absurd, let us look at the realities. Some talk about juggling with money, let's look at the realities of the creation of wealth, that is what we must do today.' Happily for him – unhappily for us – the monetarists were the first to be exiled. They were received, of course, with that courtesy with which we always receive refugees. They settled in Oxford, in Cambridge and in Whitehall, and, it is rumoured, even in Downing Street.

To understand Macmillan in his glorious Indian summer and his Downing Street years it is necessary to make a journey back to that prewar society of which, as Lord Hailsham reminds us, his administration was so strongly redolent. Harold Macmillan, a son of the great Macmillan publishing house, was a shy, bookish boy. He absorbed history through his pores and it shaped virtually every paragraph he wrote or spoke, as Lord Hailsham recalls: 'There would be quotations from Homer. There would be vague historical analogies: the trade union leaders as medieval barons in the period of the Wars of the Roses. Some of them would be relevant and some of them would be mildly misleading, but they would all be amusing, detached and carefully thought out.'

Macmillan himself showed his grasp of history when explaining the great events encompassed in his memoirs:

The particular period in which I have lived is one of the most extraordinary in the world's history. I was born as a child in the Victorian age with all its solidity, its sense of security, and I've lived through two wars, intervals of war, and seen perhaps the greatest evolution in the world – in the balance of power, in the relative strength of countries, in the life of the peoples – there's ever been, perhaps since the fall of the Roman Empire.

The man to whom Macmillan spoke these words was Professor Bob McKenzie, a political scientist from the London School of Economics with whom, in his anecdotage, the old Prime Minister struck up a remarkable rapport, and to whom he reminisced about his formative years at university, in the trenches and as a young MP for a depressed area. 'He went up to Oxford immediately before the First World War,' recalls McKenzie, 'and fell in love with the place; some claim that he was as proud to be elected Chancellor of the University half a century later as he had been to enter Number Ten Downing Street.'

Macmillan's own account of the cornucopia Oxford represented is marvellously evocative:

> Well, you see, after the rather narrow life of an old-fashioned English home – I have no sisters, so we hadn't many friends, except one's own – suddenly to come to Oxford in those days, Oxford before the industrial revolution, before Lord Nuffield, before science, with the horse trams and just the old colleges, and a little city – little town – its extraordinary beauty to start with, and then suddenly to meet chaps from all over the world – Rhodes scholars like Vincent Massey, with whom I made a great friendship, lasted all my life, and boys from all sorts of schools; and to enter, for me, into a much wider world, ranging from the reading men to the hunting men to the political chaps – and I loved it. We didn't then work much during the term. You had some books and a few lectures and did a few things, but you worked during the vacation. For me the two years at Oxford opened up a completely new world.

In the First World War Macmillan served with the Grenadier Guards on the Western Front, and came close to sharing the same fate as hundreds of thousands of young men of his generation who did not return, as he told Bob McKenzie.

> We went out and attacked and then we occupied the green line, or the red line, or whatever it was. But the people on the left were rather held up. It was a bit of a botch-up. It wasn't too bad, we captured a German trench and most of the position. There was a machine gun on the left, probably some kind of pillbox or something, making a lot of trouble for us. So I went out with some chaps to try to deal with it, but it hit me, when I was sort of half crawling and half running, and that knocked me out altogether. So I could do nothing but pull myself down into the deepest shell hole that I could find. Although I was wounded in the right knee and absolutely my whole pelvis was destroyed and everything, I did manage either to run or to crawl through to the other side of the village.

'He was in hospital on and off for two years,' continues McKenzie, 'and throughout his life he never wholly recovered from the effects of his war wounds. By 1924 Macmillan was Conservative MP for the north-eastern industrial constituency of Stockton-on-Tees; but the events of 1914–18 were to have a profound and continuing effect on his political attitudes.'

I was thrown first into a different society among the officer class – I didn't care about hunting and that kind of thing – then I saw the great mass of our splendid . . . of the ordinary private soldier. Then I went up to Stockton – well, there were just the same chaps in trouble and you tried to help them as you had in the war. It was quite easy to get on with them. I'd learnt that from the war, it altered my life. And then there came the problem. Up till thirty-one we felt we could alleviate – with all the things we were trying to do and what the government were doing. But after that I felt we must adopt a more radical approach. I think that was the great thing that happened after the National Government and the economic collapse of 1929–31.

As a young MP, Macmillan learned how to make a speech from a master craftsman, David Lloyd George.

He said, 'First of all, your speech was an essay. It covered fifteen, twenty points. A good economic essay, make a good article in the *Economic Journal*. But it wasn't a speech.' He said, 'Now, you're a young Member, there won't be many people in the House when you speak. What you want to do is, somebody goes out of the House, goes into the smoking room or the dining room and says, "You know, that fellow Macmillan made rather a good speech," and the other chap says, "Well, what did he say?" Well, in your speech you said twenty things. He wouldn't know what to say. When you're a young Member you should say one thing and one thing only in a speech. Of course, you say it wrapped up in this way, and that way, a little story, little jokes, solemnly, jokingly, but it's all one point, and people know what you've said.' And this was very good advice. Then he said, 'Of course, your speech was like a gramophone record. A professor reading out a thing. Of course, there must be slow, solemn bits, there must be the quick, allegro, little joking bits, there must be the argumentative bits. And remember, the most vital thing in a speech, if you can do it, is the pause.' That's quite true, just that wait, hold the audience, if you've got an audience. But vary the pitch and the pace.

In the Thirties, Macmillan may have sparkled on his feet but he still wrote like a professor. His political and economic testament, *The Middle Way*, is earnest and heavy going, for all its hints of things to come and its progressive tone.

The Second World War transformed Macmillan's political fortunes. It swept away the 'Old Gang' Conservatives who had kept the Tory rebel out of office in the Twenties and Thirties, and his hero Winston Churchill made him a minister two years before his fiftieth birthday. During the war he narrowly escaped death in an air crash at Algiers airport. His horrified aide, John Wyndham, already free from the wreck, watched his trapped master's moustaches burn with a blue flame. Had he died, Macmillan would have been but a footnote in political history, if that. As it was, his experiences as Churchill's 'viceroy' with the British Army as they moved across North Africa and up Italy to Austria at the end of the war cast a long shadow into the 1970s and 1980s when grave accusations were made by some historians about his personal culpability in the forcible repatriation of Russians and other nationals from within the Soviet Union by British troops in southern Austria (an issue which continues to be fought in the courts).

The years of Labour ascendancy after 1945 were irritating and fretful ones for Macmillan as he pined away what should have been his political prime in the exile of the opposition benches. Churchill's return to power in 1951 brought the offer of the Housing Ministry rather than the glittering prize of the Foreign Office or the Ministry of Defence; but this appointment was to be the making of Macmillan. He recalled how his brief emerged.

> We'd promised in a rather vague way to build 300,000 houses a year – it had been up to then about 180,000 – and all the experts said it was impossible. But the Tory conference at Blackpool had demanded it, and fortunately Woolton, who was in charge, had stopped the bidding at 300,000, otherwise we might have promised 500,000. Then Churchill told me to do this. And I thought about it and said, 'Oh really, I know nothing about it.' So I went for a walk with my wife in the garden and I came back and said, 'Well, I've always done everything you asked me to do, so I suppose I shall have to do it, but I must do it in my own way.' He said, 'My dear, you can do it in any way you like.' 'Yes, but,' I said, 'you don't realize,' and he said, 'You do it in your own way.' So then I set about it in my way, which, of course, was to turn it into a War Department and really set about the job. It was quite interesting. I've never enjoyed three years more in my whole life, I think.

By the time Macmillan moved to the Defence Ministry in 1954, he was an established politician on the national stage. His Cabinet papers from the mid-1950s, which can now be read at the Public Record Office, have an extraordinary vitality. Not for him the bureaucratic language of Whitehall. His memos on housing policy read like punchy pieces from the *Daily Mirror* in its glory days. And as Foreign Secretary in Sir Anthony Eden's Cabinet in 1955, Macmillan turned to the music hall for inspiration on the handling of Burgess and Maclean, the missing British diplomats who had just surfaced in Moscow. Macmillan proposed a committee of inquiry, 'on the principle', he told the Cabinet, 'of Albert and the Lion: "sum one 'ad to be summoned, so that was decided upon".'

Macmillan moved rapidly through the great offices of state. By the time Nasser nationalized the Suez Canal Company in July 1956 he was Chancellor of the Exchequer, and a firm supporter of Eden's policy of resisting the Egyptian leader. Macmillan believed that if Britain did not meet Nasser's challenge, the country 'would become another Netherlands' (a comparison which still had the capacity to shock in 1956). Four months later, it was the same Macmillan who from the Treasury in effect brought the Suez invasion to a halt as the United States government, critical of the venture, engineered an attack on sterling.

Suez destroyed Eden, three years Macmillan's junior, enabling the older man to slake his burning desire for the premiership – though Macmillan's account of the meeting at which Eden told him of his plan to resign is more Mills and Boon than a story of decline and fall:

> I see him now – it was in that little room, the only room in Number Ten that gets the western sun – January it was; and he still looked just the same, elegant, gallant, always with a rather Elizabethan figure – he looked just like a young officer in the First War, still. I think he is one of the most wonderful figures in my life, and I always think of him as the same. He never changed – had beautiful manners and elegance, almost of the world that's gone now, absolute loyalty, absolute straightforwardness.

The succession was a straight fight between Macmillan and R. A. Butler. There were no elections in those days: Tory grandees, like Lord Salisbury, 'took soundings' and a new leader 'emerged'.

> Salisbury reported that this was the view with, I think, only one exception of all the Cabinet, for me. They then asked, I think, some of the party – the party leaders – and in the party organization they seemed to have the same view. This was the advice that they gave. But that night I did nothing. There was nothing I could do. And so I just sat in my room and read *Pride and Prejudice* – a very good book. I heard nothing at all about it until about eleven o'clock on that next day I got a message from Sir Michael Adeane, the Queen's Private Secretary: would I go to the Palace at half past two. She appointed me Prime Minister. I said to her, 'We are at a pretty tough time,' and said, 'I can't guarantee to run it more than six

weeks' – which she reminded me of about six years later, with some amusement. I then motored home and sat in the Cabinet room and began to operate.

The man who greeted the new Premier at the door of Number Ten was the Principal Private Secretary he inherited from Eden. Sir Freddie Bishop remembers how the Macmillan style suffused Downing Street.

He was very widely read, of course, and a wonderful raconteur, able to quote immediately from almost anything. The famous one, of course, is the quotation he stuck on the Cabinet Office door, at a time when his private secretaries were – I don't remember over what – showing some signs of strain. He wrote out in his own hand this quotation – which I didn't immediately spot, but I believe it comes from Gilbert and Sullivan: 'Quiet calm deliberation disentangles every knot.' That stayed pinned up on the Cabinet door for quite a long time, until he thought that we'd got over our little tremors, and then he took it down and gave it to me.

Over time, Sir Freddie learnt more about his new master.

There were a lot of things, of course, that I gradually discovered. His character was in a way a rather austere one, his behaviour reserved; I hardly ever heard him use a swear word. He wasn't particularly interested, for example, in food. He was austere and thrifty. It's well known that when he first took on the job of Prime Minister – which was a fairly courageous thing to do, of course, immediately after the difficulties of 1956 – he didn't know whether he would last for thirty days or thirty months. He also said at one stage, I recall, 'I don't think I shall be very good at this job. I'm afraid I'm no good as an actor.' Of course, the fact is that one gradually discovered that he was an extremely good actor in quite a number of parts.

In his first year as Prime Minister, Macmillan hardly put a foot wrong. Where Eden had fussed, Macmillan was calm. He repaired the Anglo-American relationship with remarkable ease, playing up his wartime friendship with President Eisenhower. The cartoonists christened him 'Supermac'. The economy boomed so noisily that his entire Treasury team resigned in January 1958 uttering dire warnings about inflation in a pre-echo of debates that were to rend the Tory Party in the Seventies and Eighties. At the time, Macmillan, setting off on a Commonwealth tour, dismissed the resignations of Peter Thorneycroft, Nigel Birch and Enoch Powell as 'a little local difficulty'.

Macmillan was good at defusing dissent. He handled his Cabinet with skill and aplomb, as Sir Freddie Bishop remembers.

Cabinet proceedings were, as no doubt they still are, quite formal. There wasn't any question of Christian names, or anything like that. There was a great atmosphere of reasonableness and politeness, coupled with a readiness to make as much fun out of it as possible. It was a serious matter, and I think in fact he acted like a very good chairman. Occasionally, of course, he deliberately made something of a joke in order to defuse a situation which might otherwise have been difficult. But you have to remember that in these days he had a team of people who were largely his friends. On the whole ministers in the Cabinet were then very considerable people, who thought in the same way, and there was definitely an atmosphere of team spirit. This was extremely important. If there was any strong division of views, it was possible to deal with it in a reasonable way.

Above all, Harold Macmillan was a performer, whether his audience was in the Cabinet room, the House of Commons – or a Russian city, as Lord Barber, his former Parliamentary Private Secretary, recalls:

He went in his white hat, the first statesman of the Western world to visit Moscow after the end of the war. He was tremendously thrilled when his invitation came along. I remember in Moscow wherever we went there were quite large crowds, and he would say something to them and they would just wave back silently, and he said, 'I wish I could say something to them.' We had a man called John Morgan, who was the Foreign Office interpreter, and I said to him, 'John, what can the Prime Minister say, you know, when he comes to a crowd of people?' And he said, 'Why doesn't he say "Good day" or "Hello".' And I said, 'Well, what is it in Russian?' He said, 'dObri dyen.' So I went back to Harold Macmillan and I said, 'Why don't you try it?' He said, 'What is it again?' and I said, 'dObri dyen.' He repeated it to us a number of times and got it absolutely right: dObri dyen. The next time he went out, he put his hands up in that rather patronizing sort of air that he adopted now and again and he said, 'Double gin, double gin,' and everyone clapped and cheered. And off we went down to Kiev: 'Double gin.' 'It's worked again, Tony,' he said, 'it's worked again.'

As the general election approached, Macmillan wielded his international experience like a weapon. He was shameless in using President Eisenhower for electoral purposes. Setting up a statesmanlike exchange in Number Ten, he addressed Eisenhower thus:

Mr President, I thought we might start by saying a word about Anglo–American relations. In our lifetime, we've been pretty close together, our countries. Of course, there have been differences, there's no use denying them, there have been serious differences – before the war, after the war, two or three years ago about the Middle East, sometimes about the Far East – but the great thing about us is, we know the job backwards. We look forward, I think, and you and I have tried to do that. Now we're up against the biggest job in the world, how to keep peace and justice. And I want to say to you, if I may, that I think your visits to these three European capitals and the interchange of visits that you're going to make with Mr Khrushchev are a very fine contribution to peace.

To which Eisenhower replied:

Well, Prime Minister, I'd like to say a personal word about this business of Anglo–American relations. Except for the two years that I was in Columbia University, ever since 1941 I've been engaged in activities where one of my principal concerns has been the state and the strength of the relationships between your country and ours. And I can say from that long personal experience that those relations have never been stronger and better than they are now.

At the 1959 election Macmillan played the prosperity card. 'You've never had it so good' was his phrase. It worked: he was returned with a majority of 100, the disaster of Suez but a faded memory buried beneath a cornucopia of consumer goods. The economy continued to boom.

Buttressed by his huge parliamentary majority, Macmillan hastened the withdrawal from Empire after his 'Wind of Change' speech to the South African parliament:

And the most striking of all the impressions I've formed since I left London a month ago is of the strength of this African national consciousness. In different places it takes different forms, but it is happening everywhere. The wind of change is blowing through this continent, and whether we like it or not this growth of national consciousness is a political fact.

His words were both prescient and progressive. But of equal significance for the future was Macmillan's success in turning his party's eyes away from Empire and towards Europe. For Macmillan, the Common Market held the promise of much more than a mere trading relationship:

What role can we play alone – Italians, French (even), Germans? But together – I'm not thinking only of the economic role, I mean the role in the world. To lead the world to right and good things, to have power and authority. Together, equal to the United States; together, equal to Russia; and together, acting more and more in a harmonious leadership. That's really what the European movement is about. And that's what Churchill meant it to be about. It isn't just fixing a price for prunes and a suitable method of marketing bananas; it's not about sovereignty, what the House of Commons can do, what the Queen; those are small things. The real thing that matters is: can we put ourselves to this job, and are we ready to do it?

But even as Macmillan began to prepare Britain's case for entry into the Common Market, tarnish began to appear on the glitter of his premiership. The 1960 East–West summit on which he had banked so much was ruined when the Russians shot down an American spy plane. The pay-pause of 1961 brought growing electoral unpopularity. In the summer of 1962, rattled by a series of by-election reverses, Macmillan sacked a third of his Cabinet. His unflappable image was gone for ever, though in later years he put a brave face on his panicky butchery: 'If you think they're overworked or failed or tired out – you see, it's a cruel life, politics. Somebody's got to be in charge. So it's a very cruel life. We had nearly fourteen years of continuous office, and a lot of my older friends were worn out.'

But it was Macmillan himself who came to look worn out. The Sixties satirists had a field day as the setbacks piled up. In January 1963 General de Gaulle vetoed British membership of the Common Market, an enterprise on which Macmillan had set his heart. The summer of that year was a nightmare for the Prime Minister as the Profumo scandal burst on a prurient public: Macmillan's War Minister had been carrying on with a call-girl whose favours were shared by a naval attaché at the Soviet Embassy. Lord Barber defends his old chief's willingness to accept Profumo's initial assurances that he had behaved properly.

After all, he had the absolute assurance from Profumo that he hadn't done what he was alleged to have done. Profumo was seen by the Chief Whip, Martin Redmayne, who was a very tough egg – I served in the whips' office with Martin, he was absolutely as straight as a die. Iain Macleod, who I think was at school with Profumo, also cross-examined him, and there was somebody else there, I think the Attorney-General. These people were all convinced that Profumo was telling the truth; and they reported to the Prime Minister. Macmillan believed them. I don't think we've got any reason to be critical of Macmillan for the attitude which he took with Profumo. What he would say, I am sure, would be that if he had seen Profumo himself he would have been less likely to have got the truth out of him than three or four of his contemporaries who interviewed him and tried to get the truth out of him and who wanted to help him.

The final blow came that autumn. Macmillan's health broke. In great discomfort, he was admitted to hospital with prostate trouble. The Conservative Party, gathering for its annual conference, was thrown into hysteria by Macmillan's resignation. From the mêlée emerged a new Prime Minister in the calm, aristocratic form of Sir Alec Douglas-Home. The Macmillan years were over.

Did his health really force him to go? Or was that prostate operation a convenient cover for a dignified departure after a year or more of political reverses? His grandson Alexander had no doubts; the doctors had told Macmillan that he was unlikely to last the year. And after all, as Alexander points out,

> you have to remember that he was a mass of scar tissue from the neck to the knees. To his dying day he had great chunks of Krupp steel still in his body from the First World War. He'd had gall bladders, he'd had operations for his stomach, he'd had operations for his colon; he was very badly burned in the second war when an aeroplane ran off the end of the runway at Algiers – all those sorts of things, so he wasn't considered a good health risk. But I think he recovered so well that there was always that feeling – 'if I had just stuck it out'. The next election was so close. Would he have just been able to pull it through for Alec and win through? It was so close, it was absolutely knife-edge.

By the time of the 1964 campaign, Macmillan was fit enough to justify his stewardship at a rowdy election meeting in Lord Barber's Doncaster constituency. He pointed with pride to the prosperity of his period and to the British nuclear deterrent which he had modernized by securing Polaris from the Americans in his last year of office.

> My message is very simple tonight. I'm thinking of a lot of people, young people, old people, middle-aged people, because we've had so many years when we have been able to make our country so much happier and better off than we ever dreamt of when I was young. We mustn't take it for granted. It's not something that nature gives us, it's not something that comes out of the sky. It comes out of the cooperation of a sound, sensible, energetic people with a wise government. It's hard to win prosperity, but it's very easy to throw it away. And I warn you, I warn you sincerely, for I

know how hard it has been to fight for this prosperity, I warn you, if you throw it away it will take long, arduous efforts to restore it. That's my first message to you. My second is, no one has worked harder for peace, for some arrangement between the Soviet Communist powers and the Western world. Sometimes in my efforts I have had to work against – or rather, without the full approval of – some of the most powerful governments in the world. Britain is not, of course, in wealth or population equal to Russia or the United States. But she has something to give, something unique, that comes from our history. That comes from centuries and generations of effort and triumph. Comes from our knowledge and experience. Comes from what we can contribute to the search for peace. And I say to you, it will be a black day when a Prime Minister, of whatever party he is, is told he is not wanted at these conferences, because his country is no longer prepared to make the effort to keep it great.

Alexander Stockton believes there was one last achievement for which his grandfather hankered.

He would have loved to have had the total abolition of nuclear weapons [tests]. He was getting very close. The Soviets had agreed to a number of inspections, for tests, underground tests – having already signed the Test Ban Treaty – and the Pentagon insisted on the number being forty-eight, I think it was, which was clearly out of the question. And he deeply regretted that that initiative which he and Jack Kennedy and Khrushchev had taken failed – in a strange way, the trauma and the tension of the Cuban Missile Crisis had brought those three men very close. He felt to his dying day that there was something there he could have done had he been allowed to go on.

In his twilight years, Macmillan would recall his friendship with Jack Kennedy, their last meeting at his home, Birch Grove, and the promise of a presidency cut short by an assassin's bullet in the autumn of 1963.

I've got the rocking chair, which is still in this room; because he couldn't sit for very long, and the pain was always there. And yet this man was a sort of hope of the world. When he went to church on Sunday morning all the village was crowded, and all the way down to the Catholic church at Forest Row there were great crowds of people. After the tragedy, quite voluntarily, our little village here put up a memorial, Forest Row put up a memorial to this man, who they'd only seen once. It was rather moving, the sense of hope that somehow he would achieve something which perhaps we old people would not be able to do.

And he was charming. He had that wonderful combination of apparently a young man on holiday, with a crew cut, not very well dressed, and yet the dignity of the President of the United States, and the Supreme Commander of their armies. He had a wonderful royal way of combining the two things: simplicity, and unbending, with dignity. And nobody could take a chance with him, or try it on.

When he finally went off, I can see him now walking out, when we went out, he said goodbye, and we had arranged to meet either at the end of October or the beginning of November to discuss the next plans, for the world. We felt sure we'd get this Test Ban Treaty, but after that – well, China, Russia . . . we'd have another meeting. I had still got a bit of life in me. Perhaps I could win the next election, he could win another. We might have five or six years together, to work on our plans. They were beginning to come off at last. Something was going to happen. And so he got in, and he sailed out over the valley. Lovely day, in June. And before the leaf had fallen, he had gone. By a most brutal and terrible act.

Macmillan's retirement years were rich in memoir and anecdote. The pace of economic growth in the years of his premiership seemed fabulous when seen from the drab perspective of the late Seventies and early Eighties – a golden memory that even strident attacks from the newer, harder breed of Tory, critical of high public spending and softness on the unions in the Fifties and Sixties, could not dim. Macmillan himself was unrepentant. In his maiden speech in the House of Lords, he made no concessions to the new monetarist ideology:

Many of your noble Lordships will remember it appeared in the nursery. How do you treat a cold? Nanny said, 'Feed a cold' – she was neo-Keynesian – and Mother said 'Starve a cold' – she was a monetarist.

Lord Stockton delivered this speech at the height of the 1984–5 miners' strike.

It breaks my heart to see. I can't interfere or anything at my age with what is happening in our country today. This terrible strike of the best men in the world, who beat the Kaiser's army and beat Hitler and never gave in; it is pointless, endless. And we can't afford that kind of thing. And then this growing division (which the noble Lords just mentioned) of a comparatively prosperous South and an ailing North and Midlands – that can't go on. Then the sort of general sense of tension . . . it's a new kind of – I can only describe it as wicked hatred that has been brought in among different types of people.

How did Lord Stockton get on with the latest standard-bearer of Conservatism, Mrs Thatcher? His grandson Alexander recalls two memorable vignettes:

There were two marvellous occasions, one of which was photographed when she literally sat at his feet at the Carlton Club. The other was when she had been leader for about six months and she came to have lunch at Birch Grove. She was getting to grips with her foreign policy brief, and she talked at great length and at great speed about all matters to do with foreign policy and my grandfather just nodded sagely; and after a monologue for over an hour they drove away and he turned to me and said, 'Do you ever get the feeling you've just failed Geography?'

But at the greatest crisis of her premiership Mrs Thatcher sent for the old statesman, as he later revealed to Ludovic Kennedy. Although, he said, 'I can't say I'm intimate with her at all,' he confessed:

I did try and help her about how to run a war, because it's such a long time since anybody's run a war. I mean the technical methods of running a war, which she did very well. You have to have a War Cabinet. You have to have a Committee of Chiefs. The Secretary of the Committee of Chiefs must not be the Secretary of the War Cabinet. They must be kept separate. You are bound to have a lot of rows, and so on. And just tips on how to run it from the government's point of view – which I learnt from Churchill, of course.

Two years after the Falklands War, Harold Macmillan began a new political career, at the age of ninety. Why in the end did he take an earldom, a hereditary title? After all, as Prime Minister he'd invented life peerages. Alexander Stockton proffers three reasons.

First, on the purely personal level, he was by then very blind already, he couldn't read any more, and he was getting very frustrated and felt that he didn't have any method of playing a part, even in the background. The second thing was that my father had already announced, privately, that he wasn't going to stand in the forthcoming election; and so there was no question of his inhibiting my father's career, which had been a consideration back in 1963, because he had after all retired through ill health and was told by his doctors that he was unlikely to survive that year, and he would probably have done some damage to my father's career. And the third reason, I think, was a sort of romantic one. Here was his ninetieth birthday and two women whom he admired enormously, in the shape of the Monarch and the Prime Minister, put it to him that it would in a sense be a birthday present from the nation to him. This appealed to the Celtic, romantic streak in him and he accepted it for that reason.

So Her Majesty the Queen was the trump card?

Oh, I am sure of it. He's always been enormously fond of her, because he was in a sense very much her mentor – Churchill was a kind of awe-inspiring figure and Anthony wasn't there very long and then he sort of brought her up in politics. They were very, very close – and still were, really, right up to the end.

Was there a single theme – a view of his country and its people – that ran through Macmillan's life? His grandson Alexander expresses it as

the same way as he regarded his business. It was a family business. He stayed very close to the family business and very close to his property. His concerns were the concerns of the patriarch rather than the concerns of an employee director, if you like. He felt very deeply that the people who looked to him, be they people on the estate or publishers, or the authors, or the people in his constituencies, or even the people in the country as a whole, he had an obligation to them which was a personal obligation; not a public obligation, but a deep, personally felt one.

13

A Countryman in Downing Street

'I think if you stopped, not the first hundred people you met in the street but the first ten thousand people you met in any street in any city in Britain, and asked them, "Who was Alec Douglas-Home?" it would surprise me if you got an answer from even two or three of them.'

This must be one of the cruellest verdicts passed on any postwar Prime Minister. But the man who delivered it, the long-standing left-wing Labour MP the late Ian Mikardo, wasn't so sure: 'I wonder if he might be rather proud of it in a funny old way.'

Perhaps he was right. For those under forty, it's very hard to believe that Sir Alec Douglas-Home, the fourteenth Earl of Home, was, or could have been, a British Prime Minister – even a Conservative one – in the years since 1945. For those over forty, the image is of a kind of tweedy blur on the polit-ical landscape, of a Scottish laird with a clipped, aristocratic voice and half-moon glasses. He looked dreadful on television – like a living skull, said one make-up artist – and he gave the satirists of *That Was The Week That Was* a field day. Both as Prime Minister and during the long Indian summer of his political career, Lord Home often gave the impression of being personally rather surprised at finding himself in Number Ten. Even during his short premiership, which lasted from October 1963 to the general election nearly a year later, those close to him thought he would always rather have been elsewhere, on his beautiful country estate in the Scottish Borders near Coldstream. Lord Home readily acknowledged his willingness to forsake the fascinations of state in Downing Street for the more timeless pleasures of the Hirsel: 'At a moment's notice I was ready to go. And thankfully it was a relax-ation, even a couple of days up here. One came back refreshed. I think most people feel that. Unless of course you're bred in London. But I was bred in the country and never used to the town life.'

He even pleaded guilty to being 'the most reluctant premier of the twentieth century'. He was certainly the most surprising. His lack of ambition, the unexpected nature of his arrival in Number Ten with his wife Elizabeth – *his* whole life had not been a preparation for that hour – created a singular atmosphere in Downing Street. Sir Derek Mitchell, his Civil Service Private Secretary, recalls the idiosyncrasies of the Home occupation:

He was extraordinarily kind and courteous. He had, I think, a sort of aristocrat's genuine ease in sizing people up, making them comfortable and generally inspiring affection. People also liked the high degree of informality. The girls in the Garden Room liked the fact that there'd be a grandchild parked outside in a pram. I think Cabinet ministers enjoyed having grandchildren tripping up on them as they waited to go into the Cabinet. And in the flat where he and Elizabeth almost camped out during the week, one saw the flowers that had been brought down from Scotland, the suitcase that lay on the floor, opened but not unpacked, ready for the lid to be closed again on Friday evening when they retired, with some obvious relief, back to the country, where they liked to be.

So reluctant, so unexpected a premier: how did he ever get to Number Ten? When his predecessor, Harold Macmillan, stricken with prostate trouble, conveyed to the 1963 Conservative party conference in Blackpool his intention to resign, the betting would have been on almost anyone but Alec Home succeeding him – on R. A. Butler; on Quintin Hogg, who had renounced his peerage as Lord Hailsham; even, perhaps, on Reginald Maudling from the younger generation; but not on 'the amiable Lord', as Clement Attlee once called him. After all, the Foreign Secretary, as he then was, sat in the House of Lords. He knew nothing of economics and little of home affairs, apart from the experience of a spell in the early 1950s as a Scottish Office minister. He appeared never to have fought for any glittering prize in his life, and gave not the slightest impression of aspiring to the top job.

These were the days when new leaders simply 'emerged', before Conservative MPs actually voted on such matters; and even now, when a new memoir or biography of a politician involved in that frantic party conference of 1963 appears, dark accusations are still made that Harold Macmillan 'fixed' it. It's often said that the outgoing Prime Minister was determined that at all costs his own old rival, Rab Butler, shouldn't get the prize, and that he weighted his advice to the Queen accordingly. Sir Edward Heath was Lord Privy Seal at the Foreign Office when in 1963 the Queen invited Lord Home to form a government, and he was given twenty-four hours in which to try to construct a Cabinet. According to Sir Edward, 'It was originally comparatively well known that Harold Macmillan would like to have seen Quintin Hogg become Prime Minister, to follow him as leader of the party. But I don't think there's ever been any evidence to suggest that the answer that Alec Home should be called for was a fix by Harold Macmillan.' He describes the famous meeting at Enoch Powell's town-house in London, where 'a certain small group did get together and thought they were going to be able to control the situation':

The conclusion which arose from the number of persons who met in this house and the opinions which they expressed was that there was not a majority of Cabinet ministers in favour of Alec Home, but that there was a majority in favour of Rab Butler. It seemed, therefore, to those persons that it was material that Rab Butler should know that such a majority in his favour existed, and I was invited by them to convey that information to him. And I remember very vividly what his reaction was. It was very early in the morning, and he said, 'The Prime Minister must be told of this.' A very characteristic, a very arcane and a very defeatist approach, not the reaction of a man who was determined to fight for what he could get.

What does the outcome of that Cabinet cabal at Mr Powell's place tell us? Perhaps that he who is given the Queen's Commission to have a first stab at forming a government is, to all intents and purposes, already Prime Minister. The outcome was beyond doubt once Butler, in the interests of party unity, agreed to become Foreign Secretary in a Home Cabinet. Enoch Powell and his colleague Iain Macleod, however, declined to become members of a Home Cabinet. What kept Mr Powell from joining the new administration?

What made me refuse was that I had already refused. After all, a person who is approached by a potential Prime Minister has one power, and that power is to say 'no' to him. And I had, in exactly those circumstances, said 'no' to Alec Home. And when, having received what he regarded as sufficient assurances to accept the Queen's Commission to form a government, he addressed the same question to me, I said to him, 'Alec, you don't expect me to give you a different answer today from what I gave yesterday. I'd have to go home and turn all the mirrors to the wall.' And he said, 'Enoch, I didn't expect you to.'

A very characteristic Home reply, without a trace of animus. But what were the particular qualities in the amiable Earl's character that enabled him to win the day? Former chairman of the party and his Minister of Defence, the late Lord Thorneycroft, points to that very amiability:

I think it's certainly true to say that he had no enemies. He was therefore the natural compromise candidate. Anybody there, if they were asked, would it be a disaster if Alec was Prime Minister, would answer no, it would not be a disaster. He wasn't a runner in the real sense of the term, and he wasn't taking trouble to make various announcements or pledges or anything of the kind. He was just Alec, available as the Duke of Omnium and others have always been available, as aristocrats: perfectly happy to serve his country but equally happy to hunt a pack of hounds.

Looking back, was this perhaps a soft option for the Conservative Party? Replacing Macmillan with Home – 'Alec will see us through,' 'Alec's all right' – was, in a way, taking no decision at all. Or, as Lord Thorneycroft tellingly put it, 'It was taking the decision to be the Conservative Party.'

However, while it is true that such easy-going, aristocratic charm disarmed potential enemies, there was steel in the man. Once it became apparent to him that he had a chance of the premiership, he moved with a deftness and a determination that wrong-footed his allegedly more professional rivals. As well as toughness, there was a consistency of views which made him anything but a trimmer capable of being all things to all men. Home was a veteran of Munich; and, unlike some in his party, he never tried to explain away the history of his appeasing past as Neville Chamberlain's Parliamentary Private Secretary. He was also unrepentant in his support for the Suez expedition. As the Anglo–French invasion of Egypt reached its ruinous climax in November 1956, with the Americans destabilizing the pound and putting the warships of their Sixth Fleet alongside the Royal Navy vessels to harass them, Lord Home, as Commonwealth Secretary, wrote to the exhausted Prime Minister, Sir Anthony Eden: 'If our country rediscovers its soul and inspiration, your calm courage will have achieved the miracle.'

In the 1980s, looking over the declassified Suez papers, Lord Home reiterated his old conviction of the rightness of trying to topple the Egyptian leader, Colonel Nasser.

Hindsight tells me that Nasser probably couldn't have dominated the Middle East. Nobody has been able to unite the Arabs and therefore the chances are that perhaps Nasser couldn't have done it. But it was a horrible combination, you know. The Russians were there – and that was new, you have to remember that was new – and they've always wanted the Gulf area. If Anthony Eden's instinct was right that Nasser's operations really were going to cause very great trouble and could lose us our oil, then we had to try something of this kind. Some would say, and I'd be inclined to agree, that we ought to have contemplated a much bigger operation and taken the whole of Cairo, made sure that Nasser fell.

He did not think that the Suez débâcle hastened the end of empire: 'It illustrated to people that Britain was no longer a great power and couldn't mobilize sufficient force to subdue a country like Egypt. This was the damaging thing, really. But it was inevitable that the empire should dissolve.' However, it did, he thought, teach future Prime Ministers – including himself – that Britain could never again mount a serious military or economic initiative without the agreement of the United States. And he remained critical, though in characteristically measured terms, of the actions of the US government in the crisis: 'It was unnecessary for them, to put it no more strongly than that. We'd been allies in the war and all that kind of thing, we understood each other and basically all stood for the same things. It was quite unnecessary for them to demonstrate their hostility with the Sixth Fleet movement. That was what stuck in my gullet.'

For all his calm acceptance of a new reality, Lord Home remained a strong Commonwealth man, constantly and openly worried by the rapid pace of decolonization after Macmillan's 'Wind of Change' speech in 1960. At this very time the Cabinet was agreeing to apply for British membership of the European Economic Community. Sir Edward Heath, as number two at the Foreign Office, led the negotiating team in Brussels. Did he see his number one, Lord Home, as a reluctant European?

> No, because he believed that our membership of the Community was the best possible thing for the Commonwealth. He realized that there were certain things we had to try to negotiate for the Commonwealth in their particular economic interest, but that our membership of the European Community was for the future and this was bound to be for the benefit of the Commonwealth. If we were outside Europe we could have no influence whatever, and that couldn't be of any help to Commonwealth countries. And at the end of his life he said to me he was more convinced than ever that we were right.

The word 'influence' in this passage is significant. Lord Home may have realized that after Suez Britain's *great* power days were over but, like nearly all Conservatives of that generation, he was determined that Britain should remain a player in the world game at the highest level possible.

Lord Home's preoccupation with foreign affairs during the early 1960s should have made him economically aware, because diplomatic clout was increasingly bound up with industrial strength. It was never clear that it had, and both commentators and party colleagues wondered whether this was not a serious gap in the portfolio of experience he brought to the premiership. Only when he became Prime Minister did he realize how much the economy would impinge on his office:

> It oughtn't to have done, but the thing that did take me by surprise was the amount one was supposed to concentrate on the economic affairs of the country. I'm a natural devolver and I always thought that if you appointed a very competent Chancellor of the Exchequer that was it. Not at all. The economic side was always overflowing into the Prime Minister's programme.

And the famous phrase about getting the box of matchsticks out when he was solving economic problems; was that actually true, or was it a little joke on the hustings? 'I don't think I ever actually got them out. It was purely a chance remark at lunch, because Kenneth Harris said to me, "Do you think you could be Prime Minister?" and I said, "I really don't think so because I have to do all my economics with a matchstick." But it stuck, of course. Harold Wilson wasn't going to miss something like that.'

It was his misfortune to find himself facing, in Harold Wilson, the first leader of the opposition with a professional training in economics and statistics. The argot of Keynesian demand management was foreign to Lord Home. Was there more to his distaste for such modern economic techniques? Was he, perhaps, a 'sound money' man by instinct? The late Lord Thorneycroft, briefly Macmillan's resolutely anti-inflationary Chancellor of the Exchequer, saw his approach rather as one of practical judgement, that of the steward of the nation's land and resources:

> I've never seen Alec as a 'sound money' man, or a money man at all. He hated economics. I don't think he expressed passionate views about the economic situation, though I used to tell him that I respected his judgement very much indeed. I think he was a very sensible man. He thought about money as a great aristocrat thinks about running an estate, but it wasn't the sort of chat you get today. He would want to preserve what was worthwhile in a country. He was a natural Conservative.

Every Prime Minister for the last thirty-odd years has chaired the Cabinet's Economic Policy Committee; but not Lord Home, who left this to the Chancellor of the Exchequer, Reginald Maudling. 'But I used to talk to him regularly, of course, about what he was doing. I was not familiar with economics. It had never come my way. Nor have I been encouraged ever since to think that it is an exact science. But it was a weakness. If I had thought I was going to be Prime Minister I would have taken more trouble to understand the various theories.'

Lord Home's problems on taking over the premiership were not confined to unfamiliarity with the slide-rule and Keynes's *General Theory*. The House of Commons was not the House of Lords, where he'd led his political life since inheriting his father's earldom in 1951, and the Commons had changed a great deal since he had last been there. In later life he would talk about the shock, the noise the opposition made as they tried to trap him during Prime Minister's Questions. To make matters worse for him, in 1963–4 Harold Wilson was the most effective leader of the opposition anyone could remember. Lord Home must have struck the Labour Party as a gift. Lord Healey, then a member of the Shadow Cabinet, recalls him as 'an ideal target, especially of course for Harold Wilson who really made mincemeat of him every time they met in the House'. This is not to say that the opposition had no respect for him; quite the contrary, as Ian Mikardo explained:

I could never feel highly critical of Alec Douglas-Home, I don't know how anybody could. He was a good guy. Contrary to what most people think, decency counts for a lot in politics, especially in relationships between people on opposite sides of the House. I could never have said Alec Douglas-Home was a bad egg and that maybe he was still living a century back and on those grounds he ought to be burned in a socialist fire or something. Nobody could ever think that way about Alec.

Perhaps this palpable decency, with its cross-party appeal, explains why Sir Alec came so close to saving the 1964 election. Nevertheless, faced with the numerate, rhetorically agile Harold Wilson, those equally tangible short-comings on economic and domestic policy told against him. Could there be a reason for this that goes beyond his concentration on foreign affairs? Unlike many of his Cabinet colleagues, he never seemed entirely at ease with the postwar consensus, with its emphasis on economic planning and public spending. His own economic thinking, such as it was, had been fashioned in the pre-Keynesian era, a point fully appreciated by a young economics journalist working with him in Downing Street: Nigel, now Lord, Lawson, who was to become Chancellor under Mrs Thatcher.

Alec Home may have been a little uneasy with the particular consensus in which he found himself slightly unexpectedly Prime Minister, but he accepted it. You needed, I think, to challenge it, a degree of bloody-mindedness, which wasn't a particular characteristic of his, and you also needed a freedom from guilt to challenge the ever-greater power of the state. To say that people should have much more freedom to make their own way, stand or fall – of course there would be the safety net for those who really couldn't cope with society, but everybody else should make their own way, do the best they can with their own talents and abilities, and that way the society and the economy will do best – that could be made to look very heartless, and it could look as if it's all very well for people with privi-leged backgrounds, but it's harder for others. And therefore people with privileged backgrounds – and Alec Home *par excellence* had an extremely gilded background – would have felt a little bit awkward in challenging it because of the feeling that people would say, 'Well, it's all right for you.'

Even if he'd won the 1964 election, then, it would, Lord Lawson believes, have continued to be what one might call a *noblesse oblige* premiership, with no fundamental change of direction. We should be wary of the connotations of language. One man's 'guilt' is another man's 'duty'; recall Lord Home's treating the whole country as if it were a great landed estate.

There was, however, one parliamentary monument to his brief premiership that has won applause from free-market economists like Lord Lawson: the abolition of resale price maintenance, the system which kept the price of a packet of cornflakes the same in the corner grocer as in the then still novel high street supermarket. Edward Heath was the minister determined to stride in where previous Presidents of the Board of Trade had feared to tread. Not all his Cabinet colleagues were happy to follow, as he recalls.

> There were some people who were very strongly opposed to it, not only for political but for economic reasons. They thought it was a good thing to have fixed prices. There were others who said no, we've got to move into the modern age and really give people the opportunity of competing. The small shopkeepers and such are not going to suffer because people are still going to do local shopping as well as go to the supermarkets on the Friday evening or Saturday when they want to. And they backed me.

One of his backers was the Prime Minister:

> I happened to think that Ted Heath was right on that occasion, so I backed him. It wasn't popular, particularly because I think a majority of the Cabinet would rather it hadn't been pressed, and certainly our majority in Parliament didn't like the resale price maintenance Bill. But it was not far off an election and I thought we'd better settle it one way or the other and go for it. It possibly lost us an odd seat or two; I don't think very many. But then, there was only an odd seat or two in it at the end of the day; we lost by four seats.

Conservative Party legend has it that the abolition of resale price maintenance did lose them the shopkeeper vote and the 1964 election, putting Lord Home on the path to retirement from the Tory leadership. Pressure had been building for some time in favour of a more 'modern' man to take on Harold Wilson; in July 1965 he stood down and Conservative MPs, using the – for them – novel device of a secret ballot, elected Ted Heath to replace him. Lord Lawson takes a slightly jaundiced view of the circumstances of his replacement.

> During the end of his period there were a number of people within the Conservative Party working very hard to get him to go, and eventually he did go. He didn't have to go; it was a voluntary act by him. He enjoyed,

on the whole, being Prime Minister. He never liked being out of office, and particularly he never liked the job of leader of the opposition. And when there was so much bitching about him – quite wrongly, I think – he decided to pack it in and stand down. And then, of course, all those people who had been trying to get him to go were then the people who were applauding him and cheering after he'd gone and saying what a wonderful man he was and we'll never see his like again and so on. That hypocrisy did irk him rather, but he never let it show.

The retrospective gilding of previous Tory leaderships is something of a party tradition. However, in Lord Home's case it had much to do with the courtesy he extended towards Ted Heath, who made him shadow Foreign Secretary and, after the 1970 general election, sent him back to the Foreign and Commonwealth Office, always his natural political home. The warmth of his welcome back at the FCO also went beyond the standard courtesies. Sir Antony Acland, former Head of the Diplomatic Service, who served for two spells as Lord Home's Foreign Office Private Secretary, recalls the priorities that earned him such widespread esteem.

He had a Christian sense of right and wrong; and then what was right for his country. And he believed in democracy and free enterprise and hated Communism and totalitarianism and oppression. Then, of course, much lower down the scale – didn't really feature very much! – what was right for the Conservative Party. Although he believed in Conservatism he wasn't a party political figure at all. You had occasionally to say to him, 'Well, how do you think the party will react to this?' 'Oh yes,' he'd say, 'oh, that's right. Of course, I must think a little about that.' And never, ever, in all the time I knew him, did I ever hear him say, 'How will this affect *my* standing? Is this right for me, for my reputation?' Just didn't enter his makeup.

One thing Lord Home always knew was right for him: the regular escape from public duties. Unlike some of his successors, he had a rich and fulfilling private life.

Well, first of all one's wife keeps one sane. And then children or grand-children. I always made time for them whenever I could. And then hobbies. Fishing is one. If you're wading in running water you can't think of anything else. That's a very good secret: get away and fish. And then gardening. And so all the sporting side of things, the games, all of that. I always used to pop up to Lord's. When Sir Robert Menzies was Prime Minister [of Australia] and I was either Foreign Secretary or Prime

Minister, we managed over fifteen years to make certain that the meetings of the Commonwealth Prime Ministers coincided with the first Test Match at Lord's.

He was also, apart from being that rarity of recent times, an aristocrat in Downing Street, the most famous flower arranger in British political history. And he was a collectors' item for another reason: he was a man who appeared to have taken Baldwin's advice to new backbenchers, someone who *had* grown a new skin and thrown away his press cuttings. Such serenity is striking. Though Alec Home was not the same without his wife, Elizabeth, who predeceased him, it's almost certain the reluctant premier died a happy man; can that be said of any other Prime Minister in the postwar period? Lord Hailsham, one of his rivals for the leadership in 1963, thinks the odds are probably against it: 'I've known every Prime Minister to a greater or lesser extent since Balfour, including Balfour, and most of them have died unhappy . . . It doesn't *lead* to happiness.'

How should we remember Lord Home? Sir Edward Heath emphasizes his achievements in a short period of office.

He was only Prime Minister for less than a year, and it was very difficult for him to make his mark during that time, but those who have followed events closely will always say that as Foreign Secretary he was outstanding, because he handled foreign policy very soundly. And they would pay tribute for that and for the fact that in the time he was Prime Minister he did support major changes, first of all in economic affairs, with the abolition of resale price maintenance, and secondly from the point of view of regional development, in which he believed passionately, as indeed I did.

It has often been said that in his short time at Number Ten he showed he was a very decisive Prime Minister, very good at running Cabinet business. Sir Edward links this with his personal qualities: 'He was certainly good at handling Cabinet affairs, in the same way that he was good at handling foreign affairs; people respected him for his knowledge and for his integrity and the fact that he wasn't creating, or trying to create, a great public personal image.'

So successful was Lord Home as a *non*-image maker that history, wrongly, will find it immensely difficult to recall at all the understated premier amid the clamour of those who claim to have changed everything. Lloyd George was once asked how posterity would remember Arthur Balfour. His reply was: 'He will be just like the scent on a pocket handkerchief.' Will the memory of Lord Home be as fleeting? He didn't close down the Empire like

Harold Macmillan. He didn't reorient our geopolitics by taking us into Europe like Ted Heath. He didn't curtail the power of the unions or redraw the boundary between the public and private sectors like Margaret Thatcher. And yet there is a personal legacy: the touch of decency in public life, almost above the party battle, as rare as it is endearing. It is easy to undervalue those quiet virtues. But although, as Sir Edward Heath pointed out, he supported a few important economic initiatives during his brief premiership, it has to be said that he changed the direction of neither his party nor his country.

14

The Scarlet Thread

Earlier this month came the Treasury figures for the second quarter of this year on the balance of payments, showing a balance of payments surplus of £190 million. Britain's friends applauded these figures. But not the leader of the Conservative Party. This is what he said – and I quote his words: 'The second quarter's always a good quarter. If we are to keep the thing in perspective we have to recognize that this comes at the end of five years of Labour government.' So let us see what was the balance of payments surplus in the seasonally favourable second quarter of 1964 when the right honourable gentleman himself was in charge of the nation's overseas trade. Now what was their surplus? There was *no* surplus. Their achievement was a deficit of £184 million. Their achievement after nearly thirteen years – thirteen years – *thirteen years* – was to produce a quarter's results which were £374 million worse, in a single quarter, than what we have just published after less than five years, and done it, of course, in the second quarter. The second quarter is always a good quarter! That's what the man said. Not when *he* was in charge it wasn't.

This was Harold Wilson at the Labour party conference in the autumn of 1969, an absolute pig of a year for him when the list of the Labour government's woes ran off the page. It was vintage stuff and very revealing of Wilson himself: a blend of statistics and a carefully crafted reworking of the recent political past, an oratorical style which could dance straight from sub-Churchillian statesman's talk to a Northern comedian's patter that was pure Eric Morecambe, all the while rubbing the nose of his hapless Tory opponent, Edward Heath, in the paradoxes of his own leaden prose. The Tories in Parliament knew they were up against a truly formidable opponent, as Lord Whitelaw, Ted Heath's Chief Whip in the 1960s, readily acknowledges:

'Oh, there's no doubt that he was. When he was the Prime Minister between 1964 and 1966 and then after he won the 1966 election, he undoubtedly was. People feared what he would do in Parliament and they were right to fear it. He was a very powerful parliamentary figure.'

It is hard now to recapture just how Harold Wilson bedazzled his political generation. He seemed the complete professional politician, with good reason. The late Ian Mikardo, like Wilson, arrived at Westminster on the Labour tide of 1945; and as he recalls, his colleague gave the appearance of having charted his course for Downing Street from that moment at least: 'I have no doubt, and I didn't have any doubt from the early days, that somewhere in a drawer in Wilson's residence there was a sheet of paper headed "Ways to the Top", and it listed all the things he was going to do in the sequence in which he was going to do them. That is the constant thread, the scarlet thread running through it all.'

Initially, that scarlet thread was detectable only by the true insider. As Attlee's youngest Cabinet minister – he was only thirty-one when he went to the Board of Trade in 1947 – on the surface he was donnish, technocratic and precocious. His Parliamentary Private Secretary, Barbara Castle, now Lady Castle, was none of these things, but her initial impressions of him were strongly favourable:

'First was his absolute geniality. He'd got no side, you see. He'd been the wonderboy, you know, during the war. It was obvious he'd got a first-class brain and all that, but he was so accessible and from the very beginning what I liked about him was his lack of stuffiness, his "cheeky chappie" streak, which was a very refreshing change from the pomposity of some other politicians I knew.'

The moustachioed Wilson first came to public attention with his clipped, mannered newsreel presentations on Guy Fawkes Day 1949, when he ended wartime restrictions on a range of clothing and consumer goods. With that flair for a headline for which he was later famous, he called it 'the bonfire of controls'. Not everyone was impressed. Left-winger Ian Mikardo, for one, saw him removing the kind of controls which, if Britain was going to have a peacetime socialist economy, would still be necessary – and, worse, doing it with enthusiasm:

'This was a man doing something which theoretically we ought not to have been enthusiastic about even if it were necessary; he did it enthusiastically. This was a man looking for popularity; and a pragmatist looking for popularity is going to let you down in the end, isn't he? The bonfire of controls was as good as saying "I don't believe in socialism."'

In ideological terms, Wilson travelled light. His detractors always suspected that his early Liberal affiliation at Oxford was a truer guide to that elusive phenomenon, the real Wilson, than any rhetorical devotion to the public ownership creed, Clause Four of the Labour Party constitution. Michael Foot, a real Clause Four man in the 1945 Parliament, swiftly sensed the thread of ambition, and the economic pragmatism, which would take him to the party leadership.

I think he obviously had the calculation – and to pull off the calculation, by the way, if that's what it was, took a hell of a lot of doing. But it was something more than that. He really was a politician to the fingertips. After all, let's look at the elections that he won – and there's no political leader in recent times who's won as many elections as he did – looking back, people think, 'Oh well, it was easy.' But it wasn't. Nobody thought so beforehand. So although, of course, there was this very strong element of calculation, of him calculating what was going to be beneficial for himself, also he had ideas on many of these matters. Many of them are not exactly socialist ideas, but they were expansionist ideas, they were Keynesian ideas many of them, and the economic affairs – I think he had a full grasp of it.

So the earlier thread was more Keynesian pink than Red Flag scarlet. How, then, did Wilson acquire his reputation as a man of the left? At a stroke, by resigning with Nye Bevan and John Freeman in April 1951 over the cost of Hugh Gaitskell's Korean War rearmament budget. There were those who detected cool personal calculation in even such a seemingly principled act – Denis Healey among them:

I think in fact he did feel strongly about the unwisdom, to put it at its lowest, of Gaitskell's decision to pay 10 per cent of our national product on defence; he thought, as the Tories later proved, that it could not be done even if you wanted to do it, but it was wrong to want to do it. I think this was a very genuine feeling. But I doubt whether he would have had the courage to resign over it if he hadn't felt that the government was nearing its end and it was a way of establishing, for the first time in his political career, a clear political personality as a member of the left.

It was Wilson's misfortune that his tactical brilliance led both left and right to suspect him – suspicion to which he was especially sensitive as the premiership beckoned:

I always made clear, long before I became leader, that I thought the job of the leader of the party was to represent the whole party and to work with all sections, and when I became leader, I said, 'I am not going to be the prisoner of any part of the party,' and that was fully understood. I think some of the troubles and some of the arguments about me in the past have been because I wouldn't say, 'Yes, I am a Bevanite,' 'No, I am not a Bevanite.' I would say, 'The issue we're talking about is a rearmament programme. We're talking about raw materials; we're talking about German rearmament; we're talking about nationalization of building land'

– whatever it was, and I'd be more interested in the issue than in the personality.

Perhaps it was less a matter of sacrificing principles he never had, more an acquisition of the skills and persona he needed to capture first his party and then the government. It's as if he were still a Boy Scout in his native Huddersfield, sewing new badges to his shirt. By the time he succeeded Hugh Gaitskell in 1963, the erstwhile backroom boy could hold any audience, smother any party difficulty, be it nuclear weapons or nationalization, with a captivating phrase. His long-time political friend Peter Shore watched the final transformation, and was in no doubt that the end result was the most successful leader of the opposition this century.

No question! And as every year goes by the claim to be by far the most brilliant leader of the opposition becomes more clearly established. But in fact he used the House of Commons very effectively as a platform. It's very important for a leader of the opposition to establish at least equality of performance with the Prime Minister of the day. Harold took on Harold Macmillan, in his declining days, and certainly was his equal. Then he took on Sir Alec Douglas-Home, and quite frankly he beat him on virtually every occasion; and so he established himself very clearly as the obvious leader, the dominant personality, in the House of Commons, and then backed it up at the same time with a nationwide campaign. And he projected the Labour Party's policies to large audiences in the country as well as in the House itself, and that enthused the Labour Party, at least as far as I could see, in a way that certainly hadn't happened before and probably hasn't since.

At the 1963 party conference in Scarborough, Wilson found the perfect rhetorical vehicle. It bore the shining badge of modernity: science and technology.

Mr Chairman, let me conclude with what I think the message of all this is for this conference, because in this conference, in all our plans for the future, we are redefining and we are restating our socialism in terms of the scientific revolution. But that revolution cannot become a reality unless we are prepared to make far-reaching changes in economic and social attitudes which permeate our whole system of society. The Britain that is going to be forged in the white heat of this revolution will be no place for restrictive practices or for outdated methods on either side of industry.

'White heat' caught the mood of the restless Sixties. The Conservatives, under Sir Alec Douglas-Home, looked like a crumbling *ancien régime* after thirteen years in office. But Wilson only squeaked into power in October 1964 by a majority of three; and immediately he was confronted by the kind of problem which yielded not an inch to the cleverest of phrases – the weakness of the British economy, as reflected in a balance of payments deficit of £800 million, with all the stress that placed on the pound, then locked into a system of fixed exchange rates. Within hours of stepping into Number Ten, Wilson, his number two, George Brown, and his Chancellor, Jim Callaghan, had to decide whether to maintain the $2.80 parity bequeathed by the Attlee government after the 1949 devaluation or to take the rate down. Treasury man Sir Derek Mitchell was working for Wilson in Downing Street as his Principal Private Secretary when the new administration came down on the side of maintaining parity.

> It was always said to have been a political rather than an economic decision, and I think that's probably an apt description of it. And the politics of it were dictated, I believe, by Harold Wilson's own determination not to go up this particular creek again. He felt, more strongly than anyone else there, that this would represent a broken promise, a change of direction which would reflect on him subsequently – as indeed, eventually, it did.

That decision set the government's course for the next three years. Some people believed that Labour's social programme, its plans for regeneration, white heat and all, were sacrificed to that sterling parity. Barbara Castle, Wilson's left-leaning Minister for Overseas Development, thought the decision ill-judged.

> I believed that the earlier the devaluation had come, the better. Obviously I would have liked it to come immediately we took over in 1964, and that would have put an entirely different complexion on what we did, and I think it would have enabled us to win the support of workers in the factories, rank-and-file trade unionists. We could have said to them, 'Look, we are engaged on a growth policy and to help us you've really got to pitch in, lads, and not make excessive wage demands.' But when all they were offered was deflation, deflation, deflation on the old Tory formula of financial orthodoxy, we lost their sympathy. Now, I don't know that it would have made a very dramatic difference if we had devalued in 1966 as against 1967. The key date was 1964 and we should have set the stamp on our government then.

This view was echoed on the right of the party – by, for example, Roy Jenkins, who was Minister of Aviation in 1964.

> I think it would have been better to have devalued when the Labour government came in. It inherited a very bad economic position, inherited a massive balance of payments deficit, and so there would have been a perfectly good scenario in which to do it, though I can understand a counter-argument for saying we've got to have an election within a year, eighteen months, better try and get that over first. I wouldn't think I'd have accepted it myself, had I been in a position of power, but I could understand that argument. But once the election was over then the summer of 1966 was a great mistake, a major mistake which hobbled a lot of the effectiveness of that government.

Wilson was later asked in an interview whether he'd been tempted to break free earlier. He remained unrepentant:

> I think if we'd done it immediately in 1964 – it was a temptation – it would've been easy. We could have said, 'Look, we've suddenly discovered what no one knew': there was an £800 million deficit which the country hadn't been told about. This would be a wonderful opportunity to do it and to blame our predecessors; there was a political temptation to do it. The reason why I was very much opposed to it was that I knew it wasn't going to be such a nice, easy thing as some of my colleagues thought, but secondly, I thought if we did that the overseas world would say, 'Look at this government, every time they get into trouble, even a small trouble, they devalue.' Then, of course, it would be expected next time. I believe, absolutely categorically, the case was stronger in 1966. Had we done it in 1966 I believe we'd have had to do it again in 1968 because of the problem we were facing at that time. 1967 it was. I regard it as a defeat. I fought hard to prevent it and really we had no alternative by that time, particularly since the French were talking the pound down all the time.

Characteristically, in his devaluation broadcast, Wilson tried to gloss over the setback with a form of words that came to haunt him and left him with a reputation as the most devious occupant of Number Ten since Lloyd George: 'From now on, the pound abroad is worth fourteen per cent or so less in terms of other currencies. That doesn't mean, of course, that the pound here in Britain, in your pocket or purse or in your bank, has been devalued. What it does mean is that we shall now be able to sell more goods abroad on a competitive basis.'

Yet the 'if only' approach to political history is a dangerous one. Even if the pound had been devalued in 1964, is there any convincing reason to suppose that the postwar economic miracle would have been there for the taking? After all, it had eluded every premier who came before Wilson and all those who have come since.

Wilson was always growth-minded, and his experience at the Board of Trade told him that the Treasury would invariably sacrifice production on the altar of finance. His solution in 1964 was to weaken it by creating a competitor, the Department of Economic Affairs. The new body, however, started off at something of a disadvantage, as Sir Ronald McIntosh, who transferred to it from the Treasury, explains.

> I don't think there was anything wrong with the concept of the Department of Economic Affairs. I think actually that it was one of the most constructive and imaginative administrative innovations of the postwar period. What I do think about it is that the people who were responsible for bringing it into being and operating it in the early stages had almost no first-hand experience of government. The civil servants had no real cohesion – they were all enthusiasts, but they came from different parts of Whitehall with different kinds of experience and they had to build up quite quickly a group feeling and a team spirit and so on – and not nearly enough thought was given to the handling of the absolutely inevitable and predictable power struggle, both within the Cabinet and, more importantly perhaps, within Whitehall between the Treasury and this upstart new department which looked as though it was going to try and take over many of the Treasury's functions.

Peter Shore, former DEA minister, homes in on this last point as the crucial one:

> The real weakness of the DEA from the start was the division of powers between the Treasury and the DEA, with the Treasury being, as it were, entrusted with the short-term management of the economy and the DEA with the medium-term, and when the short-term got in the way of the medium-term, I'm afraid it was the medium-term that had to give.

Planning was *the* big idea of the first Wilson government. The National Plan, unveiled by George Brown in September 1965, anticipated annual growth of 4 per cent, well above the postwar norm. Within a year it had collapsed. The consequences of a seamen's strike had put pressure on the pound, causing the Cabinet to rein back on expansion; but wasn't there more to it than that? Ian Mikardo, socialist and management consultant, thought the government hadn't equipped itself for the job in hand: 'There was no mechanism for planning at all, and there was nothing like the French agreements between the government and private industry, the planning agreements. The government couldn't do what it had promised because it didn't have the tools to do it with, and showed no sign of desiring to create the tools to do it with.'

Such setbacks brought to the fore Wilson's insecurities, never altogether concealed even in the three and a half years of remarkable political success between his taking over from Gaitskell and the economic measures of July 1966. He needed the comfort of cronyism, the company of his political intimates. Among them was Peter Shore, who notes the crucial support the fabled 'kitchen cabinet' provided for the sometimes beleaguered Prime Minister:

> The importance of the kitchen cabinet to Harold was not just a form of relaxation. It was really him consciously accepting that, 'Yes, I am enclosed in my prime ministerial office and role. I have only two ways out of this. One is when I go to the House of Commons and I meet that lot over there, and that sometimes is a very shaking and bracing experience, but secondly, if I deliberately build into my political life a place for the party.' And really his office was about the Labour Party rather than anything else.

The name forever associated with the kitchen cabinet is that of Wilson's long-time political secretary, Marcia Williams, later Lady Falkender. The rumour mills hummed – erroneously – with talk of an intimate relationship between the two. What was undoubtedly true, though, was the special blend of political counsel and personal loyalty that bound them together over four decades. Sir Derek Mitchell had celebrated turf fights in Number Ten with Lady Falkender, but he appreciated why she mattered to Wilson. 'He needed desperately to be able to rely on the loyalty of one or two people and Marcia was pre-eminently the one whose loyalty was never in question in any way whatsoever. He told me on one occasion that he knew she was difficult, but the fact was that when he was no longer Prime Minister she was the one who would still be there, backing him and helping him'

If the kitchen cabinet provided solace of one kind, playing the international statesman offered another. Far from making a radical break with the thrust of postwar British foreign and defence policy, to the fury of the left he kept the Polaris nuclear force and became a keen exponent of the 'special relationship', only jibbing at the commitment of British troops alongside US forces in Vietnam. He found no difficulty initially in keeping British troops east of Suez as the price of American support for sterling. He was almost Lord Curzon-like in his talk of Britain's frontiers being on the Himalayas, though he made a brave attempt to end white minority rule in Rhodesia after Ian Smith's Unilateral Declaration of Independence. Can he be faulted for overestimating British power, not least its capacity to bring the Rhodesian rebellion to an end in weeks rather than months? Sir Derek Mitchell, who was at his elbow in every high-level meeting, sees some justification in such criticism.

> In some ways this was an extreme example of the lure of foreign policy for any Prime Minister who finds domestic policy hard going. It was in many ways a God-given opportunity to exercise what Wilson regarded as some of his great skills. He'd always prided himself, rightly or wrongly, on being a very effective negotiator. Here was a long-running negotiation. He enjoyed it most of the time, but it went on far longer than he'd intended and it was not on the whole successful.

Sir Derek, in the comfortless role of candid counsellor, did try to offer private warnings on these trips to Salisbury, but with variable effect: 'One always tries to do that, but knowing that at times one's going to find the person you're advising more receptive than at other times.'

On racial injustice there remained a genuine streak of Wilsonian conviction. Even in the fraught aftermath of devaluation, he was prepared to forgo much-needed British exports by refusing to restart major arms sales to South Africa. He prepared for what were perhaps the nastiest Cabinet meetings of his first premiership in characteristic fashion, as Barbara Castle recalls:

> I'd already been called into secret consultation by Harold over that issue. He said, 'Barbara, I can talk to you because I know you never leak. Only this time I want you to.' And he told me that at this Overseas and Defence Policy Committee, this attempt was being made to sell some arms to South Africa and that would totally discredit him politically. He'd be finished. And he wanted me therefore to get a move going among the backbenchers in the House of Commons to play into his hands and stop it. Now, that produced one of the most bitter periods I can remember in Cabinet with George Brown and others having apoplexy, blaming Harold for all these great stories that were circulating and all the rest of it – and of course to some extent they were right. But then Harold was fighting very hard and I think it was partly because he felt he'd lost credibility over devaluation and he wasn't going to lose credibility over a big left-wing issue like arms for South Africa.

For all his political manoeuvring, by this time Wilson was past his best. Paradoxically, his verve began to drain away almost from the moment he won his huge majority in the 1966 general election. Denis Healey, then Defence Secretary and an increasingly powerful figure in the Cabinet, thinks that personal insecurity once more came to the fore.

> I think in his first period, until the election in 1966, he was brilliant. After all, it was a tactical situation he inherited. There wasn't much room for strategy because we were looking to consolidate our victory at the first possible moment, and he handled it very well. I certainly had no complaints, because we had to take some very difficult decisions on defence at that time and he always supported me. I think the difficulties arose when he had a secure majority. He knew he was there for four or five years and that was the period, I think, when he began to be suspicious of everybody else as wanting to supplant him and started packing the Cabinet with people not of Cabinet calibre in order to command a majority, and in my view that's a mistake.

As always with Harold Wilson, matters are never quite that simple. Roy Jenkins, by this time at the Treasury, offers another analysis: 'One of his great qualities was that he had very good nerve in a crisis. He never recriminated in a crisis and he never panicked in a crisis, and those are two very high qualities in a Prime Minister. It was when things were going better that he got suspicious and difficult.'

The Prime Minister and the Chancellor, however, needed each other. The two men, though both grammar-school boys groomed for great things in prewar Oxford, had very different tastes and lifestyles. Jenkins grew less Welsh and more Whiggish by the year; Wilson remained determinedly provincial, almost a professional Northerner. Nevertheless, for a time at least the relationship remained strong, as Jenkins recalls:

> Although we weren't in a way socially very close, we could gossip together with pleasure and interest, certainly on my side. One would have long, long meetings with him, two and a half hours or something like this, in which one would sort of ramble round some of the ramparts of political reminiscence, as it were. He had a very good statistical mind and I was rather interested in that sort of detail. He could always remember who lost three by-elections running in what year, or whatever it was, and liked that sort of gossip. And we also had an interest in railway timetables and railway stations!

During the great crisis of 1969, however, over trade union reform, not even a gossip about Bradshaw or the swing at Fulham East in 1933 could fill the gap which opened between Jenkins, Wilson and Barbara Castle over her proposals in the evocatively named White Paper *In Place of Strife*. Joe Haines, Wilson's Downing Street Press Secretary, describes the disarray which ensued.

> There were people like Roy Jenkins, who were happy to go along with it at the beginning, and then lost their nerve. There was Peter Shore, who said memorably to Harold, 'I thought you didn't mean it, Prime Minister.' There was Tony Crosland, who knew little about the unions and was scared of them, and believed the myths about powerful unions. Len Murray, who was TUC Assistant General Secretary at the time, said to me at one point during the negotiations with the unions, 'Why doesn't the Prime Minister understand that we're a paper tiger?' Well, *he* understood it but his Cabinet didn't. They were scared of the unions, they were scared of the vote back home, they were scared of the general election coming the next year. They thought that they could carry on with a kind of cosy, occasionally hostile, union–Labour relationship and that they could always, if it came to it, do a deal. I think Barbara Castle and Harold realized that the relationship between the government and the party and unions had to change.

By subsequent standards, the proposals to curb unofficial wildcat strikes, Wilson's latest ploy for tackling the root of Britain's economic weakness – pre-strike ballots, cooling-off periods – were tame. So why did pivotal figures like Roy Jenkins trim? Lord Jenkins admits that

> I didn't think I covered myself with glory. I thought most of the other people in Cabinet behaved still worse, though! But what I said from the beginning was that you will not be able to get this through if you do it on the very leisurely timescale which you have in mind. For a Labour government to do trade union reform is a very difficult thing and it's got to be done on the run, with momentum, whereas the original plan was to do it over about eighteen months. So I did have a consistent position on that, and as one got on into the summer and the negotiations became of a more and more Byzantine nature, it really became, I found, impossible to follow them. Meanwhile the Cabinet, led by Jim Callaghan, of course, who mounted a great revolt against the Prime Minister and Barbara Castle's policy, began to slip more and more into a hostile position to this, and eventually it became clear that one had negotiated too much, that the momentum had gone out of the thing and it simply couldn't be carried through.

Lady Castle thought her colleagues had been feeble:

Lily-livered lot they were! I wanted my Cabinet colleagues to learn the lesson of what we were trying to do, and what I was trying to do was to save the trade union movement from the destruction I could see coming upon it unless it was prepared to accept certain responsibilities about controlling its own membership and accepting a positive role in helping the government to save the economy.

In Place of Strife could have broken the government, but in the end Wilson opted for survival. His gift for the vocabulary of face-saving added yet another phrase to the political lexicon the moment he went on air to explain away his defeat at the hands of his Cabinet and the trade unions:

Yesterday we made one more effort to get them to meet our requirements. We told them that if they could not do so, we would proceed at once to legislation. And yesterday evening we reached agreement, not just in words, not just in a statement of intentions, but in what the TUC themselves described as a solemn and binding undertaking unanimously agreed by the whole General Council. I was left in no doubt about their determination to carry out this undertaking.

'Solemn and binding . . .' All this, and Northern Ireland too. A recrudescence of the Troubles led an emergency meeting of the Cabinet – this time united – to deploy troops in Belfast and Londonderry. Another of the great intractables of British politics had resurfaced. The whole government must have felt under siege. Peter Shore sums up the frustrations besetting the Prime Minister:

Things just wouldn't come right. All the investment he made in trying to get Ian Smith to renounce UDI, the terrific investment he put in with the trade unions trying to get *In Place of Strife* adopted. Then, remember, no one was more involved in devaluation, in trying to prevent it and then handling the consequences of it, than Harold Wilson. So he had a cluster of huge problems of that kind, and in a way, and one felt very sorry about it, they were almost personal defeats. And yet the resilience of the man and this extraordinary rubber-ball capacity of bouncing back was there all the time. I've never seen him in despair.

That resilience was indeed extraordinary, enabling him to turn rumours of his political demise into yet another well-turned soundbite: 'For the benefit of those who have been carried away by the gossip of the last two days, I know what is going on. *I* am going on.'

Without that rubber-ball quality, he might well have left the premiership earlier. Certainly he would have had no chance of casting aside a string of mighty by-election defeats in 1968 and 1969 and creating a chance of winning the next general election. When he called that election, he built the campaign around his personality rather than policy. Tony Benn, his Minister of Technology when the poll took place in June 1970, characterized the almost hubristic approach:

> He was 'Doctor Wilson' who would do it for you while you could get on with your daily life and not bother about politics. It was Labour, the natural party of government; it was Wilson, the constitutional monarch who in the end believed that a walkabout based on the Queen's walkabout in Australia would win him the 1970 election. There were these illusions that came into it.

Shattered by defeat, Wilson retreated to his study to write his memoirs instead of giving Labour a lead, while left and right fought for the party's soul with increasing bitterness about the record of 1964–70. A worthy story of liberal reforms on abortion, homosexuality and equal pay? Or a betrayal of socialism?

Europe became the battleground for the left–right divide. Notwithstanding the subsequent French veto, Wilson had made a genuine effort to get Britain into the European Economic Community in 1967. Now, however, he sacrificed all to the needs of party unity and opposed the terms under which the Heath government took Britain into Europe in 1973. Deeply traditional about British constitutional practice, he nevertheless reached for a referendum to keep the party together. The idea came from Tony Benn, who describes the initial opposition to it:

> I had, of course, first mentioned it in 1968 in a speech in Wales, and there was an attempt to get rid of me from the Cabinet, at the party meeting, because I'd mentioned the word 'referendum'. I came back to it again in 1970, took it to the Shadow Cabinet in December; Wilson wouldn't look at it. I was in a minority of one. And then Callaghan used this phrase that got into the history books: 'Tony may have launched a little rubber life raft into which one day we shall all wish to clamber.' Wilson was very sceptical about it, but I kept the campaign going. I produced a Bill, sent it to every constituency. It got through the 1971 conference, as policy, and then, of course, when Pompidou came out with typical French contempt for a referendum in France as to whether he would have Britain in, the argument was over! But by the time we came to the European Communities Bill of 1972, where I was speaking for the opposition, the referendum was entrenched and, of course, we later introduced it.

Wilson probably thought the question of a referendum was academic. Even when the Heath government began to stagger under a succession of blows – inflation, strikes, a quadrupling of the oil price, the three-day week – few people thought Heath would lose if he went to the country early, and Wilson was not among them. This Heath did, in February 1974. Wilson's political astuteness, however, convinced him that Europe offered at least the glimmerings of electoral opportunity, and, as an old pro, he couldn't resist trying to exploit it – particularly, given his love of the conspiratorial, because it involved an undercover arrangement with Enoch Powell. Joe Haines describes the cloak-and-dagger stuff:

> Harold did have a conversation with him in the men's lavatory at the House of Commons, and Powell said that he would be making speeches against the government and it seemed only sensible that the speeches should be coordinated. There was that kind of general agreement while two elderly men settled their business. And then Enoch Powell got his chief assistant, who was Andrew Alexander – later City Editor of the *Daily Mail* – and myself to meet. There was one hilarious occasion where he emerged from the shadows of a hotel in Cardiff to beckon me, and we discussed the timing of the speeches so that Powell and Wilson wouldn't make major speeches on different subjects on the same night.

Haines takes the view that, with the election result so marginal, this collusion 'may have had a significant effect'.

Despite Powell's eleventh-hour advice to the electorate to vote Labour, only at the last moment did Wilson sense the possibility of forming a new government. Lord Donoughue was with him in his Huyton constituency as adviser on opinion polls:

> I went for a walk with him in Huyton, a dreary wet evening through bleak housing estates, and I was convinced that we would be the largest party. As a pollster, that's what the numbers told me; I'm no genius. And I told him I thought this would be the result. He perked up a bit and began to discuss the kind of government he would have, and that's when he used his football analogies to me about how he was going to be a sweeper-up at the back and let the other ministers do the attacking, and it would be different from 1964 when he had had to score all the goals.

Could all this talk of the centre half have been a cover for a loss of appetite as well as a failure to prepare for a return to power? Not only did he lack both a majority and a strategy for government, some of the big figures around his Cabinet table were a touch ambivalent. Roy Jenkins, for example, was struck by the contrast between the defeated government of 1970 and the incoming Labour administration of 1974: 'In 1970 we had put the economy into a fairly decent shape and we would have gone on and been a sensible government, whereas in 1974 we had no real policies and we had become a coalition of incompatibles. It was a very uneasy Cabinet, that Cabinet of 1974, and there was nothing we really wanted to do.'

This lack of direction was the more significant given that the new government inherited a domestic crisis without parallel in the postwar period. Apart from settling the miners' strike and repealing Heath's industrial relations legislation, the Wilson of 1974, in sharp contrast to the Wilson of 1964, had no fresh ideas to offer, least of all, it seemed, on the economic front. Despite inflation heading towards 20 per cent, the Cabinet talked about everything but economic strategy, as the Cabinet Secretary of the time, Lord Hunt of Tanworth, recalls.

> The Cabinet devoted a fairly small amount of its time to economic affairs, partly because it was at first preoccupied with ending the three-day week, getting the country back to work, etcetera, then preoccupied with Europe and preoccupied with devolution, both of which took quite an inordinate amount of time. I think the Prime Minister and other ministers saw wider economic difficulties looming but they hadn't perhaps the time to grapple with them, and I think also to some extent they didn't know what to do about them and were waiting until they were forced to deal with them.

There were occasional signs of the old Wilsonian fire, as when he taunted Ted Heath or, later, patronized Mrs Thatcher at Question Time. But that was all. By the mid-1970s Wilson seemed largely burnt out. Joe Haines, then back in Number Ten as his Press Secretary, thought he had been at the top too long:

> There hadn't been any pause; from university it was straight out into being Beveridge's assistant and then the War, and then pretty early on into the Cabinet once he got elected. Apart from a brief spell on the back benches after his resignation with Nye Bevan and John Freeman, he had never been out of the top flight. His ambition, after losing in 1970 – and I think he would have gone in 1972 or so had he won in 1970 – was really to get back so that he wasn't just another defeated Prime Minister. I think he had run out of ideas on what he could do for Britain. He thought the country needed a bit of peace and quiet after the miners' strike, and he could certainly deliver that, but we hadn't got North Sea oil then, it was just a promise for the future, and it was racked with the old problems and he had only the old solutions.

There was, however, one intriguing and perhaps even courageous exception to this lassitude: Northern Ireland. Lord Hunt describes his search for the elusive alchemy:

> Wilson at that stage did believe that somewhere in this tangle of problems there was a key to it all and that if only you could find the right constitutional gimmick or solution or whatever, this would solve it – you'd do it at a stroke, one bound and we're free. I think his inclinations were always towards disengagement of Britain and British troops and thus his inclinations were more towards a wider Irish solution. But certainly dominion status was a phrase he used and certainly he did ask for all sorts of options to be prepared. By feeling that there was a sort of golden key – that if only you could find the right constitutional solution everyone would agree with it – he didn't allow sufficiently for the really considerable mistrust and fears and apprehensions on both sides of that community.

But it was the politics of another community, the European Community, which dominated both domestic and foreign policy in the first fifteen months of Wilson's final premiership, especially after the October election of 1974 had returned him with a hairline overall majority. This was the one issue which could have broken this last Cabinet and split the party. Avoiding both fractures demanded a classic Wilsonian operation. Shirley Williams, then the fiercely pro-European Minister for Prices and Consumer Protection, acknowledges his skill.

> From the point of view of holding the party together and from the point of view of sustaining the government, it was a brilliant operation, no quarrel with that. He made it quite plain that in allowing each one of us to express our own views this was strictly limited to the campaign itself, it was limited to discussing the terms of the referendum, and once the referendum was held and was over, that was to be the end of it. And I actually think that the entire Cabinet lived up to the spirit of that.

Lord Hunt, connoisseur of Cabinet government and present at every meeting, is less glowing: 'It was a very strange experience and I think the lesson of it was that it shouldn't be repeated.' Furthermore, he says, it came home to roost later:

> The Labour government came in with a very clear division of view on Europe. Harold Wilson knew that during the first two years of his

premiership – and I think this ties up with the date of his resignation, because he wanted it settled before he left office – he had to settle the Europe issue one way or the other. I think he increasingly came to the view himself that it had to be settled in the direction of staying in the Community, but he knew that he couldn't get Cabinet agreement over this. So you had first of all the formula of renegotiation so that the government could show they had got improved terms – possibly not dramatically improved but nevertheless a bit improved – and then you had the agreement to differ so that those ministers who were against the Community could argue against it. The campaign was conducted in a reasonably fraternal and gentlemanly way, but I think the damage which in fact it did to relations within that Cabinet *ex post facto* was very great.

Could it be that the long-term cost of the Labour Party's survival in the 1970s, despite its tensions on Europe, was the split in the centre-left vote in the 1980s which gave that decade and more to Margaret Thatcher and John Major? But in June 1975 Wilson wasn't thinking in terms of decades. A week, to echo yet another of his famous phrases, must have seemed a pleasantly long time in the aftermath of the referendum, with two-thirds voting to stay in Europe. Now, behaving as if he had won a third election in quick succession, he moved Tony Benn from industry to the Department of Energy. Mr Benn's proposals for planning agreements between government and large private-sector companies, and a powerful role for the state-owned National Enterprise Board, had alarmed not just industrialists but the Treasury and the occupant of Number Ten. There were also broader differences of approach, as Mr Benn explains:

I took the case to the public. The very thing that Wilson had never been prepared to do in 1964, I did in 1974. I'd learnt from that and therefore, for example, I went to the National Executive and I produced a paper called *The Work Programme of the Department of Industry*, and not only did I put the whole strategy before them for implementing the policy but I published it, with the consent of the National Executive, and Wilson was absolutely furious. He said, 'Once you get into government, government policy is only what's been through the Cabinet.' I said, 'Not at all, government policy is how you're getting on with the manifesto.' And we had huge arguments about collective responsibility, about this. But don't think there wasn't great support, there was enormous support, and I think one of the things that really made life difficult for him was that he couldn't contain the support there was and therefore in the end he got rid of me.

There was a dash of hysteria in the political climate in 1975 as inflation peaked at 26 per cent. There was talk of Britain becoming ungovernable, of right-wing private armies ready to thwart a hard left takeover of the state. It wasn't just Tony Benn's advocacy from the Department of Industry of boosted state ownership; there was a feeling that trade union power was excessive, symbolized by the 'social contract' between the political and industrial wings of the labour movement in which, as Joel Barnett, Denis Healey's number two at the Treasury put it, 'The unions took and we gave.' Jack Jones, as leader of the Transport and General Workers' Union, was an architect of both the 'social contract' and the incomes policy which Wilson had recourse to in 1975, once the European question was out of the way. In his view the unions did make considerable efforts to cooperate with the government:

> First of all we tried to ensure that pay claims would not exceed the retail price index figure on a voluntary basis. That wasn't easy to secure in the first period of that Labour government, partly because inflation was rising so rapidly – 25 per cent then, going up towards 30 per cent. At least, that's what our members thought it would go up to, and they were making their claims accordingly. To try to break that situation, I offered the proposal of a flat-rate increase across the board. I first suggested about eight pounds and came down to six, in discussions with both the Trades Union Congress and people like Denis Healey. Then I went out into the country, on a voluntary basis, trying to persuade masses of workers that this was a sensible and reasonable approach to getting our country back on its feet, and there was not one breakage in that voluntary arrangement. People said the unions couldn't deliver. *We* delivered. In point of fact it was the government who didn't deliver because later, when it came to economic pressures on the government, the first thing they looked at was reduced public expenditure.

With hindsight, Wilson's post-referendum initiative was the last attempt to rescue the dominant postwar idea of a mixed economy and a welfare state from the stress upon it caused by stagflation and relative economic decline. In November 1975 he called the leaders of industry and the unions to Chequers to unveil his last major contribution to British politics – a new kind of partnership which would pick future winners in British industry. This was but a faint echo of the Wilson of 1964, too vague even to deserve the name of a national plan, let alone the epithet 'corporatism'. At the heart of this final Wilsonian rethink lay an enfeebling contradiction, as Peter Shore, by this time Secretary of State for Trade, explains:

The industrial strategy and the 'social contract' were very difficult to reconcile, in particular with the rapid growth of unemployment that was taking place. Should the industrial strategy be primarily aimed, as it were, at picking winners for the future, or should a great part of it be aimed simply at preventing disaster afflicting existing industries through unemployment? When one looks back at the industrial strategy and looks at the actual sums of money that were spent, clearly it was helping, for example, the motor car industry to survive that took up the greater part of those funds which were under the industrial strategy, and it should really not have been deployed in quite that way.

To this policy weakness was added a physical weakness. To those who saw him every day, there were worrying signs that Wilson was ailing. Bernard Donoughue remembers indications quite early on in the premiership that all was not well: 'When we went to Paris to discuss the EC, I think it was at the beginning of December 1974, he had some heart-racing and the doctor had to intervene a bit, so he was pacing himself, and he certainly ran down more; there was a point in the second half of 1975 where he asked to have fewer papers and actually asked to attend fewer committees.' This creeping disengagement inevitably had its effect on the conduct of government business. Lord Glenamara, a long-time admirer of Wilson and, as Ted Short, his party deputy, recalls 'a Cabinet meeting one afternoon, an awful Cabinet meeting, when we were going to alter the secrecy laws and it got into the most hopeless confusion. Everybody was absolutely exasperated and angry and furious about it. Nothing emerged from it at all.'

There was, too, a trace of paranoia, not this time about Labour rivals but about something far more sinister. It's impossible for outsiders – and, indeed, most insiders – to reach an informed judgement about the alleged Security Service plot against Wilson. Lord Hunt, as Cabinet Secretary, was overseer of the secret services and as near to an authoritative voice as any:

Harold Wilson was a person who, I think, had always been fascinated by the realms of intelligence and spying and security. And his interest, and I suppose his concern, his apprehension, manifested itself not just as to whether MI5 was conducting some sort of vendetta against him, but when one went abroad: he was suspicious and apprehensive that he was being watched or monitored by hostile intelligence services. I think he also felt that in this country he was occasionally being watched or monitored, observed, by both hostile and some friendly intelligence services. He had this interest and fascination with that sort of world. When you come to his concern over MI5, which is well documented, I think you have to distinguish between what one knew then and what one has since learnt through the *Spycatcher* affair, through other people's memoirs and stories. But undoubtedly I think Wilson *was* concerned – and perhaps increasingly concerned during his second government – that some people in the Security Service had something against him and were concerned to damage his reputation and possibly even to remove him. I didn't think then, and I don't think now in the light of all the evidence and books and things we've read since his government, I don't think that there was anything to smear him with. I've never heard anything against him about his trips to Russia, or anything else, which could possibly throw doubt on him as a security risk. I don't think, either, that there was a deliberate campaign to do him damage. I think it is much more likely that there were a few people – and I really do mean probably two or three people – who were in the Security Service at the time who perhaps shouldn't have been there but who were malcontents – a lot of them had been missed over for promotion themselves – who were out of sorts with everyone and who were probably right-wing in their political attitudes and who talked against not just Harold Wilson but members of the Labour government, and who talked to the newspapers.

But for all Lord Hunt's measured assurances, the alleged Wilson plot is a story that will not die. It is always linked with the question: why did he really resign in March 1976? – almost the only question the public asked about Harold Wilson during his long, sad twilight of physical infirmity and political near-irrelevance. As so often, the truth seems to be far more prosaic than fiction: his resignation was long contemplated to coincide with his sixtieth birthday. There is at least one attic in southern England where a copy of the game plan is secreted, as Joe Haines confesses:

> At the Labour party conference in 1975, Harold Wilson asked me to draw up the timetable for his resignation the following year, which was to be announced at the end of February, indeed, the afternoon of the last Wednesday in February, the reason for that date being chosen being that the Labour Party National Executive met on the morning of that day and, as he said to me, 'I'm not going to let those buggers have anything to say about it.' And I drew up the timetable and, although it was to be one copy only, I did actually retain a copy for my own memory. It's here in this house.

There was in fact a slight delay from the planned schedule before Wilson took the nation's breath away by announcing his intention of forsaking the practice of government for the pleasures of writing about it.

How will history remember him? Will Wilson's trace be more than the faint smell of pipe smoke in the long-closed Lime Grove studios of the BBC where he puffed and evaded his way through countless crisis interviews? Even the arch-critic of his 'Doctor Wilson' style, Tony Benn, is generous in acknowledgement of both his achievements and his personal qualities:

> People who've held office go into the darkest of all pits between the headlines and the history books, and we're much too near him to see. I suppose his achievement is his imagination and winning for Labour, his capacity to keep the party together, his relation of science to the technological revolution, his foundation of the Open University – by *any* test the greatest of his achievements. What I think is important to remember is that he was a kind man and a man of imagination and a man of a great deal of drive, and although he's very badly hammered and I criticized him and he criticized me for that matter, I think I look back on my association with him with a great deal of – tenderness.

This surprisingly warm epitaph is perhaps a fitting tribute to Wilson's overriding purpose of holding Labour together. He was first and last a party man; everything would be sacrificed to that central requirement. Wilson's Cabinet veteran, Lord Glenamara, sees his success as party leader in this relentless pursuit of compromise:

> Harold Wilson was a man – and this is why he was a success as leader of the Labour Party – who believed you could reconcile anything; black and white, oil and water – anything. The leader's job was to find the common ground in between. Only rarely did he come out and say, 'This is what I want.' There was always a formula somewhere in the middle. As it was reconciling opposites, quite different points of view, different philosophies, it was the lowest common denominator between the two.

But if this is a virtue, it is also a failing. It keeps Harold Wilson out of the top flight of twentieth-century British premiers. All that shining promise; but to what end? Lord Whitelaw thinks that, when it came to being the leader of a nation, he didn't quite measure up to it. What was the missing ingredient in this failure to make the grade as a truly national leader? 'He enjoyed, I think, this battleground of party politics too much.'

Winning three elections out of four, keeping Labour in business, just being there, is not, in the end, enough. Modern British Prime Ministers face a tougher test, especially if the claims they made were large: did they do anything substantial to tackle the fundamental weaknesses of Britain as a producer and a trader, a nation locked tightly in relative economic decline? If the answer in this case is 'no', Peter Shore would not lay the blame entirely at Wilson's own door:

> Perhaps the ambitions to do that were too great, and, at that time at any rate, the British people were not in the mood, as it were, to regenerate themselves in the way that Harold Wilson and others wished them to do. But it can be looked at in a different way, in a way of saying, for example, that these were the problems, these were the dangers that threatened Britain, the kind of dangers we're only too familiar with at the present time. What Harold did was to hold them at bay.

He delayed the decline, then, but didn't halt or reverse it. Maybe the kindest, perhaps the most guileful occupant of Number Ten since 1945, a prospect brimming with brave claims who occupied the premiership for nearly eight years – and yet the verdict on Harold Wilson must verge on the harsh. Delaying decline is no real defence; the times called for more, much more, than keeping the show on the road and his party intact. By the time of his death, the glow of the Sixties white heat had long faded into cold, grey ash.

15

Be Prepared

British government is a huge enterprise. Its Civil Service manpower, its budgets, its range of responsibilities dwarf the activities of the largest multinational company; yet very few politicians are natural administrators. They don't launch their careers with management in mind. Edward Heath was an exception. He has always enjoyed talking about the reforms he introduced to make Whitehall more efficient. He was closer than any other postwar British Premier to the technocratic type of politician the French so often produce. But there was passion, too, in his premiership, especially when it came to making Britain a member of the European Community. Our place in Europe is the lasting legacy of his four years in Downing Street, troubled as they were by industrial strife and by the quadrupling of the oil price which hit all the world's advanced economies.

Yet when Mr Heath began looking for a seat in the late 1940s, the idea of occupying Number Ten did not enter his mind; not only because 'when you're trying to become a candidate you don't usually look as far ahead as that' but because he thought it was just not possible; that his background was not suitable. Not until after his election as Conservative leader in 1965, as his own star rose and his party seemed to be changing, did he actually begin to think that he might make it to the very top.

By then he had seen four Prime Ministers in action from the inside: Winston Churchill, Anthony Eden, Harold Macmillan and Alec Home. What did he learn from them about the art of being Prime Minister?

Each of them had his own way of being leader of a party or being Prime Minister, and in a way this was extremely valuable, because it gave me different aspects of the job which I could either accept or drop. Churchill, of course, was an exception, because he'd been Prime Minister in wartime and had an enormous standing which he could use to good effect. On the other hand, he had difficulty in mastering a detailed approach to domestic affairs when in the House of Commons. Eden was really mainly concerned with foreign affairs. It was unfortunate, I suppose, looking back on his political career, that so much of it had been spent in the Foreign Office and in similar activities. But whatever one may judge about Suez, he was really a genius in the way he handled diplomacy, and to see him working on telegrams from ambassadors all over the world was very illuminating. Macmillan, of course, had an interest in both and knew the domestic scene inside out because in the Twenties he'd been very much more concerned with it than he had with foreign affairs. His methods were always to try to bring people together and to avoid clashes of any kind. Alec Home wasn't Prime Minister for very long, only for a year, but he always was very clear about what he wanted and he supported those who were doing a difficult job. Never let them down.

As, indeed, he did not let Heath himself down over the question of resale price maintenance, supporting his minister against considerable opposition within the Cabinet.

Edward Heath is said to have prepared more thoroughly for government than any previous leader of the opposition, both in terms of the machinery of government and in terms of policy. This, he feels, paid off hugely when he actually won the 1970 election.

After we were defeated in 1964 Alec Home, who was Leader of the Opposition, leader of the party, made me responsible, as Chairman of the Conservative Research Department, for policy. And what I said to them was – and they're a brilliant lot – 'We've been in power for thirteen years, it's really time that we had a look at the whole thing. And so my instructions to you are to look at it as thoroughly as you can, as impartially as you can, and don't exclude any idea, however horrific it may seem to some people, from the point of view of formulating policy.' This they did, very, very thoroughly. This meant that when we came into power in 1970 we were extremely well prepared. There have been those since 1979 who have scoffed at the fact that we were well prepared; if they'd been as well prepared they wouldn't be making such a mess of it as they are now.*

From the point of view of the machinery of government, I'd watched it ever since 1951 when I became a whip and I don't think any of my predecessors would deny that they very often made appointments to suit the personnel rather than to suit the departments or what was required from the point of view of administration or policy. Sometimes, I suppose, this is unavoidable; but what I set out to do was to try to rationalize the government machine and ensure that it did carry out policy to the best effect. And I think we got a long way with that. Then I set up the two additional institutions. The first was called the 'think tank', in colloquial jargon, to give us a running commentary on how we

---

* This conversation took place in 1989, when Mrs Thatcher was still Prime Minister.

were doing. That they did every six months at three meetings – Cabinet level, Minister of State level and Parliamentary Secretary level – showing what we'd promised to do, what we'd set out to do and where we had got to. That too, I think, was invaluable. It also saved a great deal of time in the Cabinet. One of the jobs the 'think tank' had was to take the memoranda of different ministers and point out where they were contradictory, point out where they conflicted with statistics provided by the statistical departments and so on, and then say to the ministers, please reconcile these before you actually come to Cabinet. That had a very healthy effect.

The second institution Heath created was the Programme Analysis and Review mechanism, for dealing with expenditure in government.

What I wanted power to do was to start with the departments and their existing expenditure, the oldest sort of things on which they'd embarked, and say yes, that was fine at the time but is it really necessary any longer? Of course, to have that you had to have the cooperation of ministers, and some ministers weren't very happy about having these things looked at in their departments and that's why we didn't get further. But we got a certain way and I still believe it's the right thing to do. You must review departmental expenditure from time to time.

Edward Heath is remembered as the Prime Minister most interested in such matters since Lloyd George – indeed, it's about all he had in common with Lloyd George. William Armstrong once said, 'Ted would have made a super Permanent Secretary.' Heath himself, however, does not see himself in the slightest degree as a Permanent Secretary *manqué*.

It's perfectly true that I passed out top of the administrative Civil Service after the war, but I left simply because I wasn't that type. I want to get things done. It's also true I wanted to go to the Treasury first of all, but having seen the Civil Service – I won't say 'in action', but having been in the Civil Service, I knew it wasn't really for me. The only thing it did do was give me the satisfaction of saying, if ever I wanted, to a Permanent Secretary, 'Now look here, come along, I could be in your place if I'd wanted to, but I didn't.'

He is remembered as being a bit of a disciplinarian – though he himself calls it simply common sense – in Cabinet, almost reminiscent of Clement Attlee in his impatience with waffle. A Heath Cabinet was a businesslike affair, run as a tight ship. It wasn't jovial in the way that some of Macmillan's Cabinets had been – and it didn't leak, either. Heath puts this down to more than discipline: 'That's because people were responsible. It's because people were happy and because they knew their views were respected. People only leak when they're fed up with the way they're being treated in the Cabinet.'

He also pioneered a different system of running the Cabinet committees, putting together what were called 'mixed committees' of ministers and officials, again to be more businesslike and to save time. Not everyone was convinced this worked; some thought the officials were so conditioned not to be political that they wouldn't say anything. Heath doesn't think this detracted from the value of the idea:

> Even if they didn't say anything it was a very good thing for them to hear what the politicians had got to say. I felt that officials were very often too isolated, living in their ivory towers, and that it was good for them to hear the discussions between members of the Cabinet and some junior members of the government on certain committees. It put them in the picture, and they could then form better judgements than they would otherwise do. That's why I had them there. Any argument that the Civil Service was taking over power from the ministers is complete nonsense.

Getting Britain into the European Community was very much Heath's priority as Prime Minister. It might seem that negotiations towards such a major step must inevitably take up a great deal of Cabinet time, with the intricacies of the deals that had to be struck, and perhaps dissent occasionally if one minister or another thought that the pace of negotiations was wrong, or even that the whole enterprise itself was misconceived. Not so, says Heath.

> That certainly wasn't ever raised in the Cabinet because we all were entirely agreed that our future lay in Europe and we should become a member of the European Community. There were obviously discussions in Cabinet. It didn't really take up a great deal of time in the Cabinet because we had the European Committee, and Geoffrey Rippon, who was negotiating for most of the time – Tony Barber started it off but Geoffrey did most of it – was able to deal with the more detailed aspects of it in the European Committee. Of course, we had a negotiating team in London; we had a negotiating team in Brussels. They sorted all this out before it ever came to Cabinet, so the Cabinet only had to take decisions on the major issues, and that's how it should be. That's what a Cabinet is for.

And, he adds, as they were all agreed in principle, this was relatively straightforward.

Getting Britain into Europe was not seen as the end of the process, but as a beginning. Given longer in Number Ten, Heath would have wished to continue his reform of the British central government machine in a European direction, bringing about a more European way of doing business, a more open system.

One of the difficulties – and it still exists, I constantly trip over examples of it – is that the departments which don't deal directly with Community issues really don't see things in a European way at all. We've got to overcome this. I think we'd have to have had committees on which representatives from the departments not directly involved were sitting, and therefore could have a more European outlook but also, perhaps, put their own subjects more into line with European thinking.

At home, Heath had to face a succession of economic and industrial crises of great intensity. In 1972 there was the first miners' strike, then that of the Pentonville dockers associated with the industrial relations legislation. How did he cope with the unremitting pressures? What was his respite from the press of business?

Sailing. Of course, there were a number of people, certainly in the press and the rest of the media and among the voters – though not my constituents – who said, don't we pay you twenty-four hours a day, seven days a week? What are you doing sailing? This is very short-sighted, because if politicians don't have outside interests then they just drive themselves into the ground. Who are the people who suffer? Not the politicians but the people of the country. So I had a recreation in the summer, from the spring until the autumn, of racing at sea, and for the rest of the year the recreation of music and opera and ballet and the other things in which I am interested.

On one occasion at Chequers, it is said, the CBI were somewhat taken aback when after lunch the Prime Minister said, 'Before we start again, can I play you some Mozart?'

To help his colleagues cope with times of great stress and pressure of work he made it known that they could always come and talk to him at any time; 'and they constantly did. Sometimes I would say, "I think we had better bring so and so in as well on this, because he'll be affected, but in any case he knows the background and he may be able to help us as well." I think that's the best way of dealing with these problems.' And did he tell them to go on holiday occasionally as well? 'Fortunately, most of them didn't need telling.'

As a result of the experience of 1972 he radically reviewed the emergencies organization for handling industrial disputes that threatened the essentials of life and set up the Civil Contingencies Unit. How useful was this in helping the Heath government to get through the three-day week and other major disruptions?

It was extremely helpful. It really put us on to an entirely new basis. Looking back on it, I suppose one can say it was extraordinary how out of date the machinery was for dealing with internal problems of any kind. This gave us a fresh start. There were those who unfortunately produced a lot of false figures – the nationalized industries weren't free of that – saying how much it was hitting them. Whereas in fact the general overall production of the country during the three-day week only dropped by a very, very small percentage, something like one and three-quarters or one and a half per cent. Of course, what this showed was that if we had the will we could do in three days what we normally took five days to do. That was the lesson.

It sometimes seems as if a blight hits a government after a few years; however well conceived its strategy, however good its people, the unexpected strikes. Nineteen seventy-three was the equivalent of a political plague year. The Heath administration had to deal with the quadrupling of oil prices by OPEC, a miners' strike and an electricity go-slow; they were trying to do something about Northern Ireland with the Sunningdale discussions, and it was a very difficult time in Europe with the Copenhagen summit coming up. In terms of the intensity of pressures on the Prime Minister and Cabinet it was almost like wartime.

I think it's much worse than wartime. In wartime you're operating on one front, which is the war, and you have to deal with other things, like rationing and supplies of food and so on. But most people regard winning the war as their main objective and they're prepared to commit themselves to it. And so it is very much a problem of the Prime Minister and his Chiefs of Staff and advisers as to how you carry on and win the war. In peacetime, in the situation you've just described, you had a wide variety of problems and the people who were concerned with them didn't have any common interests in solving those particular problems. They each regarded their own as crucial. From that point of view I think the strain on the Prime Minister and the Cabinet is very much greater.

The media are inevitably critical of whoever is in power, and it might be thought that Heath would have found it particularly difficult dealing with them in the early 1970s. In fact, however, far from having to force himself to spend more time on this than he thought it merited,

> I suppose I would be accused of spending less time on it than some people wanted. I thought the people to deal with that were the people at Number Ten and the people in the departments whose responsibility it was. And I still think it's right to leave it to them. What I wanted was a much broader approach to public opinion, and that's why I wanted to abolish the lobby system in the House of Commons. I have said in the House that it is a corrupt system, and the Number Ten press office has made it even more corrupt. I don't believe that's right at all. What I wanted to do, and what I did do, was to broaden the whole contact with the media.

Ironically, the people least pleased with the Prime Minister's move towards open press conferences were the Westminster press corps themselves.

> This was particularly true on prices and incomes policy. I said then that I would personally put the whole thing before the press and the media because it covered such a wide field. So many departments were involved, but I didn't want to shift the burden on to the Chancellor or Trade and Industry or any other particular department, and if I was going to do this I wanted not only to have the press there but also television and radio and the Europeans and the rest of the world. This produced a minor crisis because the lobby said they wouldn't come. Then they said they would come but they wouldn't ask any questions. Then when they found the rest of the world was asking all the questions they suddenly found they had got questions to ask. On two occasions we did this and threw it open to the world. I'm sure that's right today. Look at Washington. There's the President doing an open press conference. The whole world can not only hear what he says but see what he says and the way he says it, and they form a judgement about the President as well as about the policies.

> Dealing with Parliament and the party in Parliament and the country as a whole is a very time-consuming business for a Prime Minister. Aside from the pressure of other work, Heath is not regarded as the most clubbable of Premiers, and the inference is easily drawn that he might therefore have found this side of the job difficult – lacking, perhaps, the bonhomie of Macmillan in assuaging difficult people on his own side. This inference, says Sir Edward, would be quite wrong.

> There's a certain amount of myth about that. I found going round the country always immensely stimulating. That I thoroughly enjoyed. I

enjoyed meetings with the party in the country. Of course, they were all mass meetings of party members; in many ways I prefer a meeting which has got the opposition there as well. As one has in one's own constituency. But I never regarded that as a misuse of time, not for one moment. And I used to enjoy meeting members of the party. After all, as Chief Whip I spent a lot of time in the smoke room and was always hearing everything about our members and knowing a lot of things which I ought not to have heard about them. This naturally remained a habit. This unclubbable idea is a myth which has grown up.

One of the special tasks that fall uniquely to a Prime Minister is dealing with the Queen at the Tuesday evening audiences. Mr Heath found his Sovereign a most rewarding interlocutor, both formally and informally.

As far as the agenda is concerned, that's a combination of things which the Queen wants to discuss, which her Private Secretary puts forward, and things on which I feel I ought to report, which go through my Private Secretary. So it's a combined agenda – or was in my time. Then afterwards informally we discussed almost everything, in my time. It's very valuable because the Queen is so well informed. Of course, it's in the definition, it's said one of the monarch's duties in the modern world is to give advice when wanted. I was always only too grateful for advice, and the Queen has, after all, been on the throne for a very long period and she is getting reports all the time from her representatives across the world – Governors-General and Governors of individual colonies and so on. And so with all that knowledge anything which she has to say is immensely valuable. Added to that, she gets around our own country a great deal, and when talking informally gives one a very wise account of what people are really thinking and how they're behaving.

Another personal duty that falls to the Prime Minister is looking after the secret services. Sir Edward homes in on the central problem for the government here, namely that even the Prime Minister cannot always know what is going on deep in those secret agencies, and yet he has to carry the can.

I always felt this was a very real problem. Of course, it doesn't only affect the Prime Minister because the Foreign Secretary is responsible for one of them and the Home Secretary for the other. I was fortunate in having colleagues who were first of all able to judge the things which went beyond themselves and secondly only too ready to come and talk to me about it. And so whether it was Alec Douglas-Home or Reggie Maudling or Robert Carr or whoever it might be, they knew that there were things with which I was bound to be involved. Then all three of us were affected by this question: do you really know what's going on? This remains a problem today, and it hasn't been solved by recent legislation.*

In order to improve this uneasy position, Sir Edward would like to see in being 'some sort of group which can make its own enquiries the whole time as to what is going on'. Who would be its members? Privy Counsellors?

As soon as you say 'Privy Counsellors', they say, 'Oh yes, a lot of old duffers; first of all they can be hoodwinked, and secondly they'll always report to the Prime Minister that everything's all right.' So I don't specify any Privy Counsellors. But I think you could have a working group who have got the right to enquire. Now, again there's absolutely no guarantee that this will produce what they asked. If you discussed this in Washington – what does the Congressional Committee do? Is it really worthwhile? – a lot of people will express doubts as to whether it really is effective or not. But I think that here we could make it effective, and we need to have something like that. I've said in the House of Commons that I've seen so many of these reports and alleged happenings from people who obviously were so biased and bigoted that if they saw anybody reading the *Daily Mirror* they would run a mile and say 'the Communists have taken over.' You're not going to get the proper material that you want for dealing with these problems from that sort of people. That means you've then got to go back to the actual recruitment of these people. And that may very well be where most action needs to be taken by some supervisory group.

Perhaps the most awesome responsibility that falls to a British Prime Minister attaches to the finger on the nuclear trigger. If war broke out, it would be a prime ministerial decision whether nuclear weapons were used or not. Mr Heath, like other Premiers, went through the motions in the exercises of the transition to war; but it was not a constant source of anxiety to him.

We did have our exercises, of course. It didn't worry me in so far as we were never in my time at the point at which this looked likely, but you have to appreciate that you may always be taken by surprise. Probably the biggest problem of all is what happens if they first of all get the Prime

---

* Since Sir Edward spoke, the Intelligence Services Act 1994 has come into force and an 'oversight' committee on Intelligence and Security has been created which consists of parliamentarians of all three major parties from both Houses.

Minister and his colleagues and then there's a lot of nuclear material left lying around.

A problem over which Prime Minister Heath did not lose sleep. Indeed, he did not lose sleep over anything – much: 'I only lost sleep when the Australian Prime Minister rang me up early one morning to complain about the way his Attorney-General had been received in London. Otherwise I didn't lose any sleep.'

Are there things that Sir Edward, looking back over 1970–4, would do differently about the way he ran the system of government, or Cabinet, or about his own job in Number Ten?

I think there are probably things one would have done differently, but it's very difficult just to pinpoint them and say: this was the thing which was wrong, or that was the thing which was wrong. We were obviously developing, and developing very fast. We were trying to do it on a rational basis which met the needs of modern times. This was true, of course, of local government. Since 1979 the government has gone back on all of this, but it'll have to come and there will come a government which will then reconstruct our local government. First of all, to the extent that it's worthwhile being a local councillor and you feel you have got something to do, a job to do, and you've got the powers and the money to do it with; and secondly, to have local government on a scale which deals with the requirements of a modern country, and that includes roads and transport, for example, not only over your little borough or bailiwick but over a wide area in which communications form one unit. That's what we were about at local government, and it was on the way to succeeding. When you make changes like this you can't expect to get the results in three months or six months.

What pieces of advice would Sir Edward give to a future Prime Minister who was as interested as him in the structure of government, efficiency in government?

One would be that they'd better get as much experience of government as they can before they become Prime Minister. I think it's a limitation if you only have one department or two departments in your experience. Certainly as far as the leader of the Labour Party is concerned at the moment,* he must feel very limited, never having been in a government department at all. And then I think you need to be able to work with a

---

* This was Mr Kinnock.

team to rationalize the whole business and see that it does fit modern requirements. I keep putting the emphasis on modern because we're just not modernized in this country and there are so many different spheres in which we've got to get up to date. Other people have got way ahead of us. You can only do it by working with a team who have got a very wide experience and that was what we had.

Part of this team consisted in people brought in from outside – people like Derek Rayner from Marks and Spencer.

There's nothing new about doing that. And we had them trained for two years before we actually became the government. And of course you come up again against a natural problem: that you're calling on business, professional organizations, to provide the personnel. There are those who say 'Yes, this is of vital importance and we'll pick our ace men and when they come back they'll be even more use to us'; and there are others who say, 'Oh well, this is a jolly good opportunity to get rid of old so-and-so; he'll be annoyed if we don't promote him and he's not worth promoting so let's pass him off over there and with a bit of luck he'll never come back to us.' I think we had twenty-four recruits and one had to recognize that they were a combination of both, and the ones we wanted were the high-flyers. Now, in exchange we said, 'Yes, of course we'll send you some high-flyers from Whitehall and they can learn how you work in the City or in business.' And the trouble about that was that none of those came back to us at all. They were all kept by business in the City, because they said, 'These are higher flyers than we've got at the moment.'

The last piece of advice, then, seems to be that a future Prime Minister should be very sceptical of the gifts that were passed from the private sector to the public? 'Very.'

What will be special, distinctive, about the Heath memoirs? 'They'll be a full account of events for the whole of my life, but politically from 1950 onwards. And they will be absolutely frank and honest and a lot of people won't like them at all.'*

---

* In the spring of 1996 Sir Edward was still at work on his memoirs.

16

Knowing Their Little Tricks

The premiership is *the* glittering prize of British political life. Winning it must be doubly gratifying if you succeed a younger man, as James Callaghan did when he replaced Harold Wilson in 1976. But the trophy probably lost a bit of its shine quite rapidly. Callaghan soon saw his wafer-thin majority disappear and economic troubles arrive with a severe sterling crisis which caused his government to trim its spending programmes in return for a loan from the International Monetary Fund.

James Callaghan, however, had more experience than most new arrivals in Number Ten. He had held several of the prime posts in government, and had been a dominating figure on his party's National Executive for many years. The contest which made him Labour leader and Prime Minister for three years was not his first attempt to head his party. After Harold Wilson beat him for the Labour leadership in 1963, did he expect that he would ever make it to Number Ten?

> Harold Wilson always said he never intended to fall under a bus, but he thought that if he did fall under a bus I might succeed him. That wasn't true after 1967, but between 1974 and 1976, when he did resign, and I was Foreign Secretary, I didn't believe that he was likely to resign, even though there was talk about it, and I thought that he would come to me one day and say, 'Look, you've done a very good job as Foreign Secretary, very good of you, I'd now like somebody younger to take over,' and I really didn't believe then that I was likely to become Prime Minister – and, indeed, the ambition to do so was fading slightly as I got older.

As a minister, Callaghan had seen two Prime Ministers in action at close quarters. He was a middle-ranking minister under Clem Attlee and a Cabinet minister throughout Harold Wilson's governments. What did he learn from them about how to conduct Cabinet business, or how to do the job of Prime Minister?

> From Attlee, the advantage of keeping your mouth shut, and of not exposing your point of view if you wanted to get your business through

rather quickly in the Cabinet. I must say, although I observed the lesson, I'm not sure that I learnt, and I'm not at all sure that I followed Attlee in that particular way.

Attlee did, however, advise Callaghan about dealing with people he might have to negotiate with: 'When I was appointed first of all in 1947 as Parliamentary Secretary to the Ministry of Transport, he said to me in that crisp way of his, "Remember, if you're going to negotiate with someone tomorrow, don't insult them today. That's all. Goodbye."'

And from Harold Wilson?

Well, of course, I learnt. I think one unconsciously absorbs what other people do very much. Harold was a master again, I think, at being able to persuade people and convince people that he understood their point of view very well, and he was very good at avoiding taking a decision if it was going to create a lot of dissension in Cabinet, and I suppose I observed that, and unconsciously absorbed it. And probably practised it, especially as I had to; the difference between myself and other Prime Ministers was that I never really had a majority. I think the biggest majority I ever had was two, and eventually we didn't have a majority at all. When people talk about my period of office, they seem to think that it was on a par with the Labour government of 1966, with a majority of a hundred, or on a par with Mrs Thatcher, with a majority of eighty, or Harold Macmillan, with a majority of a couple of hundred, whatever it was.* I never had, unfortunately, a position like that; I only wish I had.

Uniquely among recent Prime Ministers, before he got to Number Ten Callaghan held all the other great offices of state: the Treasury, the Home Office, the Foreign Office. How much of an advantage was that?

A tremendous advantage. I knew what the departments were up to. I knew their little tricks. I knew – at least, I thought I knew – when they were trying to pull the wool over my eyes, and I knew how to get behind that wool and uncover what they were really wanting to do. And I also knew what were their legitimate interests, and where I would find problems with them and their ministers.

What might an example be of a trick that one of these great departments of state might play on a Prime Minister who didn't know their ways?

---

* Mrs Thatcher's largest majority (in 1983) was 144; Harold Macmillan's (in 1959) was 100.

The Treasury were probably the biggest practitioners of it. They know the work of every department because they have to examine their expenditure. They know how to play off one department against another; how to divide and rule. They're also very good, because of their great expertise and knowledge, in presenting what I might call the worst scenario. Every time a problem comes up, they don't present – I won't say they never present a balanced view, but they always present the point of view that's going to get to their solution and nobody else's solution, and that is inevitable, I suppose. I don't blame them for it, but you've really got not only to know that this happens – a lot of people have a prejudice against the Treasury – but how to counteract it. I think I did know how to counteract it. I don't want to denigrate the Treasury, it would be quite wrong, I think it's a wonderful department, a great department with very able people in it, but they are a department that really want their own way if they can get it. And I talk about the department, rather than the Chancellor.

Wilson's resignation in 1976 wasn't quite the unexpected event that many people seemed to think at the time – not, at least, to a few insiders. He'd given a game plan to the Queen when he returned to Number Ten in 1974, and let Callaghan into the secret before he told the whole Cabinet; so his successor had some warning.

I had a warning from Harold Lever at Christmas 1975; not from Harold, who never gave me any indication of it until about a week before it happened, when he told me; and certainly I think I was one of the first, if not the first, of his Cabinet colleagues to know – except Harold Lever; I don't know what the source of his information was, three months earlier. Harold Wilson told me on a car journey back to the House of Commons to vote from his birthday party one evening, that he wanted me to know this, and he thought that I ought to start to prepare, and it was very obvious that he was telling me because he thought I would be his best successor. It was very kind of him.

When Callaghan found himself in Number Ten, actually doing the job of Prime Minister, he found very little to surprise him about it, very little he hadn't anticipated; after all, he had already seen the work of the Premier very closely 'from a number of angles':

As Chancellor you're always very closely in touch with the Prime Minister; as Foreign Secretary you obviously are; and in the period 1974–6 on party matters, because I was Chairman of the National Executive's Home Policy Committee. Harold and I used to set aside

Friday mornings, and I would go and see him with the Chief Whip and others, and discuss the business for the following week with him, because I was working with him very closely politically, and he no longer felt, as I think he had at some time, that I was trying to take over from him. There was a certain amount of reserve on his part, because he felt that I had great ambitions. He was probably right; I certainly hoped to become Prime Minister in the early days, but then those ambitions, frankly, weakened as I got older, and between 1974 and 1976 I don't think he really felt that I was a rival so much as a colleague who was ready to aid and support him; and indeed, that was true.

So I was very much in his confidence, and we used to go over a whole range of matters on a Friday morning. We'd discuss the business for the following week – how to handle the party; how to handle the House of Commons – and discuss foreign affairs, in which he was interested, and so I had a very good picture of his mind, and I don't think I was surprised by anything very much, although I did break one or two resolutions when I became Prime Minister that I had intended to keep.

And what were they?

The first one was that I hadn't intended to get myself immersed in economic affairs. I'd had enough trouble with that when I was Chancellor of the Exchequer, and we had a very experienced Chancellor in Denis Healey, whose intellectual command and whose sheer brute force in argument enabled him to hold his own, and I just thought that my job would be to support him, and allow him to get on with it while I did other things. But I found, as other Prime Ministers had done before me, and presumably after me – Mrs Thatcher found the same – that a Prime Minister can't keep himself or herself aloof. So that was one resolution that I had to break pretty quickly.

Anyone who observed politics, however remotely, in 1976 knows that the new Premier's immediate inheritance was an intense and punishing workload, with the pressure on the pound, public expenditure – and only a toehold on power. How did he organize his routine to cope with all this?

There wouldn't have been so much pressure if we hadn't had the parliamentary difficulties. If I'd had a parliamentary majority, life would have been a lot easier, and one could have afforded to have disregarded a number of things that I had to take into account, and that cost me a lot of energy and a lot of time.

When I was Chancellor I used to work very well at night, and I would work until one or two in the morning. But when I was Prime Minister, I was already in the middle sixties. I wish I'd become Prime Minister ten years earlier, or fifteen years earlier, when I was fifty. Harold Wilson was only forty-six or forty-seven when he became Prime Minister; Mrs Thatcher in her fifties. I never had that good fortune; I wish I had, I would have had much more energy.

As it was, I couldn't work late at night, so I used to put my box beside the bed, and I would deliberately wake up, or get woken up, at about half past six in the morning, and I would do my box then, of all the telegrams that had come in during the previous day, and the submissions from ministers and my private secretaries, and try to clear that. My wife was very nice, she used to bring me breakfast in bed in those days, and she really looked after me so well when I was Prime Minister. She did try to shield me from all the domestic problems. I used to lie in this very big king-sized bed, and scatter the papers around, and do them all, then get up around half past eight. In other words, I would have spent an hour and a half or so on what was in the dispatch box, have a look at the papers, then get up, and I would go downstairs – because we lived over the shop – downstairs into my study at that time, by about half past nine, quarter past nine, and be ready to start the day.

All those papers; and yet he didn't take any measures to reduce the flow – for example asking people to brief him orally, by discussion, instead of sending him endless long submissions.

My private secretaries were very good, headed by Sir Kenneth Stowe. I'm not sure which way I really like it. There are times when I want to listen to what a minister says, but I tend to be so forgetful that on the other hand I want to see it on paper, and so I really don't absorb things, I find increasingly as I get older, and I think it was true then; unless I see the three or four points put down on a bit of paper, somehow they don't register in me. I understand them when I'm told them by somebody sitting opposite me, but then I tend to forget them, so that I really needed both.

Despite the deluge of daily business, he did make time now and again to get his main departmental colleagues in to talk about their departmental problems, and where they thought they were going.

That was something I did. I'm not sure that other people did, but it was my way of conducting business. I remember so well that I'd had, when I was Chancellor of the Exchequer, daily discussion and meetings with the

Prime Minister, just by walking through the door from Number Eleven to Number Ten, and we saw each other regularly. I remember a feeling of remoteness and feeling cut off when I went to become Home Secretary. I had somehow thought when I was over in the Home Office that I could ring up Harold Wilson's office and say, look, I want to come and see the PM, and I found that I couldn't, that I was somehow shut off. I got slightly resentful about that, I think, and it was obvious when I did see him, on the particular problem, I can't remember what it was, that he was pretty well uninterested in it, and I felt somehow outside the magic circle. I don't think he understood this at all; it probably didn't even cross his mind

When I became Prime Minister I remembered this, and I decided that probably other ministers would feel the same. There was no doubt the Chancellor had always been able to see Harold Wilson; the Foreign Secretary could always see him, and there were one or two confidants he had, like Barbara Castle and Dick Crossman, they could always see him, and I thought, well, perhaps other ministers would feel the same about me. So what I did was to select a small group of ministers who rarely saw the Prime Minister, if ever, unless they had a terrible problem, and I said to my private secretaries, tell them I want to see them, one by one. I want to see them without officials, and I want them to come and tell me what their problems are; what the job is they're trying to do; what is their strategy; what's stopping them from doing it; and how they hope to achieve it. And I found that very useful for myself, because it informed me. I used to get briefed by my private office and by the think tank under Bernard Donoughue – not the Cabinet Office but my policy unit which thought more politically;* they used to brief me with a series of questions, some of which I used to use and others of which I didn't, and I would then have a heart to heart, sitting in the study with the two of us in easy chairs, and I found out a lot about the work of various departments, and I've been told since that the departments thought this was a rather cocked-hat affair, put on their best uniform, and they used to prepare very thoroughly, tell their minister everything that was going on, in order that they might come out with a clean book with the Prime Minister.

In terms of dealing with Cabinet, some observers have detected a disparity of style in Callaghan's approach. During the autumn of 1976, the IMF autumn, there were endless Cabinet meetings at which ministers went

---

* This was the Prime Minister's Policy Unit, not to be confused with the Cabinet Office's 'think tank', the Central Policy Review Staff, with which under Callaghan – as under Wilson, who invented it – it coexisted.

through all the options together, including the siege economy one, and eventually, after a punishing series of meetings, the Prime Minister carried everybody with him. Once the IMF business was over, by contrast, he is said to have reverted to a kind of two-track way of doing business. On sensitive issues related to the currency he would have Harold Lever and officials in – what he used to call his 'economic seminar' – and then report to the full Cabinet; and on highly sensitive nuclear matters he would keep the discussion within very small groups of ministers. Were there two separate approaches?

It's for others to make up their minds about that. As far as the position of sterling in 1976 was concerned, that seemed to me to be the crisis point for that government. There were some people who were saying – forecasting, indeed, from the very moment I became Prime Minister in the previous April – that Harold had got out in good time, and that there would be an election by the autumn of 1976, partly because they thought I wouldn't be able to handle it, partly because of the economic situation, partly because we had no majority, and they thought the government would break up. Now, I thought the government could break up in the autumn of 1976. There were reductions in the proposed expenditure for future years that had to be made, I had no doubt about that, irrespective of the International Monetary Fund or anything else, although it's easy for people to say, 'Oh, the IMF did it.' The IMF, of course, were an instrument in it, but they certainly didn't do it. I myself was convinced after a few months as Prime Minister that we could not go ahead with the levels of public expenditure that were projected.

I knew it was quite possible for the government to break up, and it could have been another 1931, so I was determined that we should allow the Cabinet to talk itself out. They could talk and talk and talk as long as they liked, everybody had a fair chance, and I told them to put in memoranda; we discussed their memoranda, we re-discussed their memoranda and so on, and eventually, by allowing them to talk themselves out, they all came to a common conclusion. Some were unhappy about it, but they did come to a common conclusion, and we preserved the unity of the Cabinet and of the party. It would have been a tragedy if we had split, and it was quite possible we might have broken up, as in 1931. I don't put that as an impossibility, and I regard it as one of my minor triumphs – and goodness knows, I had few enough of them – that the Labour Party did not split in 1976, as it might have done.

As regards the situation afterwards, well, we did have a number of seminars on sterling, but they weren't issues that were going to break up the Cabinet. We didn't have to discuss all these things in the full Cabinet, there were a lot of other things to talk about, and as they didn't affect the Cabinet's existence, it wasn't necessary to take things there. It wasn't a case of excluding the Cabinet; by tradition the Cabinet didn't discuss day-to-day matters of handling sterling. I don't know whether they do now; I very much doubt it.

As regards having a small group on the nuclear situation; on broad strategy that would not be true. On the question of the possible creation of a successor to Polaris it was always traditional, and nothing new, for nuclear issues to be discussed in a small group. This was not related to strains of pacifism or anti-nuclear feeling in the Cabinet; it happened under Conservative governments too. It was because of the belief, I think expressly encouraged by the Ministry of Defence and by the Cabinet Office, that these matters were so sensitive and so secret that they ought to be kept to a small number of people; and that arose from our relationship with the United States, because there they felt that they were giving us information that should not be conveyed to the French, although I believe they did it themselves – the Americans themselves told the French. But formally we weren't supposed to tell the French or the Germans or anybody else. So I think those are the reasons that that happened.

The absence of a parliamentary majority for much of Callaghan's government was compounded by difficulties within the Labour Party. There were a lot of people on the National Executive Committee – indeed, a majority of its members – who were not entirely sympathetic to some of the things the government was doing. Having constantly to watch both Parliament and party was a great drain on resources and energy alike. Lord Callaghan draws the contrast between these circumstances and those of Neil Kinnock in the late 1980s.

A number of members of the National Executive Committee at that time, people like Eric Heffer and so on, seemed to think that the party, not the Cabinet, ought to run the government, and so I had this continual struggle. One of the great things about Neil Kinnock was that he managed to change, or the party has changed, the party's attitude for the better, and gained a majority on the National Executive Committee. This enabled him to take a much more relaxed view.

Towards the end of his period in office, with an endless series of very demanding crises to cope with, the job of Prime Minister, especially without a majority, must have felt very nearly impossible. By this time an element of fatalism – or foreknowledge – had entered Callaghan's view of the future.

I keep a regular farm diary* of what's growing and what isn't growing and what's happening and so on. In the winter of 1978–9 my farm diary has a note in it which says: 'By this time next year I shall have been relieved of other responsibilities and can concentrate on these.' I was quite certain that we weren't going to win the election at the time, so it was never a despairing period for me. I very much wish that we could have done it differently, but I knew that it would turn out the way it did after the Ford settlement in October 1978, when the Ford management gave about 18 or 19 per cent; and then we had a period in Parliament in which it was quite clear that the Conservatives were going to gun heavily, and thought they'd really got a good chance. I was totally opposed, of course, to a settlement at that level, but I could see that the thing had got out of hand, and there was no chance of us winning.

One of the special tasks of a Prime Minister is the weekly audience with the Queen. Mr Callaghan's Tuesday evening meetings with Her Majesty were generally of an informal flavour:

There was always an agenda which had been prepared by our private secretaries, the joint Private Secretaries to the Queen and my own Private Secretary. I used to be given a card before I left Number Ten, and she, I believe, was also given a similar card, with three or four headings of things that we ought to raise. I'm bound to say my card tended to remain in my pocket, and I sometimes saw her fish hers out of her handbag at the end of the meeting between us. We would talk about anything; we'd always start off on non-official business, and gossip about either the weather or the crops or the family, or something of that sort, and then we would get on to something in which she might be interested, or I might be interested, or I felt I really ought to explain to her. So the conversations tended to be very informal; sometimes we would discuss what was on the cards, which our Private Secretaries had agreed should be discussed, and sometimes we wouldn't.

A much less comfortable duty that also belongs exclusively to the Prime Minister is the power of decision to launch a Polaris missile: the 'finger on the button'. Mr Callaghan took a sober but calm view of this burden.

I don't think I ever sat down and contemplated it. It was one of the things that one had had to face for many years, and I took part in exercises that would lead up to the point where either you discharged the missile or you

---

* Lord Callaghan owns a farm in Sussex.

capitulated. Those exercises were not very pleasant occasions, but it's one of the matters that you have to live with, and I found no difficulty in living with it, although I would have found great difficulty in having to take the decision. Nevertheless, that is your job, that is your responsibility, and I would have taken whatever decision was appropriate.

There were other parts of the globe, too, to keep an eye on; what one might call the 'colonial residuals'. Callaghan had a map brought to him every weekend of where the ships of the fleet were, in case the Argentines invaded the Falklands.

I didn't regard that as a little local issue; I regarded it as a very important one. After all, it led to a war. In my view it led to a war because the government of the time took its eye off the Falklands. I kept my eye on them; I had Ted Rowlands in the Foreign Office deputed specifically to keep a very close eye on the matter, because it's always the small problems which can lead to big results. The Cold War went on for years, the possibility there didn't change, we were in a frozen attitude; but with the Falklands, or with problems like Gibraltar and other problems like Belize, small tiny pimples, as it were, if they'll forgive me using that word, on the whole of the world, they could nevertheless precipitate, as they did in the case of the Falklands, a very big situation.

   I think you have got to keep your eye on small things; but I think I was not like Harold, more like Clem Attlee in that I did let my own ministers get on with things. Harold let people get on, but he was full of insatiable curiosity, and he knew, he wanted to know, everything that was going on; I was lazier than he was, and I used to let them get on with it to a great extent, and only interfere in the things that I thought were necessary.

If Lord Callaghan had to tell the next Labour Prime Minister just what the job was about, and give him a few words of sage advice, what would they be?

I think I would resist the temptation. Every man has to suit the job to his own temperament. Speaking for myself, and only for myself, as to the way I would conduct these matters, in my opinion you've got to act not only as Prime Minister arising from your party, but as leader of the nation. That, I think, is part of the job, that you should not dismiss your opponents as being unworthy of consideration. You should not regard them as enemies within. You should not feel that their views are not worth listening to. Secondly, of course, and just as importantly, you must keep your party with you if you can. You must let your backbenchers feel that you haven't forgotten all about them. There's a great tendency to do so in the rush of events, not because you're actively spurning them, but because your day is so busy.

Also, stand back if you can. It's very difficult, because your private secretaries will fill up the day for you; there are always too many people wanting to see you, too many papers to be read, too many problems they want to put under your nose – but stand back, refuse to see them, go upstairs and have a nap, which is what I often did in order to get free of them. I well remember being in the House of Commons one day, sitting there, just in order to escape them, although I knew they'd have some problem for me. Stanley Baldwin used to do that, he used to sit in the House in order to escape problems, and a lot can be said for sitting back and allowing things to take their course for a bit, and reflecting a little, and not rushing in and hitting everybody with your handbag.*

---

* Mrs Thatcher was still Prime Minister when this conversation took place.

17

The Last Retreat of Fame

Mrs Thatcher as History

Names which hoped to range over kingdoms and continents shrink at last into cloisters and colleges. Nor is it certain that even of these dark and narrow habitations, these last retreats of fame, the possession will long be kept.

Samuel Johnson[1]

Time, even a short span of it, can be very cruel to the once-mesmeric. Margaret Thatcher, like David Lloyd George (the twentieth-century Premier to whom she is most comparable), seemed to pass almost in a trice from colossus to the 'Where Are They Now?' column. Come with me to the House of Commons on Tuesday 19 March 1991 – Budget day – the first for eleven years not to bear the imprint of the most celebrated corner shop in economic history (surely her father, Alderman Roberts of Grantham, had more influence on her thought than Friedman or Hayek?). There she sat, *The Economist*'s 'Bagehot' noted, 'a few rows behind Mr Lamont's right shoulder, clad in puritan black and muttering a running commentary on his speech. It was not complimentary. Hardly surprising really: the budget, with its return to deficits and its U-turns on the poll tax, child benefit and higher-rate mortgage tax relief, was described by one senior Treasury person as "the end of Thatcherism". After it, she hurried away, looking dismayed and confused.'[2]

And how this paragraph of Alan Watkins' a few weeks later must have hurt (if she read it) a woman who liked to say she had 'changed everything': 'Large claims were made for Mrs Margaret Thatcher as a great Prime Minister; but they are melting before our eyes like the snows of spring. My prediction is that history will judge her as just above average, below C. R. Attlee and H. H. Asquith, who has better claims than she to being a great peacetime Prime Minister, but above Harold Macmillan and Harold Wilson.'[3]

Such instant revisionism, the Ozymandias syndrome of reducing the once-mighty to a pair of decaying pillars of stone in the pitiless desert, is, I think, as misguided as those who placed her on a permanent, weather-proof plinth in the years of her ascendancy and as those who thought the

Department of Education and Science in the early 1970s would be the pinnacle of her career. Mind you, the early detractors can be more easily forgiven. If in, say, early 1973 you had taken the most sophisticated political observer on one side and afforded him or her the following insights as 'givens' in the future –

(a) that Edward Heath would be deposed from the Conservative leadership within two years,
(b) that his successor would be Prime Minister in another four, and that eleven years of Conservative hegemony would follow under that person's leadership, and
(c) that that person was already in the Cabinet,

where would the Education Secretary have come, the minister so disliked by Heath that he placed her in the Cabinet room's equivalent of a coalhole[4] (on his right, beyond the Cabinet Secretary, the hardest place from which to catch his eye without doing an awkward Quasimodo impression)? She would have been seventeenth or so. Only the peers would have been lower down the list of probability.

To my knowledge, only one person truly saw her potential. Roy Langstone, her agent in Finchley, told me during the first of the two 1974 general elections:

> Normally, women in politics are a bloody menace. But she is the most fantastic person I've ever worked for in twenty-seven years as an agent. She gets more done in a day than most MPs do in a week. The greater proportion of this constituency would be very, very proud to see Mrs Thatcher as the first woman Prime Minister of this country. I know she's got the capabilities. One of these days, maybe; one never knows.[5]

One does not. Of all the postwar premiers, only once has the clear heir apparent made it to Number Ten: Sir Anthony Eden. And look what happened to him. Talking of the occupants of Downing Street since 1945, I have to declare an interest. I was never a fan of the lady. I have a theory that we tend to 'go native' on the Prime Minister with whose contemporary life and words we first became familiar as we grew up and started reading the newspapers. In my case it was Harold Macmillan. Ever since I have expected British premiers to be sophisticated, self-ironic, witty and marinated in the juices of the past. I have been severely disappointed. When Macmillan, in his anecdotage, would dismiss Mrs Thatcher as 'a brilliant tyrant surrounded by mediocrities',[6] I would be only too prone to concur. Allow, please, for a certain sourness of perspective in what follows.

The greatest distorter of perspective, however, is hindsight. The best antidote to this is to adopt the approach pioneered by Robert Rhodes James in his *Churchill: A Study in Failure*.[7] Assume the Thatcher odyssey had ended at various points in her career before Sir Geoffrey Howe launched his unexpected torpedo at her great dreadnought of a premiership in the autumn of 1990. Had she retired or lost her seat in 1964, 1966 or 1970 she would, for example, have been remembered outside Whitehall (if at all) as the rather beautiful (in a bunged-up sort of way) housewife who had briefly held the lowest form of ministerial life as Parliamentary Under Secretary at the Ministry of Pensions and National Insurance, and inside Whitehall as the lady who wore a hat even when sitting at her desk working.

It is said that it was Peter Walker who persuaded Edward Heath to include a woman in his 1970 Cabinet and that it had to be Mrs Thatcher. (There is no corroboration for this; if it is true, it could explain why Mr Walker survived so long in the Thatcher Cabinets despite regular and public bursts of dissent from the substance and the style of her administrations.)

Her time as Education Secretary, even if the story had finished there, would have guaranteed her more, but not much more, than a passing paragraph in postwar political history. Her ending of free school milk led to a spate of 'Thatcher the milk snatcher' headlines; and, irony of ironies, the cognoscenti noticed just how plentiful were the comprehensive reorganization schemes for which she gave approval and how skilled she was at extracting large sums of money from the Treasury for projects she held dear, such as an expansion of nursery education.

It was the speed, manner and success of her 'constitutional coup' (to borrow a phrase she used to the Soviet Ambassador about her own downfall[8]) against Edward Heath that secured her a permanent place in political lore and legend as well as the record books (she was the first woman to lead a British political party). If Sir Keith Joseph had decided to run and had not damaged himself severely by an ill-worded speech about the propensity to breed among the 'lower' social categories, the Thatcher challenge would not have been mounted. Had Willie Whitelaw not felt unable, in all honour, to stand against Mr Heath in the first ballot, there is little chance that the trajectory of time and chance would have carried her into the leadership of the opposition. Few leaders have ever arrived by a more curious set of chances, as Gilbert and Sullivan might have put it.

In her early incarnation at the despatch box at Prime Minister's Questions, Mrs Thatcher did not shine. James Callaghan's 'There, there, little lady' style was as effective as it was patronizing. Had Mr Callaghan postponed Labour's decade of civil war by a year and squeaked back into Number Ten in 1979 (to make way for Denis Healey in the early 1980s), it is unlikely that her party would have given her a second chance at a general election. How would she be remembered? Among her more worshipping supporters rather as Hugh Gaitskell is still recalled by his. No doubt a free-market-right equivalent of Philip Williams[9] would have been found to make the case for her as the-best-Prime-Minister-we-never-had. (He or she would have found the competition severe, with the name of R. A. Butler as well as that of Gaitskell in the historical frame.)

Office is a great amplifier. It is not just the guaranteed media attention, twice-weekly Question Time, the endless round of telegenic domestic trips and foreign summits. It is as if every new Premier relives Churchill's experience in the early hours of 11 May 1940 when he retired to bed as Prime Minister, convinced 'that all my past life had been but a preparation for this hour and this trial'.[10] They believe that their arrival at Number Ten vindicates their personal convictions (and the system which had the 'wisdom' to make them number one; which is why so few, Mrs Thatcher included, are constitutional reformers) and almost requires them to convert those beliefs into an indelible mark on British history – though Clement Attlee, Mrs Thatcher's only rival as a shaper of the postwar period, would have none of this. 'I had not much idea of destiny,' he said, recalling 26 July 1945 when he presented himself to a surprised King George VI to kiss hands.[11]

Mrs Thatcher behaved from first to last as if the opening bars of Beethoven's Fifth Symphony were constantly ringing in her ears. She was determined to follow the beat of her own destiny whatever the external or internal circumstances (the occasional U-turn on the Vietnamese boat people or Zimbabwean independence apart). Above all, she would not flinch on the economy. Squeezing out inflation and the painful construction of financial stability had absolute priority. Her Cabinet was first ignored on economic strategy and purged progressively in its service. Her 1981 Budget, deflating still further in the pit of a severe recession, was the crucial moment when Whitehall, the City, the world's money markets and her own party realized for the first time that she really would not turn. Even the summer riots of 1981 did not dent that resolve. They – and soaring unemployment – did, for a time, make it seem quite possible (despite Labour's internal feuding and the feeble leadership of Michael Foot) that she would be a one-term Premier. The Falklands War (its psephological impact real enough, but still furiously debated by those whose business it is to measure these things[12]) and Labour's continual ritual suicide – in Parliament, on television, in virtually every constituency in the land, everywhere – put paid to that. She came back in 1983 with a majority of 144, only two short of Attlee's landslide in 1945.

If she had not – if the nascent SDP had surged and produced a hung result – how would historians have treated the first and last Thatcher premiership? She would have achieved very little that was not, at that stage, easily reversible. A start had been made on the weakening of trade union power, but the new legislation had not been put to the test. She shrank, initially, from taking on the miners over pit closures in February 1981, waiting until coal stocks were higher and new contingency plans in place. The sale of council houses had begun, but had yet to become a cascade. She had begun to reform the Civil Service along the managerial lines suggested by her efficiency adviser, Sir Derek Rayner of Marks and Spencer. But this rolling programme of change was still subject to the Whitehall 'disbelief system'[13] and could easily have followed previous attempts in running into the sand if the electorate had brought Mrs Thatcher down in 1983. Perhaps most significant of all, privatization was still but a political glimmer. It had scarcely featured in the 1979 manifesto.[14]

The second term began, ironically enough, with accusations that the steam had gone out of 'Thatcherism' (never a term I liked, believing with that former Permanent Secretary to the Treasury, Lord Croham, that 'most "isms" are shambles'[15]). And yet the years 1983–7 are the ones in which the configurations of Britain's political economy really were refashioned. The biggest benchmarks of all were:

1 Privatization. Once British Telecom was floated successfully in 1984, the boundaries of that highly disputed frontier – the public/private sector divide – were to be changed for ever (not even a Labour government with a majority would revert to Morrisonian public corporations of the late 1940s marque).*

2 The defeat of the miners in 1984–5, which exorcised the demon let loose at Saltley in 1972 when massed flying pickets during the first coal strike since 1926 swung the balance of power heavily in the direction of organized labour.

3 The passing of the Single European Act in 1986, marking a step (little noticed at the time) towards a Europeanized Britain second only to the statute which paved the way for our accession to the Community in 1973 – and, incidentally, beginning to lay down the incendiary material which brought her premiership to an end five years later.

All three events will rank high in *national* history even when Mrs Thatcher's *personal* history has gone through the scholarly mangles in those last retreats of fame.

The second term, too, saw the start of processes, on both the domestic and the external side, which will carry a distinctive Thatcher hallmark however rough the revisionists are with her reputation. For example, the

---

* This judgement was penned in 1990, long before Mr Blair arrived to displace Clause Four.

Foreign Office picked up the potential of Mr Gorbachev ahead of his rise to power in the Soviet Union, a piece of intelligence of which Mrs Thatcher made sustained and substantial use. At crucial moments in the late 1980s, her influence was considerable in shifting perceptions in President Reagan's Washington about the credibility of Mr Gorbachev when he repeatedly asserted his intention to end the Cold War.[16] That mercurial, much-discussed phenomenon, the 'special relationship', enjoyed an extraordinary revival during the 1980s, with – 'slips' like the US invasion of Grenada in 1984 apart – the Thatcher–Reagan partnership outstripping all but the prototype Roosevelt–Churchill duo in its warmth and importance. ('Isn't she marvellous?' he would purr to his aides even while she berated him down the 'hotline'.[17])

On the domestic side, phase three of the Thatcher agenda, the assault on the 'dependency culture', the inevitable by-product of the welfare state, as she saw it, was dreamed of in the second term and implemented in the third. It was as if, having disposed of Keynes in her first pair of Parliaments, she was determined to see off Beveridge in the next pair she had in mind for herself (if her 'going on and on' interviews were to be believed). From this sprang the Fowler review of benefits, much of 'cardboard city' (the grimly photogenic image of the homeless that will feature in all reprises of the Thatcher years), the 'opted-out' schools, the Health Service hospitals with 'trust' status, the GPs with budgets. Here, the opinion surveys suggested, she would encounter electoral resistance;[18] and she did, second only to that engendered by the soon-to-be-scuppered flagship of the 'poll tax' or Community Charge.

Within months of her ejection the poll tax had gone. The fate of the benefits changes and the NHS reforms was far from clear. But the third term contained another public service change – prosaic, little noticed but of great significance to the efficiency of the state – the 'Next Steps' programme for converting large chunks of Civil Service work into free-standing public businesses, or 'executive agencies', as they were called. Within a few months of her leaving, fifty agencies were established with over 200,000 officials working in them. If the cross-party consensus holds (and the signs are that it will), three-quarters of the Civil Service, in terms of numbers, will be employed in agencies by the turn of the century, the most significant reform of Whitehall this century by far. Without her initial backing and personal impetus in the first two and a half years of the programme, the 'Next Steps' simply would not have been taken.

'Next Steps' was a semi-constitutional change as well as a managerial one. It could well be that 'Mrs Thatcher as History' will be as much a constitutional issue as a matter of political economy. The *Spycatcher* case and the forcible de-unionization of GCHQ will find their place in constitutional textbooks. But future editions of Wade and Phillips will also require their chapters on the Cabinet and the Civil Service to be substantially rewritten.

I do not believe that Mrs Thatcher politicized the senior ranks of the Civil Service, despite one or two well-publicized cases and a widespread impression that she had[19] (the quango world is a different matter, and here a case can be made for suggesting that the 'one of us' test *did* apply). Impressions can be enough in politics, however, which inevitably is something of an evidence-free zone. And if a future Labour government came in and did indulge in an element of deliberate politicization at permanent secretary level (the prospect looks unlikely), they could cite the Thatcher effect as an alibi, despite the authoritative and independent Royal Institute of Public Administration exonerating her from the charge.[20]

The Thatcher effect on the niceties of Cabinet government is equally difficult to demonstrate conclusively either way, even given the deluge of memoirs and media interviews from ministers removed in successive purges after the turn of 1980–1.[21] At the very worst, I think, Mrs Thatcher was enabled by largely supine Cabinet colleagues to put Cabinet government on ice for large stretches of her prime ministerial stewardship. But to say that our processes of government tilted decisively towards a prime ministerial, let alone a presidential system is to overstate the case to a ludicrous degree. It is, however, significant that John Major made it quite plain from his first Cabinet meeting that he was anybody-but-Margaret, and won great kudos among his appreciative colleagues for so doing.[22] The PhD mills will grind for decades on this subject, given the sacred place afforded the 'Cabinet versus Prime Ministerial Government' question on Politics 'A' level and degree level papers.

History is a ruthless sifter, however. Time reduces even the greatest reputations to a few sentences on a single side of A4. What will remain on the Thatcher ledger? Five entries, I suggest:

1   The breaking of trade union power. The balance will never again tilt so far in favour of the labour movement as it had by the late 1970s.
2   The public/private boundary will not return to the *status quo post* Herbert Morrison or *ante* Margaret Thatcher. The argument from now on will be more about regulation than about ownership.
3   With two-thirds of state assets sold off in her first ten years, the spread of shareholding from 3 million individuals in 1979 to 9 million in 1989 will have a significant, permanent place in British economic history.[23]
4   That other significant form of public asset disposal – council house sales – saw a million homes transferred to private ownership on very favourable terms,[24] a substantial shift by any standards towards that

'property-owning democracy' of which Conservatives have spoken since the nineteenth century.

5 By playing midwife to the 'Next Steps', Mrs Thatcher put the kind of mark on Britain's 'permanent government' that Gladstone left when he turned the Civil Service from a patronage society into the country's first meritocracy by establishing the principle of recruitment by competitive examination in the late nineteenth century.[25]

At its cruellest, history reduces the Ozymandias effect to a single one-liner. What will be Margaret Thatcher's? Her celebrated 'Truth can be stranger than fiction' remark at the time of the Westland affair? 'It's a funny old world,' her opening remark at her final Cabinet? No. Surely it is 'We are a grandmother,' that immortal use of the royal 'we'. But, as history showed in November 1990, the British Constitution has room for only one Queen, the one who lived at the western, not the eastern, end of St James's Park.

Epilogue

There is something distinctive and recognizable in English civilization . . .
Moreover it is continuous, it stretches into the future and the past, there is
something in it that persists, as in a living creature . . .

George Orwell, 1940[1]

It is no longer a case of one party fighting another, nor of one set of politi-
cians scoring off another. It is the case of successive governments facing
economic problems and being judged by their success or failure in the duel . . .
The compass has been damaged. The charts are out of date.

Winston Churchill, 1930[2]

Apply Orwell's continuity test to the fifty-one-year span between the parliamentarians' short walk from the Palace of Westminster to St Margaret's to give thanks for their nation's deliverance on VJ Day to the publication of this volume and, of course, it both holds and falls. Not one among the political generation of 1945 would have – could have – contemplated the slippage from status and influence of the UK over the two generations to follow. Apart from the Soviet Union's dramatic collapse, there has been nothing to equal it among the world's more substantial powers since Germany and Japan were defeated in May and August 1945.

Yet, rereading the documentaries and articles put together in this collection, I am struck by the persistence of certain core difficulties – above all, the economic and industrial underperformance, in relative terms, which has placed such stress on our society, our political system and our desire to cut an influential dash in the higher councils of international affairs.

For almost the whole period our Euro-ambivalence, our emotional deficit with an integrating Continent, has placed its own special kind of stress on our domestic affairs and our international aspirations. And each time that European Question has intruded into mainstream British politics and government since Jean Monnet came across the Channel with the Schuman Plan in his pocket in May 1950, the stress has intensified. Combine it with that other great postwar destabilizer – the weakness of the pound sterling – and the effect can be (will continue to be until single-currency day?) lethal.[3]

To some extent all postwar British Premiers, including the grand old man himself, would (had they known of it) have agreed with Churchill's despairing cry about the broken 'charts' and 'compasses' and the pitiless opponents faced by every Prime Minister, only their battle-order changing from time to time. And yet, as a country the United Kingdom, again in relative terms, has remained throughout an island (Northern Ireland apart) of tranquillity and political civility compared to much of the world – its governing systems and its ancient and mysterious Constitution largely unaffected by the tribulations and disappointments of the years since 1945.

One other factor stands out. The United Kingdom is a nation much discussed by those to whom it belongs. Our broadcasting – especially on those frequencies where radio and the spirit of public service meet – has given us the most marvellous capacity for thinking aloud in a sustained and careful fashion. Historians should shy away from offering 'lessons' from the past. But here I must make an exception. If we ever lose that shared BBC Radio Four-style capacity for thinking together, a very terrible kind of impoverishment awaits us.

Notes

Preface

1 'The Head of His Profession', *New Statesman Profiles* (Readers' Union, 1958), pp. 35–42.
2 John Redcliffe-Maud, *Experiences of an Optimist* (Hamish Hamilton, 1981), p. 51.
3 Gillian Reynolds, addressing a Royal Society of Arts symposium on 'The Future of UK Radio', 10 April 1989.
4 Mr Powell delivered this remark during the recording of 'Diminished Responsibility?' on 21 November 1990, broadcast the following day on the BBC Radio Four *Analysis* programme. It was published as Peter Hennessy and Caroline Anstey, *Diminished Responsibility? The Essence of Cabinet Government*, Strathclyde *Analysis* Paper no. 2 (Department of Government, University of Strathclyde, 1991).
5 Brian Redhead died on 23 January 1994. I was part of his general election *galère* on the night of 9–10 April 1992.
6 Bernard Ingham, *Kill the Messenger* (HarperCollins, 1991), p. 254.
7 See Margaret Thatcher, *The Downing Street Years* (HarperCollins, 1993), pp. 634–8.
8 Private information.

Introduction

1 J. Enoch Powell, 'The Causes of the English Revolution', *The Spectator*, 5 December 1987.
2 Quoted in Tom Ackland, *The Disobedient Servant* (Gollancz, 1996), p. 8.
3 See e.g. Eric Hobsbawm and Terence Ranger (eds), *The Invention of Tradition* (Cambridge University Press, 1983).
4 Paul Addison, 'The Religion of Winston Churchill', in Michael Bentley (ed.), *Public and Private Doctrine: Essays in British History Presented to Maurice Cowling* (Cambridge University Press, 1993), p. 245.
5 See p. 40 below.
6 Private information.

Introduction to Part One

1   Private information.
2   See Peter Hennessy, *The Hidden Wiring: Unearthing the British Constitution* (Gollancz, 1995), pp. 71–2.
3   Sir Robin divulged this information while chairing my inaugural lecture as Professor of Contemporary History at Queen Mary and Westfield College, University of London, 1 February 1994.

Chapter 1

1   Walter Bagehot, 'The Monarchy', in Norman St John-Stevas (ed.), *The Collected Works of Walter Bagehot*, vol. 5 (*The Economist*, 1974), p. 243.
2   Ibid., p. 229.
3   Ibid., p. 243.
4   This was a slight misquotation of Bagehot, who wrote: 'the sovereign has, under a constitutional monarchy such as ours – the right to be consulted, the right to encourage, the right to warn': ibid., p. 253.
5   Tony Benn's conversation with the Queen is recorded in his diary entry for 11 July 1969; see Tony Benn, *Office Without Power: Diaries 1968–72* (Hutchinson, 1988), pp. 190–1.
6   For Tony Benn's lunchtime exchange with the Queen's Private Secretary, Sir Martin Charteris, on 21 January 1974, see Tony Benn, *Against the Tide: Diaries 1973–76* (Hutchinson, 1989), pp. 94–5.

Chapter 2

1   Walter Bagehot, *The English Constitution*, intr. R. H. S. Crossman (Fontana, Library edn, 1963), p. 99.
2   E. C. S. Wade and C. Godfrey Phillips, *Constitutional and Administrative Law*, 9th edn, ed. A. W. Bradley (Longman, 1977), pp. 223–8.
3   See Vernon Bogdanor, *No Overall Majority: Forming a Government in a Multi-Party Parliament* (Constitutional Reform Centre, 1986), p. 17.
4   *The Times*, 2 May 1950.
5   Public Record Office (PRO), PREM 11/2654. 'Arrangements for announcement of date of general election'. See T. J. Bligh, 'Note for the Record', 21 August 1959; Harold Macmillan to HM Queen, 21 August 1959; 'Programme of Events', undated, in the same file.

Introduction to Part Two

1 Ferdinand Mount, *The British Constitution Now: Recovery or Decline?* (Heinemann, 1992), p. 89.
2 House of Commons Treasury and Civil Service Committee, Fifth Report, Session 1993–4, *The Role of the Civil Service*, vol. 1, HC 27-I (HMSO, 1994), p. v.
3 For the creation of this convention see A. Aspinall, 'The Cabinet Council, 1783–1835', *Proceedings of the British Academy*, vol. 38, 1952, pp. 166–7.
4 For the development of the career Civil Service see Peter Hennessy, *Whitehall* (Fontana, 1990), pp. 30–52.
5 The lecture was first published as *The 25 Series*, no. 1 (Civil Service College, 1996).

Chapter 3

1 Lady Gwendolen Cecil, *The Life of Lord Salisbury*, vol. 2 (Hodder, 1921), p. 153.
2 Hugh Dalton, *High Tide and After* (Muller, 1961), p. 16.
3 Tessa Blackstone and William Plowden, *Inside the Think Tank: Advising the Cabinet, 1971–83* (Heinemann, 1988), p. 185.
4 The phrase is Professor David Marquand's, himself a former MP.
5 Lord Bancroft, speaking at the Gresham College Seminar, 'In the Steps of Walter Bagehot: A Constitutional Health-Check', 13 March 1995.
6 Private information.
7 Following Herbert Marcuse.
8 SPATS stands for the Senior Professional Administrative Training Scheme. See Peter Hennessy, *Whitehall* (Fontana, 1990), pp. 529–30.
9 Ibid., pp. 525–30.
10 Conversation with Richard Wilding, 22 February 1995.
11 George Orwell, *The Lion and the Unicorn: Socialism and the English Genius* (Secker & Warburg, 1941), pp. 11–12.
12 *The Civil Service: Continuity and Change*, Cm 2627 (HMSO, 1994).
13 Lord Radcliffe, *Power and the State*, the Reith Lectures, 1951, no. 1: 'On Plato's Idea of the State', first broadcast on the BBC Home Service, 4 November 1951.
14 Harold Wilson, *The Governance of Britain* (Weidenfeld/Michael Joseph, 1976), p. x.
15 Conversation with Lord Bancroft, 9 January 1995.
16 The phrase is Sidney Low's. See his *The Governance of England* (Fisher Unwin, 1904), p. 12.

17 Douglas Hurd, *Vote to Kill* (Collins, 1975), p. 12.

18 House of Commons Treasury and Civil Service Committee, Fifth
     Report, Session 1993–4, *The Role of the Civil Service*, HC 27-I (HMSO,
     1994); *The Civil Service: Taking Forward Continuity and Change*, Cm 2748
     (HMSO, 1995).

19 Anthony Montague Browne, *Long Sunset: Memoirs of Winston Churchill's
     Last Private Secretary* (Cassell, 1995), p. 107.

20 Private information.

21 Peter Hennessy, 'Whitehall Watch: Why New Masters Could Mean
     Wholesale Change', *The Independent*, 9 January 1989.

22 *Standards in Public Life: First Report of the Committee on Standards in
     Public Life*, vol. 1, Cm 2850-I (HMSO, 1995), pp. 58–60.

23 Sir Robin Butler, 'The Themes of Public Service Reform in Britain and
     Overseas', Policy Studies Institute Seminar, 13 June 1995.

24 Tony Benn MP, briefing the Queen Mary and Westfield College
     Department of History 'Cabinet and Premiership' course, House of
     Commons, 1 March 1995.

25 Ian Beesley, now a partner with Price Waterhouse, addressing the
     'Hidden Wiring' seminar of the Queen Mary and Westfield College MA
     in Contemporary British History course, 1 March 1995.

26 *Report of the Machinery of Government Committee*, Cd 9230 (HMSO, 1918).

27 *The Reorganisation of Central Government*, Cmnd 4506 (HMSO, 1970).

28 Rhys Williams, 'Birt Warns of "Media Frenzy" Causing Instability',
     The Independent, 4 February 1995.

29 Thomas Balogh, 'Civil Service Reform', paper for Harold Wilson, May
     1963 . Tony Benn has very kindly allowed me to see his copy of it.

30 Obituary, 'John Bruce Lockhart', *The Times*, 10 May 1995.

31 Lord Bancroft, 'In the Steps of Walter Bagehot'.

32 See Hennessy, *Whitehall*, p. 190.

33 See Hennessy, *Hidden Wiring*, pp. 132–6.

34 House of Commons Treasury and Civil Service Committee, *The Role of
     the Civil Service*, vol. 1, p. lxxvi.

35 *The Civil Service: Taking Forward Continuity and Change*, p. 35.

36 Private information.

37 Butler, 'Themes of Public Service Reform'.

Chapter 4

1 Enoch Powell, *The Parliamentarians*, BBC Television, 4 February 1979,
    reproduced in Rex Collings (ed.), *Reflections of a Statesman: The Writings
    and Speeches of Enoch Powell* (Bellew Publishing, 1991), p. 261.

2 House of Commons Debates, *Official Report*, vol. 969, 25 June 1979, col. 36.

3 For the Haldane findings see Ministry of Reconstruction, *Report of the Machinery of Government Committee*, Cd 9230 (HMSO, 1918), p. 15. For their adoption by the Procedure Committee see Select Committee on Procedure (Session 1977–8), *First Report*, vol. 1, *Report and Minutes of Proceedings*, HC 588-I (HMSO, 1978).

4 For the Crossman reforms see Priscilla Baines, 'History and Rationale of the 1979 Reforms', in Gavin Drewry (ed.), *The New Select Committees: A Study of the 1979 Reforms* (Clarendon Press, 1985), pp. 18–23. For the Expenditure Committee see ibid., pp. 24–5.

5 Select Committee on Procedure (Session 1989–90), *Second Report: The Working of the Select Committee System*, HC19-I (HMSO, 1990).

6 Ibid., pp. xciii–xcv.

7 Select Committee on Defence (Session 1985–6), *Fourth Report. Westland plc: The Government's Decision-Making* (HMSO, 1986).

8 Dr Judge's critique of the Procedure Committee's work is published as 'The "Effectiveness" of the Post-1979 Select Committee System: The Verdict of the 1990 Procedure Committee', *Political Quarterly*, vol. 63, no. 1, 1992.

9 Prime Minister's Questions: Written Answer no. 236, 4 November 1991.

10 *The Working of the Select Committee System*, government response to the Second Report of the House of Commons Select Committee on Procedure, Session 1989–90, Cm 1532 (HMSO, 1991), p. 15.

11 For an account of Mr St John-Stevas's difficulties with the Cabinet in May–June 1979, see his *The Two Cities* (Faber, 1984), pp. 54–7, 104–7.

12 The latest version of the 'Osmotherly Rules' can be found in *Memorandum of Guidance for Officials Appearing Before Select Committees*, which is available from the Cabinet Office.

Introduction to Part Three

1 PRO, CAB 134/1929, 'Study of Future Policy 1960/70', FP(60), 1st meeting, 23 March 1960. I am grateful to my student, Nahdia Khan, who discovered this minute while preparing her undergraduate research project in the Queen Mary and Westfield College Department of History on 'Harold Macmillan and Foreign Policy Rethinks, 1957–60'.

2 Private information.

3 An unknown wit scrawled the following piece of doggerel during the negotiations for the American loan in 1945:

In Washington Lord Halifax
once whispered to Lord Keynes:
'It's true *they* have the moneybags,
but *we* have all the brains.'

See Richard N. Gardner, *Sterling–Dollar Diplomacy*, expanded edn
(McGraw-Hill, 1969), p. xvii.

4   Sir Brian Fall, British Ambassador to Moscow, 1992; see Peter Hennessy,
    'Does Britannia Rule the Waves?', *Director*, March 1992. Sir Brian was
    High Commissioner in Ottawa when he made this remark.

5   Lord Greenhill, former Head of the Diplomatic Service, 1988. See Lord
    Greenhill, 'British Foreign Policy, 1945–70: Could We Have Done
    Better?', Institute of Contemporary British History/London School of
    Economics summer school, 8 July 1988.

6   Conversation with Lord Franks, quoted in Peter Hennessy and Caroline
    Anstey, *Moneybags and Brains: The Anglo–American 'Special Relationship'
    since 1945*, Strathclyde *Analysis* Paper no. 1 (Department of
    Government, University of Strathclyde, 1990), p. 10.

7   According to the Scottish *Daily Record*, this took place on the night of 13
    December 1994, though no official announcement was made.

Chapter 6

1   See Peter Hennessy, 'How Bevin Saved Britain's Bomb', *The Times*,
    30 September 1982.

Chapter 8

1   Quoted in John Dickie, *Inside the Foreign Office* (Chapmans, 1992),
    p. 42.

2   Noel Coward, 'Mad Dogs and Englishmen (Go Out in the Midday Sun)',
    1932.

3   Geoffrey Smith, *Reagan and Thatcher* (Bodley Head, 1990). Mr Smith
    delivered this judgement during a seminar at the University of London's
    Institute of Historical Research on 30 January 1991.

4   Christopher Bellamy, 'Rifkind Looks to Elite Defence Role', *The
    Independent*, 8 July 1992.

5   Keith Robbins, *The Eclipse of a Great Power: Modern Britain 1870–1975*
    (Longman, 1983).

6   The view attributed to Harold Macmillan.

Introduction to Part Four

1 John Grigg, *Lloyd George: From Peace to War 1912–1916* (Methuen, 1985), p. 474.
2 Lord Donoughue, speaking to the 'Hidden Wiring' seminar of the MA programme in Twentieth Century British History since 1939, Queen Mary and Westfield College, London, 25 January 1995.

Chapter 17

1 Samuel Johnson, quoted in Jonathan Steinberg, *All or Nothing* (Routledge, 1990), p. xv.
2 'Bagehot', 'June's Budget, in March', *The Economist*, 23 March 1991.
3 Alan Watkins, 'Our Prime Ministers Have Been a Funny Lot', Political Diary, *The Observer*, 7 April 1991.
4 James Prior, *A Balance of Power* (Hamish Hamilton, 1986), p. 117.
5 Peter Hennessy, 'Mrs Thatcher Shimmers through the Hustings', *The Times Higher Education Supplement*, 22 February 1974.
6 Quoted in Peter Hennessy, *Cabinet* (Blackwell, 1986), p. 94.
7 Robert Rhodes James, *Churchill: A Study in Failure, 1900–1939* (Weidenfeld, 1970).
8 'The Fall of Thatcher', *The Economist*, 9 March 1991.
9 Philip Williams, *Hugh Gaitskell* (Cape, 1979).
10 Winston S. Churchill, *The Second World War*, vol. 2: *The Twilight War* (Cassell, 1964), pp. 238–9.
11 *Clem Attlee: Granada Historical Records* (Granada, 1967), p. 29.
12 See Mark Franklin and Lawrence Freedman, 'Controversy: The Falklands Factor', *Contemporary Record*, vol. 1, no. 3, Autumn 1987, pp. 27–9.
13 The phrase belongs to Les Metcalfe and Sue Richards. See their *Improving Public Management* (Gower, 1987), pp. 18–19.
14 See Peter Riddell, *The Thatcher Decade: How Britain has Changed during the 1980s* (Blackwell, 1989), p. 8.
15 Quoted in Peter Hennessy and Caroline Anstey, *From Clogs to Clogs? Britain's Relative Economic Decline since 1851*, Strathclyde *Analysis* Paper no. 3 (Department of Government, University of Strathclyde, 1991).
16 See Geoffrey Smith, *Reagan and Thatcher* (Bodley Head, 1990), pp. 227–41 and 146–7.
17 Ibid., p. 26.
18 See Ivor Crewe, 'Has the Electorate become Thatcherite?', in Robert Skidelsky (ed.), *Thatcherism* (Chatto, 1988), pp. 25–50.

19 Hugo Young, in his superb *One of Us* (Macmillan, 1989), pp. 336–8, gives
    more credence to the politicization argument than I do; see Peter
    Hennessy, 'Mrs Thatcher's Poodle? The Civil Service since 1979',
    Contemporary Record, vol. 2, no. 2, Summer 1988, pp. 2–4.

20 *Top Jobs in Whitehall: Appointments and Promotions in the Senior Civil
    Service* (Royal Institute of Public Administration, 1987).

21 Peter Hennessy, 'Whitehall Watch: Myth of the Discussion-Free Zone',
    The Independent, 19 November 1990; Peter Hennessy, 'Mrs Thatcher, the
    Cabinet and Power-Sharing', in Philip Norton (ed.), *New Directions in
    British Politics* (Edward Elgar, 1991).

22 Peter Hennessy, 'Whitehall Watch: War Gives Major a New Gravitas',
    The Independent, 21 January 1991.

23 See Riddell, *The Thatcher Decade*, pp. 113–26.

24 Alan Murie, 'Housing and the Environment', in Dennis Kavanagh and
    Anthony Seldon (eds), *The Thatcher Effect: A Decade of Change*
    (Clarendon Press, 1989), pp. 218–21.

25 Peter Hennessy, 'Whitehall Watch: Legacy of "Next Steps" Will
    Endure', *The Independent*, 26 November 1990.

Epilogue

1 Orwell wrote these words in 1940, though they were published in 1941:
   George Orwell, *The Lion and the Unicorn: Socialism and the English
   Genius* (Secker & Warburg, 1941), pp. 11–12.

2 Quoted in Peter Clarke, *A Question of Leadership: Gladstone to Thatcher*
   (Hamish Hamilton, 1991), p. 135.

3 This is brought out in all its painful beauty in Philip Stephens' *Politics
   and the Pound: The Conservatives' Struggle with Sterling* (Macmillan,
   1996).

Index

The letter 'e' after a page reference indicates an epigraph.

Acheson, Dean, 184
Ackland, Sir Antony, 243
Addison, Dr Paul, 189-203 *passim*
Alexander, A. V., 99
Alexander, Andrew, 259
Algeria, 135
Allen, Graham, 64, 69, 77-8
Anstey, Caroline, 15, 98, 170
Armstrong, Lord, Of Ilminster, Sir
   Robert Armstrong, 37-8, 40-1, 42,
   50-1
Armstrong, Sir William, Lord
   Armstrong of Sanderstead, 270
Ashdown, Paddy, 44, 45
Asquith, H. H., 169e, 290
Atlantic Pact, 182
atomic bomb, *see* nuclear weapons
Attlee, C. R., 171-86
    and Anglo-American relations,
      102, 104, 182-3,183-5
    and the atomic bomb, 102, 103,
      104, 105, 183, 184, 190
    and Cabinet, 175, 190
    and economic affairs, 171-2,
      172-3, 178-9, 180-1
    and Europe, 176-7
    and poverty, social conditions,
      171-2, 172, 173-4, 179
    as Prime Minister, 171, 173, 175,
      279-80, 290, 293
    mentioned, 23, 207

Bagehot, Walter, 16e, 16, 28, 34
Balfour, Arthur, 244
Balogh, Thomas, 60
Bancroft, Ian, 55-6, 57
Barber, Lord, 227, 229-30, 271

Barnett, Sir Denis, 137, 138, 143, 144
Barnett, Joel, 263
BBC, 9-11, 14, 299
Beaufré, General, 143
Beeley, Sir Harold, 140, 142
Beesley, Ian, 59
Benn, Tony, 16-17, 32
    on the Civil Service, 59
    on Parliament and the royal
      prerogatives, 15,17-33
    on Wilson, 258, 258-9, 262, 266
Berrill Report, 163
Beveridge, Sir William, 179-80
Bevin, Ernest, 99e, 103, 104, 128,
   176-8, 182
bills, government, scrutiny of, 76
Bishop, Sir Frederick, 226, 227
Blackett, Patrick, 103
Blackstone, Baroness, Tessa
   Blackstone, 164-5
Blue Streak missile, 109
Bogdanor, Vernon, 39, 43
Bondi, Sir Hermann, 118, 119-20,
   122, 128
Bourn, Sir John, 74
Bowsher, Chuck, 73-4
Boyd-Carpenter, Lord, John Boyd-
   Carpenter 188, 202
    on Churchill's postwar
      government, 188-203 *passim*
Boyle, Sir Dermot, 132-3, 138, 144,
   146-7, 147, 149
Bridges, Sir Edward, Lord Bridges,
   145, 192-3
Britain, 13e, 13-14, 298-9
    world role, 97e, 97-8, 99, 104,
      150-67, 181-2

British Council, 164-5
broadcasting, 9-11, 299
Brook, Sir Norman, Lord
    Normanbrook, 110, 192-3
Brown, George, 115, 250, 252
Brundrett, Sir Frederick, 108
Bush, President George, 157
Butler, Lord, R. A. Butler, 188, 201,
    225, 236-7
Butler, Sir Robin, 15, 91

Cabinet committees, 271
Cabinet government, *see under
    individual prime ministers*
Callaghan, Lord, James Callaghan,
    170, 279-89
        and Cabinet, 284-6
        and economic affairs, 282, 285-6
        and general election of 1979,
            38-9
        on Heath's departure in 1974,
            35-6
        and nuclear weapons, 115, 120-1,
            123, 125-7, 129, 286, 287-8
        on the powers of the sovereign,
            51
        as Prime Minister without a
            majority, 44, 45-6, 282
        and trade union reform, 256
        mentioned, 33, 250, 258
Camp David, 110
Carr, Lord, Robert Carr, 204-5, 206,
    207, 208, 211, 213, 214, 216
Carrington, Lord, 120
Carter, President Jimmy, 125, 126
Castle, Lady, Barbara Castle, 247, 250,
    254, 256, 257
Central Policy Review Staff, 163
Chevaline, 118, 120-4
Cheysson, Claude, 160-1, 164
Christmas Island, 107-8
Churchill, Sir Winston, 187-203, 298e
        and Anglo-American relations,
            101, 195, 198, 199

        and Cabinet, 189-91
        and the Cold War, 187, 193-4,
            196, 197
        and economic affairs, 199-200,
            202
        and Europe, 198-9
        on the House of Commons, 6e
        and nuclear weapons, 101, 105-6,
            190, 198
        mentioned, 58, 171, 205, 206, 268
Civil Contingencies Unit, 273
Civil Service, 53e, 53, 55-62, 73, 77,
    192-3, 294, 295-6, 297
Civil Service College, 54, 55-7, 60-1, 62
Clark, Alan, 84, 86, 93
Coates, Simon, 15, 54, 170
Cockroft, Sir John, 105
Cold War, peaceful coexistence, 187,
    193-4, 196-7
Colville, Jock, 192
Common Market, *see* Europe
Commonwealth, 162-4, 193, 239
Conservative Party, 238, 269
Constitution, 15e, 31-2, 39-40, 67
        permanent ballast in, 57
        written, 28-9
        see also Crown; government;
            Parliament; Prime Minister
Continuity and Change (White Paper),
    57, 58, 61
Cook, Bill, 108
Cooper, Sir Frank, 99, 104, 113, 118-9,
    127, 128
council house sales, 296-7
Coward, Noel, 150e
Cradock, Sir Percy, 82, 83, 85, 85-6,
    88, 90, 93, 152, 157-8
Cripps, Sir Stafford, 103, 177-8, 178
Croham, Lord, Douglas Allen, 294
Crosland, Tony, 256
Crossman, R. H. S., 178
Crown, monarchy
        government must be carried on,
            38, 39

royal prerogatives, 15, 16–33, 34–43, 49–52
sovereign not to be embarrassed, 36, 49–51
sovereign not involved in political controversy, 23–6, 38, 39
see also Elizabeth II
Cunningham, Jack, 58

D'Abernon, Lord, 13e
Dalton, Hugh, 103, 183
Darling, General Sir Kenneth, 143, 146
de Zulueta, Sir Philip, 110, 110–11, 112, 112–13
defence spending, military power, 133, 151–2, 158–60, 166–7
deference, in British society, 78–9
Department of Economic Affairs, 60, 252
'dependency culture', 295
Diefenderfer, Bill, 65
disarmament, 116, 119
dockers, London, 171–2
Donoghue, Lord, Bernard Donoghue, 169e, 259, 264, 284
Duff, Sir Antony, 123
Dulles, John Foster, 135–6, 212, 214

Eden, Sir Anthony, later Lord Avon, 204–19, 225
    and Cabinet, 210–11
    and economic affairs, 204, 207, 208
    and Europe, 216–17
    health, 200–201, 211
    as heir apparent, 191, 195, 200–201, 205
    becomes Prime Minister, 204–6
    as Prime Minister, 206–9, 217–19, 268–9
    and Suez, 130–49 *passim*, 193, 204, 209–16, 217, 219
    mentioned, 197

Edward VIII, King, 20
Eisenhower, President Dwight D., 108, 110, 135–6, 137, 198, 214, 227–8
electoral reform, 36–7
Elizabeth II, Queen, 15e, 50, 51, 234, 275, 287
Emery, Sir Peter, 64, 72
Empire, British, 162, 181–2, 193, 228, 238
Europe, Common Market, European Economic Community, European Community, 17–18, 160–2, 298
    Britain attempts to join, 110–11, 148–9, 160, 258
    Britain joins, 258–9, 271–2
    see also under individual prime ministers

Falkender, Lady, Marcia Williams, 253
Falklands, 18, 81, 162–3, 288
Fielding, Sir Leslie, 154–5, 159, 162, 167
Foot, Michael, 173, 247–8
Foreign Office, 142, 150, 154–5, 194, 197
France, 152–3, 160–1
    and nuclear weapons, 110–11, 113, 125–6, 159, 286
    and Suez, 135, 139–44, 148–9, 204, 210–11, 121, 215
Franks, Lord, 97–8
Frisch, Otto, 99–100
Fuchs, Klaus, 104
Fulton Inquiry, Fulton Report, 56–7, 61

Gaitskell, Hugh, 213, 248
Garel-Jones, Tristan, 88
Gaulle, Charles de, 110–11, 160
general elections
    1945, 171
    1950, 45, 174
    1951, 45
    1955, 209

1959, 228
1964, 114, 241, 242, 250
1966, 255
1970, 258
February 1974, 35-8, 259
October 1974, 261
1979, 38-9
1983, 293
George V, King, 23
Gladwyn, Lord, 135, 148-9
Glenamara, Lord, Ted Short, 264, 266
Gorbachev, Mikhail, 295
Gordon Walker, Patrick, 115
government
    to be carried on, 38, 39
    executive courts, 80, 89
    executive and legislature,
        separation of powers, 53-4,
        67, 69, 73, 78
    machinery of, 269-70, 277-8
    minority, 44, 48-9
    see also Constitution; Crown;
        Parliament, Prime Minister
government, local, 277
Griffith, Professor John, 67
Guadeloupe summit, 125, 126
Guiringaud, M., 125
Gulf War, 156-7, 158, 166-7

Halisham, Lord, Quintin Hogg, 205,
    207, 210, 211, 214, 220, 236
    on Eden, 205, 210-18 *passim*
    on Macmillan, 220, 221
    on the premiership, 244
Haines, Joe, 256, 259, 260-1, 265
Haldane Committee, Haldane Report,
    59, 63
Hale, Julian, 11, 170
Haley, Sir William, 9e
Harris, Kenneth, 172, 173, 174-5, 177,
    179, 181, 183, 185-6
Hazell, Robert, 65, 76
Healey, Lord, Dennis Healey, 282
    and defence spending, 151, 166-7

and nuclear weapons, 114-5, 116,
    121, 123, 124, 159-60
on Wilson, 240-1, 248, 255
Heath, Sir Edward, 170, 268-78
    becomes leader of Conservative
        Party, 242
    becomes Prime Minister, 23
    defeated in 1974, 35-8, 259
    and Cabinet, 270, 270-1
    and Civil Service, 59, 270
    and economic affairs, 272, 273
    and Europe, 239, 258, 268, 271-2
    on Home, 236, 244, 269
    and nuclear weapons, 118, 276
    as Prime Minister, 243, 268-78
    and resale price maintenance,
        242
Heffer, Eric, 286
Herbert, Alan, 173
Heseltine, Michael, 83
Hinton, Sir Christopher, 105
Hogg, Quintin, *see* Hailsham, Lord
Home, Lord, Sir Alec Douglas-Home,
    235-45
    becomes Prime Minister, 23, 51,
        230, 236-8
    defeated in 1964, 114, 242
    succeeded by Heath, 242-3
    and Anglo-American relations,
        111-12, 112, 137, 149, 238-9
    and economic affairs, 239-40,
        242
    and Europe, 239
    and nuclear weapons, 111-12,
        112, 114, 129
    as Prime Minister, 235-6,
        239-40, 244-5, 269
    and Suez, 130-1, 132, 134, 137,
        139, 141-2, 144-5, 145-6, 149,
        238-9
    mentioned, 249
Houghton, Douglas, 24
House of Commons, 6e, 17-19, 29-33,
    63e, 78, 92

Standing Orders, 48-9
see also Parliament
House of Lords, 33
Howe, Lord, Sir Geoffrey Howe, 86-7, 155, 161
Hunt, Lord, of Tanworth, 260, 261, 261-2, 264-5
Hunt, Sir David, 173, 174, 176, 177-8, 178, 181-2, 183-4, 185
Hurd, Douglas, 58, 152
Hyde Park Agreement, 101
hydrogen bomb, H-bomb, 105-9, 190; *see also* nuclear weapons

immigration, 207
In Place of Strife, 24, 256-7
industrial relations, 204, 208; *see also* trade unions
Ingham, Sir Bernard, 10
intelligence services, secret services, 80, 83, 85-6, 157-8, 264-5, 275-6
Iraq, arms for, 80-95
Ismay, Lord, Sir Hastings 'Pug' Ismay, 189
Israel, and Suez, 138-45, 147-8, 210-11, 212, 214-15, 215-16

Jay, Lord, Douglas Jay, 172
    on Attlee, 172-86 *passim*
Jenkins, Arthur, 179-80
Jenkins, Roy, Lord Jenkins of Hillhead, 45, 251, 255-6, 260
Johnson, Samuel, 290e
Joint Intelligence Committee, 85
Jones, Jack, 263
Jones, Jim, 71
Jordan, 138-9
Joseph, Sir Keith, 292
Judge, Dr David, 67-8
judges, judiciary, 28-9

Keightley, Sir Charles, 143
Kennedy, President John F., 111, 111-13, 231-2

King, Tom, 81, 85, 87-8, 90, 91, 92
Kinnock, Neil, 277, 286
'kitchen cabinet', 253
Korean War, 183-4, 184

Labour governments, pre-war, 23, 44
Labour Party, 24, 33, 44, 249, 266, 285, 286, 293
Laity, Mark, 98
Lang, Ian, 80-1, 84
Langstone, Roy, 291
Lascelles, Sir Alan, 34-5
Lawson, Lord, Nigel Lawson, 241-2, 242-3
Lee, Sir David, 134, 138
Lennox-Boyd, Alan, 130
Lever, Harold, 281, 285
Liberal Democrats, 43, 44, 45, 47-8
Liberal Party, 36-7
Lloyd, Selwyn, 136, 140-1
Lloyd George, David, 223, 244
Lockhart, John Bruce, 60
Logan, Sir Donald, 136, 140-1
Longford, Lord, 172, 173-4, 175-6, 176, 179-80, 182-3, 185
Lyell, Sir Nicholas, 80-1, 82-3, 84-5

MacArthur, General Douglas, 184
McIntosh, Sir Ronald, 252
McKenzie, Professor Bob, 222, 222-3
Macklen, Victor, 106, 108, 117, 118, 122
Maclean, Donald, 104
Macleod, Iain, 229, 237
McMahon, Senator Brian, McMahon Act, 102, 108
Macmillan, Alexander, 2nd Earl of Stockton, 220-1, 230, 231, 233, 233-4
Macmillan, Harold, 1st Earl of Stockton, 220-34
    and Anglo-American relations, 107-8, 110-13, 115, 116, 227-8, 231

on Attlee, 173
on Britain's role in the world, 97e
and Cabinet, 190, 220, 226, 227, 229
his earldom, 233-4
and economic affairs, 224, 226, 228, 232
and Eden, 205, 225
and Europe, 110-11, 161, 228-9
health, 222-3, 230
as housing minister, 224
and nuclear weapons, 107-8, 110-13, 115, 116, 190, 231
becomes Prime Minister, 225-6
as Prime Minister, 220, 226-30, 269, 290
resignation, successor, 51, 230, 236
as speaker, 220-1, 223, 230-1, 232
and Suez, 137, 145-6, 214, 225
and Thatcher, 233, 291
mentioned, 249
McNally, Tom, 45, 49
McNamara, Robert S., 111, 113, 116
Major, John, 46, 47-8, 69, 80, 296
Makins, Sir Roger, *see* Sherfield, Lord
Mann, Tom, 69
Masani, Zareer, 98
Mason, Sir Ronald, 122-3, 123-4, 128
Matrix Churchill trial, 81, 82-5, 86, 89
Maud Committee, Maud Report, 100
Maudling, Reginald, 240
media, the press, 60, 206-7, 273-4; *see also* BBC
Meyrick, Nichola, 54
MI5, 264-5
Middle East, 130, 131, 148, 153, 217, 238
Mikardo, Ian, 235, 241, 247, 252-3
Millard, Sir Guy, 130, 136, 139, 147-8, 206-7, 209, 211, 212, 215, 217, 218-19

ministers, 53e
accountable to Parliament, 80-2, 88, 91, 95
MIRVS, 118, 119
Mitchell, Sir Derek, 235-6, 250, 253, 254
monarchy, *see* Crown
Monckton, Sir Walter, 199, 199-200, 208
Moncrieff, Anthony, 170
Montague Browne, Anthony, 188
on Churchill's postwar government, 188-203 *passim*
Morrison, Herbert, 172
Moscow Criteria, 119-20, 124, 125
motorways, 202
Mount, Ferdinand, 53e
Mountbatten, Lord, 114, 138, 144
Mulley, Fred, 123
Murray, Len, 256

Nailor, Professor Peter, 108-9, 113-14
Nassau Agreement, 111-13
Nasser, Colonel, 130-2, 135, 149, 209, 217, 238
National Audit Office, 72, 74
nationalization, public ownership, 172-3, 180-1
NATO, 176-7
Northern Ireland, 37, 47, 257, 261
nuclear weapons, 10, 98, 99-129, 133, 159-60, 183, 184, 190, 198, 276-7, 286, 287-8
Nuffield, Lord, 207
Nunn May, Allan, 104
Nuri Said, 148
Nutting, Sir Anthony, 131-2, 142, 148

Oates, Peter, 192
oil, 130, 131
Olivier, Lord, Laurence Olivier, 221
Orme, Stan, 44
Ormsby-Gore, Sir David, Lord Harlech, 111

Orwell, George, 57, 298e
Osmotherly Rules, 77
'Overlords', 188, 189
Owen, Dr David, 40-1, 117-18, 123, 124-6
Oxford, 222

Palmerston, Lord, 150e
Parliament, 16-33, 53e, 63e
    committees, scrutiny, 63-79, 87, 89-92, 95
    dissolution, 15, 17, 23-33, 34-52
    hung, 25, 35-52
Parliament Bill (1911), 23
Parsons, Sir Anthony, 152-3, 156-7, 162-3, 163-4
party politics, multi-party system, 35, 39, 40, 45
peerage, 30, 33
Peierls, Sir Rudolph, 99-100
Penney, Sir William, Lord Penney, 102, 105, 108
Perrin, Sir Michael, 103
Peston, Lord, Maurice Peston, 56
Plowden, Lord, 105, 105-6, 107
Polaris, 98, 110-17, 160, 253, 287-8
    improvements, replacements, 117-29, 286
Portal, Lord, 103
Poseidon, 117, 118, 120
Powell, Enoch, 9e, 13e, 23, 236-7, 259
    on Parliament and the royal prerogatives, 15, 17-33, 47, 63e
Powell, Sir Richard, 107, 133-4, 134, 142
prerogatives, royal, *see under* Crown
press, *see* media
Prime Minister, 293
    advised by monarch, 16
    appointment of, 15, 17, 23-4, 34-9, 42
    how to do the job, 268-9, 279-80, 288-9
    power, 29, 30-1, 169e
    premiership enjoyable?, 44, 220, 244
    and select committees, 92
Prior, Lord, James Prior, 165-6
privatization, 294, 296
Procedure Committee, 64, 72, 75, 77
Profumo scandal, 229-30
Programme Analysts and Review mechanism, 270
Public Accounts Committee, 69, 72, 74, 75, 122
Public Interest Immunity certificates, 81, 82-5

Quebec Agreement, 101, 102, 104, 184
Quinlan, Sir Michael, 151-2

Radice, Giles, 81, 87, 89-90, 91-2, 94
Ramphal, Sir Sonny, 163, 164
Rayner, Lord, Derek Rayner, 294
Reagan, Pesident Ronald, 71, 295
Radcliffe-Maud, Lord, 9e
Redmayne, Martin, 229
Reischauer, Bob, 70, 71
resale price maintenance, 242
Reynolds, Gillian, 9e
Rhodes James, Robert, 205, 213, 292
    on Eden, 205-18 *passim*
Rhodesia, 163, 254
Riddell, Peter, 66, 80-1, 84-5, 88-9, 89, 91, 94
Rifkind, Malcolm, 151, 159
Rippon, Geoffrey, 271
Robbins, Keith, 153-4
Roosevelt, President Franklin D., 101
Rowan, Sir Leslie, 145
Russia, *see* Soviet Union

St John of Fawsley, Lord, Norman St John-Stevas, 63e, 63, 64, 67, 68, 75, 76, 77, 78
Salisbury, Lord, 3rd Marquis, 55e
Salisbury, Lord, 5th Marquis, 191, 225-6

Scott Report, 80-95
Scottish National Party, 46-7
Scrivener, Anthony, 82, 84, 86, 91, 93-4
SDP/Liberal Alliance, 40-1
secret services, *see* intelligence services
Security Council, 152, 155
shareholding, 296
Sheldon, Robert, 72, 75
Sherfield, Lord, Sir Roger Makins, 100-101, 101, 102, 104-5, 135-6, 145
Shore, Peter, 249, 252, 253, 256, 257, 263-4, 267
Shuckburgh, Sir Evelyn, 198
Sillars, Jim, 46, 48-9
Skybolt missile, 109-11
Smith, Frank, 54
Smith, Geoffrey, 150
Soames, Lord, Christopher Soames, 192
South Africa, 153, 254
Soviet Union, Russia, 104, 105, 106, 109, 116, 117, 119-20, 124, 231; *see also* Cold War
Steel, Sir David, 40-1, 43, 47-8
sterling, devaluation/parity, 250-2
Stewart, Michael, 115
Stockton, Lord, *see* Macmillan, Alexander *and* Harold
Stockwell, General Sir Hugh, 143, 144
students, overseas, 164, 165
Suez, 97-8, 130-49, 193, 204, 209-16, 217, 219, 225, 238-9, 253
Sunningdale Agreement, 37
Super Antelope, 117-18

Teller, Edward, 108
Templar, General Sir Gerald, 134
Test Ban Treaty, 116, 231
Thatcher, Margaret, 170, 290-7
    and Anglo-American relations, 157, 295
    and the BBC, 10
    and Cabinet, 296

and the Civil Service, 295-6, 297
and economic affairs, 293-4, 296-7
and Europe, 294
and Macmillan, 233, 291
and nuclear weapons, 126-7
and trade union reform, 293-4, 294, 296
and the welfare state, 179
Thorneycroft, Lord, Peter Thorneycroft, 237-8, 240
Thorpe, Jeremy, 36-7
Tizard, Sir Henry, 103-4
Trade and Industry Select Committee, 87, 89, 90
trade unions, 207, 208, 256-7, 263, 293-4, 294, 296
transport, motorways, 202
Treasury, 197, 252, 281
treaties, power to make, 18
Trident, 98, 124, 125, 126-8, 159
Truman, President Harry S., the Truman Doctrine, 183, 184

Ulster Unionists, 37, 47
United Nations, 166, 183-4; *see also* Security Council
United States of America
    Anglo-American relations:
        Korean War, 183-4; nuclear weapons, 100-129 *passim*, 159-60, 184, 231, 286; 'special relationship', 111, 116-17, 136, 155-8, 182-3, 184-5, 195, 198, 199, 212, 227-8, 253, 295; Suez, 135-7, 146, 147, 149, 212, 214, 238-9
    Constitution, Congress, 29, 31, 64-79 *passim*

V-bombers, 107, 108, 109, 110, 111, 116

Waldegrave, William, 80-1

Walker, Peter, 292
war, power to declare, 18
Watkins, Alan, 290
welfare state, 172, 179–80, 199
Westland Affair, 65–6
Whitelaw, Lord, William Whitelaw, 246, 266, 292
Wilding, Richard, 56
Wilkinson, Ellen, 9e
Williams, Francis, 174–5
Williams, Baroness, Shirley Williams, 261
Wilson, Harold, Lord Wilson, 246–67
   as leader of Labour Party, 113, 266
   wins 1962 general election, 114
   wins 1966 general election, 255
   defeated in 1970, 258
   returns to power in 1974, 23, 37, 259–60
   resigns, 262, 265, 281
   and Anglo–American relations, 116
   and Cabinet, 175, 261–2, 262

   and economic affairs, 24, 240, 246, 249–53, 256, 260, 262–4
   and Europe, 258–9, 261–2
   'kitchen cabinet', 253
   and nuclear weapons, 113, 114–16, 120–1, 253
   as opposition leader, parliamentarian, 240–1, 246–7, 248–9
   as Prime Minister, 252–8, 261–4, 266–7, 280, 281–2, 284, 288, 290
   alleged Security Service plot, 264–5
Windscale, 102
Wyatt, Woodrow, 192
Wyndham, John, 224

Zelikow, Professor Philip, 155–6, 157, 158
Ziegler, Philip, 13, 39–40, 49–50
Zilliacus, Konni, 178
Zuckerman, Lord, Solly Zuckerman, 114, 119, 124, 125

THE HIDDEN WIRING

Peter Hennessy

'Hennessy's discussion of his separate themes is . . . brimming with scholarship and erudition. He writes, as he speaks on both radio and television, with pace and verve'   Anthony Howard, *Spectator*

Peter Hennessy is a demystifier who for twenty years has been searching for the concealed codes of state power, and in THE HIDDEN WIRING he unravels the mysteries of the British constitution to expose the true nature of the relationships between the five institutions at the core of public life: Monarchy, Premiership, Cabinet, Whitehall and Parliament. This paperback edition is fully updated and includes a new chapter on the constitutional implications of the Scott Report.

   With the conduct of public affairs under scrutiny as never before, Peter Hennessy's characteristic wit, zest and incisiveness have never been deployed to better effect.

'The vibrant tones of the author's infectious enthusiasm ring from every page'   Julia Langdon, *Glasgow Herald*

'Characteristically timely, lively and provocative'
                                        David Cannadine, *Observer*

£7.99   0 575 40058 7

IND/GO

CAMPAIGN 1997
How the General Election was Won and Lost

Nicholas Jones

'Pain in the neck though he may be, Jones constitutes a persuasive argument for the role of the journalist as useful nuisance. Long may he and his tape recorder flourish – but, if he doesn't mind, as far away as possible from me'   Gerald Kaufman MP

From the day the Conservative Party grafted those demonic eyes on to Tony Blair's grinning face when unleashing its controversial 'New Labour, New Danger' campaign, to the day when Labour party workers were instructed to stage 'a spontaneous outpouring from offices and factories to greet the new Prime Minister', the 1997 general election was fought as much by the spin doctors as by the politicians.

Veteran BBC political correspondent Nicholas Jones, whose book SOUNDBITES AND SPIN DOCTORS was described by Anthony Howard as 'an essential primer for all who want to understand the strange no man's land between politicians and journalists', chronicles the political media machine cranking up to full steam as the election approached and gives a doorstepper's-eye view of a campaign which, whatever the outcome, was always going to represent a watershed in British politics.

Incisive, revealing and funny, CAMPAIGN 1997 describes the cut and thrust of political street-fighting through the most intense general election in living memory.

£8.99   0 575 40116 8

*IND*I*GO*

Out of the blue..

INDIGO
the best in modern writing

FICTION

Nick Hornby *High Fidelity*	£5.99	0 575 40018 8
Geoff Nicholson *Footsucker*	£5.99	0 575 40027 7
Joe R. Lansdale *Mucho Mojo*	£5.99	0 575 40001 3
Stephen Amidon *The Primitive*	£5.99	0 575 40017 x
Julian Rathbone *Intimacy*	£5.99	0 575 40019 6
Kurt Vonnegut *The Sirens of Titan*	£5.99	0 575 40023 4
D. M. Thomas *The White Hotel*	£5.99	0 575 40022 6

NON-FICTION

Nicholas Jones *Soundbites and Spin Doctors*	£8.99	0 575 40052 8
David Owen *Balkan Odyssey*	£8.99	0 575 40029 3
Peter Hennessy *The Hidden Wiring*	£7.99	0 575 40058 7
Elizabeth Jenkins *Jane Austen*	£7.99	0 575 40057 9
Jessica Mitford *Hons and Rebels*	£6.99	0 575 40004 8
Louis Heren *Growing Up Poor in London*	£6.99	0 575 40041 2
Stuart Nicholson *Ella Fitzgerald*	£6.99	0 575 40032 3
Nick Hornby *Fever Pitch*	£5.99	0 575 40015 3
Victor Lewis-Smith *Inside the Magic Rectangle*	£6.99	0 575 40014 5
Jim Rose *Freak Like Me*	£6.99	0 575 40033 1

*IND*IGO books are available from all good bookshops or from:

> Cassell C.S.
> Book Service By Post
> PO Box 29, Douglas I-O-M
> IM99 1BQ
> telephone: 01624 675137, fax: 01624 670923

While every effort is made to keep prices steady, it is sometimes necessary to increase prices at short notice. Cassell plc reserves the right to show on covers and charge new retail prices which may differ from those advertised in the text or elsewhere.